Colección Támesis

SERIE A: MONOGRAFÍAS, 235

A COMPANION TO GOLDEN AGE THEATRE

Spain's artistic Golden Age produced Cervantes's great novel, *Don Quijote*, the sublime poetry of Quevedo and Góngora, and nurtured the prodigious talent of Velázquez, and yet it was the theatre that captured the imagination of its people. Men and women of all social classes flocked to the new playhouses to see and hear the latest offerings of their favourite dramatists, and to be seen and heard. As well as dealing with the lives and major works of the most significant playwrights of the period – Lope de Vega, Tirso de Molina, Miguel de Cervantes, Calderón de la Barca – the *Companion* focusses on other aspects of the growth and maturing of Golden Age theatre, reflecting the interests and priorities of modern scholarship. These include: the sixteenth-century origins of the *comedia nueva*; the lesser-known dramatists, including women playwrights; life in the theatre; the Corpus Christi street theatre and minor genres; performance studies; and the critical reception of the drama. The *Companion* also contains a guide to *comedia* versification, a full bibliography and advice on further reading.

JONATHAN THACKER is a Fellow of Merton College, Oxford.

JONATHAN THACKER

A COMPANION TO
GOLDEN AGE THEATRE

TAMESIS

First published 2007
by Tamesis, Woodbridge
Paperback edition 2010

Transferred to digital printing

ISBN 978-1-85566-140-0 hardback
ISBN 978-1-85566-209-4 paperback

Tamesis is an imprint of Boydell & Brewer Ltd
PO Box 9, Woodbridge, Suffolk IP12 3DF, UK
and of Boydell & Brewer Inc.
668 Mt Hope Avenue, Rochester, NY 14620, USA
website: www.boydellandbrewer.com

A CiP catalogue record for this book is available
from the British Library

CONTENTS

For Claire
'no hay sin ti el vivir para qué sea'

FOREWORD

This *Companion* is intended to be an up-to-date and reliable guide to the extraordinary flowering of Spanish theatre between the late sixteenth century and about 1680. It provides an account of the nature and development of this theatre from the time when the first permanent playhouses were created in Spain until the death of Pedro Calderón de la Barca, the last major playwright of the time – a hundred-year period which Spaniards justifiably call their artistic *Siglo de Oro*.

Although Golden Age theatre is studied as part of university Spanish courses and tends to be admired and highly valued by those who have read or seen plays from the period, it is not a well-known area of European culture beyond the academy. The reasons for this are several: in Spain, the drama, which became known as the *comedia nueva* (or simply the *comedia*), has been successively, although never universally, mistrusted, rejected as formally inept, re-written, abused for political purposes, and misunderstood. It is not possible to talk of a performance tradition for the *comedia* the way it is for English or French drama of the same period. Abroad, despite the attentions of pockets of admirers in different parts and in different periods, it has tended to suffer because of its foreignness: the polymetric poetry in which it was written (in which verse forms change, often to suit different speakers or circumstances) is an obstacle to successful translation, and the concerns of the plots have seemed to some to be rather particular to Spain. In recent years, however, both within and outside Spain, there is some evidence of a renaissance in Golden Age theatre, and the more consistent testing of these plays on the stage, and the renewed interest which accompanies it, should begin to erode the misconceptions and ignorance that so often surround them.

A *Companion* is not strictly a history and this one is no exception. Fine literary histories of Spanish Golden Age drama already exist as single volumes or parts of a larger series. A good *Companion* should be simultaneously authoritative and individual. This may at first seem a contradictory notion but a guide must have a foundation built on a body of knowledge and analysis that is already there and has played a central part in past thinking about its subject. A simple example should demonstrate this point: it is true that a small number of plays from the Spanish Golden Age have come to represent – some would say misrepresent – the whole of the period's drama, and it would be a perverse guide which ignored these fundamental works. Accounts of most of what scholars and critics have taken to be the major works of Golden Age drama are included in these pages despite misgivings about the justice of their standing for the whole. The authority of the guide depends on its author's choice and fair representation of the views of those many scholars and writers who have dedicated time to thinking about Golden Age drama. And yet the most pressing reason for the writing of a *Companion to Golden Age Theatre* at this time is that the field of study has changed so much so quickly. The past cannot be ignored but neither should it obscure the present. In choosing how much space to devote to developments in areas of investigation which touch upon staging, performance, women's writing, lesser-known plays, minor genres and critical reception, I reveal my own predilections and make judgements on their relative importance for the future. As the array of reactions to the *comedia* over the centuries proves, however conscious one may be of the pitfalls, one can never avoid some degree of enslavement to one's own time and subjective viewpoint.

A couple of further points are worth making to those about to take up this *Companion*: first, in addressing individual works or groups of works, I have attempted to avoid the value judgements that scholars often make about Golden Age plays or playwrights, and that often come back to haunt them as fashions change. I hope that some of the short analyses of the many works under consideration will encourage readers to explore the plays themselves and make up their own minds about them; secondly, I have not become embroiled in the often thorny issues surrounding the dating of plays but have given, in parentheses, the most generally accepted date of composition for each work, when it is examined. At times the date is approximate or is that of the play's first known performance. I have included, in the Bibliography, editions of all the plays that I mention in my text. In citing from a play I give its author, a short title and a reference to either line numbers or page numbers in the edition listed. Where two editions of the same play are recorded in the Bibliography, I also provide the editor's name. Where an editor chooses to recommence line numbering at the start of each act, a roman act number (e.g. II) is included. Orthography has rarely been modernized and when it has been, this is indicated in a footnote.

Finally, I am grateful for the guidance of many scholars whose work on the Spanish Golden Age I have read and admired. In particular, though, for their encouragement and willingness to read drafts of the chapters that follow, I would like to thank Jack Sage, Mike and Sarah Thacker, Victor Dixon, John Rutherford and Alejandro Coroleu. Especial thanks are due to Charles Davis for his thorough reading of the final typescript.

Jonathan Thacker

LIST OF ABBREVIATIONS

AC	*Anales Cervantinos*
AHCT	Association for Hispanic Classical Theatre
ALEC	*Anales de la Literatura Española Contemporánea*
ALV	*Anuario Lope de Vega*
attr.	attributed to
BAE	Biblioteca de Autores Españoles
BCom	*Bulletin of the Comediantes*
BHS	*Bulletin of Hispanic Studies*
CGST	Critical Guides to Spanish Texts (Grant and Cutler)
CNTC	Compañía Nacional de Teatro Clásico
Cov.	Sebastián de Covarrubias, *Tesoro de la lengua castellana o española* [1611], ed. Martín de Riquer (Barcelona: Alta Fulla, 1993)
Crit.	*Criticón*
CSIC	Consejo Superior de Investigaciones Científicas
CTC	*Cuadernos de Teatro Clásico*
GRISO	Grupo de Investigación Siglo de Oro
HR	*Hispanic Review*
JIRS	*Journal of the Institute of Romance Studies*
MLR	*Modern Language Review*
MP	*Modern Philology*
RABM	Revista de Archivos, Bibliotecas y Museos
RAE	Real Academia Española
RSC	Royal Shakespeare Company

INTRODUCTION

The early-modern period in Europe, broadly the sixteenth and seventeenth centuries, is regarded, as the epithet suggests, as critical in the development of the way Western cultures view themselves today. Spain experienced the tensions of this period with a particular intensity: its Empire, which had expanded confidently, providentially to some eyes, within the Old World and the New, fell into crisis and gradual but unrelenting decline. The Spain of Philip II (1556–98), Philip III (1598–1621) and Philip IV (1621–65) bred a succession of painters, poets, prose-writers and dramatists, who confronted and engaged with the issues at the heart of the period through their art. This flowering of the arts came to be known as the Golden Age – and for good reason.

The sixteenth century, which began with the kingdoms of Castile and Aragón newly united under Ferdinand and Isabella, and proceeded with expansion in the New World and military hegemony in Europe under Charles V, boasted considerable accomplishment in the arts. It had opened with Fernando de Rojas's extraordinary 'dramatic' work, the *Tragicomedia de Calisto y Melibea* (or *Celestina*); Garcilaso de la Vega had expanded the horizons of Spanish poetry in the 1520s and 1530s with his lyrical verse inspired by classical and Italian models; and the second half of the century would see the flowering of epic and religious poetry, the former represented by Ercilla's *La Araucana*, and the latter by Fray Luis de León and the mystics, San Juan de la Cruz and Santa Teresa de Ávila. Prose writing, dominated for a time by romances of chivalry, also developed in innovative directions as the picaresque was born. In the theatre two traditions, religious and popular, developed alongside each other, as we shall see. In painting this is the age of El Greco, in which Philip II attracted some of Europe's most prominent artists to his court.

However, in the last years of the reign of Philip II and the entirety of those of his son and grandson, a new sensibility is evident particularly in the form that art takes. This period, not quite congruent with the Golden Age itself, is often referred to, especially within Spain, as the Baroque (*el Barroco*).[1] The extent to which the emergence of Baroque art and literature in Spain is due directly to historical developments in the period is debatable, but it seems likely that the events and currents of the reign of Philip II in particular brought about cultural

---

[1] Throughout this *Companion* I tend to apply the broader term 'Golden Age' to the theatre of the period.

changes and sparked questions that held artists' attention and therefore influenced their works. The future promised by enthusiastic attitudes towards
humanism (which included the attitude of Charles V towards Erasmus) in the
third decade of the sixteenth century had failed to materialize, in part because of
the association, in Spanish minds, of Erasmus with Luther's Reformation. Some
of humanism's legacy remained evident in the arts in Spain, especially in
Cervantes's prose works, but the Catholic renewal, pursued under the austere
Philip and epitomized by the deliberations of the Council of Trent (1545–63),
saw Spain turn back in on itself, and back to its past, to assert conformity through
orthodoxy within its territories. The promise of progressive Renaissance
currents, though they had mostly run dry, left a trace, and ensured that
post-Tridentine Spain could not return unperturbed to a world-view dominated
by medieval Catholicism and a concomitant system of hierarchies within
society. The tensions, including an uncertainty which resulted from a subsidence
of faith in traditional sources of authority, are clear in the period. Some groups
did not, or did not want to, accept their allotted place in the world: Spain was not
a homogeneous whole but a country with a large population of *conversos* (from
Islam and Judaism) and a good number of intelligent and perspicacious individuals who could see fault-lines in the world as it was presented to them. The
repressive activities in the New World did not go unquestioned, as the salutary
works of Bartolomé de las Casas prove; although monarchy was not seriously
questioned as a system of government, individual kings were criticized and the
conditions for regicide were discussed; although Machiavellianism as an ideal of
government was resisted on principle, there was a creeping acceptance that
ruling was not a straightforward business; although the relative positions of the
sexes and the classes within Spain were defined by tradition, there were those
who were not comfortable with them; new ideas were thrust into the great square
of the republic by *arbitristas*. Open dissent, however, was not a sensible option.
    Artistically the period, as we noted, is one in which formal limits are
exceeded, in which containing skins are sloughed, in which innovation is
presented as a challenge to the audience, whether reader or spectator. A
consciousness of the pretence inherent to the maintenance of the social status
quo, even to the presentation of self (if that is not to go too far), and of the moral
and epistemological questions that are raised as a result, leads to a culture of
excess, of difficulty and complexity, which dazzles the senses and engages the
intellect provocatively. Art requires sophisticated interpretation. In poetry,
Góngora and Quevedo, though literary opponents, both experimented with
linguistic and conceptual sophistication and exhibited a coruscating wit; in
prose, Cervantes's *Don Quijote* lays down a gauntlet to the notion of authority
and merges the worlds of reality and fiction; in painting, Velázquez and Murillo
question the very nature and authority of representation; in the theatre, playwrights of the generations of Lope de Vega and Calderón de la Barca all but
abandon classical norms and expectations to create a world in which performance and identity are often at loggerheads. Meanwhile the 'moralists', notably
the Jesuit Baltasar Gracián and Francisco de Quevedo, use their prose works to

shock their readers out of mental complacency, pointing to alarming differences between appearance and reality, and investigating the human capacity for deceit and self-deception.

The theatre of the Golden Age was, it should go without saying, engaged with the society that brought it forth and is a particularly interesting facet of this world of art because of its reach. Unlike poetry, prose and much painting, theatre was able to command the attention of a cross-section of the population, not just a literate minority or social elite. Spaniards from the royal family to the *mosqueteros* (who stood to watch the play), men and women, clergy and laity, the literati and the illiterate, all became connoisseurs of the rich dramatic menu served up to them. This accessibility ensured that the world of the theatre was closely regulated. Its popularity ensured that writers who could satisfy an audience were in demand and produced huge numbers of plays. And yet, in spite of the privileged place that theatre had in Golden Age life, from our standpoint we can only ever know it partially, through texts and documents related to it that have come down to us. The precise ways in which a knowledge of contemporary performances of these play-texts would affect our understanding of their meaning and their purpose have escaped us forever. However, this should not mean that we read Golden Age plays without envisaging them as drama.

Several hundred of these plays, of perhaps 10,000 that were written in the period, have been preserved either in manuscript form or more usually as printed editions, either in *partes* (collections, usually of a dozen plays) or in *sueltas* (unbound quarto editions of single plays, printed in two columns usually on four sheets of paper). Many of these works, whose editing is usually a complex matter thanks to the changes made to them by theatre companies and printers after they left the desks of their creators, are still little read and remain unperformed since the seventeenth century. The sheer scale of the task of reading the extant plays makes it difficult for any individual to form a clear picture of the whole of Golden Age theatre. Indeed, only a small number of plays have tended to form part of a Golden Age canon at any one time, meaning that no century since the seventeenth has been allowed to appreciate the richness and variety of this dramatic blossoming. These difficulties have two implications for the modern-day Golden Age drama enthusiast: first, they complicate the task of writing a full guide to the drama; and second, they mean that there remains a great deal to be discovered and added to the sum of knowledge.

The seven chapters that follow are written with these points in mind. The first four attempt to provide a useful brief account of the emergence of the *comedia nueva*, of Lope de Vega's drama, of that of his contemporaries including Cervantes and Tirso de Molina, and of his successors' works, especially those of Calderón. And the final three explore and comment on the staging and performance of this drama, its generic variations, and its reception over the centuries. The *Companion* also includes appendices on the main verse forms Golden Age dramatists employed, and the *comedia* in English translation. It ends with a list of suggestions for further reading aimed at those keen to explore in more detail issues, plays and dramatists mentioned and discussed in these pages.

1

The Emergence of the *Comedia nueva*

When he appears ghost-like from the sack of flour in which he has been hiding, Lope de Vega's peasant-turned-captain, Peribáñez, fatally stabs the proud *comendador*, Don Fadrique, his feudal lord. The shocking murder is committed with the very sword that this noble warrior, scourge of the Moors, has girded on the peasant. However, our sympathy for the *comendador* is limited as the wily and principled Peribáñez has just crept into his own house under cover of darkness in order to prevent Don Fadrique from raping his wife, Casilda. For a moment, flour-encrusted and hesitant, he cuts a comic, even farcical figure, but the natural desire to laugh dies in the audience's throat as Peribáñez avenges his honour like a nobleman, and then coldly hunts down both the *comendador*'s servant, Luján, and Casilda's cousin, Inés, adding their blood to the flour that has adhered to his perspiring body.

In many ways this scene and this play typify the new kind of drama being written in Spain at the turn of the seventeenth century. The recourses of comedy rub shoulders with those of tragedy, combining 'Terencio con Séneca' as Lope self-consciously put it. The separation of noble and peasant characters and their respective values is called into question. The deaths occur on stage. The characters speak here in verse, in one of nine distinct forms employed in the play, and the same octosyllabic form that Casilda and Peribáñez had used in Act 1 when innocently exchanging their alphabets of love. The night-scene would have been first performed in afternoon sun-light on a permanent but highly flexible stage: the location of the action moves between town and country, palace and peasant dwelling. Some of the characters in the play are figures from Spanish history, although its 'source' is probably a popular verse. Unlike in Shakespeare's England or seventeenth-century France, Casilda, Inés and all the female characters are played by actresses. The lively and socially mixed audience in the yard-turned-theatre will be united in their attention to the play, but divided over the evident upheaval in the social order: may a cat look at a king? How should one deal with a rebellious vassal? Can a marriage survive such turmoil for happiness to return?

Lope de Vega (1562–1635) most likely wrote *Peribáñez y el comendador de Ocaña* when he was in his mid- to late forties, towards the end of the first decade of the seventeenth century, shortly after the publication of Part 1 of Cervantes's *Don Quijote* (1605) and when the so-called *comedia nueva* had become the dominant type of theatre in Spain. The play, and perhaps this key scene in particular, serve as good examples of how far and how quickly Spanish drama had developed under Lope de Vega's guiding force. Many of the features of Lope's drama outlined in the description above will hardly seem novel or adventurous to an audience some four hundred years after *Peribáñez* was written, but their emergence and development made a large and sometimes controversial impact on the late sixteenth and early seventeenth centuries in Spain. The flourishing new theatres, known as *corrales*, attracted the attention and interest not just of Spain's legislators, churchmen and intellectuals, but also of municipal authorities, charities, entrepreneurs, artisans, artists, the aristocracy, the bourgeoisie, and criminals, because of the central place they assumed in Golden Age society and culture. The combination of celebrity, money, and questions of morality was clearly sufficient, as it is today, to provoke an acute interest and emotional reaction.

In chapter 2 we shall look more closely at the ingredients of Lopean theatre, and in chapter 5 at the theatres themselves and the passions they aroused. The subject of this chapter, however, is the hundred-year journey which takes us from the relatively simple form of drama we know to have existed in the time of Ferdinand and Isabella, to the fully-fledged *comedia nueva* of which *Peribáñez* is a fine example.

The search for the origins of and influences on what became the norms of Spanish Golden Age drama needs a cautionary preface. Traditionally literary histories of Spanish drama have begun with speculations about the extent to which a medieval liturgical drama existed in Castile, and gone on to trace the increasing sophistication of dramatic works from Juan del Encina and the Salamancan school to Torres Naharro, who wrote, largely in Spanish, for the Roman elite. This narrative passes through professional playwrights like Lope de Rueda for whom an entertained audience was the only mark of success, and proceeds to Juan de la Cueva, Cervantes and the educated Valencians, including neo-classical tragedians such as Virués. It is important to note and explore such a trajectory – one dramatist frequently does pick up and develop the ideas of another – but the dangers of over-simplification when dealing with a reconstructed chronology are manifest. The achievement of Lope and his fellow moulders of the new drama can seem like a mere 'fusion' or a simple cutting and pasting of sources and influences. At the other extreme is the equally seductive, but equally mistaken, popular image of Lope as a founding genius, creator *ex nihilo*, of a new national theatre. The *comedia nueva*, like the modern novel, developed gradually and somewhat haphazardly, and even when the basic model was established it continued to evolve.

Most of the norms that Lope and his followers adhered to when they came to create a play for the *corral* did have precedents in the playwrights of the sixteenth century. The term *comedia* itself (which has come to stand for the drama of the Golden Age: see p. 145) was in fact used by Humanist writers in the Renaissance to describe their imitations of Roman drama. It had been employed by Fernando de Rojas in the first version of his *Comedia de Calisto y Melibea* and was discussed by Bartolomé de Torres Naharro in the *prohemio* to his *Propalladia* as early as 1517. Torres, one of the most important sixteenth-century dramatists (see pp. 11–12), used this preface, amongst other things, to recommend that the number of active characters in a play should be between six and twelve, and to argue for decorum and verisimilitude. These aspects were later central to the conception of the *comedia nueva* too. He also differentiated the 'comedia a noticia' from the 'comedia a fantasía' thus allowing the dramatist to be inspired by either 'history' or the imagination. Golden Age dramatists were, by both. Polymetry (the use of several verse forms in one work) may have been roughly codified by Lope in his own dramatic manifesto, the *Arte nuevo de hacer comedias en este tiempo* (published in 1609), but he was by no means the first to vary poetic form within a single work. Other staples of the *comedia nueva*, its tragicomic mix, its division into three acts, its freedom from neo-Aristotelian rules,[1] its obsession with love as a theme, its inclusion of certain character-types, including the *gracioso* (or comic figure), were all anticipated by various pre-Lopean playwrights, some of whom Lope certainly knew. However, the path from Juan del Encina to Lope de Vega is not a straight one along which an increasingly sophisticated sequence of dramatists add judiciously to their art-form. There are branches which lead to dead ends, sections which disappear (sometimes to re-emerge later), crossroads, twists and turns which lead through foreign parts.

In the *Arte nuevo* there is in fact no mention of Juan del Encina, despite some eye-catching similarities between the father of Spanish drama and the chief architect of the *comedia nueva*. Lope earned his living for a time within the ducal court at Alba de Tormes (exactly a century after Encina had put on his entertainments there); both men were of relatively humble origins and rose well above what would be expected of their social stations through their innate talent; both were acutely conscious (perhaps as a result) of detractors and enemies who would do them down; both failed to obtain official positions within Spain only to be rewarded for their talents by Rome; and both had a sharp eye for the satirical possibilities of drama. Yet there is no evidence to suggest that Lope thought of the dramatic contents of Encina's *Cancionero*, published in Salamanca in 1496, as a key to, or the first step towards, the development of the drama which he wrote. This does not, of course, mean that we should not examine Encina's output in tracing the emergence of the *comedia nueva*. It is simply a warning that a modern perspective can impose a narrative that is misleading or comfortable, and a recommendation that the whole question of sources and origins needs cautious handling.

In his *El teatro del siglo XVI*, Alfredo Hermenegildo makes the additional point that theatre history should not be treated like literary history. The develop-

---

1 What began life in Aristotle's *Poetics* as recommendations or observations on dramatic form tended to be interpreted in Italy (and to a lesser extent Spain) in the sixteenth century as rules for drama: the unities of time, place and action; the separation of tragic and comic, high and low styles; the need for verisimilitude and decorum. The *comedia nueva*'s relationship with neo-Aristotelianism was more complex than is sometimes thought but the new form was certainly not in thrall to any set of overarching 'rules'.

ment of the epic, the novel, or lyric poetry can be traced through influences which are confined to the page; we can decide, for example, on textual evidence, what a Garcilaso sonnet owes to Petrarch. However, theatre is only in part a written text. The point is obvious, but worth underlining for the frequency with which it is ignored or underplayed. When Cervantes, in the *prólogo* to his *Ocho comedias y ocho entremeses* of 1615, harks back to his youth and the experience of seeing Lope de Rueda perform, his memory is primarily visual. Although he claims to remember still some of the verses he heard, he clearly has a strong recollection of the primitive staging, the costumes and the actions which had changed so much during his lifetime. He does not mention the available texts of some of Rueda's plays that had been published in Valencia in 1567 by Joan Timoneda and which modern scholars do consult. Like Cervantes, Lope de Vega was a voracious reader, yet both men would have seen and heard far more plays on stage than they read in books. Not long after Lope had begun to take a prominent role in the editing of his own plays, he wrote (in the guise of 'el teatro') in the *prólogo* of 1619 to his *Parte XII*: 'Bien sé que leyéndolas [i.e. *comedias*] te acordarás de las acciones de aquellos que a este cuerpo sirvieron de alma, para que te den más gusto las figuras que de sola tu gracia esperan movimiento' (Vega, *Prólogos*, p. xxii). Although the same prologue later reveals a clear understanding of the immortality granted to the *comedia* by its very preservation in print, Lope's choice of metaphor here (text = body, *performance* = soul) betrays, paradoxically, the comparative importance to this playwright of the *mise-en-scène*, remembered, it would seem, from an actual performance. Earlier, when Lope was being tried for libel in Madrid in 1587–88, it emerges from witnesses' statements that he was very frequently to be found in the *corrales*, on one occasion (we are informed in apparently superfluous detail) watching 'los italianos' perform. Undoubtedly the most important influences on Lope in his formative years would have come from contemporary plays he saw performed and heard read. Experiencing a play in the theatre and reading a play-text in the study are very different experiences, and yet the former is an area largely beyond the reach of the scholar and one which consequently cannot ever fully regain the position it deserves in the history of the formation of the *comedia*.

An awareness of the dramatists' first-hand experience of the performance of drama becomes even more important when one remembers the popularity of the *commedia dell'arte* in Spain in the 1570s and 1580s. The reference to the Italians is to one of the troupes of players, and maybe even to that of Ganassa (perhaps the most important figure in the development of theatre in Spain before Lope de Vega), which were so popular in the second half of the sixteenth century. The areas of their influence are difficult to ascertain with precision however, because of the improvised and very physical nature of their theatre, but one scholar sees the *commedia dell'arte* as 'the bridge between Lope de Rueda and the *comedia nueva* as created by Lope de Vega' (Shergold, 'Ganassa', p. 368). The *scenari* of the Italians most likely had an effect on the development of the character of the *gracioso*, and of the old man (the *barba*), as well as perhaps on the division into three acts, the sparseness of stage décor and props, and the predominantly comic tenor of the genre.[2] These influences cannot be traced through textual trails, but as with the theatre of Molière in late seventeenth-century France, certain types of characterization and plot construction and development used by Lope in his early theatre betray the Italian influence.

Another area of investigation in which it is hard to go beyond speculation is that of inaccessible plays of a different sort. There are many hundreds of plays from the sixteenth and seventeenth centuries that are now lost, with obvious consequences for the writing of the history of the emergence of the *comedia*. One of only three sixteenth-century Spanish playwrights mentioned in Lope's *Arte nuevo* is Miguel Sánchez, praised for his ability to deceive with the truth. There is very little with which to judge Sánchez, who also impressed Cervantes and Agustín de Rojas Villandrando[3] with his dramatic writing, and yet he was clearly an influential figure. Such lacunae add to the difficulty of establishing clear lines of development in the *comedia* in the crucial last third of the sixteenth century. Plays were written to be sold to actor-managers for performance, not to be preserved in manuscript or print for later reading, and much of the transmission of new ideas to practising dramatists came through what they saw and heard in the theatre itself.

Although dramatists were inspired primarily by what moved them or made them laugh, what made an impression or worked well on the boards, in short what is often absent from the black and white of a page, some plays *were* preserved and diffused through printing in Spain from the time of Encina. Whatever financial advantage, far-sighted man of letters or simple good fortune was the cause of that preservation, these works remain the privileged resource for writing the history of the development of the *comedia*. The texts reveal that the sixteenth century saw the blossoming of the tradition of popular drama (including religious drama), the growth of the nascent court drama (which soon lost its more overt religious preoccupations), and a more erudite theatre largely inspired by Italian writers, and later by the classical models with which fin-de-siècle writers became so concerned. This tripartite division does not cover every work that influenced later drama and neither does it preclude overlap, but, as we shall see, important elements of all three of these traditions found their way into the *comedia nueva*.

---

[2] Juan Oleza deduces reasonably that the companies that toured Spain 'debieron representar fundamentalmente commedia dell'arte' ('Hipótesis', p. 31), but details are lacking.

[3] Rojas Villandrando provides an interesting potted history of Spanish drama in the section of his *El viaje entretenido* of 1603 entitled 'La comedia'. He clearly does see the developments of the sixteenth century as leading to the perfection of the *comedia*, describing the early seventeenth century as 'el tiempo dorado' (Rojas Villandrando, p. 154). On Miguel Sánchez, see Crawford, *Spanish Drama*, pp. 187–8.

The Salamancans

The search for the origins of the *comedia* usually begins with the Salamancans, a little over a century before *Peribáñez* was first performed. In the 1490s at the important ducal court in Alba de Tormes, in a palace that today has only a circular tower standing, Juan del Encina (1469–1530?), a musician and poet of humble origins, began to entertain his paymasters with short *églogas*. The term *égloga* suggests a classical education and indeed Encina had 'translated' Virgil's pastoral poems. Yet these conversations between shepherds were to be spoken, 'acted' in some sense of the term, before the assembled court. The eight that were published in 1496 were intended for performance at significant moments of the religious calendar, but were not merely doctrinal in content. There is a clear movement, even in these first works, from the religious to the profane, specifically from the *Officium Pastorum* to the more classical themes of the power of human love and the relative merits of life in the countryside and in the court. What singles out the *églogas* of the *Cancionero* is the certainty and confidence of their theatricality. They may have been performed in a hall without a stage, they may for the most part lack a recognizable plot, and they may rely on interactions local to the captive court at Alba, but they do create an illusion through invented characters and engage the audience emotionally and with increasing sophistication. The first pair of eclogues are *Égloga representada en la noche de la natividad*, and its companion, *Égloga representada en la mesma noche de Navidad*. In the former, two shepherds, Juan and Mateo, praise the duke and duchess and argue comically about the legitimacy of Juan's position at court. The autobiographical figure of Juan gives a heartfelt defence of the intellectual content of his art, an echo of the poet's views expressed elsewhere faced with the accusation that he merely wrote about the pastoral world. The second short piece is really an immediate continuation of the first, in which the original shepherds are joined by Lucas and Marco, who announce the birth of Christ, leading to a discussion of the meaning of the coming of the Messiah, and prompting outpourings of joy and the decision to travel to Bethlehem for the adoration. The popular celebration of the nativity climaxes with a *villancico* sung by all four men.

These playlets are episodes rather than plots, in which the dramatist sees no need to explain the transformation of Salamancan shepherds to real-life figures or the gospel-writers and back again. Spanish drama has yet to discover the Aristotelian rules. However, their engagement with the debate about the merits of dramatic composition, their pastoral characteristics and the special rustic language their characters speak, later termed *sayagués*, and their pious devotion, find many echoes later in the century. The last of the early works, the *Égloga representada en recuesta de unos amores*, and its companion piece set a year later, are an indication of the direction that Encina's drama was to take. The dominant theme becomes human love and its powerful effects. Nowhere is this clearer than in the playwright's later *Égloga de Fileno, Zambardo y Cardonio*, in which Fileno kills himself as a result of the 'fieras passiones' (Encina, *Teatro*, ed. del Río, p. 153) he feels in his unrequited love for Zefira (who never appears). The play is rightly termed Spain's first tragedy – it ends with Fileno's companions composing a suitable epitaph for the dead lover, and is the dramatist's only play written in *arte mayor*, suitable for 'cosas graves y arduas' according to Encina's own poetic *Arte*. The sort of scene created around a pastoral *locus amoenus* is better known to students of Spanish literature from Garcilaso de la Vega's later *églogas*, which scholars tend to view as lyric poetry rather than primitive drama. The sad story of Fileno's doomed love should not disguise Encina's eye for the comic moment, however. As the self-conscious lover, Fileno, begins to unburden himself to his friend Zambardo, the latter struggles to stay awake, as he has spent a hard day protecting his sheep from predators. The contrast between the courtly world of love which Fileno inhabits and the mundane concerns of his fellow shepherd as he slips in and out of consciousness, undermines the seriousness of the former's quest for a remedy for his predicament. Fileno is reduced to checking that Zambardo is listening to what he is saying, and when his reply makes it clear that he is still thinking of his sheep, Fileno loses patience, and declares in frustration: 'No hablo en ganado, ni casa o percoyo,/ mas sólo te cuento mis ásperos daños' (Encina, *Teatro*, ed. del Río, p. 158). Such a deflationary counterpoint is never far from the surface in Spanish Golden Age drama, and indeed is immortalized in the novel in the comic dialogues between Don Quijote and his squire, and in France between Diderot's Jacques and his *maître*. Even when the slightly more sympathetic Cardonio arrives to assume the role of audience, he interrupts the story of Fileno's *amour* with an insensitively-timed defence of women.

The later plays of Encina, including the *Égloga de Fileno, Zambardo y Cardonio*, clearly owe their increased sophistication to his presence in Rome from about 1500. The musician-playwright's ambitions probably outgrew Alba de Tormes, and he was well received at the papal court as his social rise attests. It is not possible to see much development in terms of stage-craft in this period: plays in Rome were still essentially dialogues performed in halls as part of an evening's festivities. However, there are clear developments in characterization, the sophistication and scope of the plot, the variety of verse forms, and the themes dealt with. The primary influences on Encina are classical (Virgil, Ovid), Italian (Sanazzaro, Tebadeo) and a Spanish work with links to Humanistic drama: Rojas's *Celestina* (as the story of the doomed love of Calisto and Melibea became popularly known). The extent of Encina's dramatic develop-ment can be seen by comparing his first eclogues with his longest work, the *Égloga de Plácida y Vitoriano*, probably first performed at the Roman palace of the Cardinal de Arborea, the Valencian Jacobo Serra, in 1513. Again the play begins with a rustic figure, Gil, speaking in *sayagués*, but now with a definite role, previewing the events that will unfold. The practice is one that will never completely disappear in Spanish Golden Age drama, taking the guise of the *loa* in later decades. Gil quickly gives way to Plácida, lamenting the absence of her beloved Vitoriano in a fine monologue on the theme of male inconstancy. The theme of the play is love, and despite the pastoral setting, we are exposed to the highest and the lowest forms. The mutual love of the main characters survives

Vitoriano's attempt to escape Cupid's clutches, and they are rewarded when
Venus descends and has Mercury restore a moribund Plácida to the arms of
Vitoriano. The presence of the gods on stage, Plácida's consciousness of dying
in the fashion of Dido, the liturgical parody put into the mouth of Vitoriano, are
all evidence of drama written in full cognizance of the currents of early
sixteenth-century Rome. The scene between the go-between, Eritea, and
Flugencia, whom Vitoriano tries woefully to woo in order to cure himself of his
passionate love for Plácida, belongs to the world of *Celestina*, however. A
consciousness of the unadorned reality of 'love' and the sex industry in the
Renaissance world undercuts the idealization of love as it will do again and
again in the decades after the publication of Rojas's masterpiece. By 1513 we
are still a long way from the *comedia nueva*, however. Some character-types
have emerged and some themes are being worked for the first time, but,
although the audience is expected to follow changes of location, and to realize
that time has elapsed during the performance, scenes continue to be fairly static
and the plot linear and at times (to modern tastes) laboured in its development.

Lucas Fernández (1474–1542) and especially Gil Vicente (c.1465–1536?),
contemporaries of Juan del Encina (and in the former case sometime rival), are
the other two important dramatists at work within the Iberian peninsula at the
turn of the sixteenth century. Like Encina, Fernández composed short plays for
the court at Alba, pastoral in nature, some of which contain discussions of the
nativity inspired by the New Testament. His seven surviving works were
published in Salamanca in 1514 as the *Farsas y églogas*. He remained closer to
his roots than Encina although he may well have spent time at the Portuguese
court where Vicente earned his living. He was certainly professor of music at
Salamanca in 1522 and would have been responsible, as such, for the festivities
organized in the university chapel. It is his *Auto de la Pasión* that scholars have
tended to single out as his most significant piece, usually because it seems the
most powerful forerunner of the *auto sacramental*, the type of Corpus Christi
play performed in the street using carts throughout the sixteenth and seventeenth
centuries (see chapter 6). Scholars have recently differed in their views as to
whether the play was written specifically for performance in Salamanca cathedral in 1503 or for an earlier court performance like much of the rest of
Fernández's output. The question would seem to hinge upon whether the
accounts of the sufferings of Christ, especially in the mouths of Pedro and Mateo,
are designed to move a whole congregation to more fervent religious observance
still, or whether, as Hermenegildo argues, the play should be seen as a more intimate story of the conversion of a single intellectual to the Christian faith (*El
teatro*, pp. 40–2). This would turn the doubting Dionisio de Atenas into the play's
central character, and may link the work more closely to the reality of Spanish
society a mere decade after the expulsion or forced conversion of the Jews.[4]

---

[4] The question of the treatment by Golden Age drama of the reality of the *converso*'s experience is a vexed but important one. On the one hand many dramatists belonged to *converso*
families; on the other it was difficult to dramatize a *converso*'s perspective.

Gil Vicente

Gil Vicente, although Portuguese, wrote some eleven plays in Spanish – a quarter of his extant output – and a further eighteen in a mixture of Spanish and his native tongue. He wrote for the bilingual court at Lisbon, in particular for King Manuel and his queen, María, daughter of Ferdinand and Isabella, and later for John III. His first nativity play, the *Auto pastoril castellano*, of 1502, is similar in length and structure to those of his Spanish contemporaries, ending in the usual adoration of the shepherds, and is probably intimately tied in to the events of the Portuguese court (celebration of the recent royal birth). However, in this and others of his religious plays there is clear evidence of his superior dramatic gifts. Vicente's shepherds are much livelier and more individual creations than those who had until then graced the aristocratic halls of Castile: the peace-loving Gil who has his calm shattered by the insensitive Bras, in fact ends up being the most loquacious of the shepherds, with an intimate knowledge of local genealogies; Lucas lazily (or philosophically) leaves his lost sheep to their fate; and the bashful Silvestre announces his betrothal, to his interested fellows. These characters possess a ring of authenticity to them that reveals Vicente to be a shrewd observer of the world about him, but they are also affectionate comic portrayals.

In the *Auto de la sibila Casandra*, the protagonist is equally well drawn. Casandra is the first example of the strong female in Spanish drama (McKendrick, *Woman*, pp. 45–51). If she is meant to be merely a laughing stock, constantly seen as 'muy cerca de loca' (Vicente, *Teatro*, ed. Calderón, p. 101) for believing herself to be the virgin chosen by God to bear His son, she is also given a lot of reasoned lines for rejecting marriage: 'Veo quexar las vezinas/ de malinas/ condiciones de maridos' (p. 86) she explains to her would-be husband in a long defence of her decision to remain single. Whatever Casandra's real motivations for rejecting the arranged marriage with Salomón, she is an important forebear of the single-minded women in seventeenth-century drama – Inés of Lope's tragic *El caballero de Olmedo* and Marta of Tirso de Molina's comic *Marta la piadosa*, to name two of them – who use the authority of religion to avoid union with an unwanted partner.

Later in his career, rather as Encina had, Gil Vicente experimented with longer works which were more ambitious in their conception, more suggestive of what drama might become. Noting the courtly passion for romances of chivalry, Vicente sought to adapt this captivating world of knights and damsels by using characters and episodes from the romance in his drama. In the early 1520s he produced the *Tragicomedia de Don Duardos*, and a decade or so later, the less impressive *Tragicomedia de Amadís de Gaula*. The former should detain us for a number of reasons. In his prologue addressed to the new king of Portugal, Juan III, Vicente acknowledges that this work is a departure for him, being a search for a 'conveniente retórica que pudiesse satisfazer al delicado spíritu de Vuestra Alteza' (Vicente, *Teatro*, ed. Hart, p. 127). Presumably this is a reference to the pervasive language of love: human love removes every social obstacle in the play until the heroine, Flérida, can claim that 'el amor es el señor/ de este mundo' (p. 184). The play charts the love between the knight Don Duardos, an English prince, and the aforementioned Flérida, the daughter of the Emperor of Constantinople. Duardos spends most of the play disguised as Julián, newly returned son of the Emperor's gardener, in order to see and be seen by Flérida in her favourite haunt. The two lovers each go through an anguish of love which is often presented as a battle, until Flérida finally agrees to elope with Julián, suspecting, although still not certain, that he is Duardos in disguise. His test of her love, his insistence that she make her decision before he declares his identity:

> Y dezilde que, si soy rey,
> sospiros son mis reinados
> triunfales,
> y si soy de baxa ley,
> basta seren mis cuidados
> muy reales (p. 173)

seems unnecessarily cruel, but does produce a genuine rise in dramatic tension (as well as prefiguring later Golden Age plays which revolve around the theme of love across a divide).

Vicente's *Don Duardos* is a more sophisticated and forward-looking piece of theatre than Encina's *Plácida y Vitoriano* because of the more human love complication: Flérida and Duardos might have their origins in romance and might suffer like courtly lovers but for the most part they make psychologically credible decisions in pursuing one another. As Flérida's lady admits, lovers might complain of their living death but 'ninguno veréis morir/ por amores' (p. 149). There is more to the play's novelty, however, than these thematic concerns. Vicente proves to be technically innovative too. Although he allows evening to turn to morning during the course of a single speech, and on one occasion is 'reduced' to narrating how the plot has developed in a short 'stage direction', the playwright does show a concern with temporal verisimilitude. He introduces, for example, a scene between the ridiculous knight Camilote and his beloved, the ugly Maimonda, to allow Duardos to go off and add to his chivalric reputation. He also inserts a comic scene to break the tension which has been building up in the relationship between the lovers. In this his 'father', also called Julián, offers to find him a bride from his own humble class, and comes up with the willing Grimanesa, who is introduced with the suggestive words: 'He aquí la moça do está./ Esta creo que será/ buena para . . . ya sabéis' (p. 167). The implication that the exquisite Duardos's lovesickness might be cured by sex with the wholesome Grimanesa provides a comic clash of worlds that is a more gentle, and wittier, echo of Rojas's *Celestina*. The comic scene of which this is a fine early example has, as we shall see, a privileged place in later Spanish drama.[5]

---

[5] On this scene, which 'has no counterpart in *Primaleón*' (p. 68), and its excision from the *Copilaçam* of 1562, see Hart, *Gil Vicente*, pp. 68–70.

Vicente's play set in the garden of love is not, it goes without saying, as sophisticated as, say, Tirso's similar *La huerta de Juan Fernández*, written just over a century later, but the use of disguise, the love complications and distractions, the tension and the comedy are all already developing. The Portuguese playwright's fine sensitivity and facility for dramatic composition mean that he can, with hindsight, be seen to have been restricted by the tastes of the court for which he wrote.

Bartolomé de Torres Naharro

The other major Spanish dramatist of the early decades of the sixteenth century is Bartolomé de Torres Naharro (c.1485–c.1520). Although he too was probably from western Spain, and may well have had some contact with the Salamancans, Torres wrote his drama exclusively in Italy, where he lived first in Rome and then Naples. The implications of this are important: whereas the dramatists we have considered so far were entertainers first and foremost, poets and musicians who wrote mostly glorified dialogues for special occasions, Torres had a clear idea, within humanistic Italy, that he was writing theatre within, or at least related to, an ancient tradition. Even the Roman-style titles of his plays immediately betray this concern. In the *prohemio* to his *Propalladia* of 1517, an important theoretical document to which we have already alluded, Torres shows his familiarity with Cicero and Horace, but also his own practical independence: he comments of his classical sources, 'todo lo cual me parece más largo de contar que necesario de oír' (Sánchez Escribano and Porqueras Mayo, *Preceptiva*, p. 63), in a manner that would later be characteristic of Lope de Vega. The *Propalladia* was repeatedly published in the sixteenth century, which makes it surprising that it is not mentioned by Lope in his *Arte nuevo* or by Rojas Villandrando in *El viaje entretenido*. Indeed the latter attributes the division of plays into acts to Lope de Rueda rather than to Torres. In fact Torres followed the classical pattern of five acts, or *jornadas*, as he termed them (and as they remained into the Golden Age), with a spoken prologue or *introito* which was typical of the learned *comedia humanística* written in universities throughout Europe during the Renaissance.

As we have seen, Torres himself recognized that his plays could be split into two groups. The first, 'comedias a noticia', is best represented by the *Comedia soldadesca*, which dramatizes the lives of mainly Spanish soldiers in Renaissance Italy. The play is structured around a succession of conflicts, as a *capitán* and Guzmán attempt to recruit (and swindle) a group of men. The entertainment, probably an elaboration of the kind of situations that Torres knew well from his own days as a soldier, is sharply satirical, and seems to play directly on the guilt of the courtly audience, who enjoy their privileges on the back of the labours of those less fortunate. The lives of the lower classes are also elaborately depicted in the 'comedia a fantasía', *Comedia Himenea*, the 'obra capital del teatro de Torres Naharro' (Hermenegildo, ed., *Del palacio al corral*, p. 37). Here, however, we have a play that in length (some 1700 lines), plot, structure, thematic concerns, genre and characterization comes much closer to the developed form of the *comedia nueva*.

The *Himenea* is heavily indebted to the *Celestina*, especially in the depiction of the relationship of master and servant. Act 3 is deliberately dedicated to the servant class as the audience awaits developments in the main love plot, and contains a delightful scene in which the old lag, Boreas (a rough equivalent of *Celestina*'s Sempronio), patiently explains to the wet-behind-the-ears Eliso (Pármeno's equivalent) why he really should not have turned down his master, Himeneo's, proferred gift of clothing. Nevertheless the travails of the servants are a side-show in this play, as they are in the *comedia* as Lope develops it later, a point confirmed by the postponement of a decision on the possible marriage of Boreas and Doresta at the end of Act 5. The real interest is the love/honour plot, which *is* resolved. Himeneo loves Febea and constantly haunts the street beneath her window, to the annoyance of her guardian and brother, the hypocritical and blustering *marqués* ('Bien me place el festejar,/ mas no en mi casa, ¡par Dios!' (*Del palacio al corral*, p. 171)), and his over-confident servant, Turpedio. As with scores of later *comedias urbanas* or *comedias de capa y espada* (see p. 150 for definitions), the lovers end up marrying after a series of tribulations, and melodramatic twists, in this case when the *marqués* threatens to kill his sister. Although the number of acts, the rough unity of place, the simplicity of the plot, and perhaps the more blatant sexual innuendo[6] would not prevail beyond the end of the sixteenth century, there are a number of significant elements that did: the capitulation of the figure of authority to allow the happy ending, the lovers' proximity to disaster, the concern with personal honour, the cowardice of the servants, the love scenes, especially with musicians in the street at night, the discovery of a meaningful sign (here Himeneo's cape) as a spur to the plot, the structural awareness that leads to the building of suspense, and the heroine's independence of mind.

The later sixteenth century

Drama in the second half of the sixteenth century took up some of the leads suggested by these early playwrights but it also developed in other directions. Courtly, religious, humanist, university and college drama continued to be written and performed for a captive, often elite audience, by a dramatist who was often a *funcionario* (Oleza, 'Hipótesis', p. 22). However, another kind of theatre lived or died by its ability to satisfy a 'nuevo público que surge con el teatro profesional' (Hermenegildo, *El teatro*, p. 17). This democratization or perhaps vulgarization of the audience, encouraged by various social factors, is key to the evolution of the pre-Lopean theatre, most notably the disappearance of classical tragedy in Spain in the late sixteenth century (as we shall see when

---

[6] Some of the lines included in the early editions of Torres Naharro's works were suppressed by the Inquisition in later editions. In the time of Lope de Vega innuendo was still present but more subtle, as self-censorship dictated.

we look at two plays by the Valencian Cristóbal de Virués). Before we come to the dramatists who made a living by attempting to satisfy this growing public demand, we should pause to consider school and university drama, an area which has attracted serious attention from scholars only in fairly recent times. There may not be much reliable information about Lope de Vega's education, but we can see clearly when he comes to 'defend' his theatre to the academy in the *Arte nuevo* that he realizes what an educated individual would think of as proper theatre. He mentions the names of a score of classical writers and their Italian imitators, interpreters and translators (and indeed some of their works), and just three sixteenth-century Spaniards: Lope de Rueda, Miguel Sánchez and Virués. The classical dramatists he and his contemporaries knew best wrote in Latin: the comedians Plautus (fl. 205–184 BC) and Terence (fl. 160s BC), whose plays were school texts from some hundred years after his death until recent times, and the Stoic Seneca, whose tragedies were written in the first century AD. Greek dramatists were also known (Lope mentions Aristophanes, Menander and Sophocles), mostly through translations of their plays into Latin or the vernacular.

For many literate Spaniards educated from the 1540s, including members of literary academies and those who eventually turned their hand to playwriting, the first and even most significant contact with theatre was at school or university. Some university statutes (including those of Salamanca from 1538) stipulated that a performance of a classical play should take place at Corpus Christi. The Jesuit *colegios*, which were set up in many Spanish cities in a rapid expansion from 1547 in competition with the universities, used classical texts as the basis of their programme of education and also staged dramatic performances. Plays were frequently written, translated (e.g. from Italian to Latin), or adapted by the teachers of rhetoric, for a performance that formed a part of the school's engagement with the community from which it recruited its pupils. The most important of these 'dramatists' that we know about are Pedro Pablo de Acevedo (teacher of rhetoric in the Jesuit school in Seville from 1561), Hernando de Ávila (writer of the *Tragedia de san Hermenegildo* on the occasion of the opening of a new school in Seville in 1580), and Juan Bonifacio (grammar teacher at Medina, Ávila and Valladolid). Performances of their plays were put on in front of a distinguished audience, with a high proportion of relatives of the boys being educated, not all of whom would know Latin themselves. The plays were usually in prose, often a mixture of Latin and Spanish (with more Spanish used in less culturally rich towns and cities), and tended to have a large cast including a chorus which would set in motion the parts of the performance to be sung or danced. The plays' religious didacticism was the paramount concern, but comedy had an important place in the entertainment.

The importance of school and university productions in the formation of the *comedia* itself is difficult to assess, but they at least formed a background against which the new drama could be scrutinized. Their variety and flexibility must have helped, along with the Italian popular drama to which we have already referred, to prepare an audience for what they would experience in the *corral*, and certainly for the religious plays which became common on the Golden Age stage (McKendrick, *Theatre*, p. 52). We must remember too that school and university drama did not fade away as the *comedia nueva* became dominant. Unlike some forms of commercial theatre, its dual didactic purpose and its captive audience remained. Lope and his fellows were always conscious of a cultured element in the *corral* audience – plays were attended by the clergy, the nobility, and also by an educated section of the public, who would sit on stools in front of the stage. The social breadth of this audience and the consequent differences in its theatrical diet must have contributed to the development of one of the *comedia*'s most remarkable features: its ability to satisfy a number of constituencies simultaneously. If we take briefly the figure of the *gracioso*, we can often find in him a likeness to Terence's sharp-witted slaves, the socially disruptive servant with strong echoes of Rojas's Sempronio in the *Celestina*, the rustic buffoon or engagingly innocent simpleton from Encina and his followers, the backward *simple* of Lope de Rueda, and the principal clown of the *commedia dell'arte*, Harlequin, known for his ineptitude and his flashes of wit.

Lope de Rueda

To return to the main path which leads towards Lopean drama, we must go back to popular theatre and look specifically at the figure of Lope de Rueda (d. 1565?). Rueda was a native of Seville, originally a gold-beater by profession, and as such, would not have gone to school and studied Terence and Plautus. His theatre is unashamedly popular and was to indulge the Spanish audience's sweet tooth, its love of the comic, with profound consequences for the *comedia*'s future shape and direction. By 1542 Rueda had his own peripatetic troupe, and although settled in Valladolid between 1551 and 1559, he is known to have travelled widely to perform with his fellow actors. He was very well known in his day and clearly in demand for performances of Corpus *autos*, and at other festivities. In 1554, for example, he performed in Valladolid for the future Philip II as the prince journeyed to England. Towards the end of his own life, Miguel de Cervantes, who would have been 18 or 19 when Rueda died, looked back with unconcealed nostalgia to his youth and the actor-playwright's memorable performances.

Enough of Rueda's theatre was published in Valencia in 1567 by the prescient Joan Timoneda, for us to have a clear idea of what his audience appreciated.[7] Most notable amongst these works are the two dozen detachable comic scenes or *pasos*, which played a key role in the development of the *entremés* (the farcical scene played between the acts of the *comedia* – see pp. 156–8 for further discussion of the *pasos*). Most of the plays themselves were written in prose, facili-

---

[7] Timoneda also published three plays by Alonso de la Vega, a member of Rueda's troupe, who died in Valencia. Hermenegildo's discussion of the 'editing' of Rueda's works by Timoneda (*El teatro*, pp. 164–5) must be kept in mind when reading his play-texts, which were, like the *commedia dell'arte scenari*, likely to have been only the basis for a performance.

tating the addition of extempore lines, and were influenced by works from Italy. The *Comedia Eufemia*, presumed to date from the early 1540s, is a case in point, with a possible origin in Boccaccio. The play traces the fortunes of a noble brother and sister, Leonardo and Eufemia. The former decides to set out on a journey for no apparent reason and in spite of his sister's protestations. He ends up encountering, and becoming *secretario* to, the aristocratic Valiano, and his position makes him the target of a certain Paulo's jealousy. Paulo convinces Valiano that he has slept with Leonardo's apparently honourable sister, leading to Leonardo's dishonour, incarceration and death sentence. When she hears of his impending fate, Eufemia sets out to save her brother which she does by tricking Paulo (with a subterfuge and *sang-froid* worthy of Solomon) into admitting his deception. Her reward is marriage to Valiano himself.

This plot, however, is secondary. The play, sub-divided into eight *scenas* (by Timoneda, perhaps), is peopled by a series of comic characters – simple servants, lackeys, a page, a gipsy, a less-than-trustworthy maid, and a *negra* – who completely take over two scenes (2 and 7), the *pasos*, and dominate others. One can easily imagine the simple central plot providing a peg on which to hang a series of brilliant comic performances. Rueda has little concern for setting or background, for unity of place or time, or for verisimilitude, preferring his play to live for the moment and provoke laughter. In scene 5, for example, we learn that some time must have passed because Eufemia complains that Leonardo has stopped writing to her, and immediately a gipsy enters to predict that he is in mortal danger. The gipsy scene is more interesting for the light it sheds on the maid Cristina's minor misdemeanours, of little consequence to the plot, than it is for the structure of the play. In the next scene Eufemia does hear from her brother and determines, as a result of his letter rather than of the gipsy's gift of fortune-telling, to go to his aid.

In terms of mere plot structure, Rueda's drama is a backward step from the achievements of Torres Naharro, reminding us again that the journey from Encina to Lope de Vega is not a smooth one. When dramatists of Lope de Vega's era approached a plot similar to Rueda's in this play, they were advised: 'ponga la conexión desde el principio,/ hasta que vaya declinando el paso' and 'guárdense de imposibles, porque es máxima/ que sólo ha de imitar lo verisímil' (Vega, *Arte nuevo*, pp. 16 and 17). Thus when Tirso de Molina came to deal with the separation of a brother and sister in *La villana de la Sagra* (of 1611), he had to justify, within the exigencies of the plot, the hero's decision to leave home, and the heroine's donning of male disguise. Psychological motivation, an impor- tant element of what the Golden Age called verisimilitude, had an enormous influence on how later dramatists constructed their plots. The comic element did not disappear from an afternoon at the theatre, however; it is there in the *gracioso*'s (diminished) role, and most importantly in the unconnected *entremeses* which entertain the audience between the acts of the more serious *comedia* (see pp. 155–6). We can see how popular elements in Rueda's theatre retained their importance to the Spanish audience but changed their shape as the main *comedia* plot took on a transcendent significance.

Juan de la Cueva

There were two other noteworthy types of dramatist writing in Spain in the last decades of the sixteenth century, who did much to mould the future shape of the *comedia nueva*, moving it away from Rueda's pure populism, and back towards a more classically-informed drama. These playwrights were amongst the first to see their works performed in the permanent playhouses of Madrid, Valencia, Seville and other cities, which ironically owed their creation to the dedication and popularity of Rueda and the Italians. In Seville, Juan de la Cueva (1550?–1610?) was the dramatist who best sensed the direction in which professional drama was heading, writing a mixed theatre which must have run counter to the instincts produced by his own classical schooling.[8] And elsewhere, particularly in Valencia, there was an attempt at a more classical drama perhaps inspired by the translation of Aristotle's *Poetics* into Italian in 1570, and the learned commentaries that knowledge of Aristotle's 'rules' inspired. Cultured writers knew of the existence of dedicated theatres in the classical age, and it is possible that the humanistic legacy of Italy helped to produce a climate in which the very presence of permanent spaces dedicated to drama encouraged the playwright or poet to believe that his time had come again.[9]

Whether Lope would have approved or not, a search for the roots of the *comedia* must take Cueva into account.[10] The Sevillian Cueva wrote an *Ejemplar poético* of 1606 which defends the move away from classical drama, as Cervantes later did, in a more intellectually straightforward way than Lope in his *Arte nuevo*. He writes: 'Esta mudanza fue de hombres prudentes/ aplicando a las nuevas condiciones/ nuevas cosas que son las convenientes' (Sánchez Escribano and Porqueras Mayo, *Preceptiva*, p. 145). While clearly knowledgeable about, and respectful of, classical drama, he reveals himself to be an enemy of slavish imitation and an unapologetic supporter of 'novedades' (p. 143). The evidence from his fourteen surviving plays confirms his experimental tendencies and more than hints at his importance in the *comedia*'s evolution. These works were all performed in Seville between the years 1579 and 1581, that is, about the time of Lope's earliest surviving play, the four-act *Los hechos de Garcilaso de la Vega y el moro Tarfe*. Cueva wrote in four acts, which, like Torres Naharro, he called *jornadas*, and used a variety of verse forms, traditional and Italianate. However, his use of historical themes and ballad material were Cueva's most significant contributions to the *comedia*'s development.

---

[8] McKendrick postulates the existence of a 'Cueva school of dramatists' (*Theatre*, p. 57) who found equivalents in Spanish history and legend to the classical stories they knew. However, the loss of many works makes it difficult to be certain about this individual's influence and even the importance of his place in the history of Spanish drama.

[9] Although his commentary does not survive, the work of the Spaniard Pedro Juan Núñez demonstrates a healthy native engagement with Aristotle's *Poetics* in the later sixteenth century (see Alcina Rovira, pp. 19–24).

[10] Lope was always keen to praise the Valencians but is curiously silent about Juan de la Cueva.

Cueva's *El infamador*, given its first performance in 1581, is a curious mixture. It has a plot akin to that of a later *comedia urbana*, following the (doomed) attempt of the rich and boastful Leucino to overcome the resistance of Eliodora, one of the few chaste women he has encountered in Seville. In order for Leucino to be punished for his despicable attempt to slander Eliodora after she has killed his servant in self-defence, Cueva has recourse to a kind of super-plot which takes the form of a battle between Venus, outraged at Eliodora's resistance to love ('Venus no tiene en mí parte,/ y así quiero carecer/ de su fruto y su placer' (Cueva, *El infamador*, p. 44)), and Diana. Diana eventually forces Leucino to confess his dishonourable behaviour in front of Eliodora's father, whose attempt to murder his daughter has miraculously failed. As well as goddesses and other supernatural figures, Cueva brings the figure of the River Betis on stage to beg that Leucino not be thrown into its water – thus contaminating its purity – by way of capital punishment. Later dramatists would find recourses within the 'real world' to reveal the blackguard's guilt, and would have less recourse to 'allegorical' figures such as rivers.

In spite of his feeling for the direction Spanish drama would take, Cueva's plays can still seem rather elementary compared with those of dramatists writing towards the end of his own life, and even some of his more immediate contemporaries. The technique (especially prevalent in Act 2 of *El infamador*) of using a character's soliloquy to remind the audience of the plot's progress seems clumsy by later standards; similarly the 'walking-speech', where a character (for example, Felicina in Act 4) moves from one location to another during the course of a monologue – a technique copied in much early drama from *Celestina* – would disappear; characters were to gain considerably more depth; audiences would be worked harder; and the common structure of the *comedia nueva*, with its well integrated sub-plots, is no more than embryonic here.

The tragedians

In the late 1570s and 1580s dramatists from several parts of the peninsula, conscious of the need for serious drama to obey rules, and briefly confident that these rules, the *arte* that mattered, had been re-discovered, began to write in a more overtly classical style, but, unlike Torres Naharro, for the commercial stage.[11] This is the drama that has been termed *teatro del horror*, in part for its Senecan leanings. However, the new crop of dramatists were not slavish imitators but rather engaged with the 'trágicos grecolatinos', using them 'como

---

[11] In Cervantes's *Don Quijote*, I, 48, the canon of Toledo makes it clear that classical-style tragedies were once successful on the stages of Spain, mentioning works by a number of contemporary tragedians. In his reply to the canon the priest alludes to one of the factors that must have encouraged classicizing dramatists, the opprobrium of foreigners: 'los extranjeros, que con mucha puntualidad guardan las leyes de la comedia, nos tienen por bárbaros e ignorantes, viendo los absurdos y disparates de las que hacemos' (Cervantes, *Don Quijote*, I, p. 571).

pretexto para la consecución de un ejercicio de modernidad marcado por la negación del modelo inicial' (Hermenegildo, *El teatro*, p. 202). The playwrights involved included Jerónimo Bermúdez (1530?–99), the Valencians Andrés Rey de Artieda (1544–1613) and Cristóbal de Virués (1550–1609), Lupercio Leonardo de Argensola (1559–1613), and Miguel de Cervantes (1547–1616). It should be emphasized that we have only a small body of extant plays from this group, and that many plays by these figures and other admirers of classical theatre, which could tell us much more about their motivations and successes, have not survived.

No native Spanish neo-classical theorist emerged, however, to produce an *arte antiguo* around which this disparate group might congregate. Two of the important theorists, often called *preceptistas*, who did write in this period (Alonso López Pinciano and Francisco Cascales) published their works too late to influence this generation. El Pinciano's *Philosophía antigua poética* appeared in Madrid in 1596 and Cascales's *Tablas poéticas* were published in Murcia in 1617. The engagement with the old rules then was not uniform – it did not spring from a single source. There were tragedies written in three, four and five acts; some were made from classical, some from novelesque and some from Spanish material; the ancient chorus all but disappeared; and neo-classical unities prompted varying degrees of enthusiasm. The prologue, perhaps hinting at the uncertainty the authors felt faced with a paying audience rather than the relative security of a cultured academy, became '[un] escaparate ideológico y [un] vehículo de sus preocupaciones teóricas' (Hermenegildo, *El teatro*, p. 204).

Although the tragedies of this period are not all alike – except perhaps in their Senecan use of horror and their overt moral agenda – we shall limit our exploration of them to three plays written by a pair of veterans of Lepanto, Cristóbal de Virués, and Miguel de Cervantes. There are no certain dates within the period 1570–90 to which we can ascribe Virués's *Elisa Dido, tragedia conforme al arte antigo* [*sic*] or the *Tragedia de la infelice Marcela*, but it is fair to deduce that the latter, being much closer to the eventual form of the *comedia nueva*, was written second. Virués acknowledged that the purer tragic vision of the first had failed to win over the public. Neither do we know the precise date of Cervantes's *El cerco de Numancia* but it must have been performed in the early to mid-1580s.

In the *prólogo* to *La infelice Marcela*, Virués casts himself as a 'mísero piloto' (Virués, *Tragedia*, p. 118a) limping home after a storm has wrecked his ailing ship, which left the port in such good shape and spirits. He defiantly declares that even if the winds of the *vulgo* – presumably his cucumber-throwing public – destroy his proud creations, he still cares more about the views of the appreciative *discretos*. Like most artists who fail to win over a sceptical public, Virués is keen to shift the blame for failure, here by stressing his elitist credentials. His frustration must have been enormous, however, as there was an audience ready to be seduced. If *La infelice Marcela* is his last surviving play then it is an indication of this playwright's continuing attempts to find a popular acclaim. In a clever reification of the image, the shipwreck of his theatrical hopes for Spain becomes, at the start of Act 1, the 'real' ship-wreck of the play's opening, from which Marcela is saved (only to meet an equally unfortunate and undeserved end at the play's close). It is perhaps overworking Virués's despondent image to envisage the figure of Lope de Vega picking through the wreckage of Spanish tragedy's painful collision with its public, to construct parts of his own seaworthy craft with the flotsam and jetsam, but the idea has some validity.

We shall return shortly to the unfortunate Marcela, but must look first at Virués's purer tragedy. *Elisa Dido* is a remarkably static play reminiscent in some respects of the French neo-classical drama that was to blossom in the seventeenth century. The tragedy of chaste Dido's momentous rejection through suicide of marriage to Iarbas, king of Mauritania, is played out, or rather mostly narrated by, courtiers on stage. The horrors all take place away from the audience's gaze. The events of what could easily be a period of a few hours include the episodic narration by Ismeria, to the captive Delbora, of Dido's past history and present respect for the memory of her husband Siqueo. The nearest to the development of a sub-plot that Virués comes is the double-rejection of Ismeria by the Carthaginian noble Seleuco and of Delbora by Carquedonio. Both of these foolhardy courtiers meet a tragic end because of their inability to control their passion and ambition, a fault of which Iarbas is also guilty, as his moment of *desengaño* reveals (Virués, *Elisa Dido*, p. 255). *Elisa Dido* is one of the few plays even of this period to retain a chorus, which, in each of the five acts, reflects on the miseries of human existence, sending the audience on its way with the perhaps too obviously didactic: '¡Ay, esperanza humana,/ falsa, mudable, ciega, injusta y vana!' (p. 256). The play relies on the dramatist's ability to move us with rhetoric and poetry, as the alexandrines of Corneille and Racine will succeed in doing in France. In this respect it fails: the play would have been unlikely to engage an audience in late sixteenth-century Spain and would not succeed on today's stage either.

Two major faults of *Elisa Dido*, in addition to its over-egged moralizing, are a lack of verisimilitude and a failure of the poetry to perform its affective function. Unfortunately no tragic poet with the vision and control of Racine emerged to plough this potentially fertile furrow of Spanish drama. In Act 2 of the tragedy it would be almost impossible for an actor to perform successfully the part of Ismeria, who, within a couple of minutes of stage action, moves from utter dejection (and rejection of the world and its deceptions) at learning from Seleuco that his love for her has been a sham, to controlled but engaged narration of the epic story of Dido. Indeed the verse of the play is often more akin to epic in tone than to dramatic dialogue; the characters' feelings are repeatedly expressed in clichéd terms at a time when Spanish poets are alive to the possibilities of language.

However bitter Virués may have been about the damage done to his well designed and constructed tragic vessel, it would seem he was willing to undertake a radical overhaul and have her put to sea again. In *La infelice Marcela* the moralistic figure of 'Tragedia' ends the play with an exhortation to the audience to learn from its 'notables trágicos exemplos' (Virués, *Tragedia*, p. 145b). In general, however, the explicit moralizing is much reduced; the play itself is divided into three acts (here *partes*); the nobles are mixed with the lower born; the more popular octosyllabic metres, including the ballad metre, are regularly used; and dependence on reportage and to an extent on the unities is lessened if not abandoned. The plot too has an unlikely source for a tragedy – the Italian Ariosto's *Orlando Furioso* (1532) – to which Lope de Vega himself would turn again and again for dramatic and poetic inspiration in his early works. In the play, Landino, prince of León, awaits the arrival of his beloved Marcela from England, but misfortunes and betrayals leave her in the hands of a gang of bandits in the mountains. Landino and his men eventually track down and kill the offenders but not before Marcela has inadvertently poisoned herself, and her gallant rescuer of the first act, Oronte, has been killed in the mêlée. It is clear that Virués's confidence that drama should be tragic in nature remains unscathed. However, the tragic trajectory seems to work against the grain of the play, preventing it from coming very close to the new type of *comedia* that Lope de Vega might have envisaged writing. Certainly the structure and the integration of characters into the plot, as well as their more realistic motivations and reactions, belong to a theatre that has changed direction.

Cervantes probably wrote 20 or 30 plays for the stage in the 1580s, although he is not mentioned in the same breath as Artieda, Argensola, Virués and a certain Morales by Rojas Villandrando (p. 153). The mention of Morales (whose comic work, the *Comedia de los amores y locuras del conde loco*, was inspired by the spirit if not a precise episode of *Orlando Furioso*) alongside the names of these tragedians is a useful reminder that we should not assume that most of the native drama being performed in the first decade of the permanent playhouses' existence was tragic. The opposite is surely true and it is a good guess that at least Cervantes's output in this period was varied. All but two of Cervantes's early plays are now lost and his eight *comedias* published in 1615 (to which we shall return in chapter 3) were never performed in his day. One of these two, *El cerco de Numancia*, is the best known neo-classical tragedy written in Spanish.[12] This enigmatic work charts the second-century BC resistance and then mass suicide of the Celtiberian town of Numancia, besieged by the Romans under their famous general Scipio Africanus.[13] Cervantes sets his four acts now

---

[12] Cervantes's other surviving play of the early period, based on his captivity in North Africa, is *El trato de Argel*. A possible third play from the 1580s is published in Arata, '*La conquista de Jerusalén*'.

[13] The play is enigmatic because Cervantes's intentions in it are unclear. By championing the Numantians' stoicism, did he intend to criticize the notion of imperialism, with obvious ramifications for the policies of Philip II? Hermenegildo claims that the broadside against tyranny launched by Virués and other tragedians of this time, in their works, had a clear political relevance, and that this was one of the reasons why they failed to find favour with a public that was 'más conformista y menos crítica de los fundamentos mismos del sistema político' (Hermenegildo, *El teatro*, p. 225). Further research is required in this area, but this scholar's assertion that Lope's theatre, by contrast, triumphed because of its conformity has been convincingly countered by McKendrick (*Playing the King*, p. 7).

in the Roman camp, now inside the walls of Numancia, as he builds up the audience's consciousness of the diplomatic impasse. Whilst Scipio has some of the desired qualities of an ideal military man, he is eventually denied the capture of the prisoners he needs to take back to Rome, perhaps as a punishment for his uncompromising, even inhuman attitude, perhaps additionally as a lesson about the potential effects of colonization and imperialism.

The didacticism of Cervantes's play is much subtler than that of Virués, and he has a surer touch in his control of structure, especially the building of ominous suspense towards the youth Bariato's leap from the tower to join his fellows in death:

> Yo os aseguro, ¡oh fuertes ciudadanos!,
> que no falte por mí la intención vuestra
> de que no triunfen pérfidos romanos,
> si ya no fuere de ceniza nuestra.
>
> (Cervantes, *Numancia*, lines 2385–8)

The playwright's conception of tragedy possesses a similarly classical remorselessness but there emerges a sense of purpose, of Providence, which adds a triumphant silver lining to the dark clouds that are gathered. The horrors of a siege and the desperation it provokes are depicted on stage; characters at times simply represent a feeling one-dimensionally; the personified figures of war, disease and hunger appear, as do Fama, España and the River Duero, the latter (in Act 1) to announce the 'future' glories of Spain, thus contextualizing this grim episode in her history, and offering a ray of hope.

If the theatre performed in Spain in the century leading up to the arrival of the *comedia nueva* appears to evolve inexorably from the primitive towards its apotheosis, then the pages of this chapter (victims of the simplifications of chronology) have been misleading. Aware of the risk of generalizing further we might attempt to summarize broad developments up to the 1580s in a number of crucial areas: in plot, there has been a move away from dependence on the religious towards the love intrigue, with sub-plots and off-shoots which threaten any unity of action; structurally plays have moved from either one simple action, or a classical division into acts, to a norm of three or four acts; the 'introduction' has begun to disappear, certainly as a guide to the action of the play; as a result the audience is now expected to make informed deductions in order to 'read' the stage action much more actively than had been the case; characters are often still based on types, but there tend to be more of them in any one work, and dramatists have become less worried about mixing them against the 'arte', or having them develop during a play; verse has been established as the medium through which this drama is delivered (except, for the most part, in the *entremés*) with particular forms regularly but not exclusively being associated with particular character-types or scenarios; fixed genre boundaries have all but broken down; acting has become professionalized (see pp. 130–1) and staging has undergone a concomitant revolution with the development of permanent *corrales*, where an audience is attracted and pays to gain entrance, and where certain effects are now possible (see p. 138); finally, the intentions of playwrights are perhaps the hardest thing to gauge. A desire to entertain has always been accompanied by a corrective urge, but it is quite possible to discern a move from a general moralistic concern or desire to point out and correct vices, to a more specific engagement with what we might term, anachronistically, 'social and political issues'.

However, in any one year during the 1580s, when Lope de Vega began to write seriously for the stage, one could probably enjoy in Madrid a whole variety of theatre, simple and complex. In the *corrales* there was neo-classical tragedy and the *commedia dell'arte*, there were novelesque intrigues and urban comedies. Between the acts of these plays were short farces and they ended with a dance. Additionally, at Corpus Christi and on other important dates in the church's calendar, specifically religious plays were performed in the streets of the new capital. Schools continued to produce classically inspired plays in Latin and the vernacular. A single individual might have attended a number of these urban performances, treating them differently and expecting a distinct experience from each, just as we do today. Other urban centres (notably Seville and Valencia) might have had slightly different focuses but still experienced a similar variety of theatrical fare.

Lope de Vega, the subject of the next chapter, was heavily influenced by much that he saw on the stage at this time. He watched and listened to many different dramatic performances; he also read widely in classical and contemporary literature (especially non-dramatic writing); he studied historical works and lives of saints; he heard ballads sung; he talked to other playwrights and poets; he listened in church; and he experienced the passions of love, fatherhood, deception, jealousy, bereavement and anguish. Lope's was to be the dominant guiding hand on the tiller of the *comedia nueva*, but, however much we try to build a meaningful narrative towards him, the new theatre must have emerged somewhat messily from the hits and misses of the late sixteenth century in a way that we can still only glimpse.

Lope de Vega

Lope de Vega, as we have begun to see, is the most important figure in the development of Spanish Golden Age drama, whether we ascribe to him the god-like role of creator of the *comedia nueva*, or whether his (instinctive?) selections were responsible for a giant step in its evolution. A separate chapter must be dedicated to him. The designation of Lope by his contemporaries as *fénix de los ingenios*, or *monstruo de la naturaleza*, helped to create an image of him as a unique, superhuman genius, an image which has proved durable in assessments of his life and work. The facts of Lope's life and literary output are extraordinary, but his myth-like status has tended to prevent scholars, perhaps especially in his native country, from challenging naive assumptions about him. In fact, as Enrique García Santo-Tomás has pointed out, the attitude to Lope which has prevailed until the present day takes the form of 'un repertorio de clichés que se mantiene poco alterado durante casi cuatro siglos' (*La creación*, p. 12). The dramatist's qualities of 'fecundidad, espontaneidad, naturalidad o versatilidad' have come together to operate as 'síntomas de una esencia única de genialidad, pero también lo han hecho como paradigma de algo negativo y censurable' (p. 11).

The double-edged praise to which Lope has been subjected has a number of overlapping explanations: (1) the legacy of early scholars, including Menéndez y Pelayo in Spain, who have helped to form the canon of his plays which are read and studied; (2) his enormous fecundity, which leads to an assumption that he dashed plays off without thinking about them and that he took all his ideas and classical knowledge from *polianteas*; (3) his dependence on other works, which goes hand in hand with a reputation for merely retelling old stories from history or fiction, an explanation that ignores the fashion in which he interprets his sources; (4) his apparent inconsistency, which contrasts with the much-admired Calderón, whose works have seemed to critics to form part of a unified world-view; (5) his undisciplined personal life, which has discouraged a hunt for artistic cohesion or coherence; (6) the almost complete absence of a performance tradition for his plays (in contrast to Shakespeare, for example, whose works go through different interpretations and are tested again and again on the stage); (7) his preference for the comic genre, which has traditionally been regarded as rather light-weight compared with more 'serious' works; and (8) a reluctance to analyse with care his own statements on his dramatic theory (e.g. in the *Arte nuevo* and in his prologues and dedications).

The principal effect of this reception of Lope de Vega is to discourage his interpreters from viewing the playwright as anything more than a popular and uncritical conduit transporting the life of his people to the stage of his time. Thus, a Romanticized Lope was assumed to show in his drama unreserved support for the Spanish king and his country's political and social structure; and he was thought always to champion the dominant Christian religion at the expense of Islam and Judaism (see pp. 173–4). A critical feminization (or sometimes infantilization) of Lope, apparently the emotional barometer of his fellow Spaniards, accompanies a sometimes explicit contrast with the role in Spanish letters of the father of the novel Miguel de Cervantes, the *learned* poets Luis de Góngora and Francisco de Quevedo, or the moralist Baltasar Gracián, all controversial or dissenting voices in Golden Age Spain. Thus, to give one instance of an almost universal approach, Alonso Zamora Vicente writes in his introduction to Lope's life and works, that 'no debemos buscar en su obra el fruto de un pensador como Cervantes' (*Lope de Vega*, p. 117).

Before assessing Lope's artistic output, it is worth reviewing the major facts of his life. A warning is necessary here: there is a tendency amongst Lope's biographers to exploit his literary works, especially his poetry and *La Dorotea*, in order to shed light on his life story. In the case of most writers such a procedure is fraught with danger, but the disguised character of Lope (most frequently appearing in his drama as Belardo, Lucindo or Jacinto) and events from his life do recur frequently in his writing. Indeed, he seems to have found writing about his emotions cathartic, as in the early play *Belardo el furioso* (1586–95).[1] Nevertheless, as an artist, Lope made use of material, whether from his personal experience or from literary, historical or Biblical sources, to create poetry and drama. However prevalent or attractive it may be, the idea that there was 'a "hot-line" from his heart to his pen' (Hayes, *Lope de Vega*, p. 104), which bypassed his critical faculties, is one which should be strenuously resisted.

Lope Félix de Vega Carpio was born in Madrid in 1562, the third or fourth child of Félix de Vega, an embroiderer, and Francisca Fernández. Lope always claimed that his family was a noble one from the mountains of the north, near Santander, but this was a common claim made by those who wanted to appear to possess more noble blood than they actually did, and Lope was mercilessly mocked for his social pretensions by his literary enemies. Later in life, despite angling for the post of Royal Chronicler, Lope never achieved the kind of institutional recognition that Calderón would, and some other playwrights did enjoy, although he was awarded an honorary doctorate by the Pope (Urban VIII) in 1627.[2] In the years after 1561, when Madrid had become Philip II's permanent capital, Lope's family would have formed part of the middle classes which

---

[1] See the exemplary approach to this subject in Morley, 'The pseudonyms and literary disguises'. Dates of plays, which are often uncertain, are taken from Morley and Bruerton, *The Chronology*, unless otherwise stated.

[2] On Lope's attempts to rise socially and the reasons for his failure, see Wright, *Pilgrimage to Patronage*, for the reign of Philip III, and Rozas, *Estudios*, pp. 73–130, for the time of Philip IV.

surrounded the court. Lope was sent to be educated by the Jesuits at what later became the Colegio Imperial and was a precocious student, apparently learning Latin when about five years old and writing his first play when still a schoolboy. Later he is likely to have attended the University of Alcalá.[3]

Lope was twice married, first in his mid-twenties, then in his mid-thirties. His first wife, Isabel de Urbina ('Belisa', in Lope's verse), died after giving birth to a daughter, in 1594, and his second, Juana de Guardo, passed away in 1613. He had six legitimate and at least ten illegitimate children many of whom did not reach maturity. Of the several major love affairs of his life, perhaps the two most significant were his first and last, those involving Elena Osorio ('Filis' or 'Dorotea') and Marta de Nevares ('Amarilis' or 'Marcia Leonarda'). Memories of his intense and ultimately unhappy relationship with Elena in the 1580s continued to haunt Lope throughout his life, as the late publication of his prose dialogue *La Dorotea* (1632), in part an imitation of Rojas's *Celestina*, confirms. The end of the relationship with Elena had led to the appearance in Madrid of some scurrilous verses whose target was Elena and her family, including her actor father, and whose author was soon discovered to be Lope. The poet was imprisoned, tried and banished from Castile for two years, and from Madrid for eight. Lope's exile was characteristically full of activity: he married Isabel (against her family's wishes) and lived briefly with her in Valencia, only to leave for Lisbon and possibly sail with the Armada in 1588, an adventure from which one of his brothers did not return. Throughout the first twenty years of his writing life the *comedia* continued to evolve as Lope spent time in the 1580s in Valencia with its vigorous dramatic life, and then, in the early 1590s, in the more peaceful surroundings of the ducal court of Alba de Tormes.

Lope's later years were marked by bitterness and personal tragedy. He took holy orders in 1614, but was unable to live the celibate life of a priest, and he became a *familiar* of the Holy Inquisition, a post which meant that he could theoretically defend the Catholic faith by informing on heretics, but which also protected its holder from investigation of his own background. His last fifteen years or so were spent with Marta de Nevares, but after their early years together she went blind and suffered from periods of insanity before dying in 1632. His beloved son Lopillo (by his mistress Micaela de Luján) was drowned in action in 1634, the same year that his 17-year-old daughter, Antonia Clara (by Marta de Nevares), was 'abducted' by her aristocratic lover, who was connected to the Olivares faction at court. When he died in 1635, Lope's funeral lasted for nine days and there were 150 orations. Even in his day Lope was a hero for many Spaniards; a bright star in a world that was beginning to recognize writers as figures of individual brilliance.

---

[3] On Lope's possible presence at Alcalá, see Pedraza Jiménez, *Lope de Vega*, pp. 7–8. His first biographer was his friend and fellow playwright Juan Pérez de Montalbán, whose *Fama póstuma*, of 1636, must be treated with caution. There is a clear need for an authoritative modern biography of Lope de Vega.

In affirming that Lope de Vega had written some 1800 *comedias* and 400 *autos* in his dramatic career, Montalbán put a round figure to what Cervantes had recognized as 'muchas e infinitas comedias que ha compuesto un felicísimo ingenio de estos reinos' (*Don Quijote*, I, p. 571). Lope's astonishing levels of productivity have been a subject of debate for many years, with most critics reckoning that the number must be considerably smaller than Montalbán claims, and some finding ingenious explanations for such fecundity.[4] In 1604, in an incomplete listing of his plays, Lope records the titles of some 220 plays, and in 1618 he adds a further 210 new plays to this list.[5] Some 44 plays survive whole or in part in autograph manuscripts and scholars today tend to believe he probably wrote 600–800 full-length plays, of which some 400 are extant (some of them merely attributed to Lope). This figure would mean that he wrote on average over a play a month for fifty years.

In the early days of his dramatic writing, Lope had an apparently ambivalent attitude to his plays, claiming in court that he penned them for his own pleasure. His coyness should not be taken at face value. As a young man with pretensions in a Spain obsessed with appearances, and like Velázquez some half a century later, Lope did not want to admit that he earned his living from his art. He sold plays to the *autores de comedias* without a thought for posterity, and wanted to live in the court like a gentleman. Later, however, especially a few years after an entrepreneurial bookseller, Angelo Tavanno, had published a volume (or *parte*) of his plays in Zaragoza in 1604, Lope took a lively interest in preserving his dramas in print.[6] His dedications to individual plays and the prologues with which he introduced the *partes* in which he had a hand reveal a thoughtful, if often prickly character, who despite appearances, is justifiably proud of his contributions to his country's artistic heritage.

Lope's affected nonchalance is evident too in his *Arte nuevo de hacer comedias en este tiempo*, published in 1609, and most likely given as a speech to the Madrid Academy some years earlier. The *Arte nuevo* is one of the most important and far-reaching documents on drama of the early-modern period. In it Lope, rather like Aristotle had, describes rather than prescribes, explaining half defensively, half assertively, often with tongue in cheek, how he has gone about creating the phenomenon of the *comedia nueva* 'sin el arte', that is, riding rough-shod over the old rules. There is evidence aplenty that Lope knew (and had studied) classical theorists and their commentators, as well as the dramatists themselves. He refers to Aristotle on several occasions and paraphrases part of the *Poetics*. After all, classical drama would have formed a part of his Jesuit education, and Humanist commentators in Italy and elsewhere had by this time all but merged Aristotle's insights with the Horatian commonplaces well known even to Torres Naharro in the early years of the century. Lope recalls that

---

[4] See, for example, Aubrun's 'Las mil y ochocientas comedias de Lope', which raises the very unlikely possibility of Lope running an atelier like a master painter.

[5] See Morley, 'Lope de Vega's *Peregrino* lists'.

[6] See Dixon, 'La intervención de Lope'.

Aristotle advises that a play should not exceed the span of a day, and that Cicero saw drama as a mirror of life. He claims too that when he comes to write a play he removes his copies of Terence and Plautus from his study 'para que no me den voces' (Vega, *Arte nuevo*, p. 12). If Lope is at first apologetic in rejecting the ancient art, blaming the bad theatrical habits for which his fellow Spaniards have shown a weakness, the *Arte nuevo* does become increasingly assertive. Thus in the space of seven lines a mixed theatre which fails to keep the worlds of tragedy and comedy separate is at once monstrous (a 'minotauro') and yet 'tiene belleza' in its reflection of life, which itself is a natural blend of the comic and the tragic.

The *Arte nuevo* cannot really be described as an elucidation of a Lopean aesthetic or dramatic theory. It is not bold or insistent enough to be a defence of poetry. Neither is it properly a manifesto as it is sometimes described. It is too slippery to be such. It is rather a practical man-of-the-theatre's guide to (and apology for) what has been shown to work in the Spanish *corral* at the turn of the seventeenth century. Its lack of punctiliousness is perhaps its defining feature. Although the imperative mood is often used in the second half of the poem, it is an avuncular Lope offering advice to the would-be dramatist with his arm around his shoulders, rather than a blinkered law-giver, who is behind the text. As well as encouraging the admixture of comic and tragic elements (e.g. permitting kings in comic plays, combining the high with the low style), Lope champions a unity of action to avoid distraction of the sort to be found in Lope de Rueda's plays with their detachable scenes, and suggests that the events of each of the three acts take place in the course of a single day. He is happy for years to pass between acts, however, which increases greatly the types of stories that can be dramatized. His own practice was clearly to plan his plays by writing out the plot in prose and then to divide the action into three, so that the 'caso' can be set out in Act 1, complicated through Act 2 until the middle of Act 3, and then resolved, but not in such a way that the audience should be confident of guessing the outcome and thus lose interest.

Lope's experience is evident again when he urges the playwright not to empty the stage of speaking characters too often, not to break the bounds of verisimilitude, and to have characters speak according to their stations. Their style of speech should accord with their purposes in speaking, so that highly rhetorical language is not used inappropriately. Nevertheless in polymetric drama, different verse forms should be used at different moments, and Lope makes a few suggestions which reflected his own practice of the time: *décimas* are good for complaints; sonnets for characters who are waiting; the ballad (or *romance*) form is suitable for narration, but *octavas* can add lustre to a relation; *tercetos* are for serious moments, and the octosyllabic *redondillas* are perfect for love (see appendix 1 for further details). Lope's poem ends with various other remarks and suggestions including famously his observation that honour plots arouse the audience's emotions: although he also remarks on an audience's love of virtuous characters. He champions deceiving with the truth and speaking equivocally (an interesting area that has attracted insufficient scholarly attention) and notes the popularity of the female character in male disguise, which had become a staple of the *comedia nueva*.

Lope's Janus-like ability to look both ways is evident in the *Arte nuevo* and surely explains how the work can confusingly be taken by one scholar as a largely neo-classical document and another as quite the opposite. Recent studies of Lope's kingship drama, by Melveena McKendrick (*Playing the King*), and his strategies for seeking patronage at the court of Philip III, by Elizabeth Wright (*Pilgrimage to Patronage*), have coincidentally drawn attention to the drama-tist's ability to appeal simultaneously to different constituencies, to say one thing and mean another. Herein may lie the secret of Lope's success: he produced some works which were undeniably populist and others which were inventive and sophisticated, aimed at the *discreto*, and others still, perhaps the majority, which were both at the same time. The 1619 prologue to the twelfth *parte* of his plays contains the claim that '[e]ntre los que me siguen, unos hay que entienden, otros que piensan que entienden, y otros que dicen lo que oyen a los que entienden' (Vega, *Prólogos*, p. xxiia): clear evidence that Lope was well aware of differences within his audience. He had a rare knack of appealing to the *vulgo*, whilst satisfying the more discerning reader or audience member. It seems extraordinary that a writer should produce such a large quantity of work with so subtle a quality, but one has to remember that self-presentation was a theatrical business in Golden Age Spain, and that for the individual to learn to conceal and reveal, to create an impression for a particular social audience, became second nature.[7] It is not such a surprise that drama of the period should possess a similar quality, and that having dressed as the *commedia dell'arte* fool, Botarga, for the 1599 celebrations of Philip III's wedding in Valencia, Lope should make the figure of the plain-speaking fool and the subtle madman so central to his theatre of the time.[8]

Early plays

Most of the major works on which Lope's modern reputation has been built – *El perro del hortelano*, *La dama boba*, *El caballero de Olmedo*, *Peribáñez y el comendador de Ocaña*, *Fuente Ovejuna*, *El castigo sin venganza* – are mature plays written in the third, fourth or fifth decades of his dramatic career (that is, between about 1605 and his death). The earlier plays, of which, as we have seen, there were over 200 by 1604 when Lope was only 42, have attracted less scholarly attention and critical acclaim. They have tended to be regarded as stepping-stones towards a perfection of the formula. Whilst it is true that Lope's priorities and sense of self-confidence develop as he matures as a dramatist,

---

[7] Orozco Díaz has explored the theatricality of Golden Age life: 'hay . . . una conciencia aguda y deliberada de actuar en la vida con sentido teatral y dramático: es sentirse personaje que ha de ser contemplado por el público como en un teatro' (*El teatro y la teatralidad*, p. 112).

[8] See Wright, *Pilgrimage to Patronage*, and Thacker, 'La locura'.

many of these early works are in fact very accomplished, particularly the urban comedies from which the *comedia de capa y espada* developed (see p. 150).

Lope's playwriting practice did change over time but this does not mean that his early plays are automatically less interesting or accomplished. In looking at some of the representative or key works, and some of the themes to which he returned again and again, we should begin with *Los hechos de Garcilaso de la Vega y moro Tarfe*, his only surviving play in four acts, but one of half a dozen he claims to have written in this format as a budding playwright. The date of composition suggested for this play by Morley and Bruerton is 1579–83, that is the time that Juan de la Cueva was enjoying success in Seville, and around the date (1580) that Cervantes, now in his early thirties, was finally ransomed and released from captivity in Algiers to begin writing for the stage himself. If Morley and Bruerton are correct in the date they posit, then Menéndez y Pelayo's more romantic notion, that the play could be one of the twelve-year-old Lope's dramatic works, is undermined. There is no doubting the play's immaturity, whatever its actual date of composition. Reading it after becoming accustomed to Lope's facility for dramatic craftsmanship, one is struck by the huge shift in focus between the first two acts and the last two. The first half of the play charts the violent passion of the *granadino* Moor, Tarfe, for the resolute Fátima, who favours Gazul, her cousin. The apparently implacable Tarfe, reminiscent of characters from a number of Lope's Moorish ballads of the period, sees sense only when he wounds his former lover, Alhama, who has dressed as a man in order to persuade him not to dishonour her by neglect. Having reflected that his duty is to marry his old sweet-heart, Tarfe soon leaves her sorrowing as he rides out in order to challenge the Christians massed at Sante Fe, and bent on re-taking Granada. The eponymous Garcilaso (not to be confused with the Renaissance poet of that name) makes his first appearance in Act 3 as we move to the Christian camp, and defeats the gallant Tarfe in single combat, against the orders of King Fernando. Tarfe had incensed his enemies by tying a Hail Mary to his horse's tail, and the righteous Garcilaso, who redeems the paper and its prayer, is allowed to add 'Ave Maria' to his coat of arms after the battle.

If the first half of the play reminds us of the bold vicissitudes of love narrated in the *romances artificiosos* which became so popular as they flowed from the pens of Lope and Góngora amongst others, the second half is inspired by (and includes lines from) the older historical ballads that narrated this (spurious) tale of the naming of Laso de la Vega. The work is a fascinating melting pot of competing sources, themes, character-types, settings, and plot-lines, some of which reflect contemporary norms in the theatre, others of which Lope would develop in future works, but that here tend to trespass upon and obscure one another. The abiding impression of this play is one of a young dramatist ambitiously wanting to include all of his ideas at once: there are discussions of kingship, religion, love and honour; there are noble Moors, a woman in male attire, the disdainful lover, the disdained lover, the lover driven mad, the lamenting wife, two kings (with Ferdinand providing the necessary sense of closure), the impetuous but brave knight, the renegade Christian, and the figure of Fama (as in Cervantes's *Numancia*), who appears first in Garcilaso's dream of glory and then describes to the audience his heroic defeat of Tarfe, which takes place off-stage; there is the forest clearing as a meeting place for lovers, the prison-tower, the royal court, the vega de Granada, and the city of Santa Fe under construction and represented by the opened *vestuario* (see pp. 125–6); we see the hostility between Christian and noble Moor played out with the triumph of King Ferdinand's religion, the theme of love unrequited and then honour being restored through marriage, the chivalric-style hero coming of age, and the poetic commonplace of love as a battlefield as Alhama laments her husband's bellicose arrogance.

By the end of *Los hechos de Garcilaso* the disappearance of the unfortunate and blameless Alhama from the play (she last appears at the end of Act 3), as well as the failure to conclude the stories of many of the characters on whom the first two acts were based, seems to point to a carelessness (or perhaps simply immaturity) in the work's construction. We feel none of the satisfaction of comic resolution, little of the emotional upheaval associated with tragedy, only some of the inspiration of the epic story. In later works Lope would become a master at manipulating his audience's emotional responses, and he could, if he chose to, deliberately undermine generic endings (see the analysis of *El perro del hortelano* on p. 128 below), but here there is no ulterior purpose for the play's lack of composure. Here is a playwright bursting with ideas, but learning his craft.

Just as Virués had turned to Ariosto for the plot of his newer kind of play, *La infelice Marcela*, Lope sought for his early dramatic works the authority of successfully established literary forms. Scholars at different times have alleged as crucial to the development of his early theatre Lope's interaction with Valencian dramatists at the start of his exile in 1588, the popularity of the *commedia dell'arte* in Spain in this period, the importance of Roman comedy, and the influence of native drama. Evidence of Lope's leaning on the pastoral novel, the *romancero* (for historical plays), the Italian *novella* (as well as the *Orlando* tradition) and the *Celestina* is even clearer to see. These myriad influences help to create just one of the difficulties attached to generalizing even about the younger Lope's plays. Lope was not, as it can seem retrospectively, merely hoping to chance upon the fittest combination of elements which might survive and emerge from a primal stew: he was in fact already writing with a deliberate variety, entertaining and challenging his audience now with a historical/legendary work such as *El casamiento en la muerte* (1595–97), about the young Bernardo del Carpio, now with an imaginative romantic comedy involving, like the ballads, Christians and Moors, such as *El grao de Valencia* (1589–90?). During the 1580s and 1590s Lope also wrote his first mythological play, *Adonis y Venus* (1597–1603), pastoral plays celebrating love between shepherds and shepherdesses (such as *Los amores de Albanio y Ismenia*, of 1590–95, which probably disguises real historical figures from the court at Alba), tragedies such as *El marqués de Mantua* (1596), honour plays (*Los comendadores de Córdoba* of 1596–98), dramas based on novelesque characters (with Ariosto a favourite source), such as *Los celos de Rodamonte* (1588–95), plays set in the court amongst the mad machinations of the royals or aristocrats, for example, *El príncipe melancólico* (1588–95), and a host of comedies in a variety of settings usually charting the vicissitudes of the *galán* and *dama* as they find love in a hostile environment.

Weber de Kurlat is surely right to suggest that Lope searched for the 'sustancia del contenido' ('Lope-Lope', p. 130) in other successful works and genres at a time when the *comedia nueva* was being forged, but it is worth insisting that he was not a slavish or undiscerning imitator as a young dramatist. The point can be made with reference to *Los locos de Valencia*, one of these comedies, set in a madhouse and written probably at the start of the 1590s in Alba de Tormes. In the play Erífila, who has eloped with a servant to Valencia, and Floriano, who visits his friend there having apparently killed Prince Reinero in Zaragoza, both end up 'mad' in the Hospital de Inocentes, the city's renowned asylum. Under the pseudonyms of Elvira and Beltrán they fall for each other and are able to communicate (and suspect each others' underlying sanity) through their knowledge of Ariosto's *Orlando Furioso*. In part by assuming the speech and characteristics of characters from the *Orlando* stories they can appear mad but speak to each other in code. 'Ansí loca, bien podré/ decirle mis pensamientos' (Vega, *Los locos de Valencia*, lines 1315–16) says Erífila in the moment that dictates her future strategy. A play which perhaps takes some liberties with verisimilitude turns out to be a serious engagement with the world of Lope's day. Not only does Lope engage with the Erasmian ambivalence towards madness as the world inside the asylum at times seems more sane than that beyond its walls, he has also clearly ruminated, like Cervantes some years later, on the close relationship of fiction to real life. Even in these early comedies we find evidence of a thinker like the author of *Don Quijote*.

There were a number of features of Lope's early drama which evolved or disappeared as the sixteenth century gave way to the seventeenth. It has been claimed that his earlier drama is less dominated by a recognizable moral code, so that love tends to predominate over concerns of honour; there is a frankness about physical love, a bawdiness and recourse to sexual innuendo more akin to the atmosphere of the *Celestina*; there is a concentration on elevated social figures (which gradually give way to more populist heroes); speeches are longer and more rhetorical, and more stage directions are provided; verisimilitude is less of a priority, while casts are large and names unrealistic; the element later provided by the *figura de donaire* is commonly found in characters who are mad or foolish. Changes and developments in verse forms that Lope favoured meanwhile (for example, the establishment and growth of the use of the *romance* form in his drama) have been exhaustively explored by Morley and Bruerton. Lope's style of writing plays, his *Arte nuevo*, and thus the *comedia nueva* itself, were born of lessons learned as a practising dramatist.

One of the more extraordinary works from the years in which the *comedia nueva* took shape is the little-studied *La pobreza estimada* (1597–1603), a play which raises a number of other questions about Lope's drama. In Act 1, Dorotea, a poor noblewoman, is in a quandary as to whether to accept the advances of her equally poor but traditionally noble suitor, Leonido, or those of the rich *converso* (a man whose family has converted from Judaism), Ricardo. She seems attracted to the latter, but writes to her father, held captive in Algiers, asking to whom she should offer her hand. When the answer comes it is Leonido who celebrates marriage while the bitter Ricardo tries all manner of malicious schemes to possess the object of his passion. He even tries to rape Dorotea when Leonido is forced to enlist in order to earn some money to bring into the household. Fortune smiles on Leonido, who by chance is able to rescue his father-in-law and earn riches for himself (through 'capturing' and ransoming the king of Algiers, Audalla) and who receives further financial reward on his return to Valencia when Ricardo turns to a life of contemplation in a monastery, and gives his money away to the travelling 'strangers', Leonido and his father-in-law, Aurelio.

The play shares some of the features of the rudimentary *Los hechos de Garcilaso* and other early works. The' action moves rapidly from one world to another, here Spain to North Africa; a year can pass between Acts 2 and 3; a love story is worked out against the backdrop of mistrust and hostility between Christian and Moor. However, the narrative thread is never lost and all the characters are accounted for at the end: even Dorotea's slave, Isabel, turns out to be the kidnapped daughter of the Algerian king. However unlikely the romantic story, Lope keeps a grip on its telling and creates moments of great theatre, as when Isabel and Dorotea defend their honour with the point of a sword, faced with Ricardo and three companions who have tricked their way into the married woman's house. The comedy, if such it can be called, provides a fine example of how Lope is able to please the *vulgo*, here with an eventful story of the plucky and patriotic Spaniard who acts to overcome both Islamic and 'Jewish' adversaries to be rewarded with a noble and faithful wife, the return of the father-figure, and riches galore. Isabel even renounces her religion, as is typical of Lope's Islamic characters, to become a Christian when rescued from her predicament by her brother at the end of Act 3. And yet for those who listened carefully and were prepared to think about the play there is evidence aplenty of Lope's ironic stance towards his noble Spanish characters, and his sympathy for the hapless *converso*. As Américo Castro noted, it was not possible to make a hero of a *converso* on the Golden Age stage (*De la edad conflictiva*, pp. 24–5), but Lope raises the issue of *limpieza de sangre*, the nature of true nobility, and his compatriots' prejudices, in an extraordinary exchange between Leonido and Ricardo in Act 2, which shows his ability to perceive and present both sides of a question. To Leonido's ignoble taunts that his family were merchants before they bought their nobility, that he possesses the courage of a 'dueña de toca y faldas' (Vega, *La pobreza*, p. 151c), that his ancestors were Christ-killers, and that he wounded him treacherously in the back to steal some of his pure blood, Ricardo replies with a composure and logic that shames such ridiculous bigotry:

> Que hidalgo seáis no sé;
> pero cuando lo seáis,
> ni con hablar lo mostráis,
> ni en vuestro talle se ve.   (p. 152a)

He argues that he is 'de mis obras hijo' (p. 152a), and that true nobility will be recognized in heaven: those who have acted badly will not be saved by a coat of arms that indicates noble birth. Ricardo's pricking of his enemy's unchristian presumption is crucially underlined by his own decision in Act 3 to withdraw from the world to a monastery, inspired by Dorotea's saintly behaviour in rejecting his advances and offers of money. The title of the play may, for some, refer to Dorotea's steadfastness, but in fact it is Ricardo who takes the vow of poverty at the end when unexpected and unwarranted riches fall to the impoverished nobles, for whom working for a living is anathema.

Perhaps the most remarkable scene of the play comes at the opening of Act 2 when the captive Aurelio reads his daughter's letter to the Moorish king, Audalla, and promises to follow his advice as to whom Dorotea should marry. When Audalla chooses the poor Leonido, arguing for the superiority of true nobility and despising Ricardo's Jewish ancestry, Aurelio protests that in Spain there is no nobility without money, echoing his daughter's appreciation of why Ricardo's hand is so sought after by the Valencian nobility, despite his impure blood. He goes on to argue that all are ultimately descended from the same man, and that in the past slaves have risen to become kings (which prompts Audalla to admit to his own lowly origins). However, against his better judgement, Aurelio honours his word and takes the advice of the king. The irony of an old Christian father accepting the advice of a *parvenu* North African Muslim not to marry his daughter to a Christian man of Jewish origins would not be lost on the thoughtful audience member. The tradition of the figure of the noble Moor in Golden Age Spanish literature would hardly offset Audalla's unsuitability for a match-making role. In asides, Aurelio mocks the Islamic faith. The play, in highlighting Aurelio's own unworthy abdication of responsibility for his daughter's future, in removing the veil from the Spanish nobles' reluctance to work, in allowing the *converso*'s tragic complaint to be heard, and in casting aspersions on the noble qualities of Leonido, the traditional hero, presents us with a Lope deeply and ironically engaged with issues central to his society.[9]

Religious plays

To suggest that Lope would undermine his own and his country's Catholic religion would be a grave mistake. As a playwright, and an observer of and participator in the life of his time, however, he was able, as Cervantes was, to note inconsistency, unfairness and hypocrisy. The sympathy for the *converso*

---

[9] See Herskovits, *The Positive Image*, for further consideration of the *converso* in Lope's drama.

character arguably evident in plays such as *La pobreza estimada* and *La villana de Getafe* (1610–14), as well as evidence of understanding of the plight of the Jews expelled or converted in 1492, in *El niño inocente de la Guardia* (1604–6), are a result of his compassion. His active engagement with his Catholic God, however, is evident in his taking of Holy Orders (the room where he said his daily Mass is preserved in the house he purchased in 1610 in the then Calle de Francos and can be visited to this day), and is expressed in his devout poetry and his religious theatre. In addition to writing *autos sacramentales*, Lope wrote some twenty-five saint's plays as well as several works inspired by books of the Bible.[10]

Of the saint's plays his *San Isidro, labrador de Madrid* (1604–6) is the first of three he wrote on the life of the twelfth-century patron saint of his native city, who was canonized in 1622, partly, it has been claimed, because of Lope's dedication to his cause, and certainly because the saint was thought to have helped cure the illness of Philip III in 1598. The others, *La niñez de San Isidro* and *La juventud de San Isidro* (both 1622), were commissioned (and comprise only two acts apiece) to be performed before the king and queen as part of the celebrations for Isidro's canonization. The earlier work, like many saint's plays, defies to a large extent Lope's established generic and structural norms for the popular *comedia*. And yet these religious plays were obviously enthusiastically received by Golden Age audiences. Although the 'action' is spread over the usual three acts, episodes do not necessarily require a particular order. The aim is to illuminate the miraculous events of the life of the farm-worker and his wife María (the angels ploughing the fields as Isidro prays; the saint's quenching the thirst of his master Iván de Vargas; his feeding of the poor with his own portion of the *cofradía*'s dinner; María's crossing of the river to reassure the saint of her chastity). As further miracles were attributed to his uncorrupted body the action moves forward in time at the end of Act 3 to after the saint's death. We witness Isidro's admirers miraculously prevented from taking relics from his resting place and see an angel caring for the lamp that burns by his body. To add dramatic interest, Lope includes comic episodes at regular intervals: the figure of the greedy *sacristán* in Act 1, and the accident-prone Bartolo on a number of occasions. The figures of the Devil and Envidia, more usual in the *auto sacramental*, appear regularly in a vain attempt to cast aspersions on Isidro, but their failure is never in doubt. And Lope follows the tradition of Juan de la Cueva and Cervantes, in bringing onto the stage personified rivers: here the Manzanares and the Jarama eulogize the labourer and prophesy his canonization.

The curiosity, the piety and (in the case of *San Isidro, labrador de Madrid*) the pride of the Madrid theatre-going public is sufficient to explain the enthusiasm for saint's plays. The *corral* audience, after all, contained many who would flock to see the *autos sacramentales* performed in the street at Corpus

---

10 There is evidence of increased interest in this group of plays, not least in Morrison's *Lope de Vega and the* Comedia de santos, from which this figure is taken, and Canning's *Lope de Vega's* Comedias de tipo religioso.

Christi, and who, in a world in which Christianity was at war with Islam and itself, would be moved and inspired by the stories of martyrs who had died for their faith.

Many *comedias de santos* were set in Roman times during the persecution of the Christians. *Los locos por el cielo* (1598–1603) is one such play. Set in Nicomedia in the time of Emperor Maximiano, and with its source in Alonso de Villegas's *Flos sanctorum*, it charts the conversion and subsequent martyrdom of Dona and Indes, but contains eight saints in total. The play is much more complex than the pastorally-set San Isidro works, with its exploration of the relationship of madness to religion in Act 2 and the play-within-the-play in Act 3, performed in the church in which 20,000 Christians will die at the hands of the Emperor and in the name of his Roman gods. The fate of the innocent protagonists, who make up a persecuted minority in a would-be monolithic empire, is a persuasive argument against any religious or ethnic intolerance. Whether or not Lope's Spanish audiences thought about the responsibilities as well as the apparent rights of belonging to the dominant (and intolerant) religion in the peninsula is an interesting question. This particular work is also interesting for the defence of religious theatre it provides. As the *auto* within Act 3 begins, the character Terencio explains how devotional works have an ability to move their audience toward the truth:

> Representar los pasos y misterios
> de tales Sacramentos, es muy justo,
> porque a mí me mueven y enternecen,
> y he visto en sólo verlos, convertidos
> algunos que a los dioses adoraban.
>
> (Vega, *Los locos por el cielo*, p. 144a)

Lope's greatest *comedia de santos* is undoubtedly *Lo fingido verdadero* (c.1608). This work on the life of San Ginés (St Genesius), the patron saint of actors, is set in the same period as *Los locos por el cielo*, and ends with the saint martyred at the hands of the Emperor Diocleciano. The play, although probably written only a few years after *San Isidro, labrador de Madrid*, is much more complex in its conception and seems strikingly modern in its metatheatricality. The apparently episodic and disconnected first act, which follows the future emperor on a campaign in the eastern reaches of the Roman territory, and cuts to the poetically just end of the cruel Emperor Carino in Rome, in fact prepares the audience for the later full exploration of the notion of the world as a stage. Carino, as he lies dying, explains:

> Representé mi figura:
> César fui, Roma, rey era;
> acabóse la tragedia,
> la muerte me desnudó:
> sospecho que no duró
> toda mi vida hora y media.   (Vega, *Lo fingido*, p. 67a)

The later acts each contain a play-within-a-play composed and performed by Ginés for Diocleciano. In the first the actor-manager tries to engineer a happy ending to his real-life love for his leading lady, Marcela, but succeeds only in instigating her elopement (during the performance) with her lover, Octavio. Art and life merge, in a comedy that turns sour and leaves the uncomfortable audience doubting what is true and what fictitious. Ginés finds the perfect merging of art and life in Act 3 when he is converted by a real angel who joins the play in which he has taken the role of a Christian. When he insists that the end of the metaplay is the truth – he *is* a Christian – he angers the Emperor, and ultimately pays the highest price for his art with his martyrdom.

Lope in one sense urges his audience to be moved to piety and Christian truth, as Terencio of *Los locos por el cielo* had envisaged the process, by witnessing Ginés's miraculous conversion, but he is also well aware of the philosophical implications of the *theatrum mundi* topos. There are times in the play when the actors are unsure whether they are acting in someone's play or dealing with reality. Similarly the on-stage audience cannot be sure whether other characters are acting or not. The confusion and self-consciousness, the removal of the frame around the stage which points to the presence of a larger frame around an individual's life, is food for profound thought. What is the source of one's social role? How should one play that role? Where does one's moral framework come from? Who is the audience's audience? Roman emperors will continue to be created and to fall in rapid succession but the actor, Ginés, has a guiding truth to cling to and leaves the confusion of earthly life behind. As his disgruntled troupe leaves Rome they discover an impaled Ginés delivering his final lines:

> ya soy
> cristiano representante;
> cesó la humana comedia,
> que era toda disparates;
> hice la que veis, divina;
> voy al cielo a que me paguen.   (Vega, *Lo fingido*, p. 107b)

Lope de Vega was clearly inspired to dramatize the lives of saints, so popular in the early-modern period, but these are by no means his only religious plays. We shall look in more detail at the *auto sacramental* in chapter 5, and shall analyse Tirso de Molina's House of David tragedy, *La venganza de Tamar*, in chapter 4. However, it is worth noting that Lope, too, frequently based dramas on Biblical history, mainly Old Testament books, as the figure of Christ was not thought suitable for the *corral* stage. Notable amongst these works are *La historia de Tobías* (c.1609), *El robo de Dina* (1615–22), and the fascinating *La hermosa Ester* (1610). There remains a great deal of work to be done on these little-studied plays, not least the search for an answer as to why Lope was inspired by a particular story and what he took its relevance to be.

Political plays

These questions have begun to be answered where Lope's dependence on Spanish history, from ballad or chronicle, is concerned. Many episodes from his country's past are brought to the boards in order to engage with the burning issue of the day, the role of the king within the Spanish monarchy. A large number of kingship plays give the lie to the notion that Lope merely toed the party line. As Melveena McKendrick has convincingly shown, throughout the reign of Philip III (1598–1621) and in the early years of Philip IV's government (1621–65), Lope echoed the concerns of *tratadistas* and satirists in his depictions of monarchs unable to match their behaviour to the role demanded of them. That dramatists writing plays about kings usually got away without being censored was in part because of their 'use of complex and diffused stratagems of criticism' (McKendrick, *Playing the King*, p. 70). It was common, for example, to displace the action of the kingship play geographically or historically (transforming events, for a particular purpose, in the case of historical kings) so that any obvious relevance to contemporary events might be denied.

A plethora of treatises on the subject of kingship and reason of state were published at the turn of the seventeenth century and during its first few decades. Although the well-intentioned writers of these treatises stressed idiosyncratically the importance of different aspects of the role of the king, and did differ in their understanding of the monarch–subject relationship (for example, on the question of the legitimacy of tyrannicide, or the degree to which the king is subject to his own law), as an institution monarchy was not really questioned. The reasons for the penning of so many similar *tratados* were several: the need to confront the economic and military decline of Spain; the education of the prince; a consciousness of the weakness of Philip III and his son; a need to define the role of the *privado*, or favourite/first minister, in the days of the Duke of Lerma and then the Count-Duke of Olivares; nostalgia for the heroic monarchs of the sixteenth century; and a serious objection in the climate of the Counter-Reformation to the political philosophy epitomized by Niccolò Machiavelli. These treatises perhaps also reflect the post-Renaissance demythologization of the king, the realization that, after all, he is a man, not a god. The intellectual (and often religious) elite who produced the works shared with the populace a desire to be ruled by a powerful king. I. A. A. Thompson writes that 'the popular demand, as expressed in the mass of satirical pamphlets of the seventeenth century, was not for less, but for more and stronger royal government' ('Castile', p. 94). At issue was not the nature of government, but the nature of the man who would govern.

In some ways dramas on kingship might be seen as popular versions of the more esoteric treatises. Scholarly tradition has tended to deny that the theatre is part of the theoretical literature aimed at correcting the behaviour of the errant monarch, but issues of good kingship were well known even to the illiterate members of the *corral* audience, via the pulpit, *refranes* and *romances*, and so dramatic works could be understood by the audience as mirrors for princes.

Lope's *El duque de Viseo* (1604–10) is one of a substantial number of king-ship plays he wrote from relatively early in his dramatic career. It demonstrates that the life of the social master, the monarch, must be exemplary in its adher-ence to the social norm. To be born a king is to be denied the chance to experi-ment with identity, with self-conception: it is to be one's role. (By contrast the roles of young men and women, the stuff of comedy, are of less grave import.) Golden Age drama on the subject of kingship stresses this fact whether it be satirical (like some plays by Guillén de Castro and Tirso de Molina), didactic in a more orthodox fashion (like Tirso's *La república al revés*), or laudatory (as Lope de Vega's has traditionally been taken to be). An influential and highly visible figure must also be an exemplary one.

El duque de Viseo twists historical truth in order to dramatize the destructive passion of King Juan II of Portugal. He envies his cousin, the Duke of Viseo, who is clearly more regal than he is. The play charts the king's destruction of Viseo, together with his *privado* Don Egas's revenge against the four noble Braganza brothers, one of whom has cast aspersions on his *limpieza de sangre*. Egas cynically uses the king's hostility towards the blameless Viseo to pursue his own vendetta. Egas has been seen as a kind of Iago figure who delights in the downfall and death of Viseo. In fact he does not persecute the Duke but uses him as a necessary, plausible element in his fabrication, which convinces the king that the four Braganza brothers are plotting his downfall. His protestation of the much admired young man's innocence, 'de todo está inocente' (Vega, *El duque de Viseo*, p. 425a), is ignored by the king, who sees an excuse for the outpouring of his own jealousy:

> Sospechas me da el duque de Viseo.
> Y ¡vive Dios, que si el amor que tengo
> a la reina, su hermana, no me atara
> las manos, que el castigo que prevengo,
> en mi primo primero ejecutara!   (p. 425a)

The point of Lope's tragedy, and many of his other related plays, is to show that the potentate who allows his personal desires to interfere with the execution of his monarchical duties, his social role, has to be shocked into the realization that his improper behaviour is held up as an example to his subjects. In this play the final scene, in which Juan II's authority is resisted by the queen and in which Don Egas also dies violently, begins to teach the monarch a lesson (p. 442c). He must adhere to his part or risk disaster, personal and national. The monarch, according to Lope's play, must *be* God-like in his actions. Thus will he be seen to be just and virtuous in his exercise of power. The man who is invested with the role of king is not distinct, in his physical or psychological make-up, from the rest of humankind: he possesses no extraordinary abilities and has had no divine grooming. When Viseo and the Condestable are discussing the person-ality of Juan II of Portugal in the first scene of the play, the newly-arrived commander is reticent about criticizing his monarch:

> No hablemos desto yo y vos,
> y esta máxima se crea:
> que cualquiera que el rey sea,
> al fin representa a Dios.   (p. 421b)

The same character later restrains his brother, who reacts belligerently when hearing of the Braganzas' punishment by exile, with the words:

> Quedo, conde de Faro; que del modo
> que al cielo no podemos preguntarle
> por qué nace uno pobre y otro rico,
> ansí a los reyes en decretos suyos.   (p. 431a)

King Juan's failure arises when his jealousy of his cousin, Viseo, clouds his perception of justice. As supreme judge in the state, the king is expected to maintain Christian principles in exercising his power to decide the fates of those below him. His desire to be rid of Viseo, with scant evidence to suggest that he is guilty of high treason, unsurprisingly appears to Egas as diabolic in its Machiavellian logic. Juan attempts to hide his personal insecurity and jealousy behind a smoke-screen of justifiable reason of state.

Not all kingship plays depicted a monarch behaving badly but audiences must have thrilled to those that did. *El mejor alcalde, el rey* (1620–23?) dramatizes an idealization of the role of the king and thus allows its audience to admire virtue as Lope said they liked to. The drama begins with the perfect peasant love of Elvira and Sancho, who aim to marry. Their noble lord in their native Galicia is Don Tello and he agrees to the wedding and offers Sancho a gift of livestock. However, when he arrives for the ceremony, Tello is overcome by Elvira's beauty and invents a pretext to postpone it. He returns with a mask and abducts her before she and Sancho have had a chance to consummate their relationship. The next morning Sancho and Elvira's father, Nuño, appeal to Tello courteously to release the bride, who has resisted Tello's attempts at seduction. He has them removed from the palace and a despairing Sancho is advised to appeal to the king, Alfonso, who is in León. This perfect monarch hears his suit and gives him a letter for Tello. When Sancho politely enters Tello's palace, the nobleman again has him banished, refusing to bow to the authority of the king on his own land won from the Moors. The unabashed Sancho returns to the king, who comes to Galicia dressed as a gentleman and pretends to be a magistrate. He challenges the despicable Tello, who only relents when he realizes that he has Alfonso himself in front of him. He has just raped Elvira, having been unable to persuade her to forget her sense of honour and accede to his wishes. The king sadly metes out his justice. Don Tello is married to Elvira and then beheaded. Elvira as a widow is able to marry her beloved Sancho, who is given half of Tello's inheritance.

The play, which dramatizes an incident from Spanish history taken from the *Crónica general*, harks back to the days when the court was peripatetic and the monarch was able to dispense justice to all. An individual subject has rights under the law which cannot be alienated by the passions of someone higher up the social ladder. A peasant has as much right as a nobleman to legal protection. Don Tello knows he is acting ignobly and immorally but simply thinks that a peasant's honour is not the equivalent of his own. Although he wears a mask when he abducts Elvira, he is hardly worried about keeping his identity a secret. He is taught a sharp lesson by a perfect monarch, a king who listens to the most insignificant of his subjects even when he has finished his day's work. When his letter is ignored, King Alfonso realizes that he must act himself. He teaches Don Tello that his justice is represented by his judiciary all over Spain and that to show a lack of respect for that is to insult him. Tello's claim of exemption from royal authority is roundly refuted. The play's probable date is an indication that it was meant as a lesson in kingship to the young Philip IV, who was only 16 when he took to the throne in 1621.

Peasant plays

The plays on kingship and statecraft tend to be serious in intent as they often dwell revealingly on the consequences of Machiavellianism or the human failings of the monarch. And serious events dominate the action of three other mature works, usually known as peasant plays. *El villano en su rincón* (1611–15) is a play about the values of the rustic Juan Labrador, his clash with the king of France, and importantly how different estates might or might not be harmoniously united. Lope shows that both the monarch and the peasant who would stubbornly resist him have something to learn from each other, although he withholds a neat set of answers to the questions the play raises (see McKendrick, *Playing the King*, pp. 187–99). *Peribáñez y el comendador de Ocaña* (1605–8), with which we opened chapter 1, and Lope's best-known play (at least outside Spain), *Fuente Ovejuna* (1612–14), will be examined in more detail.

The hero of *Peribáñez y el comendador de Ocaña* is a well-off peasant who is marrying his social equal, Casilda, as the play begins. Their festive, colourful wedding is interrupted by the fall of the young and popular *comendador* (local lord) from his horse. (The interrupted wedding and the fall from a horse are both bad omens suggesting impending disaster.) The unconscious *comendador*, Fadrique, comes to in the company of the beautiful Casilda and the play then charts his pursuit of her and his increasingly desperate attempts to seduce her. Peribáñez learns of the *comendador*'s immoral and antisocial intentions when he sees a portrait of his wife, made on the instructions of Don Fadrique, in a painters' workshop, when he is going to have the figure of the local saint repaired. He bides his time but after the *comendador* has knighted him and sent him off on a military campaign against the Moors, he returns at night to discover that through Casilda's cousin, Inés, the *comendador* has entered his house. He runs him through, taking advantage of his newly acquired social status, and wins over the king, Enrique, with his explanation that his honour was compromised by his social superior and he had no choice other than to kill him. Ironically Don

Fadrique's cunning scheme to rid himself of his inferior rival provides the means for Peribáñez to punish him with death.

At about the time the play was composed, Spain's sense of crisis was at its height. Famine and plague had driven up food prices and forced many to abandon the fields and head for towns. In its historical and political context *Peribáñez* can be read as an advertisement for life outside the city. This may be for no more suspicious a reason than that a good percentage of Lope's audience would enjoy the nostalgia of the descriptions of country life, such as Peribáñez's early speech in praise of his bride, in which she is compared to the good things of country living: olive oil, wine, grape juice, pippins and so on. The play can also be read as a propagandistic attempt to keep the peasant in his place, in part through flattery of his old Christian blood, in a swiftly changing world. It may be for this reason that Peribáñez's prudence and discretion within his social role are so highly praised.

Whether Lope, either consciously or not, created figures with a macrocosmic significance, he certainly did create a work with three dramatic characters with whom we can engage profoundly. At the heart of the play is the contrast between this particular peasant and this particular nobleman. The two central characters are initially defined by the way they think about and react to Casilda, the character who inadvertently brings them into conflict. Peribáñez, as we have noticed, ties her inextricably to the natural world. His wedding speech in praise of Casilda presents a picture of the couple as part of the harmony of the natural world: the images he associates with her belong to all four seasons. The verse is in *quintillas*, a traditional octosyllabic form. The *comendador* can only think of her in terms of the flowers of the spring-time: she is not an integral part of his life, but a fancy which becomes an obsession. His speech is much more formal in its Italianate *lira* verse form, a (regular, in this case) mixture of seven- and eleven-syllable lines (see pp. 184–5). Her husband's images also reveal a complete sensual understanding and appreciation of his wife whilst the *comendador* becomes obsessed with the visual; his attraction is superficial. Similarly, when Peribáñez offers Casilda the town of Ocaña, he means its fields and olive groves, its physical reality with which he is at one. By contrast, when the *comendador* offers to give up the town, his *encomienda*, he shows how his passion has upset the social order. He is abusing his power over his vassals. He uses the conventional terms from courtly poetry to describe Casilda and his description of her is replete with mythological references, unsuitable for a woman of her class. The lack of harmony in his speech and subsequent actions prejudices the audience against the *comendador* and his ignoble motives. He is at his most despicable when he disdains his vassals' class. He is one of a number of Lope's characters who fall for a woman of a class below them and are punished when (or after) they try to seduce or rape her.

The only times when the audience's sympathy for Peribáñez is in jeopardy are when he appears to aspire to a higher social level. At first he seems keen to avoid giving himself airs: he turns down Casilda's suggestion that he wear a hat. However, we cannot help noticing a certain arrogance in him, an excessive confidence in his own good fortune on his wedding day. He obviously decides to keep the *comendador*'s hangings in his bedroom after they have been used on his cart. He understands how inappropriate their presence is only after seeing Casilda's portrait, and realizing the dangers to his honour (and thus his life) of mixing with his social superiors. He replaces them, with obvious symbolism, with gifts of nature and religious images.

The justice meted out at the end of the play, Peribáñez's promotion and the *comendador*'s killing, can most accurately be described as 'social'. The play becomes a test of the individual's conformity to his or her social position. The *comendador*'s assault on the hierarchy is a double one: he raises Peribáñez above his station with his mischievous knighting of him, and simultaneously lowers himself through attachment to a peasant. The death-blow he is dealt by Peribáñez awakens him to this reality and he admits that the peasant's action has been justified. Peribáñez's eventually prudent adherence to the social role he is expected to play, even when surprised by his social elevation, shows him to be a worthy member of society. As a loyal vassal, duty-bound to obey the *comendador*, he accepts the commission to lead a hundred men against the Moors. However, ultra-sensitive to social niceties he forces the *comendador* to knight him personally, and is able to warn him eloquently of the duties he has towards his absent vassal. Any breach of social decorum, any threat to Peribáñez's honour, can now be personally punished by a noble equal. Whilst for the *comendador* the knighting scene is insignificant, for Peribáñez it is deadly serious. As a vassal he can feel dishonoured by the *comendador*'s approaches to Casilda, but cannot do much about them, except worry and observe (which he does prudently). The social raising of Peribáñez to noble status allows him the freedom to act, to kill his adversary.

Peribáñez does raise questions of some subtlety which were almost certainly discussed by the play's first audience, and which remain difficult to resolve today. The *comedia nueva*, as we have suggested, does not merely provide an opportunity for an audience to escape reality. The society depicted on the Golden Age stage is recognizably related to that of the day, even when a work is set in the past, in the reign of a different monarch, as this play is. There is no doubt that the drama comments on the milieu that brought it forth, but not so much as part of a propaganda machine, as the Maravallian school has suggested (see pp. 176–7), as critically, often satirically – as a corrective and subversive force.

The play asks, and partially answers, the question: can a social inferior judge and kill his superior, when unable to appeal to a higher authority? (The same issue is approached somewhat differently by Calderón in *El alcalde de Zalamea*, as we shall see in chapter 4.) The question relates to the difference between peasant honourableness (as we might call it) and noble honour. The former is earned by leading a good life and is evident in the respect one earns amongst one's fellows: the latter is inherited through birth and equates to rank (see also pp. 99–104). Does Peribáñez possess an honour socially valuable enough to allow him to end the productive life of a highly regarded member of society? Is his worth equal to any other individual's worth? The king's answer is initially negative. He is amazed that a humble peasant should possess and defend his honour, and his first reaction is to have Peribáñez killed without ceremony. Yet the peasant's story persuades him to reward this exceptional individual, even if it does not shatter his world-view. In another way the question is avoided, because when he kills the *comendador*, Peribáñez has become a nobleman and is therefore entitled to defend himself. Or is he? The ceremony has been a farce, as we have observed, and Peribáñez must realize this even if he has tried to make his master take it seriously. To what extent, then, can we say that Peribáñez is the *comendador*'s equal? Perhaps the punishment killing itself can shed light on this matter. When he steps forward, sword drawn, Peribáñez says, in an aside:

> (¡Ay honra! ¿Qué aguardo aquí?
> mas soy pobre labrador . . .
> bien será llegar y hablalle . . .
> pero mejor es matalle.)
> Perdonad, Comendador,
> que la honra es encomienda
> de mayor autoridad.   (Vega, *Peribáñez*, lines 2843–9)

This passage seems to suggest that possession of personal worth, or honourableness, is the element which puts Peribáñez on an equal footing with his master, not rank. Peribáñez exerts his right as a human being to punish treachery. Of course, the question of whether an inferior can punish a superior takes on a new resonance in the tight hierarchical structure of the society depicted. For a crime against a superior is a kind of mini-regicide; the *comendador* is a local king who derives his authority from Enrique the Just. Hence the latter's fury at the social rebellion of the murder. If a peasant may kill a noble, then might a noble (or even a peasant) not kill a king? This idea is no more than an implication in the play but the early seventeenth century in Spain, as well as in other parts of Europe, was a time obsessed with social organization, kingship and tyranny. *Peribáñez* is perhaps not a play about kingship, but it does reflect the uncertainty which surrounds the place of the individual in society at the time and in some ways might be read as a more revolutionary play than its illustrious companion, *Fuente Ovejuna*.

Fuente Ovejuna shares some of the same themes and character-types with *Peribáñez*. It is set in the era of Ferdinand and Isabella, more precisely in 1476. The play's main plot (involving the peasants of the village of Fuente Ovejuna in the province of Córdoba) and its related sub-plot (the taking and subsequent recapture, by the monarchs, of the town of Ciudad Real) are both taken from history. Lope built on them and combined the two stories to produce a coherent whole, in which the two plots shed light on each other. (This provides further evidence of the development of Lope's structural awareness since his early days as a playwright.) Again the villain of the piece is a *comendador*, a knight of one of the three military orders (Santiago, Alcántara and Calatrava). This *comendador* is diabolically evil, unlike the young and ill-advised *comendador* of *Peribáñez*. Fernán Pérez de Guzmán, as he is called, not only advises the young *maestre* of the Calatrava Order to take Ciudad Real, in an act equivalent to treason, but he also terrorizes the local people of his own *encomienda*, Fuente Ovejuna. The peasants try to do their duty, fulfilling their side of the social bargain, but he disrupts their lives by stealing from them, abusing them verbally and physically, and above all by seducing and in some cases raping their young women (with the perverse claim that he is honouring them).

When, at the end of Act 2, the *comendador* interrupts the marriage of the young lovers Laurencia and Frondoso to arrest the latter and abduct the former, the villagers debate their course of action. It is Laurencia, however, returning dishevelled from the *comendador*'s palace, who rouses the villagers (especially the women) to rise up against their feudal lord. They storm the palace, release Frondoso and kill and mutilate the *comendador*. Of course the Catholic monarchs cannot let such civil disobedience go unpunished, however morally justifiable, and so they send a judge to find the culprits. Even the weakest members of the village in an act of solidarity and mutual love, epitomized by the natural relationship of Frondoso and Laurencia, refuse to answer the judge's interrogations under torture, other than to say, 'Fuente Ovejuna lo hizo.' The monarchs decide to withhold punishment and give the villagers their wish that the village should now be under the direct jurisdiction of the monarchy.

Although the play has occasionally been read and used as propaganda for revolution (e.g. in the old Soviet Union),[11] in fact its theme is love and the cohesion it causes when perfect in form. The villagers never look to upset the social order, but want to be governed directly by Ferdinand and Isabella. The opposite of this pure, socially-bonding love is a host of self-interested passions: lust, greed and ambition, which can be seen to be a force for evil in the play in the person of the *comendador*. This is noticeable at both the microcosmic village level and the macrocosmic republic level. Lope's play is part history lesson, showing how the Catholic monarchs united Spain at the expense of the once powerful military orders and their masters, but it is simultaneously, in the words of Victor Dixon, 'a lesson in morality, and even in metaphysics' (Vega, *Fuente Ovejuna*, ed. Dixon, p. 6). The love of Ferdinand and Isabella is deliberately juxtaposed with that of the two villagers; Mengo, the *gracioso* figure, who in Act 1 defines love as self-interest, eventually twice proves his commitment to his fellows at the expense of his own physical punishment; Frondoso, too, protects Laurencia from the *comendador*, risking his life in the process, an action which persuades the love-shy peasant girl that his intentions are noble and his aim a Christian marriage.

The peasant plays then present some of the ideal, old Christian, morally superior Spaniards of Lope's day. Their protagonists had little in common with real peasants, but helped elaborate Lope's vision of an idyllic world based on harmony and love, and his examination of elements which might disturb it.

---

[11] See López Estrada, ed., pp. 41–4, for a brief performance history.

Peribáñez and *Fuente Ovejuna* in particular have been popular with audiences and scholars, often standing for the whole of Lope's dramatic output, and seeming to fit comfortably into a cherished, if rather clichéd image of his playwriting.

Comedies

Were one to talk of a 'typical' Lopean play (a dangerous business given his variety) its spirit would be comic; it would involve a *galán* and a *dama*, in love but with many an obstacle between them and their desired marriage. There were numerous variations on this central and traditional comic staple, exploited wittily and remorselessly by Lope and his contemporaries, through the age of Calderón, who specialized in the unravelling of house-bound love affairs, to Sor Juana Inés de la Cruz, who tried to outdo Calderón in her Baroque farce *Los empeños de una casa*, first performed in Mexico City in 1683 (see p. 121).

In the 1590s, as the composition of *Los locos de Valencia* shows, most of the elements of Lope's love comedies were in place. He had become adroit at creating unpromising situations and heart-rending trials for his pairs of lovers only to have them happily extricated in the final few lines of the play. His women could be bold and inventive when following the dictates of their hearts; his men tend not to be so clever but are also capable of defending their passion to the hilt. Honour and love are often set against each other, and life itself can seem 'una estrategia de intrigas, como un maquiavélico arte de la política' (Oleza, 'La propuesta', p. 177). Jealousy and melancholy are never far below the surface.

By the first decade of the seventeenth century, a number of refinements to the comic paradigm are in place. Lope has developed what scholars have termed the *comedia de intriga*, or *comedia de enredo* and more specifically the *comedia de capa y espada*.[12] This latter subgenre has a precise set of ingredients. The characters are individuals, usually of the lower nobility, living in the city, and pursuing love affairs in this urban environment. The plays often involve an *ingénu*'s arrival in a new city, street scenes (often outside a church), love at first sight, jealousy, night scenes, trysts at a balcony or grille, disguise and cross-dressing, coincidental meetings, male posturing and even duelling, and finally the victory of youth and consequent arrangement of marriages. Time and space are constricted to suit the situation. The comedy stems from the situations created by the dramatist and their resolution, and also from the characters, particularly of the inflexible fathers or older brothers (much less commonly mothers) who jealously guard the virtue of the young woman in their charge whilst hypocritically pursuing their own agenda or desires (see also p. 149). The most obvious source of audience laughter, however, is the figure of the *gracioso*,

---

[12] For a very useful consideration of fourteen of Lope's pre-1606 urban comedies, see Arellano, *Convención y recepción*, pp. 76–106. Arellano here wisely warns against making generalizing statements about Lope's varied and constantly evolving *oeuvre*.

the comic servant, whose genealogy is mixed: the two *commedia dell'arte* fools, Harlequin and Scapino; the *pastor-bobo* of sixteenth-century theatre; the cunning slave of Roman comedy; the court jester. The *gracioso*, often loud, indiscreet, gluttonous, cowardly, and lewd, at other times loyal and shrewd, becomes, in Lope's hands, perhaps the biggest attraction for the *corral* audience through his word-play, his bawdy humour and his constant undermining of his master and often of the theatrical illusion. As Montesinos has argued, he provides a necessary counterpoint to his master's aristocratic values (Montesinos, *Estudios*, pp. 21–64).

By the time that Lope came to write his *Arte nuevo*, that is the second half of the first decade of the new century, it is fair to say that he had settled upon the ingredients of the comedy that would enrapture the *corral* over the remaining three decades of his life. Plays such as *La discreta enamorada* (1606) and *El acero de Madrid* (1607–9)[13] depict young women, Fenisa and Belisa respectively, who manipulate the world around them in order to escape their chaperons and ultimately marry the men they have fallen for. Although the comedies of this period can seem formulaic, Lope and his contemporaries find an extraordinary number of variations on the same central idea. In *El acero de Madrid*, part of the novelty lies in Lope's creation of an unusual character, Riselo, a *galán-gracioso*, whereas in *La discreta enamorada* it is the clever Hernando, Lucindo's servant, who ends up (unusually) dressing as a woman and also courting the *dama*'s mother Belisa, for different demands of the plot. These plays, and many others so eagerly bought by the canny *autores de comedias* at this time, reveal a playwright exuding confidence in his creative powers. The vibrancy of such comic works barely fades, as modern performances can demonstrate, for they deal with the perennial themes of youthful love and aged disapproval. However, the comedies are also of their time and contain numerous topical references, for example to the move of the court from Madrid to Valladolid between 1601 and 1606, royal festivities, military events, financial hardship and the economy, fellow writers' works. One might argue too that the comedies change social perceptions over time: the sheer ingenuity of their female characters suggests a proto-feminist bent in Lope: Fenisa, of *La discreta enamorada*, is cleverer than all but the *gracioso*, including her pretty but rather slow husband-to-be, Lucindo. The rise of a female voice in the *comedia nueva* is a noteworthy development, whether or not it had an actual effect on contemporary gender politics. Between them the witty female character and the *gracioso* gave Golden Age drama, in the hands of Lope, a subversive force that matched the social undermining inherent in picaresque prose fiction, and the concentration on the marginal that would play such a part in Golden Age painting.

Lope's later comedies, amongst which can be counted *La dama boba* (1613), *El perro del hortelano* (1613–15), *La vengadora de las mujeres* (1615–20),

---

[13] The dates of these two plays, which are more precise than Morley and Bruerton's estimations, come from Arata's excellent edition of the *comedia de capa y espada*, *El acero de Madrid*, pp. 17–20.

Amar sin saber a quién (1620–22), and *La moza de cántaro* (before 1627), are
the works of a playwright at the height of his comic powers, and increasingly
cynical, perhaps disillusioned at the lack of official recognition shown to him.
As so often with Lope, to generalize about the plays of a particular period or
type is to risk ignoring a host of exceptions, especially as he was capable of
writing in different veins (and indeed genres) within the same short space of
time. Clearly the problems we have dating many of his dramatic works adds to
the uncertainty. However, it would seem that these later comedies are
harder-hitting than the more overtly carnivalesque ones of his earlier days.
Although *La moza de cántaro* ends happily with the eponymous María marrying
Juan, she has had to commit murder (on stage) and run away from Ronda to
Madrid, denying her true social status, before her beauty and her lover's dedication to her bring about the happy close. *Amar sin saber a quién* re-works with a
new twist a comic staple, the so-called 'invisible mistress' plot (an inversion of
the classical Cupid–Psyche story), which Lope had so wittily explored in his
much earlier *La viuda valenciana*. However, this work begins with an on-stage
duel that leads to the death of Don Pedro and unjust incarceration of Don Juan,
newly arrived in Toledo from Seville. The female lead, Doña Leonarda, who
will eventually marry Juan, is a *mujer esquiva*: a woman who is initially resistant to the attractions of the opposite sex. The comic trajectory of the play is
overshadowed by the uncomfortable feeling of injustice, especially as Juan has
to spend most of the play in prison in place of the real killer, Leonarda's brother,
Don Fernando. The prison comes to represent social demands in general, as
character after character sees himself trapped by codes of etiquette and honour.
The image is so insistent that an audience can hardly fail to reflect upon parallels between physical and mental constriction and claustrophobia. Don Luis,
Juan's rival for Leonarda's love, characteristically begins a discussion of friendship with the words:

> Si diferencia ha de haber,
> ha de ser en las prisiones;
> que vos habéis de tenellas
> en el cuerpo, y yo en el alma.
>
> (Vega, *Amar sin saber a quién*, lines 1010–13)

The play also hinges upon the doubts that Juan and the *gracioso*, Limón, have
about the age and status of Juan's invisible admirer. As well as allowing Lope
the chance for some staple satirical jibes aimed at women who make themselves
up to appear younger than they are, there is an underlying (and characteristic)
uncertainty about whether things are as they really seem, which can be related to
the sceptical attitudes evident in other later Golden Age writers and thinkers.

Some of Lope's most memorable characters are the strong women of his
mature comedies. The prospect of writing for particular actresses, such as
Jerónima de Burgos (who played the blue-stocking, Nise, in *La dama boba*, and
to whom Lope gave or sold his manuscript, which still survives, in 1613), must
have pushed the playwright to new heights and subtleties of characterization that

were rarely matched in other national dramas. *La dama boba*, one of the few of Lope's comedies to have been seriously assessed by critics, manages to achieve a satisfying balance between the Horatian ideals of 'enseñar y deleitar', so dear to literary theorists of the Renaissance. The worldly-wise father, Otavio (in no way a caricature like Fenisa's foolish father, the *capitán*, of *La discreta enamorada*), despairs of his two daughters, the clever but self-satisfied Nise, and Finea, an ignoramus (the 'boba' of the title) who nevertheless possesses a large dowry provided by her uncle. Finea has been promised to the young *galán* Liseo. Nise's 'amado' is the impoverished Laurencio. During Act 1, both men change the object of their affections, one appalled by ignorance and attracted by intelligence, the other lured by money. Act 2 complicates the situation. There is evidence that love is educating Finea, but the two *galanes* are on the point of duelling over the confused state of the affairs of love. When, in Act 3, it becomes clear that Finea has been taught, coaxed to good sense, by her love for Laurencio and has become *discreta* instead of *boba*, the lovers' relationship is of course threatened. Liseo becomes interested in the rich sister again, making it necessary for Finea to *pretend* to be stupid, to play the role of the idiot. This time the audience knows that it is a pretence and enjoys the discomfort of the other characters and in particular the tricking of the supposedly highly intelligent Nise, who finally agrees to marry Liseo. Meanwhile Finea's mock innocence has allowed her to hide Laurencio and his comic servant in the attic, a move which allows her ultimately to compromise her father's honour and thus ensure union with her beloved.

One theme of the comedy is the power of love to educate. Lope's considered exploration of love makes use of neo-Platonism and Ovid's *Ars amandi* but also, characteristically, of his own experience of love as a combination of mental and physical desire. *Amor* is claimed to be the 'luz del entendimiento', a force which produces greater understanding, but Lope equally allows a sensual side to love, expressed through the erotic passion of Finea. One might even argue that in allowing Finea a surprising victory over her exquisitely refined sister he gives the palm of victory to the sensual lover. However, the fact the Finea 'learns' from a lover whose motivation is greed, muddies the waters, leaving the playwright characteristically uncommitted. The comedy additionally allows Lope, through Nise and her mini-academy of educated admirers, to comment on literary fashions and in particular on the fashion for writing poetry which is *culto*, i.e. in the complex and convoluted style of Góngora.

One of the advantages of the traditional comic theme of love for Lope de Vega, and a reason he wrote so many love comedies, was that (as in his kingship plays) allowing a character to be impassioned helps to strip away the norms of behaviour that social role would dictate. In Lope's comedies all are seen to be human at bottom: even the haughty Nise and her man-hating equivalent, Laura, of *La vengadora de las mujeres*, are shown to be susceptible to love like their fellow characters whom they apparently despise. As we have suggested, Lope aims to lay bare aspects of human nature, admirable and negative; not to present a thesis.

This process is most starkly revealed through the character of Diana in *El perro del hortelano*. The work is usually categorized as a *comedia palatina*, a common sub-genre of the comedy relating to its location (an aristocrat's or monarch's palace) and its theme (love intrigues amongst the higher echelons of society). Despite its darker implications its hero Teodoro calls it a 'famosa comedia'. The play's title, like those of many dramatic works of the period, is a tantalizing reference to a proverb, 'el perro del hortelano que ni come ni deja comer' (roughly in English, 'the dog in the manger'). Such titles would whet the audience's appetite, conceding some clue as to the content and genre of the play without giving too much away, and would often be referred to specifically at strategic points, such as the ends of acts, in order to leave the audience with something to ponder.

The beautifully structured plot of *El perro*, whether or not it has an Italian novella as its source, as has been suggested, seems to stem also from a theoretical concern: the sort of issue of love which might have been discussed and written about in an academy of the period. One question under consideration in Act 1 is: can jealousy lead to love? (We all know that love can lead to jealousy, but what about the other way around?) Lope's answer comes through the action of the play but also in a series of sonnets – there are an impressive nine in total – for which the action waits. The main characters are able to explore their feelings poetically, giving the lie to the critical assumption that the audience wanted nothing but a diet of action, and showing the importance of well spoken poetry as a part of the afternoon's entertainment. The countess Diana, rich, beautiful and unmarried, is courted by the aristocratic suitors Conde Federico (her cousin) and Marqués Ricardo, and is coming under increasing pressure to marry. Her secretary Teodoro is courting one of her maids, Marcela, and the play opens at night with Teodoro and Tristán the *gracioso*, as Teodoro abandons his amorous pursuits within the palace. When Diana gets to the bottom of the affair and finds out about the love suit she begins to behave inconsistently towards both lovers, cryptically allowing Teodoro at last to think that she loves him, as indeed she does. Each time that Teodoro makes a move to reciprocate she is overcome by the differences in their status and the incompatibility that entails. She gets cold feet and is thus the dog in the manger who will neither have Teodoro for herself nor let Marcela have him:

> Es el amor común naturaleza,
> mas yo tengo mi honor por más tesoro,
> que los respetos de quien soy adoro,
> y aun el pensarlo tengo por bajeza.

> (Vega, *El perro*, lines 329–32)

A state of confusion reigns and when the aristocratic suitors get an inkling of the state of affairs they plot to kill Teodoro. What could become a tragedy akin to Webster's *The Duchess of Malfi* remains comic, however, as Federico and Ricardo hire the *gracioso*, Tristán, to carry out the murder, convinced by his mock bravado. Order, happiness and a marriage only become possible because of Tristán's *ingenio*. Disguised as a beturbaned Armenian, he persuades a senile old aristocrat, Ludovico, that Teodoro is his long-lost son, allowing Diana to drop her reservations and declare her love fully and in a socially acceptable way. Even when she realizes that the proclaimed nobility is a sham, Diana is ready to embrace Teodoro for his nobility of spirit in revealing the truth behind Tristán's trick: 'que el gusto no está en grandezas,/ sino en ajustarse al alma/ aquello que se desea' (lines 3309–11).

The atmosphere of the play is often festive, verging at times on the farcical. However, there is a darker side which it is difficult to ignore: Marcela loses out and has to settle for Fabio rather than her well-matched suitor Teodoro; in her anxiety that no-one should know of their trick Diana suggests that they can murder Tristán; Ludovico is mercilessly tricked; there is a real possibility that Ricardo and Federico will discover the ruse and resume their plotting, or dishonour Diana as a revenge. The fiction, the *deus ex machina*, which allows the happy ending to take place, does not look very secure, to say the least.

Eric Bentley claimed that great comedy is in part defined by a basis in misery and the 'convention of gaiety [being] from time to time in danger' (Bentley, *The Life*, pp. 299–300). Lope's *El perro del hortelano* flirts outrageously with disaster and chaos and then transcends it with a knowing wink to the audience: 'que a nadie digáis se os ruega/ el secreto de Teodoro' (Vega, *El perro*, lines 3379–80). It is this confident self-consciousness that has led scholars to single out the comedy as one of the finest of the early-modern period.[14] Jack Sage, who looks at the play in the context of several other works which hinge on questions of misalliance (including *El mayordomo de la duquesa de Amalfi*, of 1604–6), feels that *El perro* reflects contemporary concerns about the reality of social climbing and the pervasiveness of the figure of the secretary. This it does through a novel generic mix: '*El perro del hortelano* was one of the forward-looking dramas that demanded a new critical vocabulary unacceptable to the classical theorist generally' (Sage, 'The context', p. 265). It is 'a deliberately funny play of *burlas veras*, a play which, on reflection, is to be taken as seriously as life itself' (p. 266).

It is tempting to see Lope himself in the figure of the *secretario* Teodoro: in the age of secretaries, the dramatist for many years filled the role for the Duke of Sessa, and he certainly had pretensions to rise socially. He tried and failed to become royal chronicler. But, whatever the personal interest, the play is at least, as Robert Pring-Mill has argued, a criticism of the sham of honour, evident in 'the wonderfully successful parody of a traditional happy ending' (Pring-Mill, 'Introduction', p. xxviii), and may simultaneously be a sharp satire on the demands of the statutes of *limpieza de sangre*. On paper it was impossible to be a fully free and functional member of society without a certificate of purity of blood. In actual fact the certificate could be bought or fabricated, and Teodoro's

---

[14] The play, perhaps now Lope's best known work within Spain, was turned into a popular and Goya-winning film directed by Pilar Miró in 1995.

sudden elevation is a parody of this process. Historically, as we have seen when examining *La pobreza estimada*, it is also true that many old Christian families were marrying into *converso* families who were financially successful. Lope uncovers this potential for hypocrisy within an apparently strictly orthodox society. As good comedy can and perhaps should, *El perro del hortelano* performs a satirical function as well as entertaining the masses. A high percentage of Lope's aristocratic characters are abusers of their social positions, and amongst the dramatist's favoured underdogs who best them are women, servants and peasants. Under scrutiny in this and other comedies of the period can be said to be nothing less than the authority of traditional noble values in Golden Age Spain.

Tragedies

The two broadly tragic works for which Lope is best known are *El caballero de Olmedo* (1618–21) and *El castigo sin venganza* (1631). The former, which has held a 'peculiar fascination' (Sage, *Lope de Vega*, p. 9) for scholars, is based partly on another play of the same name, of 1606, and, some have claimed, a sixteenth-century song, *El caballero*, which tells the story of the murder of a certain Juan de Vivero in 1521 between Medina del Campo and Olmedo. It is set in the early fifteenth century during the reign of Juan II of Castile. In the play Don Alonso, from Olmedo, has fallen in love with Doña Inés, a woman from the rival town of Medina, who is being unsuccessfully courted by Don Rodrigo. So love-sick is Alonso that he pays a go-between, a Celestina-like figure, Fabia, to intercede on his behalf. The atmosphere of the play, with Fabia's machinations (appeals to the devil, despoiling of dead bodies), Inés's lie to her father that she wants to become a nun, to avoid marriage to Rodrigo, and Alonso's and Tello's premonitions of doom (the dream of a goldfinch being caught by a hawk; a vision of his own shadow), leads the audience to the conclusion that the play will end unhappily. And yet, the plot with its love complications, stratagems and disguises is in some ways typical of a love comedy. (In other plays, such as Tirso's *Marta la piadosa*, a false vow of chastity is a comic ingredient.) As he returns to Olmedo to see his parents, as he does every night, Alonso, like King Pedro in Calderón's *El médico de su honra*, hears a snatch of song ('Que de noche le mataron') about his own death. Sure enough, en route, Alonso is shot in a cowardly fashion by his enemy Rodrigo's men. When the king discovers the truth of the crime, in an ironic ending in which Inés's father offers her Alonso in marriage, he prepares to have Rodrigo and his friend Fernando executed. To add to the poignant sense of waste and what might have been, we learn that the king was about to promote the gifted Alonso.

The twentieth-century concern about whether *El caballero de Olmedo* can justifiably be labelled a tragedy, whilst understandable, has distracted some attention from the fascinating questions the work raises. It is unusual for Lope to deny well-matched lovers their happy ending in marriage. In other broadly tragic works there is less teasing of the audience with the hint of a comic trajectory.

How can this ambivalence be explained? One answer is that Lope takes more literally than ever his thought from the *Arte nuevo*: 'buen ejemplo nos da naturaleza,/ que por tal variedad tiene belleza' (Vega, *Arte nuevo*, p. 15). The irony of the ending strikes a chord with audience members, who well know that in real life the best laid plans and the most ardent desires can be cruelly dashed by fate or Providence. If there is a dominant lesson in the play it is that Don Alonso must be regarded, however misty-eyed his contemporaries might feel about it, as an anachronistic hero. The exquisite lover and self-sufficient knight who wears his nobility on his sleeve and trusts to the prowess of his sword arm, dies shot from a distance by an arquebus, powerless to defend himself. Although justice is served when Rodrigo is punished for his jealousy it is too late for the knight to reap the rewards of marriage. For once the escapism of Golden Age comic resolutions is undermined by Lope in a more pessimistic frame of mind.

Lope de Vega was always aware, as we know from the *Arte nuevo*, of the fact that abroad, and for purists wherever they were, his drama was unsatisfactory. The mixture of genres and the lack of respect for neo-classical rules made it difficult for him to feel appreciated in more erudite circles. Yet Lope's pride in his dramatic ability constantly comes through in his prologues and other writing on the theatre. He was very highly regarded by his compatriots and was well aware of this fact, even when he realized that he would never satisfy the *preceptistas*, and the literary enemies who attacked him in print. An example of the respect felt for Lope by the majority comes in the censor's approval of *El castigo sin venganza*: Fray Francisco Palau writes of the play that 'es tal esta tragedia que sólo podía ser de Lope'. He stresses that '[c]on decir que es de Frey Lope Félix de Vega Carpio y que la confiesa por hija de su ingenio, queda aprobada por muy conforme a la fe y buenas costumbres y adornada y compuesta de suma erudición, dotrina, elegancia y agudeza acostumbrada'.[15]

As he neared the end of his life it seems that Lope was keen to make a statement, to leave a last great work behind him, one that would satisfy the populace but also the harsher critics. To this end he adapted an Italian novella based on a historical event, about the misfortunes of the Duke of Ferrara, turning it into a *tragedia* 'que está escrita al estilo español, no por la antigüedad griega y severidad latina' (Vega, *El castigo*, ed. Pedraza Jiménez, p. 75). Lope signed the manuscript of *El castigo sin venganza* on 1 August 1631, specifically calling it a tragedy, something he rarely did. He gives the impression that he has been working at the height of his creative powers to produce the work, and scholars have generally concurred that this is Lope's greatest play, tightly structured, persuasive, moving and ironic. In the prologue to the printed version Lope explains that there was only one performance of the play in *la corte* 'por causas que a vuesamerced le importan poco' (p. 75).

The play's protagonist is yet another philandering head of state, the duque de

---

15 Reproduced in Vega, *El castigo*, ed. Pedraza Jiménez, pp. 71–2. This edition also reproduces Lope's source, the work by Bandello translated by Belleforest.

Ferrara. He is the father of the illegitimate, but much-loved, conde Federico. His vassals persuade him, for the future security of the realm, to marry the beautiful young Casandra, from a neighbouring territory. He does so against his inclination and after Casandra and Federico have clearly been attracted to each other on meeting before the marriage formalities. By Act 2, the Duke's scandalous neglect of his young wife persuades her to pursue a relationship with her step-son, a course of action which is made easier by the Duke's absence as he leaves to fight for the Pope. On his return the Duke is apparently a reformed character determined, after his victory, to mend his ways. However, he is anonymously informed of the relationship between Federico and Casandra and he punishes them with death: Federico, alone with the Duke, is made to kill a bound and gagged figure by his father, a figure who turns out to be his lover. The Duke then accuses Federico in front of the court of having murdered his step-mother because she was pregnant with a legitimate heir who would oust him. The courtiers fall upon Federico and dispatch him, providing an instant punishment which the Duke convinces himself is not revenge. The Duke feels he has acted as a shrewd monarch by dominating his natural desire for revenge as a wronged husband and actually punishing the pair for the crime of *lèse-majesté*, as a just king should: 'No es tomarla [la venganza]/ el castigar la justicia' (Vega, *El castigo*, ed. Pedraza Jiménez, lines 3013–14). His dishonour has been (perhaps inadequately) covered up, however, by *razón de estado*, in the interests of his realm.

Scholars have tended to side with A. A. Parker's assessment that '[e]verything that happens in the play follows from [the Duke's] actions by an unbroken chain of cause and effect whose first link is forged by the type of conduct exemplified in the very first scene. This being so, it is impossible that anyone else can be the protagonist' (Parker, *The Approach*, p. 17). Parker sees the Duke as the tragic figure: he it is who brings about his own disaster, and yet ironically he has reformed by the time he is punished and is left without the hope of an heir and without the son that he loved. His errors in his private life come to have an effect on his public role which he should have foreseen. Lope makes the figure of the Duke more complex by giving him an intelligence and self-knowledge which constantly nag him, and perhaps make his later conversion (or change of character) more believable.

The lesson of the play for the Duke, as for King Juan II in *El duque de Viseo*, is that vicious actions have unexpected and long-lasting consequences. The Duke's actions of earlier in the play (his philandering, to which Parker refers, his neglect of his new bride), and earlier in his life (his reluctance to marry to ensure smooth succession in the realm, his fathering of an illegitimate child), come home to roost. He is forced to produce a mockery of justice to end the affair and is promised further trouble in the future, as well as having to live with the loss of his beloved Federico.

El castigo sin venganza can be seen as a kingship play and probably did fly too close to the sun for the liking of the court, but it is also a tragedy of passion and love, in which the emotions of the three principal protagonists are given ample expression through exquisite soliloquies and speeches to confidants. It is clear that in taking the young and beautiful Casandra in marriage by proxy, without having seen her, the Duke is merely doing his duty, feeling he should provide an heir to the dukedom, but half-wishing not to. Yet could he have foreseen the betrayal of his wife and son? His anguished final scenes produce the best from Lope, as the Duke grapples with his love, his visceral desire for vengeance and his need to show that he is in control of the state:

> Esto [i.e. killing Casandra] aun pudiera, ofendida,
> sufrir la piedad humana,
> pero dar muerte a un hijo,
> ¿qué corazón no desmaya?
> Sólo de pensarlo, ¡ay triste!,
> tiembla el cuerpo, expira el alma,
> lloran los ojos, la sangre
> muere en las venas heladas,
> el pecho se desalienta,
> el entendimiento falta,
> la memoria está corrida
> y la voluntad turbada.
>
> (Vega, *El castigo*, ed. Pedraza Jiménez, lines 2866–77)

The Duke never has much sympathy for his new bride but we do as an audience, especially at the beginning of the second act when Casandra's anguished speech to her maid, Lucrecia, alerts us to the Duke's neglect of her and the simplicity of her natural desires. She would prefer to be a low-born peasant woman just so long as she could guarantee being satisfied by her husband, just to find him there when she awakes in the morning. Her affection for Federico would have died under the duty and obligations of her position had it not been for the Duke's adulterous pursuit of other women. Her decision to enter into a relationship with Federico is taken with revenge in mind but also because she wants to be loved and respected. As Batín, the *gracioso*, suggests, the wrong pair has been brought together. Casandra knows from the moment she seduces Federico that she has signed her death warrant. And yet anything seems better than the dishonour in which she lives.

Perhaps the most tortured character is Federico, who is barely allowed to express his own feelings, to the extent that when he does so in Act 2 they emerge in an uncontrolled lyricism: an outpouring of metaphor and intense poetry reveals his pent up love. When it is already too late, Federico backs away from Casandra inflaming her even more, and desperately trying to undo what has been done. Casandra has loved him but has used him for revenge; the Duke also loves him but has him killed and his memory destroyed. The populace will believe in his infamy for ever more.

In *El castigo sin venganza* Lope barely wastes a word. His control over character, plot and theme seems effortless, and yet again, through a play which appeals on a human level to a broad audience, the playwright is able to make a sharp point to those who look beyond the tragic emotions expressed in the poetry. Although he does not die, the tragedy of the Duke's final situation is clear. He is a weakened leader, who has lost his family and probably the chance to settle the succession of his kingdom before he dies. The position of ruler is a key one and the ruler must be guided by virtue.

Most overarching assessments of Lope de Vega's drama are bound to suffer from being reductive. In this chapter some 40 plays have been mentioned (approximately a tenth of the extant works, whilst more than the complete works of Shakespeare) and only a handful have been analysed in any detail, allowing a mere glimpse at the richness and variety of the whole. The vastness of the dramatic *oeuvre* continues to be an impediment to a fuller understanding of Lope. However, the growth in recent scholarship, and the publication by the ProLope group of the complete plays in reliable modern editions, suggests that a rehabilitation of Lope de Vega as a major European dramatist is underway. One of the eventual results of this reassessment may be to see his drama, through the New Historical lens, as broadly political (rather in the way that Shakespeare's plays have been viewed in recent years), as more engaged with their social and political contexts than has hitherto been thought. Whilst such new approaches are to be welcomed, it should not be forgotten that Lope was a man who valued variety and whose sensibilities would be initially touched by a story, not a thesis or a theory. As a dramatist he was a story-teller who understood and was able to depict convincingly an array of motivations for human behaviour. Moreover he did this from his years as a footloose young man in the 1580s to his devout old age in the 1630s. To try to contain and understand Lope de Vega is a mammoth, but highly rewarding task.

Cervantes, Tirso de Molina, and
the First Generation

Among the many playwrights plying their trade in the early years of the development of the *comedia nueva*, was, as we saw in chapter 1, Spain's greatest writer, Miguel de Cervantes Saavedra. It was his works in prose, of course, which were to make Cervantes's reputation amongst his contemporaries and for posterity. He probably did have some success as a playwright, though, in the early days of the *corrales* and before Lope de Vega had begun to shape the *comedia nueva*, and his surviving drama deserves careful attention. Cervantes's failure later in life to have his plays performed has led to his characterization as a frustrated man of the theatre, bitter at the success of Lope's flawed but popular product. (In fact, had Cervantes captured the imagination of the play-going public in the 1590s and early seventeenth century, instead of Lope, there would have been profound repercussions for the development of the novel: Don Quijote and Sancho Panza might never have come to life, at least in the form of characters in a long prose work. As it is, *Don Quijote* can be described as theatrical in a number of respects, betraying a lasting fascination with the compact between audience and performance.) In the ten extant plays that certainly belong to Cervantes, we can discern a sharp intelligence and a frequently playful attitude towards the Lopean dramatic norms. We shall begin this chapter by looking at some of his representative later works.

The other playwrights whose works are mentioned or explored in this chapter are also contemporaries of Lope, who were heavily influenced by his dramatic practice, who travelled the same road, but possessed strong individual voices. They belong to the *comedia nueva*'s first generation: their work could not have developed without Lope de Vega, and they must be seen as his disciples, although not slavish imitators by any means. Cervantes was the exception in not rapidly and enthusiastically taking up the model of the *comedia nueva*. His example proves that any who might have had aesthetic doubts about Lope's *modus operandi*, who were not broadly in step with his populist agenda, would have condemned their works to silence, at best a soulless existence on the page. The quality of the plays written by the most brilliant of his followers, the Mercedarian friar Tirso de Molina (1579–1648), who championed in print the progress evident in Lope's dramatic innovations, demands separate treatment. The other main figures considered, after Tirso, are the Valencian Guillén de Castro (1569–1631), the Andalusians Mira de Amescua (1570?–1644) and

Vélez de Guevara (1578?–1644), and the Mexican-born Ruiz de Alarcón (1580?–1639). Finally, we shall come to assess the works of the several female playwrights who wrote in Spain in the Golden Age. Most also followed Lope's lead although there is no firm evidence that their plays were ever performed in the *corrales*.

Miguel de Cervantes

Cervantes's playwriting activity tends to be divided into two phases: his years of some success in the 1580s, which we examined briefly in chapter 1, when he wrote largely neo-classical plays in four acts, which *were* performed; and then his return to dramatic writing probably after the success of *Don Quijote*, Part I, in the years leading up to 1615.[1] In the latter phase the long shadow of Lope's dramaturgy is inescapable, as we shall see. From the former, only two, possibly three (see p. 20), of a score or more works survive. *El cerco de Numancia*, alluded to in chapter 1, and *El trato de Argel*, a play clearly based on aspects of his own five-year captivity in Algiers, are written in four acts and remained unpublished until 1734. His own view of his achievements on the stage in the 1580s, expressed when an old man, is rose-tinted and should be treated with caution (see pp. 123–4).

Cervantes's collection of eight full-length plays, published in Madrid in 1615, has endured a rather mixed critical reception. On balance, and in spite of recent spirited arguments to the contrary, readers of the past two centuries have tended to deem the plays failures, especially when measured against the inevitable yardsticks of both Lope de Vega's *comedia nueva*, and their author's achievements in prose genres. The very appearance of the *Ocho comedias y ocho entremeses nuevos, nunca representados* was anomalous: by releasing the works to a bookseller, Cervantes broke the fashion (which was to endure) for publishing *comedias* in groups of a dozen, a practice established several years earlier by Tavanno when he published Lope's *Parte primera*. Most unusual, however, was that the plays were not 'viejos': their very publication was an admission of their creator's failure to interest an *autor de comedias* in performing them. A practising playwright would automatically think of selling his wares to a director, not to a publisher. The status of the *Ocho comedias*, and their accompanying *entr'actes*, as 'nunca representados' is famously addressed by Cervantes in the *prólogo* to his volume, and has heavily influenced approaches to his theatre. The would-be dramatist laments the absence of 'pájaros en los nidos de antaño' (Cervantes, *Entremeses*, p. 93), that is, his difficulty in finding *autores* who still trust him as a dramatic draw. He perhaps disingenuously claims that the reason for rejection (one apparently offered him by an *autor de comedias*) is the poverty of his verse. In the *Adjunta al Parnaso* the author hints at a kind of blacklisting,

---

[1] Some suggest a third phase of playwriting in the 1590s. Cervantes is vague about exactly when he wrote the eight plays he published in 1615, and they have proved extremely difficult to date other than approximately.

perhaps implying Lope's use of his influence – certainly unproven and probably unnecessary – to block his rival's potential return to the stage. 'Miguel' also reveals to his interlocutor, Pancracio, in this dialogue, an awareness of the tides of fashion, consciousness of which may justify the claim that Cervantes felt that his theatre's time would come, that his idiosyncratic works would find an appreciative audience once the *vulgo*-pleasing *comedia nueva* had had its day.

Despite his dejection at his late drama's consignment to the page – and his practical craftsmanship provides clear evidence, however loud the dissenting voices, that his theatre *was* written with performance in mind – Cervantes's pride in his influential place in Spanish theatrical history is obvious. As well as claiming to have been the first to reduce the number of acts from five to three, he argues that 'fui el primero que representase las imaginaciones y los pensamientos escondidos del alma, sacando figuras morales al teatro, con general y gustoso aplauso de los oyentes' (Cervantes, *Entremeses*, pp. 92–3). Although it is impossible to know to what specifically, in his lost works of the 1580s, Cervantes might be referring here, he does reveal himself to be quite experimental in his later plays, for example bringing on stage characters who identify themselves with placards or by wearing numbers, and abstracting individuals' mental struggles by presenting allegorical figures on stage.

From the dialogue between the priest and the Canon of Toledo in *Don Quijote*, I, 48, one might assume that Cervantes is a classicist, or *preceptista*, when it comes to his theory of drama. He objects, if it is indeed his voice behind these characters, to the breaking of the neo-classical unities of time and place by contemporary writers for the stage. He also criticizes abuses of decorum and verisimilitude, ridiculing especially authors of 'comedias divinas' for the liberties they take with historical truth. And yet he is no classicist himself in the *Ocho comedias*, being more relaxed in the adherence to Aristotle's notion of a single action (the 'unity of action', as it has been termed, explored in chapter 5 of his *Poetics*) than Lope de Vega, for example. Indeed the fascinating and unexpected appearance of the figure of Comedia in conversation with Curiosidad, at the beginning of Act 2 of *El rufián dichoso*, at first appears to suggest that Cervantes has swallowed his objections to Lopean drama and conceded defeat to this monstrous talent. Comedia defends, albeit rather coolly, the abandonment of classical principles:

> Buena fui pasados tiempos,
> y en éstos, si los mirares,
> no soy mala, aunque desdigo
> de aquellos preceptos graves.
>
> (Cervantes, *El rufián*, lines 1233–6)

She specifically advocates the modern dramatist's right to move the action of the play across the Atlantic between acts: the story of a pimp-turned-Dominican-friar, Cristóbal de Lugo (later Cristóbal de la Cruz), begins in the Sevillian underworld and ends in Mexico. However, the ambivalent character of Comedia undermines the content of her own speech, leaving us in doubt as to the playwright's personal theory of drama. In fact Cervantes does not fit comfortably into either camp: classical or Lopean. He is certainly keenly interested in the way the theatre has developed under Lope's tutelage, but parodies the structure, the content and the superficiality often evident in the underlying philosophies of the *comedia nueva*, especially as represented by less accomplished *ingenios*. In doing so he produces a small *oeuvre* of great variety and depth. He tackles the *comedia de santos* and the *comedia de capa y espada*, using material from Ariosto, from contemporary sources, from folklore, and from his own experience. Cervantes is not a seventeenth-century playwright toying with Brechtian or Pirandellian ideas *avant la lettre*, as some have enthusiastically suggested, but his is nevertheless a far more important dramatic voice than has habitually been recognized.

A look at two of the *Ocho comedias* ought to demonstrate how and why this is the case. Although this pair of plays, *Pedro de Urdemalas* and *El rufián dichoso*, cannot pretend to be representative given the variety within the collection, they can at least introduce some of the complexity and originality (and indeed playfulness) of Cervantes's drama. The former, taking the established folkloric figure of Pedro as its protagonist, superficially resembles a *comedia nueva*, written polymetrically and in three acts. However, Cervantes pointedly ignores Lope's advice in the contemporaneous *Arte nuevo* suggesting the setting up of 'el caso' in Act 1, its complication until the middle of Act 3 and then abrupt resolution, 'mirando que la fábula/ de ninguna manera sea episódica' (Vega, *Arte nuevo*, p. 15). Instead he builds his play around episodes from the ingenious Pedro's life. The protagonist narrates his picaresque life story in Act 1 and we witness his playing a number of other roles in a series of superficially linked vignettes: he is adviser to a rural mayor, then gipsy, blind man, soul in torment, student, and finally actor. Other characters come and go as the changes in action demand. Although the romantic story of the gipsy/princess Belica, who first emerges some thousand lines into the play, and indeed Pedro's own search for a role in life, do find a kind of resolution at the end, the work is striking for its deliberate resistance to most *comedia* norms.

The love story, so dear to Lope and so central to his plays' structure, would usually involve a *galán* and *dama*, with a second pairing permitted, and a romance between servants often providing comic relief. (Indeed Lope de Vega's own *Pedro de Urdemalas*, probably written in the same period as Cervantes's, features an extended and typically complex love intrigue at its heart.) In Cervantes's play the main love story is between peasants, Clemente and Clemencia, and ends happily, if farcically, before Act 1 is complete. Pedro seems at one point destined to love Belica, but their relationship stalls almost before it has started as she is far more interested in finding her rightful social position and scorns all but the king, to whom she turns out to be related. Love, it emerges, is just one aspect of life, which may be found and may be missed. In the *comedia nueva* it has become the *raison d'être*, and contributes to the genre's perversion of a reflection of life.

There are other aspects of Cervantes's frustration with or intellectual disdain for the dominant dramatic genre evident in *Pedro de Urdemalas*. In another deliberate inversion of the *comedia* custom, the petulant, love-struck king and jealous queen provide light relief, not a serious set of values to be contrasted with those of the lower classes. Above all, no single plot-line, or *fábula*, predominates in the play. It can be said to be a mirror of the world, but precisely because it lacks order, reflecting slices of life in all its tumultuous uncertainty. Above all perhaps, the character of Pedro incarnates a quest for identity in this chaotic world. A fortune-teller has predicted great things for his future and, although he is sceptical, 'todavía veo en mí/ un no sé qué que me inclina/ a ser todo lo que oí' (Cervantes, *Pedro*, lines 761–3). Whether or not the 'no sé qué que me inclina' reminds the reader of San Juan de la Cruz's spiritual anxiety in the *Cántico espiritual*, the play can be said to chart Pedro's and Everyman's fraught quest for identity. Cervantes's surprisingly modern conclusion is that Pedro will be satisfied only by performing many parts as an actor on this great stage of the world. Pedro's acceptance of his new multiple role unavoidably points to the essential theatricality of life. Cervantes is not advocating here a world in which each individual's identity is protean: giving the starring role in his play to a social chameleon, rather than a predictable character-type, is intended to undermine the predictability of the *comedia nueva*'s so-called reflection of life. Pedro's story indicates that life does not happen neatly and justly.

One of the ways that the originality of Cervantes's conception of drama emerges is through metatheatre, the deliberate breaking of the frame or fictional illusion, so common in his prose works too. This feature of the Baroque (see pp. xi–xii) is taken, for example in paintings by Velázquez and Murillo, to be a sign of a breakdown of authority in both its key senses, social and artistic. Although metatheatre is common in Golden Age drama, especially as the genre grows old and is affectionately teased by Calderón and Sor Juana Inés de la Cruz, Cervantes's sharp dramatic self-consciousness clearly has Lope de Vega in its sights, and other possible paths to follow in mind. In his final speech of the play Pedro points out that the drama his new troupe performs 'no acaba en casamiento,/ cosa común y vista cien mil veces' (Cervantes, *Pedro*, lines 3169–70), and indeed, in other plays he ensures that standard resolutions are explicitly avoided.[2]

Although his *entremeses* have always been popular (see pp. 158–9), an increased scholarly interest in Cervantes's full-length plays has been noticeable in recent years. These plays have also caught the attention, for the first time, of major companies and directors: in 1992 Adolfo Marsillach mounted *La gran sultana* at the Compañía Nacional de Teatro Clásico to great acclaim; in 2005 the same company performed *La entretenida*, directed by Helena Pimenta, and in 2004 in the United Kingdom, the Royal Shakespeare Company (RSC)

---

[2] The ending of *La entretenida*, often taken to be a parody of Lope's drama, is a good example (see Zimic, 'Cervantes frente a Lope'). See also Trambaioli's analysis of Cervantes's borrowings from Lope in *La casa de los celos*, 'Una protocomedia'.

presented Philip Osment's English verse translation of *Pedro de Urdemalas*, under the direction of Mike Alfreds. This last production made a point of emphasizing the metatheatrical nature of the work: Pedro himself made an announcement to the audience at the start of each new 'episode', while, throughout the production, the whole cast sat in full view of the audience at the back of the stage awaiting their cues (see appendix 2 for details of Osment's translation). Cervantes had waited a long time for his serious drama to be tested on the stage and the signs are that it is engaging, witty and profound. It is certainly performable.

One play which still awaits a major *première* is the fascinating *comedia divina*, *El rufián dichoso*. Like *Pedro de Urdemalas* this work is in three acts, although Act 1, which presents episodically the dissolute life of the young Cristóbal in Seville, is disproportionately long at over 1200 lines. Acts 2 and 3 contrast greatly with the first: not only are they much shorter but their content is quite distinct. The action, such as it is, moves to Mexico with all scenes taking place indoors in the Dominicans' cells or in the house of Doña Ana Treviño, the unrepentant sinner whom Cristóbal will save by assuming her past wickedness in the form of leprosy. Actions, including the later deeds and death of the protagonist, are more often reported rather than witnessed by the audience. The chasm between the two halves of the play is bridged by the appearance of Curiosidad and Comedia, whose dialogue wittily distinguishes Cervantes's drama from Lope's *comedia nueva* (not to mention Aristotle). Despite its nod in the direction of the classical chorus, the dialogue most resembles a contemporary *loa*. In the *corrales*, the *loa* was spoken to quieten the audience before Act 1 of the play, signalling the start of proceedings (see pp. 153–4). Its content varied greatly but often enough it was concerned with artistic matters. It was a separate entity from the drama that followed. Cervantes is again being mischievous in placing his discussion of dramatic theory in a '*loa*' which interrupts the action of the play by emerging before the wrong act.

This concern with dramatic form, often playful, is evident in several other places in *El rufián dichoso*: for example, in Act 1 Cervantes self-consciously avoids pursuing a promising honour plot typical of the *comedia nueva* when a woman, simply denominated '*dama*', makes amorous approaches to Cristóbal as her *marido* appears. As in *Pedro de Urdemalas*, the playwright undermines the figures of the *galán* and the *dama* by making Cristóbal resist the attentions of two women. There are several other points at which a reader or an audience will become conscious of the play's difference from the usual fare, and thus of what the usual fare consists. Just as *Don Quijote* is a novel partly about what a novel is, so Cervantes's drama questions its own artistic form. However, *Don Quijote* attracts with its content as well as playing with form, and the story of Cristóbal's *pari* and conversion, leading to a saint-like life in Mexico, is also edifying. Cervantes shows that humans have the power within them to change, to be resolute, against the backdrop of an unpredictable and unpromising world.

Tirso de Molina

Tirso de Molina was the *nom de plume* of Gabriel Téllez, who was born in Madrid, most probably in 1579. This was the year, as it happened, of the creation in Spain's new capital of the Corral de la Cruz, the first of the two permanent playhouses which would become a hub of the city's life for the next hundred and fifty years or so and which would stage many of the monk-playwright's dramas. Little is known for certain about Téllez's early life, leading imaginative biographers to create a host of myths. It *is* documented that by 1600 Tirso had begun his novitiate in the Order of Mercy, and that he was chosen as a representative of the Mercedarian Order to travel across the Atlantic on a mission to Santo Domingo between 1616 and 1618. He had begun to write for the stage before this journey, in his late twenties or early thirties, and enthusiastically allied himself with Lope de Vega and the *comedia nueva*.

It would seem that 1621 marked an important change in Tirso's life. With the death of Philip III, whom the playwright admired, and the accession of the teenaged Philip IV and the rise of his favourite, the Count-Duke of Olivares, the playwright's drama took on a more overtly satirical edge. By 1625 Olivares's reformers were complaining about the 'escándalo' Tirso was causing 'con comedias que hace profanas y de malos incentivos y ejemplos' (Kennedy, *Studies*, p. 85), and they asked for the playwright to be removed to a far-away monastery, and to be prevented from writing such material again. It is telling that the Junta de Reformación referred in their judgement on Tirso not to the principle of a religious man writing drama, but to the content of the works themselves, which must have been perceived as threatening by the new government. Tirso did leave Madrid but in fact continued to be well regarded within his Order, becoming its *cronista general*, or official historian. He maintained some involvement with the theatre but was much less prominent than he had been, penning some new plays, such as the Pizarro trilogy (1626–9), and dedicating time to polishing his earlier works for publication. Five *partes* appeared between 1627 and 1636 (the second of which in fact probably contains only four plays by Tirso). He died in Almazán in 1648.

Tirso had presumably elected to employ a pseudonym as a young writer because of the disapproval he might evince as a religious man associated with the popular theatre. The theatrical world endured frequent criticism from moralists, some of them belonging to Tirso's own order, and so his involvement with it is a clear indication of his independence of mind. He was no slavish imitator aesthetically either: some of his arguments in favour of the new drama, outlined in the miscellany *Cigarrales de Toledo*, published in 1624, were more emphatic than Lope's guarded precepts. Indeed, free from the niceties of literary academicians, he produced through the character Don Alejo, in the *Cigarrales*, one of the most intellectually satisfying defences of the *comedia nueva* written in Spain. He expressed no regret about abandoning the classical authorities. He ridiculed the imposition of an unrealistic unity of time, and claimed that Spanish drama was evolving towards perfection, that a dramatist may build on historical truth to find something more universally meaningful, and also that a blend of the old tragic and comic genres produces 'una mezcla apacible' like a hybrid fruit.

Tirso's individuality is plain to see in the details of his life that are known, and his plays themselves are a revelation in their wit, their originality and the breadth of their subject matter. His drama benefits from the confidence that comes from a certainty about the medium employed. They are economically but often intricately structured, broadly comic in terms of genre (but without regard for the social status of the protagonists), and above all hard-hitting. For a man of the cloth who lived much of his life in monasteries, Tirso is a remarkably perceptive creator of characters, particularly women. He has an eye for psychological motivation and a sure appreciation of what will invite sympathy and what ridicule. Especially during his Madrid years in the early 1620s he must have been able to witness at first hand the 'confusión de confusiones' which was the world of the court and of the burgeoning capital city, yet draw back to the stability of his religious certainties. Tirso was well-placed to make satirical observations.

Although posterity remembers Tirso de Molina chiefly for introducing the figure of Don Juan to European drama, comedy is predominant amongst his seventy or so surviving full-length plays, as it was for Lope de Vega. He fashioned a good number of urban, courtly comedies, set in his contemporary Spain, and a handful of palace-based plays of which *El vergonzoso en palacio* is the best known. To the popular comic ingredients of the daughter forced into marriage against her will, the *indiano* returning home in search of a bride, the monstrous father, the *mujer vestida de hombre*, the *gracioso*, the jest in earnest, the 'long-lost' nobleman, the foolishness and ingenuity of lovers, Tirso tended always to add a witty twist, an irony or an absurdity. There are plays in which he seems to challenge himself to take a notion to its limits, or in which the zaniness of the idea has itself sparked the *poeta*'s imagination. Although his plots are frequently complex, apparently chaotic, he tends to be scrupulous to a fault about returning to order and justice at their end.

A host of lesser-known comedies are worth reading and deserve the attentions of a modern-day director. In 2004 the Compañía Nacional de Teatro Clásico in Madrid produced *La celosa de sí misma* (early 1620s), a play which ingeniously mocks male obsession with a literary ideal of beauty. Like most of these comedies the play also provides a satirical commentary on city life, here in particular its excessive pace and the anonymity of living in Madrid accommodation. *Desde Toledo a Madrid* (1626), set in part on the route between Spain's capitals old and new, charts the unconventional love-affair and burlesque but Christian marriage of Don Baltasar and Doña Mayor. *La huerta de Juan Fernández* is a gentler love comedy in which Tirso's characters resort heavily to disguise. *El amor médico* (1620), *La villana de Vallecas* (1618), and *Por el sótano y el torno* (1623) all also display the ingenuity of lovers able to outwit their adversaries, and overcome obstacles to future happiness through disguise or clever exploitation of their surroundings. Although the young lovers of comedy are staple figures, Tirso's comic dramas manage to avoid cliché and

remain fresh and amusing thanks to the liveliness and originality of his imagination, the sharpness of his perception, and the constant linguistic surprises of
which he is capable.

Three comedies must be considered in a little more detail: *Marta la piadosa*
and *Don Gil de las calzas verdes* (both 1615) and *El vergonzoso en palacio* (an
early play, polished for 1621?). The first of these works, occasionally inappropriately bracketed with Molière's *Tartuffe*, features a clever young woman who
elects, under severe pressure, to fake a fundamental change to her usual social
role, a decision which transforms all of her subsequent behaviour, and the
expectations other characters have of her. Marta pretends to have taken a vow of
chastity in order to avoid marriage to the *indiano*, Urbina, a rich and old friend
of her father, Gómez, and thus has to maintain a façade of piety which all but
persuades her father of her unavailability for marriage. Don Gómez is anxious to
marry her off, partly through greed and partly so that he can replace his son,
killed by Marta's lover Felipe, with a son-in-law, however old the latter may be.
The old men are frustrated by Marta's newly forged place in society ('Ni es
carne ansí ni pescado' (Tirso, *Marta*, II, line 84), complains Urbina), whilst the
clever Marta rejoices in a freedom she did not realize she could have as woman:

> ya no llamo
> a la dueña, al escudero,
> ni aguardo la silla y coche,
> ni me riñen si a la noche
> vuelvo: voy a donde quiero.   (II, lines 558–62)

The play features the usual vicissitudes of the lovers of comedy whilst poking
satirical fun at a number of aspects of contemporary society, particularly its
obsession with money, but probably also the way in which marriages were
arranged (specifically the seeking out of a husband for a daughter amongst the
extended family or social peer group, however ill-matched the couple). Tirso has
been occasionally censured for including a death in the play's pre-history and
for Marta's display of 'hypocrisy', which are seen to render the play quasi-
tragic. However, we must remember that questions of honour and religion, even
life and death, can be treated with less respect in a comedy. The audience has
different, conventional expectations of this genre, and the playwright exploits
this fact. Tirso may appear more *risqué* in his comic material than other contemporary playwrights, but his daring content, his risk-taking, is precisely what
makes him stand apart as a comic artist. His marginal position, just outside
mainstream society, allows him to ridicule the social concerns of Madrid's
middle classes, and arguably criticize the treatment of women it explicitly
endorses. The play asks some troubling questions but in doing so lives up to the
demands of its genre.

Don Gil de las calzas verdes, a play apparently disliked by Lope and unsuccessful with its first audience, is one of the most interesting and innovative
comedies of the Golden Age. Tirso seems to challenge himself to produce a love
intrigue of such complexity that it becomes almost impossible to follow except

in performance: there are generational conflicts, frequent changes of location within Madrid, disguises (at one point four characters dress as the fictitious Gil simultaneously and for different ends), mistaken identities and misunderstandings, night and balcony scenes, changes of heart, a fight, misappropriated belongings, and in Caramanchel, one of the wittiest, and most confused, of *graciosos*, all cleverly woven into a seamless plot. Behind the Don Gil of the title is the cross-dressing Doña Juana from Valladolid, whose aim in the play is to reclaim her seducer, the miserable Don Martín, who has acceded to his father's demands that he win a rich marriageable girl, Inés, in Madrid. As in all good comedy, there is a serious message lurking beneath the surface, for a thoughtful audience to ponder: here the main targets of satire are greed and hypocrisy, born of the obsession with social status. The playwright unveils the depths of immoral, destructive behaviour to which even ostensibly upright members of society will stoop in pursuit of their own comfort and security. As well as dressing as the charmingly ridiculous Don Gil, Juana invents another alter ego with a heart-rending story, Doña Elvira. Juana pursues Martín relentlessly, having her servant inform him of her pregnancy and subsequent death in childbirth, stealing his intended bride's affections, 'haunting' him, and finally having him arrested under false pretences. The lengths to which Tirso is prepared to go in undermining the credibility and authority of the *galán*, Don Martín, makes the play all the more amusing, but does cause problems for the audience, and was perhaps the source of Lope's disquiet. How can we now imagine the gibbering Martín as an appropriate husband for the admirable Juana? All of her ingenuity and energy will be wasted in a union with her pretty but spineless husband.

El vergonzoso en palacio is another play with strong comic credentials, but is a more obvious hybrid than *Marta* or *Don Gil*, exceeding generic expectations intriguingly and establishing Tirso as a greater risk-taker than his mentor. It begins with an *in medias res* dispute between the Duque de Avero and Conde de Estremoz which seems destined to end in the death of one of them, and although it deals with youthful love and ends conventionally in marriages, by no means everyone is left contented. The play has been regularly compared to another *comedia palatina*, Lope's *El perro del hortelano*, but the similarities are limited. In Tirso's play the young Mireno, brought up in the countryside, seeks his fortune at the court of Avero, where the Duke's daughter Madalena falls in love with him and makes him her secretary. Like Lope's Diana, Madalena finds it embarrassing to declare her love to a social inferior directly, and ends up leaving tantalizing hints and even pretending to talk to him in her sleep. He becomes tongue-tied – hence the play's title – and procrastinates. The difficulties of this strand of the plot are predictably removed by the discovery that Mireno is in fact the Duke of Coimbra, whose father has hidden him from the Portuguese king (Tirso boldly employs figures from history in the play but completely transforms the course of historical events).

The story of Madalena's sister, Serafina, upsets the expectation of strict unity of action by forming a separate plot-line. Serafina is one of the most interesting female figures in Golden Age drama: she is a *mujer esquiva*, but a committed one, who may fall in love eventually but only with a portrait of herself painted as a man. She it is who provides another lively Tirsian defence of the *comedia nueva* when rehearsing a play in Act 2 with her lady, Juana. She is a character able to express herself, it seems, much more fluently and passionately through playing a man. She continually loses herself in the fiction, mistaking Juana for a character in the play, and when the rehearsal is over she prefers to keep wearing her male attire:

> Ven, doña Juana; que quiero
> vestirme sobre este traje
> el mío, hasta que sea tiempo
> de representar.   (Tirso, *El vergonzoso*, II, lines 1050–3)

Serafina exceeds the norms of the *comedia*'s stereotypical characters: she may be tricked into sleeping with (and hence marrying) the count Antonio, but her resistance to love for a man and to her fate is unremitting. Her comfort in transvestism and tendency to narcissism suggest a character of an unusual complexity for the period in which Tirso is writing.

El vergonzoso en palacio shows Tirso at the height of his creative powers. Usually Lopean in terms of the *llaneza*, or plainness of his language, he here produces for example, against the grain, a fine semi-*culto* sonnet, 'Del castizo caballo descuidado . . .' (I, lines 660–73). The sonnet celebrates the confidence which the ambitious Mireno's new rich clothing inspires in him and contrasts with the subsequent satrical humour and low language of the now 'enlacayado' Tarso, who is unimpressed by the complexity of the newly soiled servant's clothes he has inherited.[3] Such juxtapositions of high and low styles of language, levels of action, and characters may not have been to everyone's taste, as the reactions of the audience of the play depicted in the *Cigarrales de Toledo* indicate, but they were a logical development of a type of theatre liberated from dependence on an ancient *arte* and the proscriptive interpretations of that *arte*'s contemporary adherents.

Tirso is most readily remembered within and beyond Spain not for his splendid comedies but for two of the moral/theological plays he wrote: *El burlador de Sevilla* (1618?) and *El condenado por desconfiado* (1625?). His authorship of both works has not been established beyond doubt, but the majority of scholars feel his claims are strong. *El burlador* is renowned for providing the prototype for the philandering trickster Don Juan, developed to different ends by Molière, Mozart and a host of other subsequent artists in later decades and centuries. The play, set in mid-fourteenth-century Spain, charts Don Juan Tenorio's 'seduction' under false pretences of four different women: the noblewomen Isabela and Doña Ana, and the peasants Tisbea and Arminta.

---

[3] See Sullivan, *Tirso de Molina and the Drama*, chapter 5, for examples and analysis of the playwright's 'prismatic' use of language.

His deflowering of these female characters causes predictable chaos in a world obsessed with honour, but is not his only misdemeanour. He deceives his friend Mota, and kills Don Gonzalo in pursuit of his sexual *burlas*. The miscreant is eventually dragged down to Hell for his sins, without the chance of redemption, by the statue of Don Gonzalo (the stone guest) whom he has invited to dinner in a moment of typical bravado. It is now common for scholars to point out that none of Don Juan's female victims is blameless in their relationships with him. This is true, but the women's immorality and inappropriate social behaviour is in turn only a part of the morally confused world that Tirso depicts, and here the historical displacement should not hide the world of seventeenth-century Spain. If even those who are expected to uphold the social and moral order – the king, the aristocrats, and the churchmen – are part of the problem (in their failure to condemn and deal with the malign influence of Don Juan) then Tirso's only solution is to bring divine justice on stage in the unusually bleak and powerful ending. If Juan's uncle, Don Pedro, the Castilian ambassador to Naples (the city in which the play begins *in medias res*) had done his duty and arrested his nephew for infringing the rules of the palace, instead of letting him escape, the subsequent misfortunes could have been averted. Don Pedro prefers to avoid his moral duty, arguing that, 'Industria me ha de valer/ en un negocio tan grave' (Tirso, *El burlador*, lines 75–6). The moral poison in society has reached the top and Don Juan exploits society's failings. Don Juan is an individual, but also representative as later artists recognized: he describes himself as 'un hombre sin nombre' (line 15) and, as such, he is what any individual can become without strong education of a moral and social nature.

El condenado por desconfiado is an even more engaging drama than *El burlador*. Its protagonist, Paulo, has devoted ten years of his life to God as a hermit, but a dream of his own damnation sent to him by the devil has worried him to the extent that he demands certain knowledge of his fate from God. As the *demonio* explains:

> Éste, aunque ha sido tan santo,
> duda de la fe, pues vemos
> que quiere del mismo Dios,
> estando en duda, saberlo.   (Tirso, *El condenado*, lines 213–16)

Paulo thinks he ought to be saved but forgets that good works are not sufficient; one also needs a constant faith, and grace from God. He is also proud of his life and his holiness, another fatal sin.

A tragically misguided Paulo believes the angel/devil's promise that his fate will be the same as a certain Enrico. He turns out to be the most abominable criminal in Naples, who has raped, murdered and robbed his way through life, and whose only saving attributes are his love for his venerable father and his constant faith in God and His saving grace. Both redeeming features are emphasized in powerful scenes. Enrico has, more specifically, an understanding that his crimes mean he deserves to be condemned to Hell, but a knowledge and belief that he always has the possibility of redemption through his faith and

God's grace. Paulo travels to Naples to discover the truth about Enrico and despairs, *knowing* now (as he thinks) that he will be condemned too. Paulo should realize that theologically nobody is guaranteed knowledge of their destiny: and so it proves, as Enrico goes to Heaven (showing an ability to resist the wiles of the devil), and Paulo to Hell after losing his confidence in God's mercy and becoming a bandit in an attempt to outdo Enrico. Instead of remaining faithful to God and to his chosen way of life, he loses the advantage of his good works. He becomes stubborn and ignores the chances he is unambiguously given by a *pastorcillo* to return to the flock, and he dies violently in confused despair. If a man does not persevere in goodness and faith, this is because he chooses not to, through the exercise of his *libre albedrío*.

El burlador and *El condenado* are sister plays, the latter depicting a man condemned for lack of faith, and the former, one who suffers for an excessive confidence in the time he will be given to repent. Don Juan has gone through his life upbraiding his side-kick, Catalinón, whenever the latter warns him about the urgency of making his peace with his maker. Both works are unusual in that they stage the descent into Hell of their protagonists, a sign perhaps that Tirso had little faith in human justice.

El condenado por desconfiado has been interpreted as Tirso's subtle reflection on the *de auxiliis* debate, which had flared mainly between Dominicans and Jesuits in Counter-Reformation Spain, and which the Pope eventually silenced. In this controversy over divine grace and human free will, the Jesuits had accused the Dominicans of a position close to Luther's in their stated view that God causes an individual's consent, and the nicety of their division of grace into 'sufficient' and 'efficacious'. The Society of Jesus argued that humans have the freedom to seek salvation or depart from God of their own volition, which is what we witness the hermit Paulo do in Tirso's play. Whilst God's grace could have saved Paulo as it saves Enrico, Paulo's choice to reject Him is respected, whatever the regrets and however perverse it may seem. It is not possible to discover whether the majority of the *corral* audience appreciated the finer points of a theological debate of this kind, despite their regular presence in church, but modern performance has demonstrated that the tragedy functions well as a study of human psychology.[4] Paulo's descent into despair has parallels in depressive conditions of the mind which have been described in the centuries since Tirso's masterpiece was composed.

What is interesting about these religious plays, whether they spoke to an audience member in primarily human terms or as a subtle contribution to a complex theological debate, is their evident success on the Golden Age *corral* stage. A dramatization of the issues of sin and redemption, free will, good works, and divine grace would echo some of the points heard more dryly from the pulpit in church, and probably engaged members of the audience by teaching them

---

[4] For example, the fine 1991 London production at the Gate Theatre, directed by Stephen Daldry.

through *admiratio*, that is through engaging them with lively, spectacular and thought-provoking stories. The theatre was a centre for entertainment but also a place where one could learn important lessons for life. In this sense the religious *comedia*, of which Tirso is a fine exponent, is quite close to the popular *auto sacramental*: an allegorical theatre which aimed to inspire devotion by wonder, and understanding by its 'preaching' in verse. It might be harder to engage with the religious side of these plays today but their appeal to the seventeenth-century Spaniard should not be denied.

Tirso based a number of other serious plays on stories culled from known history: Biblical, ancient or modern. He re-worked plots and re-drew pre-existing characters with an extraordinary panache and self-confidence, and, especially in what we might call his mature period after his return from the Caribbean, he exploited political and social resonances in the material he was re-working. While he was not the first to write *de regimine principis* plays containing flawed monarchs and problems with the succession, he was less careful than Lope to disguise his intentions. *La república al revés*, for instance, although in fact probably written just before the transatlantic voyage, depicts the assumption of power in Constantinople by Constantino in the absence of his mother, the Empress Irene. As the play's title suggests, the change at the helm leads to almost farcical disaster as Constantino consistently puts his personal desires before his public obligations. His unsuitability for high office is under-lined by his administration of justice in Act 3: he frees a thief and argues that a man married for ten years has every right to abandon his wife:

> Suficientes eran dos [años]
> para hacerte padecer
> un infierno: anda con Dios.
> Mártir eres de mujer:
> no hagáis más vida los dos.   (*Tirso, La república*, p. 416b)

So perverse a situation cannot remain unchallenged, and Constantino is eventu-ally undone as his mother escapes his persecution and returns to power, providing hope for the future of the realm.

Similarly serious moral dramas seem to abound after 1618 (although, as with most Golden Age playwrights, the dating of many works is uncertain): *La mejor espigadera* and *La mujer que manda en casa* are based on the Old Testament figures of Ruth and Jezebel; *El árbol del mejor fruto*, set like *La república al revés* in Greek history, is an enigmatic work often passed over by scholars, perhaps because of its apparent (but curiously-staged) anti-Semitism; *El amor y el [sic] amistad* is an examination of the subject of friendship, so important in the period; *Quien no cae no se levanta* explores the theme of moral responsi-bility before the world and before God, but also displays a curious mixture of generic norms. *La prudencia en la mujer* (early 1630s) has its source in Spanish medieval history. The play dramatizes the single-minded bravery of the widowed queen regent of Castile and Leon, María de Molina, faced with the treachery of three aristocrats – Enrique, Juan and Diego de Haro – who try to wrest the throne from her and destroy her son, the future King Fernando. Whilst Doña María is an exemplary figure who can teach the male nobles the value of virtue, Tirso is interested too in her excessive tendency to forgive her antagonists. There can be pitfalls involved in what appear to be Christian virtues practised by a monarch: at times justice should outweigh mercy.

Tirso's magnificent *La venganza de Tamar* (1621–24) is a third Old Testament *comedia*. It appears at first glance to be a fairly 'straight' dramatization of the incestuous rape of Tamar by her half-brother, Amón, taken from 2 Samuel xiii. The rape leads to revenge taken on Tamar's behalf by her full brother, the vain Absalón, who invites Amón, along with King David's other sons, to his estates at Baal-Hazor, where he has him murdered at a banquet. (This tragic story of the House of David was later continued by Calderón in *Los cabellos de Absalón*.) A comparison of the pithy Biblical verses with Tirso's artistic re-working of the story is instructive, however. The briefest of glimpses of character in the Bible, for example Amón's disgust and rejection of Tamar after the rape, or the hint of a comparison, such as that between the appetites for food and for sex, are skilfully developed by the Mercedarian into a cogent and powerful dramatic narrative whose universal (and Biblical) truth cannot be questioned but whose relevance is made contemporary.

The question that concerns Tirso, making use not for the first time of historical and geographical displacement, is that of kingship and good government, specifically again the themes of justice and mercy. Like the wicked Juan of *La prudencia en la mujer*, Amón does not benefit morally from the leniency or forgiveness of his monarch (in this case his father, the softened and confused old King David). Having forced himself on the protesting Tamar once, he is similarly uncompromising when uncovering the face of a shepherdess (Tamar again) who stands up to his violent demands. The monarch's weakness stems from his knowledge of his own past failings: he at first intends to deal an exemplary death to his first-born for the transgression but then remembers how he has been forgiven for his offence against Uriah by God: 'Venció en él a la justicia/ la piedad' (Tirso, *La venganza*, II, lines 374–5). He procrastinates and pardons Amón but then lets him travel to the deceitful Absalón's lands despite having misgivings about this son's intentions. David, in this incarnation, is far from the idealized Renaissance king.

For those who wanted to see it, Tirso depicted, in his re-working of a well-known Biblical story, the chaos of a world not governed by virtuous principles or edified by morally exemplary behaviour. Violence and vice breed further violence and vice. Almost nobody acts as they ought to, and most characters justify a wicked action by disguising it as a noble one. The play emerged at the same time as others, notably the anonymous *La Estrella de Sevilla*, which dramatized concerns about the guidance of the young Philip IV by the ambitious, Machiavellian and increasingly powerful Olivares. And yet those who saw the play in early-modern Spain, and those who have seen it in modern productions, are left with uncomfortable feelings that are not merely related to the kingship theme. Tirso's ability to flesh out plausible, psychologically complex characters from the Old Testament sketches moves us hither and thither in our natural search for those with whom we might identify and sympathize. Thus, whilst we understand David's anguish as he learns of the rape of his daughter: '¿Esto es, cielos, tener hijos?' (III, line 284), doubts about his behaviour persist. The suspicion remains that he knows that, incapable of taking decisive action himself, he is sending his first-born son to his death at the hands of Absalón.

The extraordinarily subtle painting of the relationship between Tamar and Amón also leaves the audience sitting uncomfortably. Without shying away from the horror and violence of the attack, Tirso certainly conceived of the siblings' bond as something more complex than an obsessive one-sided passion ending in rape. Tamar has been presented convincingly on stage, for example in Simon Usher's production for the RSC in 2004, as a highly sexualized young woman, more than half-aware of the feelings she arouses in her blood relation. She convinces the audience not that she is really in love with Joab but that she too has a passionate nature and is searching to satisfy it. Then, before and during the exceptional scene of play-acting-within-the-play dreamt up by Amón in Act 2 so that he can get physically close to Tamar, she is able to reciprocate playfully. The play can be seen to hinge on Tamar's tragic misconstruing of the nature of Amón's passion for her. What she perhaps perceived as correspondence is in fact based on mutual incomprehension and a romanticization or transformation of the notion of love in the lovers' minds. That Tirso should make a tragic story of this less obvious element of *La venganza de Tamar* too, reveals an impressive sensitivity to the subtleties of human love, a remarkable imaginative faculty in the elaboration of the source material, and above all a clear sense of the messy interrelatedness of existence on the human plane.

If Tirso's characters frequently find themselves victims of their own passions, slaves to all-too-human desires and foibles: greed, envy, the urge for instant gratification, shallowness, deceit, hypocrisy, then an alternative is presented by simple, often pastoral figures, able to see the world aright. *La prudencia en la mujer*, *La república al revés* and *La venganza de Tamar* all present such figures providing an antidote to courtly values, those of 'allá'. The shepherds Braulio, Aliso, and the aptly-named Tirso in the last of these plays, advise Tamar to forget the offence done to her, and not to see the rape as a stain on her honour, rather than seeking bloody vengeance:

> Acá [in the countryside] son espejos de agua,
> que a los que mirarse van
> muestran manchas y las quitan
> en llegándose a lavar.   (Tirso, *La venganza*, III, lines 638–41)

Tirso de Molina's is one of the surest and boldest of moral voices in the Spanish Golden Age. That he additionally not only appreciated but subtly developed the aesthetics of the *comedia nueva* means that he ranks as the outstanding practitioner of Lope's new art.

Other major dramatists of the first generation

The historic city of Valencia, as we have already begun to see, played an important role in the development of theatre in Spain in the sixteenth century. It had had a lively tradition of religious, and then palace and university theatre during the late medieval period and the Renaissance, and its own group of dramatists, some of whom belonged to the famous Academia de los Nocturnos, developed as might be expected. As well as Virués (see pp. 18–20) and Castro (see below), the city boasted Rey de Artieda, the *canónigo* Tárrega, Gaspar Águilar, and Ricardo del Turia amongst its playwrights. Valencia was also a natural stopping place for travelling players en route to or from Italy and as early as 1582 its *Hospital* had sought and been granted permission to stage plays in a permanent building. In 1584 the Casa (not *corral*) de la Olivera opened its doors for the first time, ushering in over 150 years of dramatic performances at the venue. It is no surprise that Valencia was Lope de Vega's choice of destination after his banishment from Castile in 1588. Lope set several plays in the city and whether he learned more from than he taught to the Valencians, with whom he remained on good terms, is a moot point. Valencia was a fine place for dramatic experimentation.

Lope was to dedicate a play, *Las almenas de Toro*, to his friend and Valencia's finest exponent of the *comedia nueva*, Guillén de Castro y Bellvís. Born into a noble family, Castro was Lope's junior by seven years. After his formative period in his native city he travelled to Italy and later lived in Madrid, publishing two volumes of his dramatic works (in 1618 and 1625) during his life. His total output runs to some 30 or 35 plays: problems of attribution remain over several works not published under his name in his lifetime. Difficulties with dating plays precisely, common to so many playwrights of the period, are manifest in Castro's case too. Neither is it possible to characterize all his dramatic works with broad brushstrokes, although he was less interested in writing plays on religious themes than most of his contemporaries, and one might describe his comedies as hard-hitting, with well developed characters. Thus his drama has parallels with Tirso's, but without the latter's recourse to order and the saving comedy of the absurd. Scholars have called attention additionally to Castro's preoccupation with high-born characters, particularly kings and the issue of tyrannicide, but in truth many dramatists explored this topic, which was so central to the increasingly complex political world of the early-modern court. Castro is also noted for his re-working of popular sources, from the ballad tradition, from Ariosto, and also from Cervantes: he wrote at least three plays inspired by Cervantes's prose works: *El curioso impertinente* (1605–8), *Don Quijote de la Mancha* (1605–8), and *La fuerza de la sangre* (1613–14).[5]

---

[5] Dates for Castro's works are taken from Bruerton, 'The Chronology of the *Comedias*', although the rough date given for *Las mocedades del Cid* is from Arata's edition of the play, p. xxxiii.

An exploration of three of Castro's plays will help to establish why his drama is worth dwelling on: the early comedy *Los mal casados de Valencia* (1595–1604), the mature play, also broadly comic, *La fuerza de la costumbre* (1610–15), and the drama for which posterity honours him (in fact the first of two he wrote on the figure of Spain's medieval hero), *Las mocedades del Cid* (1605–15), which was famously re-worked by Pierre Corneille as *Le Cid* in France in 1637.

If *Los mal casados de Valencia* could be more precisely dated it might be possible to discover whether it was written with a full awareness of Lope's dramatic predilections as he developed the *comedia nueva*. Assuming that Castro was a follower of Lope's comedies of the period, the play might be seen as a challenge to his formula, and even to comedy itself. The play's setting is Valencia and its characters superficially are those of a *comedia de capa y espada*. However, Castro daringly deals with the lovers of comedy after they have married, and ends the play, in a clear challenge to generic norms, with the dissolution of two marriages in which initial mutual passion has turned to indifference and even revulsion. The four main figures, Ipólita and her husband (also her cousin) Don Álvaro, and their friends Valerián and Eugenia, are individuals whose characters and motivations are persuasively drawn by the playwright. Ipólita is a depressive, eternally jealous of her husband's business trips (and with good reason); he is an inveterate womanizer who, at the start of the play, brings back a girl, Elvira, whom he has seduced and hoodwinked in Zaragoza. She dresses as his male servant, Antonio, and becomes the confidante of all the other characters, masters and servants. The treacherous and cowardly Valerián constantly woos the faithful Ipólita behind Álvaro's back, while his wife is equally shameless in her pursuit of Álvaro himself. Eugenia is an unusually unsympathetic figure, keen to destroy her effeminate husband and then also the target of her affections when he manages to resist her, but she is in good company in the play.

Castro, like Ruiz de Alarcón (see pp. 83–6), has decided to depict a comic universe in which nobody finds contentment because nobody is able to overcome their basic emotions and desires. Even Elvira, who seems to love Álvaro despite his deception, decides at the end of the play to return to her native Aragón and a convent rather than take the plunge into a marriage which might turn out like the ones she has witnessed at close quarters. Unlike the scheming women of Lope's and Tirso's comedies, she makes plans (the exchange of letters, the spreading of misinformation, the arranging of illicit couplings after dark) that are all concocted in full expectation of an ultimate descent into chaos. Although the trouble she causes, especially in her prolonged farcical battle with the old servant Galíndez, can cause general amusement, as when Don Álvaro thinks he is watching an *entremés*, Castro's comedy is of the bitterest type. His characters are allowed the soliloquies to demonstrate the perversity of their visions, the unlikeliness of any change in behaviour. Don Álvaro's heartfelt denunciation of marriage:

¡Oh, matrimonio!
Yugo pesado y violento,
si no fueras sacramento,
dixera que eras demonio   (Castro, *Los mal casados*, lines 161–4)

typifies the characters' solipsistic tendencies. The shameless frankness in the expression here is typical of *Los mal casados de Valencia*. When Eugenia propositions Álvaro in Act 1, she does so in a sexually suggestive way; in Act 3 when Galíndez and then Hipólita spy on Álvaro's apparently homosexual love-making with Elvira/Antonio, the audience is given a lengthy commentary. Performance might well indicate that physically the play owes a great deal to the *commedia dell'arte*.

Castro's very candid depiction of the power of sexual desire is one aspect of the play which separates it from the Lopean *comedia nueva* as it matures. The work also eschews polymetry, being written entirely in *redondillas*, a practice never followed by Lope. Neither have the characters formed a verisimilar unit: especially in Act 1 when they play a kind of parlour game, each choosing a letter of the alphabet and using it to invent a story; credibility loses out to ingenuity in this example of Castro's dramaturgy.

La fuerza de la costumbre, a mature work, is more the sort of comedy Lope would have admired. The latter's influence is now obvious. Castro is careful to provide a prc-history within Act 1, typical of the *comedia nueva*, to persuade the audience of his situation's plausibility. In this case he creates a family reunited after two decades of separation: the husband, Don Pedro, has been in Flanders where he has brought up the daughter, another Hipólita, more or less as a soldier: meanwhile his wife Costanza, ostracized by most of her family for the illicit relationship with Pedro, has brought up her son Félix almost as a daughter. The play charts the feminization of the unwilling Hipólita and the often brutal attempts made by the ashamed Don Pedro to make a man of his son. As well as providing a series of amusing scenes, particularly as Hipólita struggles with female dress, behaviour and customs, the comedy addresses a serious question: to what extent is one the product of upbringing and to what extent, of nature? In spite of Don Pedro's proud claim at the end of the play, 'su naturaleza misma/ volver a mis hijos pude' (Castro, *La fuerza de la costumbre*, p. 76b), the action has arguably revealed that identity is tied in closely with the presentation of a learned set of responses which depend on one's status in society. The development of Hipólita is particularly interesting in that her physical 'seduction' forms the basis for her self-discovery, or *desengaño*, as she puts it. After discovering her subservient sexual role she accepts her feminine destiny meekly.

The finest of Castro's dramas is the first play of his two-part dramatization of the story of the Cid, *Las mocedades del Cid*. (The second is often referred to as *Las hazañas del Cid* but should not be confused with the play of the same name [by an anonymous author].) The love theme demanded by the *comedia nueva* means that the play is shaped more by Rodrigo's dilemma with regard to his beloved Jimena, than by his prowess as a Castilian *matamoros*. (Similarly, in his

Dido y Eneas (1613–16) Castro ignored the chaste Dido tradition, followed in the 1580s by his fellow-Valencian, Virués, and exploited instead the Aeneas/ Dido love story from Virgil – a sure sign that, like Lope, he knew what ingredients to mix in his fare for the popular audience.)

Rodrigo, of *Las mocedades del Cid*, agonizes over the killing of the Conde Lozano, who has dishonoured his father, Diego Laínez:

> ¿Qué haré, suerte atrevida,
> si él es el alma que me dio la vida?
> ¿Qué haré, – ¡terrible calma! –
> si ella es la vida que me tiene el alma?
> Mezclar quisiera, en confianza tuya,
> mi sangre con la suya,
> ¿y he de verter su sangre? . . . ¡Brava pena!
> ¿Yo he de matar al padre de Jimena?
>
> (Castro, *Las mocedades*, lines 526–33)

He finds himself torn, as his exquisite soliloquy reveals, between the demands of honour and thus his family's status, and his tender love for Jimena. The latter's own strength in adversity and desire to maintain her own family's honour by seeking her lover's death contribute to a powerful play. The lovers' fates are not Castro's only concern however. His depiction of the untrustworthy Sancho, and the other children of King Fernando, allows him to exploit his predilection for the theme of kingship. He also depicts the disappointment of the princess, Urraca, at her own failure to win the perfect Rodrigo. Her unrequited love was well known from the ballad tradition (notably 'Afuera, afuera, Rodrigo'), if absent from the epic poem, and it acts to put the virtues of the protagonists into sharper focus. Castro's strengths as a poet and a handler of dramatic structure shine brightly in this moving and influential play.

Antonio Mira de Amescua was born in Guadix in Andalusia in 1570 or possibly 1574, the illegitimate son of a Castilian nobleman and a woman probably of *morisco* origin. He trained for the priesthood, most likely with the Jesuits in Granada, ultimately reaching the position of archdeacon in the cathedral of Guadix in 1631. Mira lived for many years in Madrid, where he was popular and highly respected as a playwright and poet. He became friends with Lope de Vega and pioneered the co-written play, collaborating *inter alia* with Castro, Vélez de Guevara, Rojas Zorrilla, Montalbán and Calderón. Unlike Castro he wrote a great deal of religious drama: there are some twenty *autos sacramentales* written for Corpus Christi, and of his seventy or so *comedias*, many are either saint's plays (such as his best known work *El esclavo del demonio*), or are based on Scripture (including the story of the rise, fall, and rise again of the young David in *El arpa de David* (1612–13?)), or are at least explicitly moralistic. In the 1625 *aprobación* for his *El ejemplo mayor de la desdicha*, Pedro de Vargas writes that the play, which is not religious in its content, nevertheless provides 'aviso y escarmiento de las confianzas humanas' (Mira de Amescua, *El ejemplo*, p. 302). Whether his material came from religious sources or medieval history or the ballad, Mira was particularly fond of exploring the theme of Fortune as it affects humankind, and relating it to both *desengaño* and Stoic values.

Despite his great success in his day and the esteem in which he was held by contemporary dramatists, Mira's star (in imitation of the fates of his great characters) fell rapidly after the Golden Age, perhaps in part because, like Vélez de Guevara's, his plays never appeared in dedicated *partes*. Both the *Próspera fortuna de don Álvaro de Luna y adversa de Ruy López de Ávalos* and its second part *Adversa fortuna de don Álvaro de Luna* appeared in Tirso's much-discussed *Segunda parte* of 1635 and have only been definitively attributed to Mira in comparatively recent times, despite their subject matter: the dramatization of the best known case of a *valido*'s fall from grace in Spanish history. Problems of attribution are particularly acute for those dramatists who did not publish collections of their plays during their lifetimes.

An analysis of two of Mira de Amescua's plays, *El esclavo del demonio* (pre-1605?) and *El ejemplo mayor de la desdicha* (1625), will give an idea of his dramatic achievements, although it should be remembered that he also wrote comedies, both urban and palace-based. The former play is often seen primarily as a source for Calderón's *El mágico prodigioso*, and indeed its protagonist's pact with the devil and moment of *desengaño* clearly inspired the younger writer. However, parallels with Tirso's *El condenado por desconfiado* are perhaps even stronger: the devil's slave of the title, Gil de Santarem, begins the play as a revered, saintly man in Coimbra, but he throws away his good works and devotion when he gives in to sexual temptation. The devil advises Gil through the mouth of the sleeping *gracioso*, Domingo, that his future is predestined and his soul condemned, prompting him after a short (perhaps less than convincing) struggle with his better judgement to conclude perversely, like Tirso's Paulo: 'Luego si estoy condenado/ vana fue mi penitencia' (Mira de Amescua, *El esclavo*, lines 605–6). His crime is triply reprehensible for not only does he despair of God's mercy, but he also deflowers the noble Lisarda in the guise of Don Diego, the lover with whom she is to elope, and then claims to her that Diego abandoned her in order to punish her family. As Diego has already killed Lisarda's brother, and as Gil has just persuaded him for the good of his soul not to seduce her and upset the family further, the claim is particularly callous. It results in Lisarda despairing and joining Gil as a highway robber close to her father's country estate. Don Diego, meanwhile, is eventually suspected of murdering Lisarda, and cruelly imprisoned by Lisarda's father.

Whilst Gil's depravity and desire in Act 2 to possess Lisarda's virtuous sister, Leonor, lead him to sign away his soul and become the devil's *esclavo*, robbing, raping and murdering as he likes, Lisarda herself stops short of total capitulation and by disfiguring herself, performing compensatory good works, and having herself sold to her father as a real slave for thirty *escudos*, she finds redemption before death. Gil too is saved after his guardian angel battles with the devil for the *cédula* he signed. A repentant Gil and the fortuitous presence of the Portuguese prince unravel all the strands of the complicated plot and sub-plot, ensuring in particular that Don Diego's innocence is established and Leonor's family honour is restored. Neither Calderón nor Tirso in their thematically similar plays takes on quite as much material as Mira, and their characterizations of Cipriano and Paulo are arguably more convincing as a result. However, the scholarly judgement that Mira, whilst producing impressive situations and some fine rhetorical poetry, was careless in his plot construction is based, like many views expressed on the *comedia*, on the reading of plays rather than on performance. In fact Mira is notable for a Shakespearean confidence in his audience's ability to follow movements in time, changes of location, and subtleties in the action. His stage directions show a marked interest in the visual presentation of the production. For example, in Act 3 when Gil emerges from the cave where he feels he has seduced Leonor, a direction reads: 'Sale Don Gil abrazado con una muerte, cubierta con un manto' (Mira de Amescua, *El esclavo*, p. 165). He addresses two triumphant *quintillas* to her before the truth dawns on him as he finally goes to look upon her beauty in the light of day. As he stands aghast this 'sombra infernal' (line 2781) disappears into the stage: 'Descúbrela, y luego se hunde' (p. 166). The message that the wilful pursuit of one's own inclinations is likely to lead to disillusionment and personal ruin is brought home to the audience with a fine awareness of how the scene would work visually. The same scene contains a divine voice from off stage, a *tramoya* with a devil and exploding fireworks and arquebuses firing, an aerial battle between an angel and the devil, and the reappearance of the angel clutching Gil's *cédula*. Mira's dramas may well have been so popular because of his appreciation of the possibilities of Golden Age performance and it is highly likely that their success could be repeated on stage.

El ejemplo mayor de la desdicha also proves Mira to be an adroit creator of memorable scenes. Set in Constantinople, the tragedy plunders sixth-century history to dramatize the relationship between the Emperor Justiniano and Belisario, who has risen through the ranks, demonstrating his exceptional military prowess, to become general. Belisario is above all a good man, loyal to his Emperor, embarrassed at the favour he is shown when the Emperor effectively makes him co-ruler, faithful to his lover Antonia, and magnanimous towards his enemies, forgiving the perpetrators of three attempts on his life. As in many other dramas of the period, notably Lope's *El duque de Viseo* and the anonymous *La Estrella de Sevilla*, the historical displacement of the action barely disguises the interest in kingship and the role of the *privado* in contemporary Spain. Mira's play picks up specifically on the early seventeenth-century interest in the nature of friendship which was in part the result of the concerned fascination with the king's relationship with his favourite in the days of Philip III and the Duke of Lerma, and then Rodrigo Calderón, and after 1621, the young Philip IV in the clutches of the Conde-Duque de Olivares. At the height of his favour as Act 2 closes, Belisario asks Fortune to 'pon en esta rueda un clavo' (Mira de Amescua, *El ejemplo*, line 1888). The Empress's malevolence causes him to fall from grace in Act 3, however, and Justiniano first takes back his ring of office, identical to his own, then has Belisario's eyes put out and forbids his courtiers to help him in any way. The Emperor's anxiety for his general's welfare while he is away (shown in Act 2) is excessive in a monarch – he cares more about one man's survival than about the military success of the African campaign – and so is the violence of his revenge when he believes he has proof of Belisario's dishonourable affections for the Empress. Characters in Mira de Amescua may refer frequently to the wheel of Fortune as if some ancient whimsical goddess presided over their fate, but the vicissitudes of life tend to have a discernible cause and effect which would have been fairly clear to the informed audience. In the case of the stoical Belisario, it is the monarch's failings which promote him and sink him.

In both of these plays, some of the actions and emotions of Mira's characters test the indulgence of his audience by pushing at the limits of verisimilitude. In *El esclavo del demonio* the sudden descent into sin of the saintly Gil, despite the presence of the devil egging him on, is less well-prepared psychologically and thus less convincing than in, say, Cervantes's *El rufián dichoso*, or the two related plays already mentioned. In *El ejemplo mayor de la desdicha* neither Justiniano's rage nor the Empress Teodora's predatory lusting after Belisario are satisfactorily anticipated. And yet to Mira's mind these unlikely turns of events are justified in part by their historical base and in full by the drama of the situations they create. *El ejemplo mayor*, for example, would have delighted a Golden Age audience with its four attempted murders, purloined love letter, use of the aside, night-time skirmish, and characters listening *al paño*. Mira also has the tragic Belisario, bleeding from the removal of his eyes, return to find that the pity of his old friends cannot outweigh their fear of the Emperor. Other popular elements of the *comedia nueva* make an appearance too: Belisario communicates his suspicions about the Empress to Justiniano through talking in his sleep; Belisario and Antonia are able to communicate their prohibited love for each other through a rehearsal of a court entertainment, the story of Pyramus and Thisbe; and the play ends beautifully with a Calderonian, split-line exchange between the desolate but resolute Antonia and the bullying monarch. If there is the risk of melodrama in Mira's plays (which their titles can perhaps hint at), it has its compensations in the creation of some fine moments on stage.

Finally it is worth mentioning the role of the *gracioso*, Floro, in *El ejemplo mayor*. Floro, like Batín of Lope's *El castigo sin venganza*, and Juanete of Calderón's *El pintor de su deshonra*, is a mature version of the stock character, who has travelled a long way from the rustic side-kicks of the early theatre. Not only does he use popular tales as parables to criticize or undermine his master but his own minor misfortunes create fine comic relief, especially in Act 3 when, after the shock of Belisario's fall, his own machinations are found out and the Emperor takes back his earlier reward of a *villa*. The tragic Belisario has ended his long lament with the words:

> El César y yo fuimos
> de la fortuna dos ejemplos vivos,
> y ya será mi vida
> el ejemplo mayor de la desdicha (Mira, *El ejemplo*, lines 2566–9)

and Floro echoes his despair, his verse form and his words, albeit with less reason to complain:

> yo y el señor Fabricio, [a soldier he has hoodwinked]
> de la Fortuna dos ejemplos vivos,
> y yo seré sin villa
> el ejemplo menor de la desdicha.   (lines 2601–4)

Floro's comic comeuppance, placed where it is in Act 3, provides a good example of one of the defining features of the *comedia nueva*: its reluctance, faced with the complexity of life it depicts, to greet the world with a single fixed expression. Playwrights who followed Lope's lead tended to provide more than one way of looking at life, an antidote to go with any set view, which reflected the flux – religious, political and social – of early-modern Spain.

Another Andalusian dramatist who unerringly found his way to the court was Luis Vélez de Guevara. He was born in Écija into a middle-class family, and educated at the University of Osuna, where he studied for free because of his straitened circumstances. After serving first the archbishop of Seville and then the crown as a soldier in Italy, he became attached to the royal household, finding patronage in the reigns of both Philip III and Philip IV. Vélez was another prolific dramatist, who wrote scores of plays: like Mira's, they were not published in *partes* under his name, leaving a host of problems of attribution and dating, and delaying a confident critical assessment of his stature.

To read Vélez's production for the stage is to be reminded of the problems inherent in attempting to generalize about plays written by a single *ingenio* over many years and for many different contexts (by no means simply for *corral* performance), or to pigeon-hole all dramatists of Lope's generation as his close followers. It is true that Vélez took the title and subject matter of his best known play, *La serrana de la Vera* (1613), from Lope, but it is equally the case that he was heavily influenced by the *culto* poetry produced by Luis de Góngora, and that it was Lope's duty to despise. Within the broad model of the *comedia nueva* there was considerable room for self-expression, for variety, for new approaches to established structures, plot-lines, poetic norms, themes and ideas. The fact that much of Vélez's output, like some of Lope's, was performed for the court or commissioned by particular noble patrons makes it harder still to divide it into recognizable categories. The three plays studied below, *Reinar después de morir*, *El diablo está en Cantillana* (dates uncertain), and *La serrana de la Vera*, are quite distinct the one from the other, and yet concentrating on these three precludes a look, for example, at *El caballero del Sol*, spectacularly performed in the Duke of Lerma's gardens in 1617, or *Virtudes vencen señales* (also of 1617), which has some strong parallels with Calderón's *La vida es sueño* (see pp. 104–6).

All of the three plays to be dealt with here are serious, quasi-tragic works, although they do have *gracioso* figures and lighter moments. Two of the stories take their inspiration from history but were popular in the *romance* tradition, and the third, *La serrana de la Vera*, which features a monstrous, murderous mountain-girl from the Plasencia region of Castile, had also been treated by balladeers. Like Mira, Vélez was happier eschewing the purer comic genres, and using the stage to its full extent to present shocking events and stories. Both *Reinar después de morir* and *La serrana de la Vera* end with female bodies revealed in the *vestuario*; all three plays would have allowed the contemporary *autor* to display the magnificence of the troupe's wardrobe, the agility and rhetorical skills of its actors, the quality of its special effects, and the talents of its musicians.

Reinar después de morir is a spare and moving version of a story involving figures from fourteenth-century Portuguese history. The crown prince, Don Pedro, has fallen for and secretly married Doña Inés de Castro, with whom he already has two sons when the play begins. The catalyst for the tragic conflict and horrific outcome of the work is the presence of Doña Blanca, Infanta de Navarra, in Portugal, come to marry the prince and supported by the king, Alfonso. Against his instinct, but for the good of the realm, Alfonso is persuaded by two of his advisers, Alvar González and Egas Coello, to murder the beautiful Inés. Alfonso himself is so shaken by his decision, which involves his separating the young boys from their mother, that he dies, leaving his son to inherit the kingdom, just too late of course for Pedro to make Inés his queen. Pedro has the two courtiers killed and Inés is posthumously crowned in the *vestuario* in the final scene. His own suffering will go on, as he explains in his final speech: 'Cubrid el hermoso cuerpo/ mientras que voy a sentir/ mi desdicha' (Luis Vélez de Guevara, *Reinar*, III, lines 757–9).

Vélez's dramatic skill is manifest throughout the tragedy and is especially impressive because the story's outcome would already be known by the audience. Suspense is created for example through the depiction of Doña Blanca, who at first seems to be the most likely candidate to try to remove her rival Inés. In Act 2 Blanca has warned Inés, through her analogy of a bird of prey chasing a heron, that she will not tolerate competition for the prince's hand. However, the dramatist upsets our expectations powerfully by having Doña Blanca first reject the idea of disposing of Inés, and then, dressed in mourning, sadly break the news of her murder to Pedro in Act 3. It has been the king, earlier paralysed by Inés's charm, who has given the fatal order:

> Con dos golpes airados,
> arroyos de coral vi desatados
> de una garganta tan hermosa y bella
> que aun mi lengua no puede encarecella,
> pues su tersa blancura
> cabal dechado fue de su hermosura.
> (Luis Vélez de Guevara, *Reinar*, III, lines 586–91)

Blanca, having witnessed the tragedy and been moved by it, decides to return to Navarre. The king's struggle between his visceral understanding of his son's choice and his concern for the future of his realm is a tragic one. However, it is the fate of the lovers, whose snatched scenes together are tender, yet full of anxiety, that will pull at the audience's heart-strings.

Unlike Mira, Vélez keeps an undistracted focus on his main plot: the promise of a *gracioso*'s role for Brito all but evaporates; there is little attempt to disguise the time taken to journey between the court and Inés's residence at Mondego with filler scenes; and the cast is consequently small. The playwright is well aware of the visual power of certain moments, particularly involving the children and the post-mortem coronation, but his poetry too is a tour-de-force. Without losing his audience in a Gongorine labyrinth, Vélez takes some of the convoluted syntax and images from *culto* poetry to help express the intensity of the love between Inés and the prince. Language itself has failed Blanca when she tries to describe (above) Inés as she dies, and Pedro too is unable to express the perfection of his love. When imprisoned by the king he asks Brito to take a message to Inés:

> Pues si preso me quería,
> ¿para qué dos veces preso?
> Que a explicar mi sentimiento
> no basto, y si a eso te obligo,
> di todo lo que no digo,
> pues no cabe en lo que siento.
>
> (Luis Vélez de Guevara, *Reinar*, II, lines 303–8)

With a paradox typical of the Golden Age, Don Pedro says all he needs to say to move Brito, Inés and the audience without actually trusting his feelings to the well-trodden paths of lovers' language.

El diablo está en Cantillana deals with King Pedro, the fourteenth-century Castilian monarch who featured in many Golden Age plays, most famously Calderón's *El médico de su honra* (see pp. 99–100), and who was sometimes known as *cruel* and sometimes *justiciero*. In Vélez's play he has moved to Cantillana, outside Seville, for the summer months, and the beauty of a certain Esperanza has caught his eye. He despotically commands her lover, his *privado*, Don Lope, to move aside so that he can enjoy her. A combination of Esperanza's virtuous determination, the jealousy of the queen, María, and the nightly return of Don Lope from the front disguised as a local ghost, prevent King Pedro from fulfilling his amorous ambitions. He believes, in Act 1, that he has the right as king to seduce his subjects and that such conquests do not betray his eternal love for the queen, 'una cosa es amor/ y otra cosa es apetito' (Luis Vélez de Guevara, *El diablo*, I, lines 1363–4), but learns his moral lesson in the presence of the queen and his courtiers at the play's end. The story is not as sparely dramatized as *Reinar después de morir*; it contains, for example, a more developed *gracioso*, Rodrigo, and an *entremés*-type scene exploiting the villagers' superstitious fear of the ghost. It never attempts to attain the status of a tragedy but does engage with the common theme of royal misdemeanours, of what makes a tyrant, and of how far a subject can resist him. Vélez's view of King Pedro is clear: he is the diabolic deceiver of the title, not the harmless 'ghost', whose presence is a direct consequence of the king's vicious behaviour.

The theme of 'tyranny exposed' in this play, as well as its setting, makes it possible, as has been suggested, that Vélez was the author of *La Estrella de Sevilla*, a not dissimilar, but more powerful play of the early 1620s, which has often been ascribed to Lope de Vega. The king in this work, Sancho, orders the murder of an innocent man so that he can seduce his sister. He too is taught the error of his ways, here by the resolution of a wronged subject, and the determination of his own *alcaldes*, who embody his royal power. The monarch scandalously has to resort to a Machiavellian *razón de estado* to prevail over the *alcaldes*, thus hiding his crime behind the authority granted to the king to take actions for the good of the state without explaining why they were necessary.[6]

The third dramatic work by Vélez that clearly deserves attention is *La serrana de la Vera*. The play was dedicated to a well-known actress, Jusepa Vaca, wife of the *autor* Juan de Morales. A stage direction in Act 1 reveals how Vélez imagined Vaca in the part, as he wrote: 'Éntrase el capitán, retirando, y Gila, poniéndole la escopeta a la vista, que lo hará muy bien la señora Jusepa' (Luis Vélez de Guevara, *La serrana*, at line 396). The work itself is one of the most distinctive of the period, demanding a versatile performance from the central actress, testing the limits of the *corral* stage, and challenging some of the norms of the *comedia nueva*.

Gila, the anti-heroine, is the daughter of a rich and proud peasant, Giraldo, and has, she feels, mistakenly been born female. Her inclinations, physical, emotional and sexual, are those considered naturally masculine in the period. Having agreed reluctantly but obediently to marry an arrogant captain, Lucas, she is then abandoned by him after their first night together, and becomes a bandit who takes the lives of all men in lieu of that of Lucas, whom she has pursued in vain. She is finally hunted down by the Hermandad, the rural police force, and by her father, who has become mayor of her village. Gila accepts her arrest and subsequent execution because she has at last cast the unrepentant Lucas over a cliff to join her other victims. Most of the many *mujeres varoniles*, so popular with the *corral* audiences over several decades, are 'tamed' by love at the end of their stories. Gila is a prominent exception: her tender side is reserved for encounters with women she finds attractive (both the famous Queen Isabella of Castile in Act 1 and the pretty village girl, Pascuala in Act 3); and her rebellion lasts until the end of the play when she bites her father's ear and provides a kind of moral to her story:

> Que esto merece quien pasa
> por las libertades todas
> de los hijos. Si tú usaras
> rigor conmigo al principio,
> de mi inclinación gallarda

---

[6] *La Estrella de Sevilla* has also been ascribed recently to Andrés de Claramonte (see López-Vázquez's edition). Most playwrights who were active in the 1620s, at the start of Philip IV's reign, wrote kingship plays, although few as hard-hitting and carefully aimed as this one.

yo no llegara a este extremo.
Escarmienten en tus canas
y en mí, los que tienen hijos.

(Luis Vélez de Guevara, *La serrana*, lines 3251–8)

The acceptance that she is monstrous does not prevent Gila from being a very attractive character with whom both King Ferdinand and the audience sympathize. She becomes a martyr, whose vengeance taken upon men, though excessive and indiscriminate, is performed on behalf of those of her sex who have suffered their deceits and infidelities.

Juan Ruiz de Alarcón, the last of the major dramatists of Lope's generation to be considered in this chapter, was born in 1580 or 1581 in Mexico. He studied in his native country and then in Salamanca, before settling definitively in the court in about 1614. He remained in Madrid until his death in 1639: his legal training and political connections earned him favour and ultimately, in 1626, the position of clerk to the important *Consejo de Indias*. It seems that the resulting financial security brought a close to his period of playwriting despite the popularity of his works at the palace through the early years of Philip IV's reign. Alarcón's social success and physical appearance (he was a short, red-haired hunchback) attracted the envy and scorn of Quevedo and some of his fellow dramatists, who derided him in print. Unlike Castro, Mira, and Vélez, he was never a friend of Lope, although he did co-write at least one *comedia*.

Twenty of Alarcón's plays were published, in two parts (a volume, unusually, of eight in 1628 and another of twelve in 1634), and a handful of other works have been ascribed to him. The bulk of his output is comic, and although his plays are obviously Lopean in form, his voice is quite an individual one as the analysis of his best-known play, *La verdad sospechosa* (1619–20?), will demonstrate. Contemporaries recognized his 'extrañeza' (to use Montalbán's term) and modern-day scholars have tried to pin down its nature and extent.[7] His status as an outsider, a Mexican who little resembled his fellow playwrights in education, experience and physical appearance, has been frequently put forward to explain the ironic detachment and the forceful didacticism which are both features of his drama. As well as comedies belonging to a number of sub-genres, Alarcón wrote historically-based kingship dramas: *Ganar amigos* (1617–18?) and *Los pechos privilegiados* (1620?) demonstrate the noble *privado*'s loyal dedication to his king, providing examples to be followed rather than avoided, and no doubt demonstrating the dramatist's attachment to and defence of the nascent political system of Philip IV and Olivares.

Before looking in more detail at *Ganar amigos*, two comic works, *La verdad sospechosa* and *El examen de maridos* (perf. 1627), deserve attention. The former, which was re-worked in France in 1644 by Thomas Corneille as *Le menteur*, is one of the high points of Golden Age comedy. Its wit stems from the

---

[7] For a fine short summary of approaches to Alarcón's theatre see Whicker, *The Plays*, pp. 1–14.

unexpectedly ignoble behaviour of Don García, a *segundón*, thrust into the family limelight when he is recalled to Madrid from Salamanca at the death of his older brother. Unfortunately García is an inveterate liar and his audacious, not to say foolhardy, stories upset the harmony and expose the fault-lines of polite society and eventually cause him to miss out on personal happiness through his goal of marriage to Jacinta. Many of the standard ingredients of Golden Age comedy are present in Alarcón's play: lovers' tribulations, disguise and misunderstanding, trysts in church, balcony and night scenes are all staples of the *comedia urbana* or *de capa y espada*; and the generational battle, satire, ideas of love inspired by Ovid, comic irony (as when García asks for Lucrecia's hand), and confusion are similarly common currency in Golden Age comedy. However, *La verdad sospechosa* exceeds the more comfortable form of comedy often practised by his contemporaries in a number of ways. Unlike in many Lopean comedies, the play lacks a controlling character who can at least pretend to pull the strings: there is no-one akin to Fenisa (of Lope's *La discreta enamorada*). Instead García's spontaneous stories, whilst excellent comic moments in themselves, simply create chaos, perhaps reflecting a moral disorderliness in society as a whole. Unusually the audience's sympathies are not always with the younger characters: Don Beltrán, García's father, is a reasonable man who would have acquiesced to his son's desires had he but expressed them:

> ¡Un viejo, que fue mancebo,
> y sabe bien la pujanza
> con que en pechos juveniles
> prenden amorosas llamas!
> (Ruiz de Alarcón, *La verdad*, ed. Reguera, lines 2916–19)

The usual generational battle of comedy is heavily undermined by the dramatist, especially when García abandons filial respect and lies about his Salamancan marriage and the birth of a grandson for his father. The witty *gracioso* with his alternative philosophy becomes, in Tristán, a moralizing figure. The play's ending denies García a victory in love despite the sympathy we might feel for him as an attractive, if psychologically damaged, individual: the lover's sins are not forgiven and forgotten in Alarcón's comedy. The playwright rather ignores the indulgence shown by his fellow artists towards their creations, in order to paint a more negative picture of a social jungle.

Truth is also an elusive commodity in another impressive comic work, *El examen de maridos*. The central idea is simple: instead of receiving detailed instructions as to who she is to marry on his death, Doña Inés is passed a note from her *marqués* father reading: 'Antes que te cases, mira lo que haces' (Ruiz de Alarcón, *El examen*, at line 32). She decides effectively to advertise for a husband, offering to marry the most perfect man who presents himself. Not only does she find, however, that her own emotions interfere with the selection procedure, but that procedure itself, so apparently transparent, is sabotaged by the clever machinations of interested parties, notably the jealous Doña Blanca. The virtuous Conde Carlos, unfulfilled lover of Inés, predicts the outcome of the *examen* when he hears it is to take place, echoing the sentiments of many Spanish moralists of the period:

> La fingida hipocresía,
> la industria, el cuidado, el arte
> a la verdad vencerán:
> más valdrá quien más engañe.   (lines 255–8)

Carlos turns out to be correct for the competition brings out the worst in some characters. And indeed, deception is ultimately used in securing the hand of Inés for the man she has fallen in love with, Carlos's great friend, the Marqués Fadrique. However, this is a deception used for a good end within the pair's friendship. If the change of heart by Carlos, who eventually falls in love with Blanca and claims responsibility for her malevolent slander, is unlikely in the real world, it at least helps to demonstrate that the strength of a perfect friendship is sufficient to defeat cynicism and produce a positive outcome in the society on stage, which is, after all, a reflection of the audience's own.

Alarcón is not the only dramatist to reflect a renewed interest in the concept of friendship in this period, but he perhaps returns to it more insistently than his contemporaries do. The interest may have stemmed from the discussions and definitions of the role of the *privado* or *valido* in the time of Lerma and then Olivares.[8] In *Ganar amigos* another Marqués Fadrique, *privado* to the medieval King Pedro (this time largely in his *justiciero* mode), benefits from the friends he has made through his own virtuous behaviour when Fortune and then the king turn against him. Fadrique's remarkable self-restraint enables him to forgive and aid his brother's murderer, give up his courtship of the woman he loves for the good of her brother's honour, and refuse to save his own skin when it involves disobeying his king. The debts of friendship owed to him are eventually repaid by the noblemen – originally guilty of murder, rape and slander – who cannot resist the pull of their obligations, and so disabuse the king of his mistaken assumptions about his *privado* just in time to save his life. As in the comic mode, Alarcón creates a character so exemplary in his moral fibre that he forces a good outcome in a society which promises injustice, confusion and the survival of the most ruthless deceiver.

As a dramatist closely connected to the court it seems likely, as has been suggested, that Alarcón's plays reflect the period's recognition of the need for moral reform in the sick *república*. He does reflect some aspects of his world that other playwrights eschew, and shows starkly, especially in *La verdad sospechosa*, the results of antisocial behaviour for individuals living in a group. And yet the unanswered questions or indigestible consequences in those of his plays with more positive endings (such as the marriage of Doña Ana to her

---

[8] See Feros, *Kingship and Favoritism*, pp. 121–2.

rapist in *Ganar amigos*, or the unsuitability of Doña Blanca for Carlos in *El examen de maridos*) are not morally robust enough to leave the audience satisfied. Within an apparently moralizing drama, Alarcón, as Whicker has persuasively argued, is well aware that strategies involving dissimulation and deception are a fact of life.

Alarcón's plays are sometimes distinctive in form as well as content: he tends to avoid Gongorine language of the sort employed by Vélez but is fond of intricate, what will become Calderonian plots, of making connections, and of characters expressing complex points of view in lengthy speeches. Occasionally he will sacrifice the sort of verisimilitude held dear by Lope in order to gain the full dividends of a situation: thus he has the *gracioso* Encinas, in *Ganar amigos*, be employed by two of the *galanes*, and pretend to be the servant of a third. By doing so he is able to ensure that a precious chain, significant to the plot, is passed 'realistically' from Fadrique to Fernando to Encinas to Diego to an *escudero* and ultimately to the king as evidence that Fadrique has committed the rape. Although clearly writing well within the *comedia nueva* tradition, Alarcón is happy to take a swipe or two at its creator and at the form itself. In *El examen de maridos*, Inés comments of one of her suitors who has pretensions as a poet, 'Buena parte,/ cuando no se toma el serlo/ por oficio' (lines 1895–7). Some were not fortunate enough to make their living other than as writers, and Lope was one of them. In Act 3 of *Ganar amigos*, Encinas metatheatrically complains about the rigidity of the negative depiction of servants in the *comedia.* He himself proves, despite serving more than one master, to be resourceful and faithful in overcoming temptation.

Minor playwrights

A host of other more or less forgotten playwrights – over 1100 during the seventeenth century as a whole (Urzáiz Tortajada, *Catálogo*) – penned dramatic works in the hope of finding favour with royal, *corral* or other audiences. Of these, Juan Pérez de Montalbán (1602–38), author of perhaps 50 plays as well as the *Fama póstuma* after his friend Lope de Vega's death, and the miscellany *Para todos* (1632), is perhaps the best known. Andrés de Claramonte (c.1580–1626), an actor and company director, has also enjoyed renewed renown in recent years as major plays such as *El burlador de Sevilla*, *El condenado por desconfiado*, and *La Estrella de Sevilla* have been ascribed to him. Several well-known poets or prose writers turned their hands to drama too: by each of Francisco de Quevedo (1580–1645) and Luis de Góngora (1561–1627), one full-length *comedia* survives. The former wrote *Cómo ha de ser el privado* in the late 1620s, and the latter *Las firmezas de Isabela* (published in 1613). Salas Barbadillo and Castillo Solórzano, better known as *novela*-writers, also tried their hands at drama.

Important figures in their day, according to their contemporaries and historical records, were: Damián Salucio del Poyo (c.1550–c.1621) from Murcia; Miguel Sánchez (born c.1563), called 'divino' by Rojas Villandrando, but much of whose work is now lost (see p. 5); Felipe Godínez (1585–1659); Antonio Hurtado de Mendoza (1586–1644); Luis Belmonte Bermúdez (c.1587–c.1650); Antonio Enríquez Gómez (1600–63), the son of a *converso*, who was forced to hide behind the pseudonym Fernando de Zárate (and possibly also Francisco de Villegas) and take refuge from the Inquisition in France, where he published his prose work *El siglo pitagórico y vida de don Gregorio Guadaña* (1644); Alonso Remón (1561–1632), a prolific Mercedarian like Tirso de Molina; and José de Valdivielso (1565–1638), a priest, whose contribution to the development of the *auto sacramental* before Calderón was particularly significant (see pp. 163–4).

The vast majority of extant works by these artists, many of whom wrote *entremeses, autos* and other short theatre in addition to *comedias*, remain unavailable in modern, scholarly editions, leaving a large number of unanswered questions about dates of composition and performance, authorship, influences, and the relationships between them. The sheer demand for theatre at court and in the *corrales*, especially in the 1620s and 1630s, the first decades of Philip IV's reign, adds to the confusion: not only might patrons specify the kind of entertainments they required for a particular occasion, but there was often pressure to write and rehearse a work in a few days, which leads to collaboration and frequent re-workings of earlier works. Some dramatists, such as Belmonte Bermúdez, became specialists in team-writing.

The playwrights mentioned in this chapter all wrote in the period when Lope was the undisputed king of the theatre in Spain and, with the exception of Cervantes (and the occasional playwrights, Quevedo and Góngora), all are usually seen to belong to his stable. Whilst it is reasonable to argue that there is a broad Lopean group of dramatists, and indeed that there is later an identifiably Calderonian cluster, mainly of *poetas* born after 1600, whose drama would have developed differently had it not been for Calderón's stature, the pigeon-holing is not without its problems. Like many attempts at classification, the critical temptation to place Golden Age dramatists into one of two 'schools', or *ciclos*, is also a simplification born of a desire to bring order to a cluttered landscape, some of which is anyway out of sight. Brief analysis of the works of the major dramatists considered so far in this chapter should show that although these men were writing within a three-act format, largely using polymetry, and free from classical norms or rules of artistic composition, they were individuals with their own minds, their own formal and thematic preferences, capable of innovation and not constantly anxious for Lope's approval. Some of them looked to the period before Lope's predominance for ideas for plots, and many of these plots were taken up in turn by the so-called school of Calderón. The problems of dividing the period's works into Lopean and Calderonian periods are illustrated neatly by the fact that at least one dramatist, Álvaro Cubillo de Aragón (1596–1661), has been placed in both camps. Cubillo, who claimed authorship of a hundred plays and collected ten of them, including *Las muñecas de Marcela* (perf. 1636), in his *El enano de las musas* of 1654, began writing in imitation of Lope and ended life a Calderonian. Like most artists he was not immune to ideas and practices of his day. The test of performance on stage as well as a great deal of further study, principally in the form of the publication of scholarly editions of works by minor playwrights of the Golden Age, is required before generalizations can be challenged and the achievements of each individual can be said to have been fairly assessed.

Female playwrights

Happily, by contrast, drama written by women in the Golden Age *has* attracted sustained scholarly attention in very recent years. Most female-authored plays are now accessible in modern editions, studies of them are published with some frequency, and several have been staged. There were in fact relatively very few women playwrights in the period, as there were few female painters and other artists: this is explained by the nature of women's roles in late sixteenth- and seventeenth-century society and their limited education. The latter was influenced by moral concerns about girls' exposure to fiction and other forms of art. It took an exceptional motivation or a highly privileged upbringing to gain the knowledge and skills necessary to write for the stage. In the world of the theatre, women's most active participation was in the roles of (occasionally) *autoras de comedias* and, crucially, actresses and audience members.

As might be expected, many of the educated women capable of dramatic composition lived in convents. Little is known about the extent of playwriting and performance within closed religious communities but the work of Sor Marcela de San Félix (1605–87), who entered the Trinitarian convent in Madrid in 1622, and her successors, suggests that there was a rich tradition in some houses. Sor Marcela has attracted interest in part because of her pedigree: she was the daughter of Lope de Vega by Micaela Luján. The drama performed in convents on certain special occasions included overtly religious works but also more festive pieces.

The first Spanish female dramatist of the Golden Age, the Sevillian Feliciana Enríquez de Guzmán (born c.1580), was the most resistant to the *comedia* form as Lope had established it. Her *Tragicomedia de los jardines y campos sabeos* (published in Portugal in 1624) is in two parts, each of five acts (subdivided into short scenes), and contains courtly and mythological figures. Each part additionally envelops two lively *entreactos*. In her forthright prologue, as well as in a 'Carta ejecutoria' and a notice 'A los lectores', Enríquez emphasizes the classical virtues of her own play (*inter alia* its attempt to respect the limitations set on time, place and action), as well as its generic denomination, and repeatedly expresses her disdain for drama aimed at the *vulgo*:

> Y con más razón me parece ahora que se me puede permitir que diga que es de tan buen parecer mi tragicomedia que puede salir en público, a ver no los teatros y coliseos, en los cuales no he querido, ni quiero, que parezca; mas los palacios y salas de los príncipes y grandes señores y sus regocijos públicos y de sus ciudades y reinos; y asimismo, con menos ruido, visitar en sus casas a los aficionados a buenas letras. (*Women's Acts*, ed. Soufas, p. 271)

This personification of her tragicomedy, which hints at the image of a young noble lady coming out into society, is a suggestive (and rather superior) way to point to its calibre, its breeding. Whether or not the play was performed (possibly over two days) for the visit of Philip IV to Seville in 1624, as has been suggested, it is clear that Enríquez's aesthetic concerns set her apart from most of the dramatists who were producing plays in the 1620s, and for whom financial reward (and so the seduction of the popular audience) was paramount.

The five other female playwrights, from whose pens we have some eight full-length *comedias*, are, certainly in terms of form, much truer to the *comedia nueva* tradition. They are: Ana Caro Mallén (dates uncertain), from Andalusia; María de Zayas y Sotomayor (1590–c.1660), from the capital; Leonor de la Cueva y Silva (d. 1689), from Medina del Campo; Ángela de Azevedo (dates uncertain), born in Lisbon, but a lady-in-waiting in Madrid, who wrote in Spanish; and the Mexican Sor Juana Inés de la Cruz, whose drama is examined in chapter 4.

Of these figures Ana Caro's work is the most likely to have been performed in the *corrales* although there are no records that confirm as much. She was a writer who was certainly paid for producing occasional poetry and dramatic works for Corpus Christi celebrations. Two plays survive from what is likely to have been a much more extensive dramatic *oeuvre*: *Valor, agravio y mujer* and *El conde Partinuplés* (pub. 1653). The former charts the journey of Doña Leonor from Granada, who dresses as a man and pursues her recalcitrant lover, Don Juan, in order to force him to fulfil his promise and marry her. Her character owes a great deal to Tirsian heroines especially in the labyrinthine confusion she causes and then helps to dissipate, and in her ability to appear seductive to either sex. *El conde Partinuplés* is not so neatly constructed as *Valor, agravio y mujer* but is ambitious in the demands it makes of the stage, dealing with an enticing plot that had proved successful for male dramatists, namely the reversal of the Cupid–Psyche myth.[9]

Only one play survives by María de Zayas, better known for her fine collections of short stories with feminist themes, linked by their outspoken narrators, and one by Leonor de la Cueva, who also excelled in another genre: poetry. The former's *La traición en la amistad* (1630s?) follows most of the norms of the *comedia de capa y espada*, and the latter's *La firmeza en la ausencia* can comfortably enough be called a *comedia palatina*. Cueva's play takes up some of the themes of her contemporaries: a tyrannical king imposing his will on a beautiful noblewoman, Armesinda; the demands of friendship (although the relationship between Juan and Carlos is a weak point in the play); and faith and virtue victorious. It also employs some of the staple conventions of the genre such as the confused night scene, the purloining of letters, the 'sleep-talking' scene, and the ending in multiple marriages.

---

[9] De Armas, *The Invisible Mistress*. Both Lope and Calderón exploit this story-type, in *La viuda valenciana* and *La dama duende* respectively.

No less than three plays survive by Ángela de Azevedo: *El muerto disimulado*, *La margarita del Tajo que dio nombre a Santarén*, and *Dicha y desdicha del juego y devoción de la virgen* were all written in the second half of the seventeenth century. They are all long by Golden Age standards, with *La margarita del Tajo* stretching to well over 4000 lines (1000 lines longer than the norm). *El muerto disimulado* in particular, a comedy of intrigue involving a brother, Clarindo, and sister, Lisarda, who cross-dress independently and for different purposes, is heavily influenced by the drama of Tirso and Calderón. Azevedo reveals the importance of the Calderonian *comedia* to her theatre not just in her themes (for example, creating a pact with the devil), and the length of her plays and their individual characters' speeches,[10] but also in the myriad metatheatrical asides with which she toys. When the father, Nuño Osorio, interrupts a lovers' tryst, in *Dicha y desdicha del juego*, the *gracioso*, Sombrero, exclaims: 'Mal haya la fantasía/ del poeta endemoniado/ que aquí este viejo ha encajado' (Azevedo, *Dicha*, lines 806–8). The playwright constantly anticipates 'aloud' the rest of her fiction, and plays very boldly with the dramatic illusion. Such breaking of the frame, common too in the works of other women playwrights, especially in Ana Caro's *Valor, agravio y mujer*, hints at a different sort of relationship with the audience than was usual. The erudition, the self-consciousness, the rapport with the audience, the wit of the poetry and the in-jokes which pervade many of these plays perhaps suggest a case for an understanding of them as pieces which were read or performed in an intimate setting (an academy perhaps) removed from the atmosphere of the *corral*.

Performance and further study of female-authored plays will help to establish the extent to which they express a feminist viewpoint *avant la lettre*. The prose writing of Santa Teresa in the sixteenth century and María de Zayas in the seventeeth, as well as the paintings by female artists such as Sofonisba Anguissola, strongly suggest that educated women of the Golden Age were aware of the limitations and restrictions imposed upon them by a patriarchal society – even if they could not have used such feminist terminology. Many male-authored Golden Age plays too are remarkable for the freedom of action given to the female protagonist: Vélez's *bandolera* Gila, Tirso's Juana/Gil, and Lope's Laura in *La vengadora de las mujeres* are hardly isolated examples. What might be seen to be novel in the plays by women is the absence on occasions (for example, in Zayas's *La traición en la amistad* and Caro's *Valor, agravio y mujer*) of a senior figure, a *barba*, to dispense justice and oversee the re-ordering of society. Female voices are sometimes louder, especially at the end of plays, and more strident, as when Violante explains to Fadrique, in Azevedo's *Dicha y desdicha del juego*, that she simply does not want to marry him no matter what her father has arranged:

---

[10] Calderón's plays did grow longer: *Las manos blancas no ofenden*, for example, stretches to 4353 lines, and Fernando's speech therein to 453 lines – supposedly the longest in Spanish theatre.

Cuán mal nos está a los dos
el casamiento, lo mire
vuestra prudencia, señor;
pues será cosa insufrible
que se obliguen dos sujetos
a casar sin que se obliguen
de amor, que es el propio medio
para semejantes fines.   (Azevedo, *Dicha*, lines 3350–7)

4

Calderón and
the *Comedia*'s Second Generation

Pedro Calderón de la Barca was born in Madrid in the year 1600 and was thus Lope de Vega's junior by a generation. The two dramatists coincided in writing for the stage from the early 1620s until Lope's death in 1635, more than enough time for Lope to become aware of the capabilities of this particular specimen of the 'pájaros nuevos', as the veteran called the fresh wave of *poetas*. Although he retained the basic structure of the *comedia nueva* as established by Lope and his contemporaries, it is certainly apt to denominate Calderón and his 'school' a second wave or generation of Golden Age dramatists. The differences in the form and style of Calderonian drama, and evolutions in its content, are striking, although whether one feels that through Calderón the *comedia* reaches its apogee is largely a matter of personal taste. Not all of the new developments can be ascribed to the influence of the poetry of Luis de Góngora (Lope's erstwhile rival, who had died in 1627) but the more *recherché* or *culto* linguistic legacy is plain to see in Calderón's verse, which scholars often label 'gongorine'. There are also important changes in the theatrical world, particularly of the court under Philip IV (1621–65) and in the subsequent reign of Charles II (1665–1700), which influence the kind of entertainment produced by dramatists (see pp. 129–30).

A significant difference between Lope and Calderón is that the latter came from a family which, whilst not belonging to the upper echelons of the aristocracy, occupied a more elevated social position. Pedro's education with the Jesuits at the Colegio Imperial, then at Spain's best universities, Alcalá and Salamanca (whence he graduated in Canon Law in 1619), was the finest available and is inescapably influential in much of his dramatic output, especially the Corpus Christi *autos*, of which he was the acknowledged master. Don Pedro's status, such as it was, came from his father Diego's position as a government *secretario*, a post he had inherited from his own father. In 1623, several years after Diego's second marriage (1614) and death (1615), Pedro and his siblings sold their father's office for financial reasons. As well as experiencing financial hardship for a time, Calderón was twice in trouble with the law along with his brothers, once in 1621, and then again in 1629 when Lope de Vega and others vented their anger at the dramatist and his associates for their scandalous pursuit of an actor, after a fight, into the Trinitarian convent where Lope's daughter was cloistered as a nun. Despite these black marks against his name, Calderón's background and education, combined with his talents, gave him the kind of access to court circles that Lope vainly yearned for: in 1634 a performance of one of his *autos* celebrated the building of Philip IV's new palace, the Buen Retiro; in 1635 he was appointed director of palace performances; and in 1636 he sought a knighthood in the Order of Santiago, which he obtained in 1637 after a papal dispensation.

The 1630s saw Calderón's dramatic creativity at its height. This is the period in which he produced most of his best known works, including *La vida es sueño* (from the first half of the decade), *El alcalde de Zalamea* (1636), and his honour dramas. His dramatic works began to be published, with the *Primera parte*, in 1636. The arrival of the 1640s, however, which saw Calderón in military action in Catalonia, proved to be a grim decade for the theatrical world. The fall of Olivares in 1643 was followed by the closure of the theatres (for most of 1644–49), initially because of the death of Queen Isabel, and then that of Baltasar Carlos, heir to the throne, in 1646. Then, in 1651, just into his fifties, Calderón took holy orders. Despite the existence of a lover and the birth of a son in the 1640s, Calderón's credentials were plain to see in his education and in the intimate knowledge of the Bible and works of exegesis demonstrated in his *autos sacramentales* and his *comedias* on religious themes. The decision took his career in a different direction: he was first appointed a chaplain in Toledo cathedral in 1653 and then 'capellán de honor del Rey' in Madrid in 1663, during the twilight years of the *rey planeta*. The pull of the church had an obvious effect on his playwriting: he continued to produce *autos* for Madrid's Corpus Christi celebrations, but left the *corral* behind, restricting his secular output to the palace plays (on mythological themes), which became such a feature of courtly life in Spain as the seventeenth century advanced.

Calderón's first forays into the literary world were works entered in 'justas poéticas': he won first and second prize in a competition to celebrate the canonization of San Isidro in 1622. However, unlike Lope, who wrote in a variety of non-dramatic genres and whose literary fame would be assured even if he had not composed a single work for the theatre, Calderón left a fairly small non-dramatic *oeuvre*. By most standards he was a prolific dramatist, however, writing some 120 plays and scores of *autos* as well as works in the shorter formats. From 1623 with the *première*, significantly in the royal palace, of the *comedia Amor, honor y poder*, until he died in 1681, working on the second *auto* for Madrid's Corpus Christi celebrations of that year, Calderón was indisputably a man of the theatre.

Calderón's theatrical education can be pieced together fairly reliably if not precisely. As a pupil of the Jesuits he would have read and imitated classical authors, including the Roman dramatists Terence and Plautus. He may have performed in, or otherwise contributed to, the Jesuit school drama. As a *madrileño* he would have regularly attended the *corral* performances of plays by Lope, Tirso de Molina, Guillén de Castro, Ruiz de Alarcón, and Mira de Amescua amongst others. His later praise of Tirso in print would seem to confirm the likelihood of an early preference for the Mercedarian's drama which is suggested by his own first plays. Calderón also had an advantage over the previous generation in that he could read far more contemporary plays in printed editions than had formerly been available. Thus works by playwrights of Lope's generation could become sources for Calderón's own plays.[1] What is sometimes forgotten in the case of Calderón is that his youthful exposure to the theatre was to all of its forms and genres: he would have heard *loas* spoken, seen *comedias* set in cities, palaces and far-off lands, comic, tragic and religious, watched the *entremeses* and other more minor forms performed as *entr'actes*, and witnessed processions and *autos* in the street. Calderón had a kaleidoscopic knowledge and experience of early seventeenth-century theatre, and wrote sensitively within certain generic paradigms as well as sometimes questioning or undermining them. The suggestion that his Catholic upbringing and undoubted devotion to his religion, or that an underlying essential seriousness in contemplating and artistically re-creating human activity on stage, mean that his drama is predictably conservative or demonstrates a monolithic world-view or relentless moralism must be strenuously resisted. The three broad types of full-length drama that he wrote – comedies, *dramas* and mythological plays – will be considered in this chapter, and this will be followed first by an analysis of what makes his drama distinctive, and secondly by a brief look at other playwrights he influenced. His *autos*, his short comic plays, and his burlesque drama will be reserved for chapter 6.

Comedies

Comic theatre, broadly understood, was Calderón's staple in his early years as a dramatist. In writing predominantly in this vein he was following in the footsteps of his predecessors who had developed, after 1600, a more 'realistic' comedy anchored in the social world of the time. The more escapist or novelesque comedies of the younger Lope de Vega had given way to a style which 'alude mucho más concretamente a modas, costumbres, fiestas, y ambientes actuales, e incluso a asuntos políticos' (Close, 'Convergencia', p. 133). To claim that the comic deals with the everyday seems problematic when one thinks of the strains made on the spectators' credulity in a play such as *La desdicha de la voz* (1639), but the notion, of Aristotelian pedigree, is a useful one. The world of Calderonian comedy is often recognizably that in which the audience lived: the settings, especially in the *comedia de capa y espada*, are Madrid and other Spanish cities; the protagonists are members of the lower or middle nobility; the events are tied to particular moments in history. It is the values and behaviour, especially the faults, idiosyncrasies, and perversities, of Golden Age society which are under scrutiny. Love and honour are opposed in a fast-moving world over which, with little room for heroism or idealism, the most practical individual presides. Nevertheless, although Calderón's comedies are

---

[1] The classic study of Calderón's use of earlier plays is by Sloman. There was in fact a decade-long ban on the publication of plays and novels in Castile between 1625 and 1634, which helps to explain why Calderón's first plays were not published until 1636.

perhaps easier to pigeon-hole than Lope's, it is difficult to make sweeping judge-ments about them as a whole. There seems, for example, to be a shift in his conception of the comic sometime between the end of the 1620s and about 1640.[2]

Consistently the most popular of Calderón's early comedies, both on stage and amongst readers and translators, is *La dama duende* of 1629. A paradig-matic *comedia de capa y espada*, the play begins with the arrival of Don Manuel in Madrid. He has come to stay with his old friend Don Juan, and has just missed the festivities for the baptism of Prince Baltasar Carlos, much to the amusement of Cosme, his *gracioso* servant. Don Manuel is immediately accosted in the capital's streets by a veiled woman (Doña Ángela), who asks him for protection. Despite the taunts of his servant, who sees him as a latter-day poor man's Don Quijote, he provides the lady with assistance by fighting off a certain Don Luis who is pursuing her. Luis is in fact Juan's brother and Doña Ángela is their sister. The comedy depends on the fact that, ever since her husband died in debt to the king, Ángela has been cloistered secretly in her brothers' house, actually in a room which gives on to the one Manuel is to stay in. An inexpertly fitted cupboard allows Ángela access to her chivalrous saviour and she uses her knowledge of the house to haunt him as a benign spirit. Her brothers never mention her existence, which adds to Manuel's perplexity about the identity of his invisible admirer. The action of the play takes place inside the house almost throughout and Ángela's success (she eventually compromises Manuel into marriage with her) depends on her ability to manipulate the space in which they all live, and create a fantastic and alluring aura about herself. The domination over interior space is reminiscent of Tirso's *Por el sótano y el torno* and the tempting of the *galán* has echoes of Lope's *La viuda valenciana* and other comic works which invert the Cupid–Psyche myth (see p. 89).

The play's comic pedigree is irrefutable. It would have entertained the *corral* audience on a number of levels: there is the traditional marriage of the young *galán* and *dama* after the vicissitudes of their 'courtship'; Juan and especially Luis act as impediments to the solution the audience anticipates, appearing at the most inopportune junctures and bringing the action close to farce; the *gracioso* provides moments of perspicacity in undermining his master, and idiocy in his credulity; the pace is maintained throughout to prevent stasis and inattention; the usual social order is temporarily turned upside down through the wiles of the predatory woman; at the same time there is food for thought, as there should be in good comedy. Recently scholars have found a kind of proto-feminism in Calderón's depiction of Ángela: 'Que yo/ entre dos paredes muera,/ donde apenas el sol sabe/ quién soy' (Calderón, *La dama duende*, lines 379–82). The widowed heroine certainly complains bitterly in Act 1 of her isola-tion and lack of freedom to express herself. She responds to her social invisi-

---

[2] Calderón scholars tend to sub-divide his comedies essentially by location, that is between city-based *comedias de capa y espada* and the more exotic palace plays, but there may be a stronger case for differentiating them by period.

bility by becoming the character most able to pull the strings of those around her (Thacker, *Role-play*, pp. 109–32). Her brothers, especially the impotent, blustering Luis, are typically hypocritical in protecting their own family 'honour' whilst aggressively pursuing another noblewoman, Doña Beatriz. At its best, comedy asks questions as well as causing mirth, and there is no reason to believe that Calderón would not have wanted his audience to reflect upon ossified social norms, particularly in the relationships between the sexes, in this and other similar plays.

Two other early comedies, both of 1629, *El galán fantasma* and *Casa con dos puertas mala es de guardar*, rely similarly on individuals' ability to take advantage for themselves of some quirk of their environment. In the former (set in foreign parts and thus not a *comedia de capa y espada*) it is a tunnel, which allows the hero, Astolfo, access to his beloved when all think him dead. In the latter the two doors to Laura's house facilitate a complex set of comings and goings, with the *galanes*, Félix and Lisardo, often in the dark about the machinations of their lovers, Laura and Marcela, who refuse to behave in the honourable feminine manner the menfolk anticipate of them. As is usual the comic genre prevents any offences to family honour from having serious consequences, however desperate and complex the situation has seemed. There is a temptation to read these comedies with the excesses of the honour dramas (see pp. 99–103) in mind, but a seventeenth-century audience would have had a more relaxed set of expectations when going to see a comedy at the *corral*.[3]

One of Calderón's strengths in his comedies was, as Menéndez y Pelayo observed (Rodríguez Cuadros, *Calderón*, p. 71), to create works that were similar yet different. As an audience member one would recognize comfortably the character-types and the plot-line of a new play whilst not knowing what clever novelty would emerge in the complication and disentanglement of the action. Thus, as the century wears on, the Mexican Sor Juana Inés de la Cruz is able to pay tribute to Calderón and simultaneously satirize his generic norms with her claustrophobic comedy *Los empeños de una casa* (1683, see p. 121), changing a single letter from Calderón's *Los empeños de un acaso* (1639?). Calderón was in fact self-conscious enough to have begun parodying himself, or at least the drama he was writing, as early as *El galán fantasma*, which refers intertextually to *La dama duende*. He was wont to refer frequently to Lope de Vega and especially to Cervantes too. Indeed, metatheatrical comment on the comic intrigue underway, often in the mouth of the *gracioso* or the lady's maid, becomes a feature of Calderón's comedy. The audience's suspension of disbelief is punctured by reference to the situation's patent absurdity, as in *No hay burlas con el amor* (c.1636) or when the maid, Isabel, in *La desdicha de la voz* warns of the approaching figures of authority:

---

[3] See Wardropper, 'El problema', and Arellano, *Convención*, esp. chapter 1, for this argument.

Que debe de ser comedia,
sin duda, ésta de don Pedro
Calderón; que hermano o padre
sienpre vienen a mal tienpo,
y aora vienen ambos juntos.

(Calderón, *La desdicha*, lines 2225–9)[4]

The blatant self-referentiality, with its inevitable breaking of the theatrical illusion, is worthy of attention as it indicates the start of the decaying of the *comedia cómica* in the Golden Age. In Calderón such moments occur regularly in what Mason has helpfully referred to as 'minor-key comedies' (Calderón, *La desdicha*, p. 66). At least five comedies, probably all from the period 1638–40, offer a more bitter conception of comedy, which, however important Arellano's reminders that comic works should be analysed within the expectations of the genre, do mark a break with the past. These plays, in addition to *La desdicha de la voz*, are *No hay cosa como callar*, *Primero soy yo*, *Los empeños de un acaso*, and *No siempre lo peor es cierto*. Mason remarks upon the disappearance of the individual, like Doña Ángela, who maintains some sort of control over the tricks and vicissitudes of the plot in Calderón's youthful comedies. Here he finds more 'a sense of precariousness, of a social fabric tottering on the brink of disintegration and anarchy' (Calderón, *La desdicha*, p. 90).

In *La desdicha de la voz* the brother–sister relationship plumbs new depths (or perhaps simply returns to the comic world of Torres Naharro's *Himenea*) when Don Pedro attempts to carry out his threat to kill Beatriz at her refusal to marry Don Diego. He knows she has put the family honour in jeopardy after hearing her unmistakable singing voice in Diego's house, and hears it twice more in Acts 2 and 3 as the action moves, with the flight of Beatriz, to Seville. His frustration mounts and he resorts again to violence at the end of the play. Although the marriage of the lovers Beatriz and Juan is allowed to take place, the comedy is marked by profound confusion. Neither the resourceful woman nor the kindly older family friend, Otavio, is able to take control at any time. The unpleasant Leonor, for whom Beatriz acts as maid in order to take cover, is cruelly mocked for her pretensions, in the final scene. There are parallels with *La dama duende*, for example in the failure of the least attractive male character to find a partner. Don Pedro, like Luis in the earlier play, is destined to be the *galán suelto*. Yet here the more carnivalesque atmosphere of comedy all but disappears: nobody remains aloof and nobody enjoys the deceptions. The threat of chaos is tangible and the prospects for human relationships pessimistic.

The plot of *No hay cosa como callar* also challenges the limits of the comic. The end of Act 1 sees the despicable Don Juan rape Doña Leonor, after his father has offered her shelter and a bed for the night following a fire. A devastated Leonor, in love with another man, keeps obstinately quiet about the rape until eventually she takes the chance to uncover the identity of her attacker and

---

4 Unusually Mason's edition of this play does not modernize orthography.

marry him. The comedy ends with only this marriage, clearly the best of a bad job, and the *gracioso* Barzoque's reminder that a servant lies injured outside the house as a result of the fighting that has helped bring the action of the play to a close:

> Cada uno a su negocio
> está solamente atento,
> olvidados de un criado
> que está herido . . .
> de los yerros ajenos
> 'No hay cosa como callar'.   (Calderón, *No hay cosa*, p. 1037b)

There is a deliberate undermining of even the possibility of a comic happy ending here. The *gracioso*'s metatheatrical attempt to call attention to the self-ishness and hypocrisy of his fellow characters is clearly an indictment of the values of Calderón's society, and one which is more damning and pessimistic than Cervantes's in his *novela*, *La fuerza de la sangre*, which deals with a similar theme. The combination of unsympathetic characters, the loss of control these experience over their lives, and the frequent breaking of the theatrical illusion, especially by the detached and witty *graciosos*, suggests that Calderón is not searching for an empathetic response from his audience, as he once had done, but looking for dispassionate criticism of their society as presented at one remove.

Calderón's comedies have not been adequately represented in the canon of his works. They still require testing on stage as well as further analysis by scholars before anything other than provisional or schematic conclusions, however suggestive, can be reached. Some less well known texts, such as *Cada uno para sí*, *La desdicha de la voz*, and Calderón's longest play, the fascinating *Las manos blancas no ofenden*, are at least now available in modern editions, facilitating their dissemination and study.

Dramas

The canon of Calderón's plays, regularly edited, studied at universities, translated, and performed on stage, comprises a handful of non-comic works, mainly from the 1630s, whose generic designation has caused much debate in recent times. The broad term *drama* covers most of these works adequately and avoids the vexed issue of which might reasonably be denominated *tragedias*, a problem to which we shall return. They include honour plays, works inspired by history, including ancient history and the Bible, and religious/philosophical works.

If *La vida es sueño* is Calderón's most widely known individual play, the concept that is most closely associated with the dramatist is the notorious honour code, inhumanly followed by the noble husbands of his three wife-murder (or uxoricide) dramas, *El médico de su honra* (early 1630s), *A secreto agravio, secreta venganza* (1635), and *El pintor de su deshonra* (late 1640s), and doggedly resisted by the peasant Pedro Crespo of *El alcalde de Zalamea* (early

1640s). Honour plots were warmly recommended by Lope de Vega, whose *Los comendadores de Córdoba* in particular revealed some of the paradoxes and emotional excesses associated with Spanish *pundonor*. However, it was Calderón's predilection for the subject which led to his notorious and long-lived association with the honour play. Although a lively concern with sexual honour was a reality in Spain, the code itself was not, at least in its extreme dramatic form, a feature of everyday life in the seventeenth century. This unwritten dramatic code was concerned with a nobleman's reputation. The infidelity of a wife, sex outside marriage practised by a daughter or sister, disrespect shown towards an individual by another man, made manifest for example in an accusation of Jewish descent, of cowardice, or of a failure to fulfil one's word, would all require remedial action, often violent. If news of the offence had not spread abroad, vengeance could be taken secretly.

The wife-murder plays, despite being written over a lengthy period, do have points in common, not least the ending in the violent death of the new bride. Nevertheless, there are important differences in each plot and above all in the characters of the married couples who feature in them, differences which should warn the reader of the dangers of drawing identical conclusions from every play. *El médico de su honra* shows the honour code in all its stark and absurd cruelty. The Sevillian noblewoman Doña Mencía has been married to Don Gutierre by her father: this on the surface is an appropriate, arranged, society wedding. Gutierre is ignorant, however, of the fact that Mencía was once loved by Enrique (later Enrique II), half-brother of King Pedro, who by chance falls from his horse outside Gutierre and Mencía's country residence. Her old passion is painfully repressed by Mencía, conscious of her new social status, but inflamed again by the ignoble Enrique, who wakes from his unconscious state to see the angelic vision of the woman he loved. Mencía's human desire to explain her apparent volte-face to the prince is abused by him, leading to a series of compromising situations which are taken by Gutierre to be proof of his innocent wife's infidelity. Gutierre himself is shown to be a man obsessed (perhaps abnormally) by his social reputation, or sense of honour. In the play's pre-history he has broken off an engagement to Doña Leonor after seeing a man jump from the balcony of her house, a decision which in turn dishonours Leonor, forcing her to take legal action against her betrothed, and ultimately appeal to King Pedro for justice. As Gutierre's anxiety about his wife's behaviour increases scene by scene he begins to apostrophize his honour, seeing it as a patient requiring medical attention: taken over by his metaphor, he turns into the doctor of his honour and cures his patient by having Mencía bled to death by a surgeon he hires (and intends then to silence). The play ends with King Pedro, aware that Gutierre has resorted to uxoricide in order to protect his social face, insisting that the widower accept the hand of the willing Leonor in a second marriage, the very idea of which Gutierre abhors.

This honour drama has evinced strong reactions from audiences and scholars, ranging from admiration for Gutierre, either for his uncompromising solution to the problem of potential dishonour, or for his self-mastery and self-possession, to uncomprehending hostility towards his barbarism, and instinctive sympathy for the victim of his society's misogynistic code. Indeed, the play's ambiguities and uncertainties open up a series of questions and possibilities for interpretation. Does Gutierre ever love his wife? Can Mencía be seen to contribute to her own downfall? What are the ironic implications of the doctor metaphor so dear to Gutierre? (Doctors were, predictably, frequent targets of satire in Golden Age drama.) How can a Christian society place so great a weight on the importance of external appearances? What does honour obsession imply (or symbolize) for the world of Calderón's audience? The fiction of *El médico de su honra* is lent increased depth by the presence of the historical figure of King Pedro, the fourteenth-century Castilian monarch who, as the primitive audience knew, was eventually killed by his half-brother, Enrique. As we saw in chapter 3, Pedro went down in history sometimes as cruel, sometimes as just. In the play he can be seen as well-intentioned but ineffective, a man who disguises his own errors and insecurities by hushing up the murder and insisting on an inappropriate union in its aftermath. The sub-plot involving the historical rivalry between Pedro and Enrique, with its lessons in effective kingship, would have intrigued an audience in the 1630s, a time when the initial promise of the Philip IV–Olivares regime had faded.

Calderón's strengths as a dramatist are evident in this honour drama: he produces an artefact which is at once beautiful in its poetry, moving in its combination of exquisite form and highly charged content, and troubling in the questions it raises and leaves unresolved. *El médico* is a work of theatre, like Shakespeare's *Othello*, in which a jealous husband, convinced that his wife is deceiving him and having a relationship with another man, ends up killing her. Like *Othello*, the play has repercussions beyond the obvious personal tragedy for the wife, and to some extent the husband. Transcending its historical displacement it raises questions about the society for which the drama is performed, in particular about the way that society allows relationships between men and women, and kings and subjects, to be conducted. Just as Gutierre hides the awfulness of what he is doing behind his metaphor, so Calderón is able to hide a play with a serious contemporary social relevance behind a historically-based entertainment. The very excess observable in the actions of Gutierre in his defence of his honour, together with the need to preserve the secret, has led scholars to feel that there is more at stake than meets the eye in this and the other honour plays. Melveena McKendrick has suggested in separate articles first that the concern with honour in the household might reflect a concern with Spain's reputation on a macrocosmic level, and then that the male anxiety about female fidelity points to an undramatizable concern over purity of blood at a time when those known to be of Jewish stock were discriminated against, especially in Castile (McKendrick, 'Calderón' and 'Honour/Vengeance'). In an analysis of Gutierre's long soliloquy placed in the middle of the play, Jeremy Robbins has persuasively argued, linking *El médico* to European intellectual currents of the period, that the work is 'a dramatic staging of the desire for certainty in a world were only probability exists, and of the consequences of such a desire being unrealizable' (Robbins, 'Performing Doubt', p. 70).

A secreto agravio, secreta venganza, like many Golden Age *comedias* whose titles would have been advertised on posters in the streets, leaves the potential audience in little doubt as to its content. Like the *lema* of an emblem, it presents a truism to go hand in hand with the honour play. Again the action is set in a recognizable past, the sixteenth-century Portugal of King Sebastian, not long before the battle of Alcazarquivir, in which the protagonist, Don Lope de Almeida, will no doubt meet his end along with his compatriots. This fine drama is the one most overtly and incessantly concerned with honour and its implications. Don Lope proleptically avenges the slight to his reputation by secretly killing Luis, his wife's old flame and would-be lover, and destroying the body of Leonor, his less-than-faithful wife, having killed her and set fire to their *quinta*. Some of the paradoxes of honour-obsession are revealed by Calderón's creation of a friend for the protagonist: Don Juan. The latter has himself previously acted 'honourably' in killing an enemy who had offended him but, despite this, finds that the suggestions of dishonour are stains difficult to erase. Most painful is the difficulty a friend has in raising a matter of honour, an issue so sensitive that it cannot be overtly mentioned. Both men, like the other wife-murderers, rail against the necessity for the code, condemning its inventor, whilst abiding by its dictates:

> ¡Oh locas leyes del mundo!
> . . .
> Yo no basto a reducirlas
> (con tal condición nacimos),
> yo vivo para vengarlas,
> no para enmendarlas vivo.
>
> (Calderón, *A secreto agravio*, pp. 61–2)

The outcomes of these first two honour dramas tellingly reveal the difficulties created even by avenging one's honour by the book. A secret is rarely kept; innocence and guilt are irrelevant concepts; the code itself is a bloody failure.

In *El pintor de su deshonra*, the honour-bound husband, Juan Roca, a Catalan painter, bears little resemblance to *El médico*'s Don Gutierre. Although he is possibly unwise to marry the beautiful Serafina later in life, he is not the kind of jealous old husband so well characterized by Cervantes and Molière. Serafina is an admirable character: she resists the temptation to return to her first love, Don Álvaro, when he makes a surprise return to Naples after being lost at sea, and becomes devoted to her husband and her new life in Barcelona. A combination of fate and human agency allow Serafina, in a state of unconsciousness after a house fire, to be stolen away by the persistent Álvaro. Having lost his honour so publicly Juan Roca shuns society, travelling incognito to Italy where by chance he is asked to paint a picture of Serafina, who, the audience knows, has remained faithful to him. When he witnesses her awaking from a nightmare and seeking comfort for the first time in Álvaro's arms, he shoots both the apparent lovers, an action that is approved by the representatives of the social hierarchy present. Nevertheless the murder is more *crime passionel* than honour vengeance. Serafina's innocence will never become known.

El pintor is a particularly rich play. It reveals Calderón's knowledge of and respect for the world of painting, which is carefully woven into the drama;[5] it again raises questions about the individual and society through the honour code; and most adventurously it self-consciously mixes the norms of the comic (a love triangle which owes much to farce, the cross-generational marriage, misunderstandings, disguise, a carnival setting, and an ending in marriage, however contrived or inappropriate) with elements of tragedy (death, the oppressive presence of the honour code, Serafina's anguish at the loss of Álvaro and then her self-control, Álvaro's and Juan Roca's anguish and the latter's fall from good fortune, irony, the role of fate). At least part of Calderón's intention in this play is to show that either genre is a simplification of life, which exceeds these bounds. For Calderón the generic admixture is not just a reflection of human life, which is neither wholly tragic nor wholly comic (compare Lope's view in the *Arte nuevo*), it is an acceptance that life is unpredictable and unrepresentable, and perhaps a step towards the realization that it takes a certain kind of attitude from an individual to cope with its unpredictability – a resilience, a philosophy for life which can leave that individual prepared.

El pintor's protagonist Juan Roca is the most sympathetic of the three wife-murderers. His actions are those of a man who is in love with his wife, and cannot believe his misfortune, rather than the result of the calculating thought processes of one who needs to find a way to survive socially, to regain his social standing. He is very much a victim of the honour code, the 'injusta ley traidora' (Calderón, *El pintor*, line 2591) which ruins his life.

None of the wife-murder dramas is a tragedy in the strict sense of the term. This has not prevented a great deal of ink flowing on either side of the debate about their pigeon-holing. Those against the term 'tragedy' tend to appeal to an Aristotelian or neo-classical understanding of what the genre implies, and argue that true 'tragedia' is not possible from the pen of a Christian playwright (see Maestro, 'Los límites'). The most influential argument in favour of a tragic categorization came from A. A. Parker and is his view of 'diffused responsibility': the mistakes of all the characters contribute to the tragic outcome, rather than Aristotle's one tragic flaw being central (Parker, 'Towards a definition'). There looms behind the debate another honour question, that of the status of Spain's national drama, one which is defused by McKendrick, who sensibly writes that:

> There seems in fact to be no good reason why great plays which engage with serious issues in the life of man should be intrinsically less great than great

---

[5] Painters in the time of Calderón and Velázquez argued for recognition of their art as an intellectual activity, not merely a trade. Both Lope and Calderón were friendly with painters, used painting and paintings regularly and subtly in their plays, and supported the artists' cause; Calderón in a legal submission dated 1677.

tragedies, just because they do not conform to certain formal requirements or to a specific vision of the human condition.   (McKendrick, *Theatre*, p. 80)

The once influential notion that a severe Calderón was recommending an adherence to the courses of action followed by his wife-murderers can be scotched with reference to *El alcalde de Zalamea*, a play that deliberately compares and contrasts a variety of social attitudes to honour. Borrowing from Lope de Vega's stock of honourable peasant characters, Calderón creates Pedro Crespo and his rich family. (Like *El médico*, *El alcalde* is re-worked from an earlier play of the same name, formerly attributed to Lope.) Pedro's pretty and prudent daughter, Isabel, is raped by the captain of a group of soldiers billeted on the town as Philip II prepares to annex Portugal in 1580. Although Pedro's son Juan instinctively goes to kill the dishonoured Isabel, now a source of shame to the family, Pedro protects her, and when he hears news that he has been elected mayor of Zalamea, he prosecutes and executes the captain, whose garroted body is sensationally displayed in the *corral* theatre's discovery space. Pedro thus defies social expectations, legal obligations and the authority of Don Lope de Figueroa, whom he has earlier impressed with his home-spun values. The tense stand-off between the two mature men is relieved by the arrival of Philip II himself to approve Pedro's actions and instate him as mayor of Zalamea permanently.

The conception of honour put forward by Crespo is at once more Christian and more egalitarian than the *pundonor* evident in the wife-murder dramas. Some scholars have tried to differentiate the two types by calling them *honra* (peasant 'honourableness', see p. 43) and *honor* (innate nobility), but whilst it is true that *código de honra* (rather than *honor*) makes no sense in Spanish, the two words are often employed interchangeably or chosen for metrical reasons. Crespo, in responding to his son's ambitious inclinations, rejects the chance to buy a patent of nobility, which would have allowed him certain social privileges and a status he regards as false. Instead he prefers to be respected by his Old Christian peers and, as he explains to Don Lope, to do his social duty and have a clean conscience before God:

> Al rey la hacienda y la vida
> se ha de dar; pero el honor
> es patrimonio del alma,
> y el alma sólo es de Dios.   (Calderón, *El alcalde*, lines 873–6)

Honour, then, through Pedro Crespo, becomes an essential 'honourableness', a manner of living which requires no social justification, but is an honesty and worthiness which will eventually be judged by God. The decision of Isabel (perhaps made for her by her father) to retire to a convent where 'tiene Esposo/ que no mira en calidad' (lines 957–8), is consistent with Crespo's outlook on earthly honour.

Although the Spanish obsession with honour has sometimes seemed to be a barrier between Calderón and a modern audience in Spain and elsewhere, these honour dramas (and other works such as *La vida es sueño* and *El mágico prodigioso*, which both have important honour sub-plots to them) have been the most regularly performed Golden Age plays in modern times. *El alcalde de Zalamea* is performed annually in Zalamea itself and is one of only two plays to have been produced twice by the Compañía Nacional de Teatro Clásico, founded in 1986 (the other being *El médico de su honra* in Adolfo Marsillach's production). British audiences have been able to see major companies perform both *El alcalde* (at the National Theatre in London in 1981) and *El pintor*, in Laurence Boswell's RSC production of 1995. In truth there is no reason why a Golden Age production with its dependence on the honour code should alienate a modern or non-Spanish audience any more than a play by García Lorca or any other dramatist whose work has crossed cultures.

La vida es sueño was the work that Calderón chose, in 1636, to head the first volume of his published plays. Despite its status as the standard-bearer and most assiduously studied play of the Spanish Golden Age, a large number of questions remain to be answered about this religious, or philosophical, or allegorical, or socio-historical work. Its date of composition remains unknown, and speculation continues about which was the first performed version as well as what the historical and literary sources were that inspired it. The play has undoubtedly continued to appeal to readers and directors because of its combination of universal themes and the possibility for new readings and interpretations that it provides. Its central figure, Segismundo, chained, dressed in animal skins and grasping a light at his first appearance, seems at first to belong to the allegorical world of the *auto sacramental*, and has a parallel in the Jesuit moralist Gracián's *El criticón*. He might represent the human condition. By the time he is glimpsed, however, Rosaura, a woman dressed as a man, and Clarín, her *gracioso* servant, two staples of the *comedia nueva*, have appeared on stage. The content of their opening conversation hints at a Lopean love comedy where the bold *mujer varonil* would pursue and eventually marry her recalcitrant lover. From the first meeting of Segismundo and Rosaura until the closing scene of the play their fates are linked, although not necessarily in the ways a Golden Age public would have guessed. The former is the Prince of Poland whose father King Basilio, after reading in the stars that his son would bring destruction and tyranny to the realm, has had him chained in a tower away from the court, educated by the noble Clotaldo. Rosaura is a Russian noblewoman, daughter as it happens of Clotaldo, come to Poland to search for Astolfo, the man who dishonoured her before leaving her to claim the Polish throne.

The play dramatizes the development of Segismundo from man–beast to perfect prince. Through the trickery of Clotaldo and Basilio, who oversee his violent and chaotic introduction to the court (to test the truth written in the stars) and then return him to the tower assuring him that he dreamed his changed circumstances, the bestial Segismundo comes to learn the importance of acting well even in dreams. When an uprising frees him and allows him to march victorious on his father's palace, Segismundo is careful not to act tyrannically a second time. He dispenses justice, speaks rationally, resists his sexual inclinations in restoring Rosaura's honour through marriage to Astolfo, marries Estrella for the good of his country, and seems a model of prudence and discretion. The prince's self-mastery is an example of the evidence of the influence of neo-Stoicism on Golden Age literature:[6] Segismundo is able to minimize the importance of what happens to him in this mundane dream-life in preparation for the reality which is the after-life. His behaviour then exemplifies a Christianized Roman philosophical outlook and is intended in some respects as an example for all humankind.

The story of Segismundo's victory over his self is undoubtedly touching. Its universal philosophical – even mythical – relevance has meant that successive generations have found meaning and inspiration in it, even when ignorant of the niceties of Calderón's 'full presentation of the Scholastic vision of providence' (Lewis-Smith, *Calderón*, p. 31). In presenting Segismundo's growing-pains the playwright exploits the public's basic philosophical curiosity about the extent to which the stories of our lives are already written. A knowledge of Counter-Reformation orthodoxy, then, which allows humankind free will to act prudently (that is, with moral responsibility) in the face of what fate has in store, is not essential for a fruitful engagement with Segismundo's story.

It may be possible to trace the Scholastic pedigree of Calderón in *La vida es sueño* with some confidence, explaining his religious/philosophical stance, but there are aspects of the play which resist closure. When the rebel soldier who has helped Segismundo to his rightful social place asks for a reward at the end of the play, the prince punishes him with a life sentence in the very tower in which he experienced a half-life himself. Such a pragmatic stance, which has seemed to some scholars to throw Segismundo's development into doubt, is hinted at earlier in Act 3 when the prince debates with himself how to react to his liberation and apparent change in fortune:

> A reinar fortuna, vamos;
> no me despiertes si duermo,
> y si es verdad, no me duermas.
> Mas sea verdad o sueño,
> obrar bien es lo que importa;
> si fuere verdad, por serlo;
> si no, por ganar amigos
> para cuando despertemos.
>
> (Calderón, *La vida es sueño*, lines 2420–7)

Segismundo keeps his options open: he sees the importance of acting morally well, as he has been taught, in case he is awake and not dreaming, and yet even in dreams (this earthly life) the pragmatic business of influencing others to be on one's side is vital. There are strong parallels here with Gracián's advice for the

---

[6] Quevedo was the figure most clearly influenced by neo-Stoicism in Golden Age Spain, having translated Epictetus and recommended self-denial to a Spain in decline.

moral negotiation of life in a potentially Machiavellian world.[7] The points in his drama where Calderón's religious answers do not quite seem to cover the questions being asked by a world becoming modern hold the greatest fascination. Behind the theatrical mask of an ordered world, or one that at least can be put in order, can occasionally be glimpsed, even in the religious plays, the hint of a vision of humankind isolated, naked, and uncertain.

Three other notable plays from Calderón's fecund early years as a dramatist further explore through individual human dramas and dilemmas some of the universal issues raised in *La vida es sueño*. They are: *La devoción de la cruz* (c.1625), *El príncipe constante* (c.1629) and *El mágico prodigioso* (1637). The last of these, partially translated by Shelley, and the inspiration for Goethe's *Faust*, was originally written for the Corpus Christi festivity of the town of Yepes, near Toledo, and re-worked with the demands of a *corral* audience in mind.[8] As a *comedia de santos* (see pp. 146–7) it features the martyrdom of Justina and Cipriano in Roman Antioch. Like Tirso in *El condenado por desconfiado*, and as in his own *La vida es sueño*, Calderón demonstrates a remarkable ability to dramatize potentially dry religious issues engagingly. In this case the student Cipriano is reading and thinking about Pliny's definition of God, without being able to make the final deduction that the deity in question must be that of the oppressed Christians. This pagan's intellectual progress worries the devil, who appears with the intention of derailing Cipriano whilst using him to destroy the impeccable Christian, Justina. Abandoning his studies, Cipriano falls so violently in love with Justina that he agrees to exchange his soul for the possession of her. However, after teaching him everything he knows of magic and witchcraft, the devil cannot deliver his side of the bargain: he conjures up nothing more than an image of Justina that turns to a skeleton, and which utters the warning 'Así, Cipriano, son/ todas las glorias del mundo' (Calderón, *El mágico*, ed. Wardropper, lines 2549–50). The devil, impotent when it comes to humans' free will, has to admit defeat and indeed has providentially hastened the conversion of the man he set out to damn.

Unlike Segismundo and Cipriano, the Portuguese prince, Fernando, the central character of *El príncipe constante*, is not seen to develop through his intellectual response to the words he listens to and the events he experiences. He has already achieved perfection in his role on earth through the realization of its inferior relation to the eternal realm. He ignores (or re-interprets positively) the omens of doom remarked upon by his fellows as he leads the Portuguese fleet against Tangiers, so confident is he of providential support. When imprisoned by the King of Fez, he encourages his fellow captives to remain true to Christian virtues in adversity: 'a la desdicha más fuerte/ sabe vencer la prudencia' (Calderón, *El príncipe*, p. 129). He leads by saintly example, refusing to exchange his own freedom for the town of Ceuta, arguing that it belongs to God

---

[7] See Robbins, 'Review Article', esp. pp. 44–5.
[8] See the composite edition of *El mágico*, by Parker and McKendrick.

and is not in his power to give. His stance leads to increasingly cruel treatment by the king, whom even Fernando's indebted Muslim friend, Muley, cannot mollify, and he eventually starves to death, a Christian martyr who then miraculously inspires the Portuguese forces under King Alfonso to a victory against the massed Moors. The body of Fernando is exchanged for the princess, Fénix, whose ephemeral beauty is contrasted with the eternal Christian values represented by the prince. Through the character of Fernando, Calderón makes his approval of Christianized stoical values plainer still (as Quevedo and Góngora had in their poetry). Self-denial, the control over one's passionate side, is possible if one reminds oneself constantly that:

> Pisando la tierra dura
> de continuo el hombre está,
> y cada paso que da
> es sobre su sepultura.   (Calderón, *El príncipe*, p. 163)

Fernando is the kind of prince that Segismundo, with the right education, should turn into. In this play we are not at all interested in the development of the ideal Christian leader of men (usually so important for Golden Age dramatists) but in the inspiration that consistently perfect behaviour, prudent acceptance of one's providential role, can have on others.

La devoción de la cruz, the earliest of these plays, but still not Calderón's first religious *comedia*, is clearly a less mature piece owing much to the dramatic norms of Lope's generation. The characters, particularly the rustic *gracioso* Gil, and the settings, are familiar from many earlier *comedias*; the central love affair between Julia and Eusebio (especially as played out in Act 1), belongs to the world of the *comedia de capa y espada*; Acts 2 and 3 are reminiscent of the bandit plays which go back at least to Virués. The overarching themes, however, might be called typically Calderonian and were to recur frequently in his serious drama. The relationship between father and son or daughter, important in *La vida es sueño* and in Justina's story in *El mágico prodigioso*, is central here. It is Curcio's jealous lack of faith in his wife, Rosmira, which begins the confusion that almost leads to incest between the separated twins Eusebio and Julia. Without realizing that the socially inferior Eusebio is his son, Curcio pursues him for killing Lisardo (his acknowledged son) in a duel, forces him into the hills where he becomes a bandit, and eventually, after discovering his true identity, witnesses him die at the hands of the peasant mob he has organized. Curcio's prior squandering of the family fortune is a further sign of his moral weakness as is his cruelty to his daughter when she resists his bullying. In lieu of his real family, it is the cross (under which the twins were born and with which both are marked on their chests) that protects Eusebio as he grows up. It is shown to be a force that can help prevent immorality when Eusebio resists the incestuous union with his sister in her convent cell on seeing her birthmark, and that can redeem sinful individuals, as Eusebio's death is providentially delayed so that he can seek absolution from a priest, Alberto. When human depravity resists the obvious exemplary lesson, as when in the final scene Curcio attempts to kill his daughter, who has left her convent to seek out her lover and become a bandit, the cross miraculously raises her to a higher level of the stage, so that she can return, chastened, to her holy life.

Although Golden Age painters were more rigorously controlled in the art they could produce than their playwright cousins, there are clear parallels between Calderón's didactic drama for the *corral* and many religious paintings commissioned by patrons during this period. Calderón revels in creating a meaningful tableau scene, sometimes in the discovery space, and provides evidence of this concern with more detailed stage directions than tended to be used by Lope. The purpose of these scenes – the first appearance of Segismundo, the martyrdom of Justina and Cipriano with the devil's words acting as *lema*, Fernando's miraculous presence with a lit torch as Fez is surrounded, Eusebio's confession to Alberto and his sister's elevation – is similar to that of the devotional paintings displayed in churches and elsewhere in the Spain of this period. Often too there are parallels with the popular emblem books, which presented a visual stimulus to the mind, and offered an interpretation in words, to ensure that the point had been understood by the viewer. When scholars refer to the plasticity that Calderón introduced to Golden Age drama (in his *comedias* as well as the *autos*, to which it is essential) it tends to be this careful engineering of meaningful scenes that they have in mind.

Calderón is best known, as we have established, as the writer of honour plays and religious dramas that reveal his casuistical turn of mind. In the period before he effectively retired from the *corral*, however, he wrote a number of other powerful works which are inspired by history (broadly understood). *El sitio de Bredá* was produced to celebrate Spinola's victory over Justin of Nassau in Flanders in 1625, and performed in the year of the end of the successful siege. The play aligns the dramatist with Velázquez, whose famous *Las lanzas* hung in the Hall of Realms in the Buen Retiro Palace, and other artists who succeeded in obtaining royal patronage in the early years of Olivares's grand projects. Both artists celebrate their country's military prowess but also capture the moment of surrender with compassion and understanding. *La cisma de Ingalaterra* (1627) dramatizes the development of Henry VIII's relationship with the wicked Anne Boleyn when married to the Spanish Catalina (Catherine of Aragon). It was composed at a time when the excitement and curiosity over the possible Spanish match (the proposed marriage of the Prince of Wales and future Charles I of England with the Infanta María) had died down. After showing an English king (Edward III) in a favourable light in *Amor, honor y poder* in 1623, the year of the unexpected arrival of Charles and Buckingham in Madrid, Calderón now uses recent English history to show how disastrous a fresh attempt to unite Spanish Catholicism with English Protestantism might be. The playwright proves to be in tune with Philip IV, and indeed with the many writers of treatises on kingship and statecraft of the period, who drew attention to the importance of a young monarch's learning lessons from history.

The purpose of some other historical plays by Calderón is more difficult to fathom, even when it is hard to imagine his subject choices to be innocent. Most intriguing is *Amar después de la muerte* (otherwise known as *El Tuzaní de la Alpujarra*), written probably in 1633. The play is set during the *morisco* uprising in the Alpujarras, near Granada, during the reign of Philip II. As in many other of his full-length works there are elements in the play of more than one sub-genre: the *comedia de capa y espada* in Act 1; and the honour drama when the admirable Álvaro Tuzaní avenges the murder of his wife Clara. What is most intriguing, however, is the sympathy with which the *moriscos* are treated in the play a quarter of a century after Philip III had ordered their expulsion. The content of the letter from Philip II reported by Malec in Act 1 is seen as provocative towards a group that is losing its old Muslim habits gradually but willingly. Malec urges:

> que se procediese
> en el caso con templanza,
> porque la violencia sobra
> donde la costumbre falta.   (Calderón, *Amar después*, pp. 140–1)

The good sense and chivalry of the *morisco* characters is contrasted throughout most of the play with the barbarity of the Old Christians and even the usually heroic Don Juan de Austria. Such *maurofilia* (or respect for the nobility of the Moor) is frequent in the ballads of the late sixteenth century and common enough in the early *comedia* with its dependence on exotic tales of the Reconquest, but is surprising when it emerges in relation to such recent historical events. It must have been a provocative work for its first audience.

Other plays from this period, inspired by history, deal with more universal themes. Calderón returns to his common preoccupation with painting in *Darlo todo y no dar nada* (1651), a fine play in which Alexander the Great is taught neo-stoical virtues by Diogenes. The limits of this and any monarch's power – Alexander is said to be 'esclavo de las esclavas' (i.e. his passions) – are exposed in part by the philosopher, in part by the exemplary forbearance of the painter Apeles, and in part by the strong-willed Campaspe who eventually agrees to marry Apeles because she loves him, not because she is told to do so by Alexander. In *Los cabellos de Absalón* (1634?) Calderón uses Act 3 of Tirso's *La venganza de Tamar*, almost in its entirety, as the middle act of his version of the story of the troubled and troublesome princes of the House of David. The play features the favourite Calderonian theme of filial disobedience, and in taking the Old Testament story on to the sack of Jerusalem and the predicted death of Absalom, to many minds Calderón creates a more unified Biblical tragedy than Tirso's.

La hija del aire (1637?) is unusual in being a two-part play, conceived in six acts. Its story, that of the legendary Semíramis, dealt with also by Virués in 1579, has obvious parallels with Segismundo's in *La vida es sueño*. The future tyrant queen begins the first part clad in furs and hidden away by Tiresias, for fear of the destructive power she will unleash on the world. This first part charts her rise to the throne, and the second her inability to give up power in favour of her son Ninias, and her eventual ironic death. The character of Semíramis is one of Calderón's most significant female roles, the greatness of which will only become clear, as is so often the case with Golden Age plays, with regular testing through performance.

Mythological plays

A move away from historical plays and other didactic dramas with an obvious contemporary relevance was sealed after Calderón took holy orders in 1651. The two patrons largely responsible for commissioning Calderón's plays from this time were the Madrid municipal authorities in the case of the *autos*, and the decadent court whose tastes were for the spectacular. This was the era of ostentatious magnificence in court theatre (see p. 129) and Calderón, as the producer of theatrical dialogue, was only one of the artists involved. It was the Italian stage designers who were to draw the biggest gasps of admiration for their technical virtuosity. Music too, always important in Calderón's early plays, came to dominate as dialogue was increasingly sung, and plays became semi-operatic, and later even full operas and *zarzuelas*. The subject matter was usually mythological, although a handful of court plays have as their source chivalric or Byzantine novels.

An early indication of the kind of court spectacular that would become frequent on royal birthdays and other occasions was *El mayor encanto amor* (1635), performed on the lake of the new palace (now the boating lake in the Retiro Park in central Madrid). Cosme Lotti joined forces with Calderón in this six-hour fiesta to celebrate the inauguration of the Salón de Armas, and made an impressive spectacle of the story of Circe and Ulysses. The *tramoya* (see p. 138) takes on a new importance in a play which many in the audience may have struggled to hear, and the end, with Circe's palace taking to the air and Ulises rowing off with his companions across the lake, certainly aims to please the eye rather than the ear.

Calderón opts for a Sicilian setting again for *La fiera, el rayo y la piedra*, performed in 1652 to celebrate the birthday of Philip IV's queen, Mariana of Austria. The work contains a mixture of mythological and invented stories, and includes both tragic and comic outcomes for the lovers depicted, which include Pygmalion. There is clear evidence of the development of the musical side of the drama by this time. Although Calderón had apparently rejected some of Lotti's ideas for the integration of music into *El mayor encanto amor*, by the time of this new entertainment some scenes are entirely sung. *La fiera, el rayo y la piedra*, *Fortunas de Andrómeda y Perseo* (1653) – for which the set designer Baccio del Bianco's drawings have survived, attesting to the new sophistication of the perspective stagings – and *La estatua de Prometeo* (c.1672) all feature sung dialogue, in the *estilo recitativo*, between the classical gods, who tended to float on clouds above the stage, whilst spoken dialogue is the norm for the mortals. Calderón collaborated closely with Juan Hidalgo (1614–85), who was responsible for court music, as well as with the designers mentioned, and was clearly aware of developments in Italian opera, as well as the views of humanist writers on music.[9]

These 'semi-operas', which placed mythological (often Ovidian) characters in idealized Mediterranean landscapes looked down upon by the classical gods, should be seen as distinct from the *zarzuela* and from full-blown opera. The term *zarzuela* is often in fact used rather broadly to cover all of Calderón's musical theatre, but originally it referred to the productions, of which *El laurel de Apolo* was the first, in 1657, performed at La Zarzuela palace outside Madrid when the king was staying there in order to hunt.[10] The form, which was frequently imitated in the final decades of the seventeenth century, was in two acts, mixed spoken and sung dialogue, had a pastoral setting suited to the real rustic backdrop, a plot involving love, classical, pastoral or mythological characters, and was easier to stage than the Buen Retiro extravaganzas. In *El laurel de Apolo*, Apollo and Cupid disguise themselves and descend to the terrestrial (pastoral) world, where their dialogue is spoken or sung.

In about 1660 Calderón wrote two operas on mythological themes, the one-act *La púrpura de la rosa* and the three-act *Celos aun del aire matan*. The first, what Calderón calls a 'pequeña/ representación', is a free version of the Venus and Adonis story. Its opening stage direction leaves no room for doubt about its nature: 'el teatro será de bosque, y van saliendo Flora, Cintia, Clori y Libia, cada una de por sí, cantando en estilo recitativo . . .' (Calderón, *La púrpura*, p. 676a). The librettist confesses, in its *loa*, that it is not an attempt to produce a sung *comedia*, for which the Spanish audience might not have the patience. However, Calderón does present the work as an attempt to introduce a new style of performance which will rival that of other nations. He was clearly aware of opera performances in Italy and France, and his experience with part-sung works perhaps made it inevitable that he would try his hand at the fully-fledged form, at least 'al estilo español', to borrow Lope's phrase from 1631. Unfortunately Hidalgo's score for the first royal performance of *La púrpura de la rosa* is not extant, but that by Tomás de Torrejón y Velasco, for the opera's revival in Lima in 1701 (the first New World opera), not only survives but exists in a modern recording made by Andrew Lawrence-King. Calderón's most ambitious opera, *Celos aun del aire matan*, was written to celebrate the Franco-Spanish wedding of the *infanta* María Teresa to Louis XIV. Calderón re-works the Ovidian myth of Cephalus and Procris, nymph of the chaste huntress Diana, and Hidalgo's score survives. It is clear that, in this entirely sung drama, the composer rose to the challenge of finding ways, through the music, of distinguishing between the different *comedia* character-types (Stein, *Songs of Mortals*, pp. 227–9) with which Calderón populated his text.

Calderón was very happy working with myth; he even used mythical figures, Orpheus for example, in his *autos sacramentales*. Other plays of interest of the

---

[9] See Sage, 'The Function of Music'.
[10] See Stein, *Songs of Mortals*, chapter 6, for the term's definition and its problems.

period, on mythological themes, are: *El golfo de las sirenas* (1657), *El hijo del Sol, Faetón* (1661), and *El monstruo de los jardines* (1661), which exploits the story of Tirso's only mythological work, *El Aquiles* (c.1626). The dramatist would be attracted by the possibility for allegorical readings of classical tales, exemplified in print by Pérez de Moya's attempts to interpret mythological stories in his *Philosofía secreta* of 1585, and displayed in the royal palaces in paintings by Velázquez, Rubens, Titian, Tintoretto, and Veronese amongst others. The choice of story and the additions to make to it, when Calderón comes to write a mythological play, are made on the basis not just of possibilities for the spectacular (a fall from the sky) and the unusual (Achilles's cross-dressing), but of contemporary equivalences, perceived parallels between the myth and the historical context. Thus, for example, in celebrating the royal wedding, *Celos aun del aire matan* rejects the chastity of Diana for the love epitomized by Venus. However, as in his earlier drama, it is possible to find artfully critical moments in Calderón's mythological court plays. Their neglect over the centuries means that there remains a need to recover and analyse this element of the sub-genre. In her pioneering study of the mythological plays, Greer sees Calderón as availing himself 'of the imperfections of those mythic figures to consider, through the tactful medium of dramatic illusion, political issues troubling the court' (Greer, *The Play*, p. 200).

'Calderonian' drama

One or two of the differences between Lope's *comedia* and that re-formed by Calderón and imitated by a new generation of poets will have become clear from this guide to some of Calderón's most important plays. However, it may be worth trying to isolate and summarize those aspects of the drama of the second generation that set it apart. In broad thematic terms, Calderón and his imitators tend to follow the lead of the first wave of dramatists. Comedies deal with love, often in an urban setting, sometimes in a courtly one, with fewer pastoral works (until the appearance of the *zarzuela*). Serious plays continue to deal with kingship and the organization of social life, honour, and religion, and can be inspired by the lives of saints, legend, secular or Biblical history, and earlier fictional, dramatic or poetic works. Not even plays on mythological themes were an innovation of Calderón's generation. What set the new playwrights apart, and seemed most novel, were the formal developments in the handling of these themes.

Most obviously distinct from the bulk of plays written by Lope and his generation is Calderón's style: his use of language, rhetoric and images. Broadly speaking, where Lope and Tirso had tended to employ a plainer style of speech in their verses, suited of course to the character speaking, Calderón was happy to make use of more overtly poetic, Latinate, or Gongorine language. A break with Lope was symbolically (and no doubt deliberately) signalled in the opening word of Calderón's most prominent play, *La vida es sueño*, when Rosaura, descending from the mountain, calls her horse an 'hipogrifo violento'. In his

Arte nuevo Lope had explicitly listed the term 'hipogrifo', an invention of Ariosto in the sixteenth century, as an offensive 'vocablo exquisito', to be avoided by dramatic poets. The result of this shift was a more self-consciously difficult verse, a drama whose meaning would at first have taken longer for an audience to digest, but whose norms could be assimilated in time (perhaps more readily by the educated audience member). As well as echoes of Góngora's *culto* poetry and lexical play, Calderón's verse is marked by his command of rhetoric, learned from the Jesuits: characters will argue logically (or sophistically) and in depth when analysing their emotions or deciding on a course of action, weighing up their dilemmas, and often finding themselves trapped by life's exigencies. Lope's characters could be introspective, but Calderón's seem intent on examining every nuance of their predicament. The complexity of the rhetoric – with anaphora, hyperbaton, chiasmus, rhetorical questions, antithesis and periphrasis amongst the most common features – reflects the delicacy or difficulty of the character's situation. At times it seems as if characters who can pin down their feelings, can control them and re-order the chaotic world about them. Gutierre's long soliloquy in *El médico de su honra* is a case in point.

At other times the truth is exquisitely avoided: language is used to eschew the hard facts. In Act 1 of *El pintor de su deshonra* we find a characteristic exchange between the former lovers, Don Álvaro and Serafina. The latter believed the former to be dead and has married Juan Roca in his absence:

Álvaro:	¿Luego . . .		
Serafina:		¡Qué pena!	
Álvaro:			. . . es verdad . . .
Serafina:	¡Qué ansia!		
Álvaro:		. . . que tú . . .,	
Serafina:			¡Qué veneno!
Álvaro:	Serafina. . .		
Serafina:		¡Qué dolor!	
Álvaro:	. . . como has dicho . . .,		
Serafina:			¡Qué tormento!
Álvaro:	. . . estás . . .		
Serafina:		¡Qué rigor!	
Álvaro:			. . . casada?

Serafina: ¿Cómo puedo, cómo puedo
decir que sí, si estás vivo,
ni decir que no, si miento?   (Calderón, *El pintor*, lines 629–36)

The scene is written in Calderón's favoured *romance* metre with the two characters dividing the octosyllabic lines between them. Serafina's desperate ejaculations break up Álvaro's simple question, making it seem impossible to ask. At the same time as delaying the inevitable question and its potentially monosyllabic answer, the sharing of the lines points to an intense intimacy that, for all her virtuous behaviour, Serafina will never experience with Juan Roca. The rhetorical question which Serafina goes on to ask is a typically Calderonian formulation of a dilemma: she cannot admit to being married if her choice of husband is standing before her, but neither can she lie now she has taken on the role of wife with all the responsibility that it entails. Conditional clauses and rhetorical tricks help her avoid uttering words of such painful finality, but only temporarily. The prolonged agony is beautifully poignant on stage, despite its odd look on the page, reminding us again that Calderón's mastery of language is not just poetic but serves dramatic ends.

The disorder or dilemma central to Calderón's plays is often, notably in the opening speeches of Rosaura and Segismundo in *La vida es sueño*, expressed with reference to the elemental world. The four elements – earth, air, water and fire – are sometimes included as characters in his *autos*, and the playwright builds up a set of images associated with each of them, giving him a shorthand manner of referring to the mutable world surrounding his characters (see Wilson, 'The four elements'). In a storm, such as that in Act 2 of *El mágico prodigioso*, these elements become confused, representing the devil's achievement in disrupting the order of Cipriano's mind. He has just declared portentously that he would give his soul to possess Justina. Repeated use of such elemental and other imagery has the effect of creating a particular discernible linguistic style and becomes another hallmark of Calderón. The style was distinctive, possible to imitate if difficult to emulate, and ran the risk of falling into cliché.

The change in the spaces in which plays were performed is perhaps the most important development for Spanish drama in the second half of the seventeenth century. This is a period of gradual decline for the *corrales*. An ambitious playwright of Calderón's day was likely to aim to write for the pleasure of the court, not for the entertainment and education of the masses, with a number of consequences for the shape and style of the plays produced. Although the circle of the court had often acted in masques, commissioned dramatic entertainments, and paid for *particulares* (private performances in palace halls) in Lope's day, the theatre and its practitioners were essentially independent of it. The construction of the Buen Retiro palace in the 1630s and then the Coliseo within it intensified the importance and influence of court patronage. In particular the introduction of a stage with Italian-style perspective scenery, the technical brilliance of the imported engineers, the paid-up presence of the best actors and musicians, and the consciousness of being the court of the greatest nation in Europe, meant that novelty and sparkle became the order of the day. Other dramatic traditions became fashionable and influential: this is, in particular, the time of the second intense borrowing from the Italian theatrical norms. The audience's ear was still important but Calderón and his imitators show themselves to be increasingly conscious of providing a feast for the eye too. Lope's fears for the future of his *comedia* were beginning to be borne out.

In practical terms, Calderón provides more stage directions, with more detail than the generation of playwrights that preceded him. These are not just provided for the complex mythological court plays and the *autos sacramentales* (for which Calderón would write a *memoria de apariencias* to guide the builders and painters of the carts and thus ensure that the full doctrinal force of these plays was seen by the audience). In his comedies and dramas too, Calderón is more careful to ensure that the full visual possibilities of a given scene are exploited, and that the space in which the play unravels is meaningful, even symbolic. Thus, when in *La devoción de la cruz* Julia stands up to her father Curcio by refusing to enter a convent, he leaves her locked in her room, entombed, with the body of her dead brother Lisardo. Curcio's chiastic words make her situation, in his eyes, stark: 'él [Lisardo] muerto al mundo, en mi memoria vivo,/ tú viva al mundo, en mi memoria muerta' (Calderón, *La devoción*, lines 789–90). The horrific presence of her still bloody brother, as the key turns in the lock, helps her and the audience to visualize her situation more starkly still. She has earlier hidden his killer and her lover, Eusebio, in the room and the stage direction reads: 'Vanse todos; queda Julia en medio de Lisardo y Eusebio que sale por otra puerta' (Calderón, *La devoción*, p. 163). Earlier playwrights might have made do with the direction to clear the stage of all but the siblings and announce Eusebio's re-emergence: Calderón insists on the precise prepositional phrase 'en medio de' to establish visually for the audience the pain of the split in Julia's mind. (The later discovery that *both* men are her brothers adds an ironic potency to the scene, and is further evidence of Calderón's signature.)[11]

The demands of working with professional set designers and engineers for the *auto* and the *comedia* must have heightened Calderón's sensitivity to the possibilities of the visual side of his work for the stage. It is true, however, that the plasticity of his drama, for example in the visual representation of a character's dilemma on stage, is a feature of it throughout his career. His stage directions regularly contain references to paintings. No doubt the enjoyment he took in deciphering images and emblems, his respect for painters' intellectual acumen, and his own thinking about the practice of art, contributed to this side of his dramatic skill.

A further feature of Calderón's generation, to which we have already alluded, is its tendency to re-write earlier works. In Calderón's case the purpose of the re-working of plays by Lope's generation, and even of some written by himself in collaboration with others, is in Sloman's phrase 'an unswerving and persistent quest for unity' (Sloman, *The Dramatic Craftsmanship*, p. 278). Unity of action in particular, often missing from the early days of the *comedia nueva*, becomes the norm. Sub-plots are bound more closely to the main story of the play and inessential characters and action are reduced. Major plays such as *El alcalde de Zalamea*, *El médico de su honra*, and *La vida es sueño* are re-workings of dramas that, to Calderón's turn of mind, were inferior. In *Los cabellos de Absalón*, as we mentioned, it is likely to have been a feeling that Tirso de Molina had failed to provide proper closure to the Biblical story that prompted Calderón to write a further act. It has been suggested that Tirso meant his *La venganza de*

---

[11] A further good example of Calderón's careful instructions for staging occurs in the final scene of *El pintor de su deshonra* when Juan Roca shoots Serafina and Álvaro.

Tamar to be part of a trilogy inspired by the House of David, but the play just as well illustrates the Mercedarian's typical interest in the development of a character's psychology, even at the expense of a more rounded work of art. Calderón will present difficult choices and their human and eternal consequences but is less concerned with psychological verisimilitude.

This Calderonian 'turn of mind' is in part a love of order, of correspondence. It led to thoughtful, finely wrought works of art but does not of course imply, as there is a danger of assuming, a blithe ignorance of or indifference to the complexities and variety inherent to life. The neatness is a formal one which often becomes a stylized way of presenting humankind's or an individual's relationship to the world. Forcing the audience to measure a character's harmony or discordance with the elemental world created by the ordered mind of God is Calderón's way of challenging us to think. It does not mean, as when the 'pintor de su deshonra', Juan Roca, casts himself into the Mediterranean in an insane attempt to swim after his abducted wife, that humans can control larger forces, or that life will be fair and equal. However, by providing symbolic or linguistic parallels and correspondences which are overtly artistic, Calderón does help his audience to make connections between characters and situations, and thus moral judgements. A good example occurs in *El mágico prodigioso*: Clarín, one of the two *graciosos* who end up sharing Justina's maid Livia, expresses his anxiety to be with her, in the play's opening scene when, poignantly, Cipriano's mind is on higher things:

> Livia es la que me arrebata
> los sentidos. Pues ya tienes
> más de la mitad andada
> del camino, llega, Livia,
> al *na*, y sé, Livia, *liviana*.   (Calderón, *El mágico*, lines 72–6)

The audience will laugh at the characteristic word-play of the *gracioso*, but will also be reminded of these words later in the drama, well after the immoral pact between the three servants has been made, but in a serious context. When, in Act 3, the devil tries to persuade Justina to give in to her sexual desire for Cipriano, he sophistically argues of her love:

> En haberlo imaginado
> hecha tienes la mitad:
> pues ya el pecado es pecado,
> no pares la voluntad,
> el medio camino andado.   (Calderón, *El mágico*, lines 2299–303)

Justina's ability to repel the devil and dominate her own human emotion by using her free will not to travel the rest of the path she has started down, reminds us, because of the coincidence of the expression, of the weakness of Livia and others who are not strong enough to resist temptation. The second use of the same expression gives the audience an inkling of the importance, even transcendence, of the lesson – one they can ideally apply to their own choices in life. Such echoes and correspondences are very common in Calderón's drama, occurring within a single speech in his parallelistic structures or built into the weave of the play as here, betraying a craftsmanship rarely equalled in other Golden Age plays, and never matched in a sustained way by other playwrights.

It may have been Calderón's rare precision that encouraged him to leave behind his practice of the 1620s and 1630s of collaborating on dramatic works with other playwrights, including Pérez de Montalbán (Lope's friend), Mira de Amescua, Vélez de Guevara, Moreto and Rojas Zorrilla. Certainly his later decision to re-write one or two of these works would support the argument that he outgrew his fellows. Twelve co-written works in which Calderón had an input survive. They are a feature of his generation (rarer in Lope's) and testament to the need to produce drama quickly for the demanding market. The existence of team-written *comedias* at this period is interesting from another perspective too. If between two and nine dramatists can produce a coherent play after discussing the subject to be dealt with and assigning each other sections, then it is clear that the *comedia* has become extremely formulaic.

The inevitable fate of any genre that becomes too familiar is a developing consciousness of its internal machinery that often becomes the object of parody. Calderón's awareness of the norms of the genre can be glimpsed in his self-referentiality and intertextual references, the metatheatrical play we have noted in his comedies. If the overworked norms of the sixteenth-century romance of chivalry were ridiculed and abused by Cervantes's metafictional *Don Quijote*, the *comedia nueva*, in its later years, at least had the consolation of being able to mock itself. Calderón's winks to the audience – his acknowledgement that the rules of his art are well known – are gentle, and their breaking of the dramatic illusion was a price the dramatist could afford in sub-genres, such as the *comedia de capa y espada*, that were losing their vitality and starting to stagnate.

Calderón's collaborators and imitators

We have had cause to mention already a number of the dramatists with whom Calderón collaborated. From the 1630s such cooperation became a feature of a group of playwrights who obviously knew each other well. The reasons for their collaboration are not well understood but it is clear that there were fewer reliable *poetas* writing in this period. Calderón's pre-eminence tended to be accepted by this group and the dramatists who came after him. In one of his plays, *La ocasión hace al ladrón*, Agustín Moreto y Cabaña (1618–69) referred metatheatrically to the brilliance of the plays Calderón was dedicating to the palace after taking holy orders (Cotarelo y Mori, *Ensayo*, p. 289). At the end of the century Charles II's court dramatist, Francisco Antonio Bances Candamo (1662–1704), was still singing the praises of Calderón as the greatest of all Spanish dramatists:

fue quien dio decoro a las tablas y puso norma a la Comedia de España, así en lo airoso de sus personages como en lo compuesto de sus argumentos, en lo ingenioso de su Contextura y fábrica, y en la pureza de su estilo. Hasta su tiempo no tubo Majestad la Cómica Española . . .

(Bances Candamo, *Theatro*, p. 28)

Nevertheless it should not be forgotten that it was *Los bandos de Verona*, a play by the highly-acclaimed Francisco de Rojas Zorrilla (1607–48), which inaugurated the Coliseo in 1640. Other playwrights flourished despite Calderón's long shadow. Rojas Zorrilla's first known play, *Persiles y Segismunda*, was performed in 1633, and, although doubts remain about the authorship of some plays attributed to him, he seems to have been almost as fêted as Calderón during a prolific decade of playwriting from that time. His best known play, *Del rey abajo ninguno*, cannot be attributed to him with absolute certainty. It has a theme that we think of as Calderonian, the recuperation of threatened conjugal honour, and a background, a royal visit to a rich *labrador*, García del Castañar, that belongs to Lopean drama. The solution provided by Rojas to overcome García's dishonour is not as ingenious or thought-provoking as that of Lope in his *Peribáñez*, however.

Although Rojas wrote over a dozen honour plays and works with tragic outcomes, including a pair of plays on the siege and fall of Numancia, he was a versatile dramatist like most of his contemporaries, penning religious and mythological dramas, as well as comedies. *Entre bobos anda el juego* (1638) belongs to this last genre. The play abides by most of the norms of the second wave of comic works. These are: a pared down cast of characters; metatheatrical references to other Golden Age works and poets; allusions to contemporary events; a consciously *culto* style of lover's speech (which goes above the heads of the servants); a love-plot driven by a father's tyrannical desire to see his daughter married to an older man for money; a night scene at an inn involving mistaken identity, drawn swords and extinguished lights; and a *gracioso* with a ridiculous name, Cabellera. Like many plays of the Calderonian era there is also at least a nod in the direction of the neo-classical unities, especially of time. Without betraying an obvious single source, this play reveals dependence upon the kind of plots, settings and situations popularized by Lope and Tirso: it is a kind of *Desde Toledo a Madrid* in reverse, but also has strong echoes of *La villana de Getafe*. However, rather than chiefly depicting and resolving a clash between the typical representatives of the generations or the sexes, as in many earlier comedies, Rojas creates a single figure, who, as in Molière's drama, dominates the events of the plot. *Entre bobos anda el juego* may be the earliest example of the so-called *comedia de figurón* (see p. 151).

The larger-than-life character in question is the older man, Don Lucas, proud and miserly inheritor of 6042 *ducados de renta*, and arranged husband for the attractive and clever Isabel, whose father Don Antonio has fallen on hard times. He is a butt of the comedy for his coarseness, his presumption, his dogmatism, his vanity, and his belief that he can control the world about him, but he is not easy to fool, like the usual older-man stereotype. He manages to catch Don Pedro, his own cousin and Isabel's would-be lover, in her bedroom at night, and is scathing about other characters' attempts to trick him. Although an audience would not sympathize with him, the dynamics of the comedy change with the predominance of a single figure. The success of the lovers in overcoming the obstacles set for them cedes centre-stage to the dramatist's skill in depicting an exaggerated character to whom many more lines are devoted. Even at the end, the *figurón* remains centre-stage and in some sort of control: Poirot-like he summons all the main characters to his presence, unravels the plot, and announces that he will punish Isabel and Pedro, not by taking their lives in vengeance, but by allowing them to marry each other:

> Pues dadla la mano al punto
> que en esto me he de vengar:
> ella pobre, vos muy pobre,
> no tenéis hora de paz;
> el amar se acaba luego,
> nunca la necesidad.   (Rojas, *Entre bobos*, lines 2733–8)

Rojas follows the lead of Tirso in particular in satirizing the greed of his society. Money means that Isabel looks to have little choice in abiding by the will of her father for financial reasons, until Don Lucas eventually rejects her, but the strength of his characterization intensifies the audience's consciousness of the wrong done to her through her father's decision. Lucas makes a direct reference to bedding her in order to provide him with an heir as rapidly as possible, gives a 'receipt' to her father when she is collected, and later complains to Don Antonio that he has been sold 'por liebre gato' (Rojas, *Entre bobos*, line 1832), when he thinks she has a lover. As we see in Molière's drama later in the century, depicting the sort of monster that society can create under certain conditions is a very effective means of providing satirical comment.

Rojas Zorrilla collaborated with both Calderón and a very young Moreto y Cabaña in the early 1630s. The latter, who was to become one of the best of Calderón's imitators, is known to have acted in an improvised play at court with his mentor on one occasion in the early 1640s. He too was regularly commissioned to write for royal occasions and came into his own in the 1650s when theatrical activity resumed in the *corrales*, and after he too had taken holy orders. Moreto was highly respected in his day for his comic work, including as a writer of *entremeses*. It is his full-length comedies that continue to be studied (if not performed) and to support his reputation today. The best of these fall into three of the sub-genres we have noted: *El lindo Don Diego* (pub. 1662) is a *comedia de figurón*; *El desdén con el desdén* (1653–54) is a *comedia palatina*; and *El parecido en la corte* (before 1650) and *No puede ser el guardar una mujer* (1659) are *comedias de capa y espada*. They deal with comic situations and types which were familiar, and tend to have a strong satirical or moralistic edge: the eponymous provincial, Don Diego, like Don Lucas of Rojas Zorrilla's play, is held up to ridicule for his presumption and his total lack of discretion.

El desdén con el desdén is one of the plays by Moreto that was re-worked for the French stage (by Molière, as *La Princesse d'Élide*, in 1664). It charts the ruse of the count, Carlos, who with the help of his histrionic side-kick, Polilla, overcomes the indifference to love shown by Diana to men who come to woo her at her father's court. He succeeds by showing her the sort of disdain she applies to her male suitors. The play's central thrust, and the characterization of the *mujer esquiva* at its centre, has inevitably reminded scholars of a whole host of earlier works involving long discussions of love, love emerging through jealousy, and the shrew tamed. Moreto's work, one of the most popular of the second half of the seventeenth century, was translated and adapted to so many languages, and has endured so well, not because it is a patchwork, or because it obviously borrows ideas, but because it is ingenious, amusing, and very satisfyingly worked.

Rojas Zorrilla and Moreto are probably the two dramatists of Calderón's generation whose works have attracted most scholarly attention. Moreto's, in particular, continued to be popular on the Spanish stage well beyond the end of the seventeenth century. That is not to say that other dramatists, often their friends and collaborators, did not produce successful plays of their own, increasingly for the court, often on mythological or chivalric subjects. The following are the most important of them: Antonio de Solís y Rivadeneyra (1610–86), a favourite of Philip IV who became Cronista Mayor de Indias and wrote the *Historia de la conquista de Méjico* (1684) as well as the plays *El amor al uso* (1640), *Un bobo hace ciento* (1656), and *Triunfos de Amor y Fortuna* (1658); Juan de Matos Fragoso (1610–92?), who was prolific on his own and in collaboration: his *El sabio en su retiro, y villano en su rincón, Juan Labrador* is a re-working of Lope's *El villano en su rincón*; Antonio Coello (1611–52), whose *El conde de Sex* deals with Queen Elizabeth I and Essex; Juan Vélez de Guevara (1611–75), son of the writer Luis Vélez de Guevara (see pp. 79–83), chiefly known as author of the *zarzuela*, *Los celos hacen estrellas*, which premièred in 1672; Cristóbal de Monroy (1612–49), who re-worked Lope's *Fuente Ovejuna*; Juan Bautista Diamante (1625–87); and Agustín de Salazar (1642–75), brought up in Mexico, and known especially for his mythological plays. His *El encanto es la hermosura y el hechizo sin hechizo* is a Celestina-inspired play, completed by Vera Tassis, who is famous for having edited Calderón's works.

The list is not by any means exhaustive. This was an age when Philip IV himself is rumoured to have tried his hand at writing plays, and dramatic pretensions were regularly mocked: Don Lucas, the *figurón* of *Entre bobos anda el juego*, has, he claims, written a hundred *comedias* that he is saving for his daughter's dowry, should he ever reproduce. For some, playwriting was a hobby, for others it was a chance to gain recognition, status and money. Many hopefuls, as Quevedo had pointed out in his picaresque novel *El buscón*, were tempted to write for the stage whether educated and talented or not. Two others amongst the myriad dramatists from the period require brief further elaboration, however: Juana Ramírez de Asbaje, better known as Sor Juana Inés de la Cruz (1651–95), and the aforementioned Bances Candamo.

Sor Juana, the sophisticated nun whose life and poetry have attracted such attention in recent decades, wrote her plays, in imitation of Calderón, for the viceroys of Mexico. Her attitude to her model is playful, even parodic, as the Calderonian title of *Los empeños de una casa* suggests (see p. 96). This *comedia de capa y espada*, set almost entirely in the house of Doña Ana in Toledo, was performed as part of a *festejo* for the viceregal couple and to welcome the new archbishop to Mexico City in 1683. Sor Juana's comedy follows the pace and contains the staple ingredients of the genre but gives fuller roles and more control of the plot to the female characters, especially Ana herself who attempts to exploit the interior space she knows so well. Noteworthy too is Sor Juana's ability to transcend the more stylized norms of the genre by drawing attention to them with the kind of metatheatrical wit that we have noted in other writers of this generation. Thus, when asked to perform the risky job of leaving the sanctuary of the house to deliver a letter, Don Carlos's *gracioso* servant, Castaño, appeals directly to the audience for help: '¡Inspírame alguna traza/ que de Calderón parezca,/ con que salir de este empeño!' (Cruz, *Los empeños*, p. 297c). The plan he hits upon, to dress in female clothes, leads to his attracting the amorous advances of his master's rival, Don Pedro, and further labyrinthine plot developments. Ludic self-consciousness is a feature of the play, as it is of the interludes which formed part of the entertainment. As well as *Los empeños*, Sor Juana wrote three *autos* and co-wrote *Amor es más laberinto* (1689), a mythological play with clear debts to love comedy.

Bances Candamo's theatre, like Sor Juana's, was written in the aftermath of Calderón's death in 1681, and his was the last important dramatic voice of the seventeenth century. The first play, of some twenty he wrote, was *Por su rey y por su dama*, and was performed at court in 1685. Soon afterwards he was named court dramatist. Scholarly debate has centred on Bances's political dramas of the early 1690s, *El esclavo en grillos de oro*, *La piedra filosofal*, and *Cómo se curan los celos*. These kingship plays have been taken to comment satirically on the weak government of Charles II and his minister Oropesa, and the difficult issue of the succession. In his unfinished work on the history of theatre, *Theatro de los theatros*, never published during his lifetime, Bances introduced the term 'decir sin decir' with reference to court drama. Because his own works would seem on the surface to be satirical, to have a political axe to grind, 'decir sin decir' has been taken as implying a subtle critique of the reigning monarch. Nevertheless, Arellano has interpreted the phrase quite differently, as being 'una llamada al necesario respeto con que hay que hablar con los reyes' (Arellano, *Convención*, p. 180). His comparison of Bances's words with those spoken on the same subject by Alexander the Great to the discreet painter Apeles, in Calderón's *Darlo todo y no dar nada*, is an instructive one, which helps to nuance the now traditional view of Bances Candamo's intentions.

Pedro Calderón de la Barca, the pre-eminent dramatist of his generation, left behind scores of plays which had charmed and educated the people of Spain and the Spanish court for over half a century. His very stature had implications for the direction of the *comedia nueva*: his collaborations, his success at writing *refundiciones* (see p. 172), his mythological and musical drama, his search for a more classical unity, his linguistic preferences and elaborate use of rhetoric, imagery and symbol, were all imitated and all helped to move the *comedia* inexorably away from what had been its norms in the early part of the century. Most notable and perhaps most unfortunate was the change in the role of the *corral*, which became secondary to the court in dramatists' eyes so that, by the time of Bances Candamo, there was only one audience that mattered.

5

Staging and Performance

The popular enthusiasm for the *comedia nueva* in Golden Age Spain, combined with the appeal of play-going within even the highest social circles, assured the success of the theatre throughout most of the seventeenth century. The theatrical world became attractive and potentially lucrative to a whole host of individuals and bodies, and with its rise came increased regulation. Although it is tempting to ascribe the confidence of actor-managers and entrepreneurs to the ascendancy of Lope de Vega's theatrical star, in fact it was as early as the mid-sixteenth century that Lope de Rueda from Seville (see pp. 14–15), and then the Italian Ganassa, began to turn potential into sustained financial success. In Spain's urban centres, even before the advent of Lope's new drama, the world of the theatre had begun to attract individuals with vision and an eye for a profit, and the inevitable accompanying law-suits. The theatrical world would change a great deal during the writing life of Lope, but some of its important structures were in place before his unique talents had come to the fore.

In this chapter we shall explore three (interrelated) areas of Golden Age theatre: the spaces where drama was performed; actors and acting; and the performance of this drama. The first two areas have benefited greatly from research undertaken in and outside Spain in the last three decades. The last area will take us into less well charted territory: the analysis of performance has never achieved anything like the importance in *comedia* studies that it has recently in, for example, the study of Shakespeare's drama.

Performance spaces

When Miguel de Cervantes came to publish his *comedias* and *entremeses* in 1615, he looked back, misty-eyed, on his youth to describe a performance he had seen by the troupe of the great Lope de Rueda. Evidently he remembered a makeshift stage set up by the company in any public or private space from which they might work a profit:

> No había en aquel tiempo tramoyas, ni desafíos de moros y cristianos, a pie ni a caballo; no había figura que saliese o pareciese salir del centro de la tierra por lo hueco del teatro, al cual componían cuatro bancos en cuadro y cuatro o seis tablas encima, con lo que se levantaba del suelo cuatro palmos; ni menos bajaban del cielo nubes con ángeles o con almas. El adorno del teatro era una manta vieja, tirada con dos cordeles de una parte a otra, que hacía lo que

llaman vestuario, detrás del cual estaban los músicos, cantando sin guitarra algún romance antiguo.   (Cervantes, *Entremeses*, p. 92)

Cervantes was not the only writer who nostalgically misrepresented the achievements of Lope de Rueda (see Shergold, *A History*, pp. 164–6). There is a hint here that he has little time for the 'carpinteros', as Lope was to call them, who ensured that by the 1610s the *corral* audience would have its fill of spectacular stage effects, thus devaluing the traditional skill of the poet. By the first decades of the seventeenth century the peripatetic company of Rueda must have seemed very basic indeed in its technical achievements. Yet there is evidence that the Sevillian gold-beater planned to set up a permanent theatre in Valladolid in the patio of a house as early as 1558, the year Cervantes was eleven. It was in this Castilian city that the young Philip II saw Rueda perform on his way to England in 1554. Certainly, although Rueda's and other companies continued to tour, Valladolid was a magnet for theatrical folk at this time and almost certainly boasted a theatrical space much more advanced and settled than that described by Cervantes.

The progressive establishment of permanent playhouses throughout the peninsula had far-reaching implications for the stability (and regulation) of the theatrical profession and for the development of the stage effects (*tramoyas*) that Cervantes mentions, and as a consequence, for the ambition of playwrights. This is in part why Cervantes was so conscious of change in the world of the theatre. However, the basic compact between actor and audience was the same in a square in Valladolid in the 1540s as in Madrid in the 1640s: the dramatists' poetry and the players' skills on the boards transported the populace to a world of familiar make-believe.

The first steps towards something akin to the theatrical spaces we would recognize today came in Seville with the building of the *corral de las Atarazanas* in 1574, possibly in the Valladolid of Lope de Rueda, and also in Philip II's new capital, Madrid, as a result of the innovative thinking of certain *cofradías*, set up in the 1560s. These charitable brotherhoods built and maintained hospitals for the needy in the city and in order to raise funds for their institutions sought and gained permission to erect a stage in certain yards between houses, effectively making them into temporary theatres from which they could take a share of the profits. A number of locations were used in Madrid during the 1570s and into the early 1580s but two permanent playhouses emerged, the Cruz (1579) and the Príncipe (1582). The immediate beneficiaries of the popularity of this theatrical activity, which included puppet-shows, gymnasts, the famous *commedia dell'arte* troupes led by Ganassa and Bottarga, the neo-classical tragedies, and most likely Cervantes's early plays, were the hospitals and the performing troupes. Despite the large sums of money spent making adjustments to the two new theatres in their early days there was a tidy profit to be had. The model for the creation of *corral* theatres caught on or developed of its own accord in most important cities in Spain: amongst the earliest were Valencia, Barcelona, Granada, Valladolid, Zamora, Burgos,

Murcia, Toledo, Zaragoza; and in Latin America: Lima (1594) and Mexico City (1597).[1]

Inside the Madrid theatres there was a yard (*patio*) where the groundlings (known as *mosqueteros*) stood facing the stage. The *corral* was unroofed but the audience was protected from the heat of the sun by a canvas awning which also served to diffuse the direct sunlight. The yard itself was surrounded on three sides by the back and adjoining walls of neighbouring buildings. There were *gradas*, terraced rows of benches along either side. The 'fourth wall', on the street, developed rapidly because it was owned by the brotherhood, and not the neighbours. This consisted of an entrance, then above it a first-floor *cazuela* where the women were seated, and then a second floor of boxes, one of which was reserved for the city's dignitaries. Along the sides development was slower as those whose properties fortuitously bordered the new theatres converted parts of their own buildings – windows and balconies – into boxes and then let them out. These *aposentos* were added gradually throughout the seventeenth century as the interior of the theatres evolved. Amongst other later additions are the *desvanes*, which were the third-floor accommodation, adding a *cazuela alta* for women and the *tertulia* for the clergy and literati. The third floor above and alongside the stage housed props and stage machinery, which developed with the century until the theatres reached their apogee in the 1630s, the age of Calderón.[2]

Golden Age stages, like Golden Age theatres, varied one from another depending upon the space from which they were created. Typically the stage was rectangular, with no curtain or proscenium arch between audience and performer: if we take the *Príncipe* as our example, the stage was probably about 1.65 metres high and approximately 8 metres wide by 4.5 metres deep. The space was adaptable but usually had benches behind a rail at either side for important spectators. Beneath the stage was an area, possibly partly excavated, which doubled as male dressing room and wardrobe. There were several trap-doors (*escotillones*) in the ceiling of this room, cut into the boards of the stage, which underwent frequent repairs. Immediately behind the stage was the women's dressing room, known as the *vestuario*, which doubled as the theatre's discovery space. It was a little over two metres deep and was closed off by a curtain which could be drawn to reveal an *apariencia*, a scene such as the revela-

---

[1] Many of these early Spanish theatres are given individual attention in Díez Borque, ed., *Teatros del Siglo de Oro*. There are also volumes dedicated to several theatres outside Madrid in the excellent series *Fuentes para la historia del teatro en España*, created by John Varey, published by Tamesis, and now running to over thirty volumes. See especially volumes 15, 17, 18, 27 and 34. *Corrales* at Almagro in La Mancha, re-discovered in the 1950s and now restored to host the annual theatre festival, and at Alcalá de Henares, more recently restored, are open to visitors and give an excellent impression of life in the *corral*.

[2] These details are taken largely from the excellent Ruano and Allen, *Los teatros comerciales*. The authors filter much of the copious information included in the Tamesis *Fuentes* series and have over sixty illustrations with detailed measurements for the two Madrid playhouses.

tion of the dead body of the *capitán* in Calderón's famous *El alcalde de Zalamea* (see p. 103), or Amón, murdered at the banquet in Tirso's *La venganza de Tamar*. The area would also sometimes have been used with props to represent another room or a change of scene, as we saw in Lope's earliest extant play, *Los hechos de Garcilaso* (see pp. 29–30).

On the stage there were two levels of balconies rising towards the *desvanes*. These were widely exploited for battlement/balcony/mountain and other scenes. Individual sections could be curtained off and opened when required, thus sharing a function with the main discovery space. Exits and entrances were made through the two curtained entrances either side of the *vestuario*. A character listening *al paño*, as the stage directions often put it, would be visible to the audience at one of these openings but conventionally invisible to the characters on stage. A good example is the *gracioso* Tristán's overhearing of Diana's plot to have him murdered, of Lope's *El perro del hortelano*.

Some visible scenery was used, though it was often imagined by the audience, as were night and day, since all performances took place in daylight. Although nineteenth-century editors of Golden Age plays tended, as well as sub-dividing acts into scenes, to add explicit stage directions where implicit ones already exist, dramatists kept direct instructions to a minimum, trusting the actor-managers to do their job.[3] Stage properties, however, were regularly used, although the pace of Golden Age plays meant they would be neither elaborate nor excessive in number. They included light household furniture, writing materials, cushions, candles, weapons, musical instruments, and clothing. The *tramoyas*, which became popular in the *corrales*, and were a staple of the court theatre (see p. 138), were often controlled from the *desvanes*, and involved sudden descents of figures by machinery and other stunts designed to impress the audience and frustrate the poet.

The audience that flocked to the Madrid *corrales* throughout the Golden Age, *oyentes* as they were called, was socially mixed. About a third of the spectators stood and the remaining two-thirds sat, either facing each other on the benches on either side of the *patio*, or in the *cazuela*, or in one of the numerous private boxes which became so popular. Those who stood did so in the *patio* itself. These were the infamous *mosqueteros*, who could make or break a play with their support or derision. Many of the *loas*, performed before the play proper, are aimed at flattering and thus calming this noisy element. In describing Golden Age Spanish audiences, scholars have tended to concentrate on their power to destroy, their ability to halt the play with whistles, rattles and soft fruit. The liveliness or the ignorance of the standing spectators should not be exaggerated, however, since the verse drama relied on the audience's ability to listen attentively and make connections, to follow complex plots and register changes

---

[3] To give one example, the opening of Act 2 of Pallarés's edition of Tirso's *Desde Toledo a Madrid*, preserves the stage directions, originally inserted by Hartzenbusch, which read: [*Campo a vista de Olías. Una venta a un lado.*], even though the characters make abundantly clear where they are and what they can see in the first twenty lines of their dialogue.

in verse form. There *were* sops for the groundlings, but one of the features of Spanish Golden Age drama is the ability of playwrights (and of actors) to cater to the different expectations of the audiences within the audience.

The average audience in the Madrid *corrales* between 1579 and 1586 has been estimated by Davis and Varey to be 636 spectators (with a highest figure of 1116 in the Príncipe and 1511 in the Cruz).[4] However, the capacity had increased to about 1900 by the 1630s. Sometimes there would have been a squash, as the presence of *apretadores* testifies. These individuals were employed to pack the audience into the *cazuela* where the women were seated.[5] Of these 1900 places in the Madrid theatres by the 1630s, some 1200 were public places for men, 380 public places for women, and the balance were spaces in the boxes.[6] Clergy too could see the play from their *tertulia*, although some refused to attend, taking a moral stand against this public entertainment (see p. 170).

The majority of the audience would start arriving after midday, still well before the start of the performance, and the social side of theatre-going would begin. There is evidence to suggest that the theatre was responsible for the spread of fashion in clothes, jewellery and musical tastes, and that the audience sometimes (as today) had problems separating fiction from reality. The male customer paid an actor's fee on the street outside, a further entrance fee to reach the *patio*, and a third tariff for a seat on a bench if desired. As he entered he would pass the stands where refreshments were sold. Men and women were strictly segregated except in the *aposentos*, which were privately hired. There was a separate women's entrance to the Príncipe theatre in the Calle del Prado, just around the corner from the façade. One of the *alguaciles* who policed the theatre was required to prevent the molestation of the female play-goers as they tried to reach the entrance. Another document reveals that there were times when women started queuing at dawn for the seats at the front of the *cazuela* for the afternoon's performance. In a neat reversal of the cases of women dressing as men, so frequent in Golden Age drama itself, there is evidence too of men dressing as women in order to access the *cazuela* and mix closely with the female spectators.

The *corral* playhouse in which actors and actresses performed to an audience divided by sex must have been a place of considerable tension and banter (good-natured or otherwise). One can imagine Teodoro, the secretary of *El perro del hortelano*, delivering his sonnet to close Act 1, conscious of the different

---

[4] See Davis and Varey, *Los corrales de comedias y los hospitales de Madrid, 1574–1615*, pp. 66–7 and 76. The same scholars produced a similar average figure for 1615 in Varey and Davis, *Los corrales de comedias y los hospitales de Madrid, 1615–1849*, pp. 18–19.

[5] There is a colourful and witty description of women attending the *corral* in the mid-seventeenth-century work by Juan de Zabaleta, *El día de fiesta por la mañana y por la tarde*.

[6] These rounded figures are based on the more precise estimates in Allen, *The Reconstruction*, p. 100.

reactions he would get from the *patio* at his feet and the *cazuela*, at eye-level, to his proposal to drop Marcela and pursue the noble and enigmatic Diana. As he ruminates on the morality of his course of action in wooing a woman above his station, Teodoro knows that his behaviour towards Marcela, his social equal and first love, is unfair. Yet his final resolution would alienate the *cazuela* he has flirted with, to be cheered by the men in the *patio* who recognize in his final tercet a truism, and feel they have suffered at female hands:[7]

> ¿Puedo creer que aquesto es verdad? Puedo,
> [*a neutral-sounding question arouses general sympathy*]
> si miro que es mujer Diana hermosa.   [*sop to the* mosqueteros]
> Pidió la mano, y la color de rosa,
> al dársela, robó del rostro el miedo.
> Tembló, yo lo sentí; dudoso quedo.
> [*general sympathy sought as uncertain lover*]
> ¿Qué haré? Seguir mi suerte venturosa,
> [*it is a dilemma, honestly, he reassures the* cazuela]
> si bien, por ser la empresa tan dudosa,
> niego al temor lo que al valor concedo.
> [*he flirts with the idea of Diana, and alienates the* cazuela]
> Mas dejar a Marcela es caso injusto;
> que las mujeres no es razón que esperen
> de nuestra obligación tanto disgusto.
> [*the* mosqueteros *groan; the* cazuela*'s faith is restored*]
> Pero si ellas nos dejan cuando quieren,
> por cualquiera interés o nuevo gusto,
> mueran también como los hombres mueren.
> [*Teodoro shows his true colours, to the delight of the men*]
>   (Vega, *El perro*, lines 1173–86)

It should not be forgotten that the *corral* was not the only place where theatre was performed in Golden Age Spain, just as Madrid was not the only city to experience a lively expansion in commercial theatre. The streets and town and city squares continued to provide the backdrop for performances by actors and other entertainers, not least at Corpus Christi when the *autos sacramentales* were performed using carts, according to well-established norms (see pp. 162–3). As in other European countries there was also a close relationship between theatre and the court. In Spain this went well beyond the kind of pageantry associated

---

[7] In the Royal Shakespeare Company's 2004 Spanish Golden Age season, the company's associate director, Laurence Boswell, experimented with a split audience in the Swan Theatre for productions of Sor Juana Inés de la Cruz's *House of Desires* (*Los empeños de una casa*) and Lope's *Dog in the Manger* (*El perro del hortelano*). The result was to provide a much sharper consciousness of the way that Golden Age playwrights wrote not for a homogenized audience but for elements within a whole who might be played off against each other to become part of the entertainment. Catherine Connor argues for a more flexible understanding of what constituted a *corral* audience, in her 'Hacia una teoría sociocultural'.

with royal entrances and other festivities, masques, carnival celebrations, bull-fighting, tournaments and *juegos de cañas*, all of which show a court obsessed with spectacle. The royal family (especially during the reigns of Philip III and Philip IV) frequently paid companies of actors for *particulares*, that is, private performances of plays in their quarters. The *salón grande* (or *salón de comedias*) in the Alcázar became a favourite place for royal performances, as during the surprise visit of Prince Charles to Madrid in 1623. The etiquette of attending a play when the king was present became in itself a fascinating spectacle.[8] Other royal residences regularly staged plays: Aranjuez saw three spectacular performances in 1622 to celebrate royal birthdays; and the hunting lodge La Zarzuela gave its name to a popular musical theatre inspired by the 1657 performance of Calderón's *El golfo de las sirenas*.

The construction of the Buen Retiro palace for Philip IV in 1633 provided a new location for drama to be performed. Plays, along with hunting, provided Philip with his pleasurable diversion, and were acted inside the new palace and on the lake. These elaborate spectacles were in large measure the result of the king's *tramoyista*, the Italian Cosimo Lotti, who arrived from Italy in 1626 to design sets and machinery for ever more impressive (and lengthy) productions. They were often open to an enthralled public after the court had seen them. (Lotti's first major production had been Lope de Vega's *La selva sin amor*, performed in 1627 and usually taken to be Spain's first opera.) It did not take long for a purpose-built indoor theatre to be added to the Retiro palace. The Coliseo, as it was known, was built in the Italian style, with a proscenium arch, perspective scenery and machinery for special effects, and opened in 1640. A plan of the theatre survives (dating from 1712) as well as a number of drawings of the sets for Lotti's successor, Baccio del Bianco's staging of Calderón's mythological play *Andrómeda y Perseo*, performed in 1653.[9] The Coliseo productions revealed a sophisticated departure from the simpler staging of the *corrales* and yet the king, who had regularly attended *corral* performances, attempted to re-create the lively atmosphere of the public theatres in the new palace. The *corral* theatres clearly had their own unique attractions and continued to form a central part of Madrid life despite the distraction of the Buen Retiro. Indeed in most respects the Coliseo was a third Madrid playhouse (see McKendrick, *Theatre*, pp. 220–2). In time, however, and despite the delicate state of Spain's finances, the amount of money ploughed into court drama began to take its toll on the original *corrales*: some playwrights and *tramoyistas* made a good living out of their association with the court, and acting troupes were frequently summoned to the palaces leaving the Príncipe or the Cruz untenanted. Nevertheless there was the consolation for the *corrales* of being allowed to stage plays that had first appeared at the court, and their decline has been exaggerated. In

---

[8] On private performances, see Greer and Varey, *El teatro palaciego*, pp. 15–19. On the king's comportment at royal performances, see Varey, 'The Audience and the Play'.

[9] See Brown and Elliott, *A Palace for a King*, pp. 206–14.

the early eighteenth century average audiences and numbers of performances per year were in fact similar to what they had been a century before.

Actors and acting

The Golden Age was necessarily the time that the acting profession in Spain became professional. This was not an overnight change, nor did it mean that nobles stopped acting in court entertainments, or that peripatetic entertainers from the one-man band to fully-fledged companies ceased to bang the drum and perform in towns and villages, making a precarious living.[10] Prose and drama of the period (particularly that written in a picaresque vein) abounds with examples of travelling players of various types: perhaps Chirinos and Chanfalla, the worldly tricksters of Cervantes's short masterpiece *El retablo de las maravillas*, best evoke this less regulated world (see p. 159). However, the setting up of more permanent performance spaces brought with it more permanent arrangements for providing the entertainment. No longer would actors be described, as the *batihoja* Lope de Rueda was, in terms of their original profession.

There were two striking differences between the worlds of the professional actor in Golden Age Spain and in England or France. First, despite official misgivings and hesitation in the 1580s and 1590s, women rather than boys were permitted to take on female roles. In this matter the example set by Italian companies performing in Madrid in the late sixteenth century was crucial. Writing for actresses, sometimes indeed for individuals whom they admired, encouraged playwrights to produce fine, extended female roles and helped to shape certain types of plot, such as those which hinged upon the machinations of a *mujer varonil*. One of the most remarkable aspects of this golden period in dramatic history is the variety and depth of parts for actresses. Secondly, the knowledge that the actors' efforts on the boards supported the *cofradías'* charitable undertakings, and that the best actors were recruited for the *autos* at Corpus Christi, to bolster the Catholic faith, meant that it was harder for those who opposed the theatre on moral grounds to succeed when arguing for its suppression.

In most respects an actor's life was subject to the same vicissitudes that it has been throughout history. The best and most attractive actors and actresses were well paid but were regarded with an ambivalent mixture of admiration for their abilities and prurient or envious suspicion of their moral conduct. Extant documents from this period show the kind of contract that was typically made between the powerful *autor de comedias*, who led the troupe, and the actor. Payment would be a certain sum per performance (dependent on the actor's seniority within the company) over a year or two years, and in addition travel expenses and even laundry bills on occasion would be paid by the company.

---

[10] In *El viaje entretenido*, Rojas Villandrando lists a number of types of performer including an individual capable of reciting *loas* and *comedias*, called the *bululú*, p. 159.

Payment would usually be made at the end of a performance (see Díez Borque, *Sociedad y teatro*, pp. 29–90). The benefits of belonging to a major company were significant: these included access to advances on salary, loans, and a daily payment even when there was no performance. Additionally *particulares* and the expanding court theatre, especially in the reign of Philip IV, could bring rich pickings, and some actresses were linked with wealthy patrons or noblemen who doted on them. At the start of the eighteenth century this practice clearly continued when a certain Ángela de Salamanca was so popular during a trip to Portugal that 'se equipó muy decentemente y se hizo de sortijas, de diamantes, collar de perlas y otras alhajas y muy buenos vestidos'. In practice, although not thought honourable enough to hold public office, actors were more than tolerated. In 1631, they were allowed to form a guild or brotherhood, like other tradesmen. Their patron was the Virgin Mary, and their brotherhood became the *Cofradía* or *Congregación de la Novena*, after a miracle-working image of the Virgin. The establishment of this *cofradía* indicated the growing social acceptance of actors and in practical terms provided support in lean times.[11]

On the negative side there were many upheavals and hours spent on the road, as no troupe was allowed to remain in the same city for longer than two months in any one year; uncertainty reigned throughout the period as moralists' arguments occasionally held sway or the theatres were closed after royal deaths; the church theoretically condemned actors to excommunication and refused them burial in consecrated ground; the players were expected to buy and wear their own expensive clothes for performances; and working life was demanding with the high turnover of plays meaning frequent rehearsals, which the actors were contracted to attend at the *autor*'s lodgings.

The seventeenth century saw increasing (though not always successful) attempts to draw up legislation covering the theatre. In 1603 the number of troupes that were permitted to perform in the permanent theatres which had emerged in Spain was limited to eight, but in 1615, the Council of Castile raised the number to twelve, with no more than two allowed at a time in Madrid and Seville. It remained at this level throughout most of the century except during the closures of the theatres, when troupes were disbanded. There were also numerous companies known as *compañías de la legua*, supposedly because they travelled a league per day, performing in small towns and villages.

Licensed *compañías* in the seventeenth century tended to comprise between fourteen and nineteen members, with sixteen the norm, as Davis and Varey have shown (*Actividad teatral*, I, p. cxxii). In addition to an average of fourteen actors there were a musician or musicians (actors were expected to be able to sing and dance), the *cobrador* or money-collector, the *apuntador* (who prompted, and

---

[11] The anonymous early eighteenth-century *Genealogía, origen y noticias de los comediantes de España*, edited by Shergold and Varey, whose principal source is the records of the *cofradía*, begins with details of its five founders, and proceeds to list and record information about hundreds of actors and actresses of the period. The information about Ángela de Salamanca appears on p. 450 (spelling is modernized here).

copied parts from the dramatist's manuscript), and often a *guardarropa* (who also acted as odd-job man). Stage hands were taken from amongst the *criados* of the troupe, who, along with family members, swelled the numbers to between 30 and 40. The troupe would have travelled widely and rehearsed constantly, having a repertoire of some fifty plays. The actors would include some specialists: at least one older man or *barba*, comic actors to play the *gracioso*, and four or five sets of *galanes* and *damas*. Their leader was the *autor*, so-called because in the days of Lope de Rueda he was also the playwright. Usually also an actor, he was responsible for administration of the company, and directing the plays. The *autor*'s busiest time of year was Lent when the theatres closed, and he had to decide upon the composition of his troupe, negotiate and draw up actors' contracts, and plan the content of the forthcoming season. Often rehearsals would start in this period. He had to negotiate with the *corrales*, arrange transport, liaise with the palace about their requirements, listen to new plays, judge, buy (or reject) and perhaps adapt them, then submit them for a licence for performance. The *autor* then, as well as catering to the needs of the actor and the audience, had to deal with the authorities, themselves increasingly aware of the political and propagandistic potential of the *comedia*. It is likely, since his appointment after the 1615 *Reformación* was in the hands of the Council of Castile (renewable every two years at the Council's discretion), that the *autor* ensured that the content of plays he bought was neither offensive nor too obviously risqué.

All plays (including the *teatro menor* described in chapter 6) were to be read and licensed by the authorities. The 1615 *Reformación* stated that every play had to be passed by a *censor* and a *fiscal* (responsible for the implementation of any cuts or changes), who were answerable to the *protector* of the hospitals, himself a member of the Council of Castile. Once passed by the Council, the play could still be objected to by the Inquisition, and risked suspension even on the point of production. The *censor* tended to read the play for indecency, irreverence, sacrilege, sedition, or personal attacks. The Inquisition looked for heresy, rather than immorality. The authorities could close down the theatres at any time if they considered the plays immoral, or if the troupe broke any laws.[12]

Although many names of actors and *autores* have been preserved and we can discover a fair amount about the organization of the troupes that first performed the plays of Lope, Tirso and Calderón, frustratingly little information about acting style survives.[13] Fortunately, acting fascinated Miguel de Cervantes, and his play *Pedro de Urdemalas* contains the Spanish equivalent of Hamlet's advice to the players, *redondillas* spoken by Pedro himself, from which we can deduce a great deal about the art. It is worth quoting at some length:

[12] The text of the famous 1615 *Reformación* can be found in Cotarelo, *Bibliografía*, pp. 626–7.

[13] In the words of Kerr: 'Not a single, adequate, contemporaneous eye-witness account of a *corral* performance has come to light to date, if in fact such an account was ever written,' 'The theory and practice', p. 7. Kerr ingeniously tries to piece together the norms of Golden Age acting from disparate sources. In her *La técnica del actor*, Rodríguez Cuadros attempts a similar reconstruction.

sé todos los requisitos
que un farsante ha de tener
para serlo, que han de ser
tan raros como infinitos.
De gran memoria, primero;
segundo, de suelta lengua;
y que no padezca mengua
de galas en lo tercero.
Buen talle no le perdono,
si es que ha de hacer los galanes,
no afectado en ademanes,
ni ha de recitar con tono.
Con descuido cuidadoso,
grave anciano, joven presto,
enamorado compuesto,
con rabia si está celoso.
Ha de recitar de modo,
con tanta industria y cordura,
que se vuelva en la figura
que hace de todo en todo.
A los versos ha de dar
valor con su lengua experta,
y a la fábula que es muerta
ha de hacer resucitar.
Ha de sacar con espanto
las lágrimas de la risa,
y hacer que vuelvan con prisa
otra vez al triste llanto.
Ha de hacer que aquel semblante
que él mostrare, todo oyente
le muestre, y será excelente,
si hace aquesto, el recitante.   (Cervantes, *Pedro*, lines 2896–927)

Of course, Pedro's words are an idealization of the Golden Age actor's skills, but the ideal can tell us much about what was expected of him. There is the general: the need for an actor to have a facility for committing verse to memory; the ability to extemporize when this memory fails him; the importance of looking right for the part (a requisite ruefully mentioned by Tirso de Molina when the first performance of his *Don Gil de las calzas verdes* flopped because the *autor*, Valdés, cast his overweight, middle-aged wife as the dashing young lover, Doña Juana). Then there are the finer points of style. The actor should not overact in terms of gesture or delivery but must endeavour to convince the audience that he has become the figure he is playing.[14] The adjective 'afectado' implies 'cuydado

---

[14] Here the sources are Cicero and especially Quintilian, who claimed that the most important element in moving others is to be moved ourselves. Lope concurred with Cervantes as we discover in his thoughts on acting delivered in *Lo fingido verdadero*. See Dixon, 'Manuel Vallejo'.

extraordinario y demasiada diligencia' (Cov. p. 46a), that is, an excessive or 'over-the-top' style which would have broken the illusion by drawing attention to the player as a performer. Cervantes looks instead for a 'descuido cuidadoso' and the application of 'industria y cordura', with the implication that becoming the part he is to play seems nonchalant but requires intelligence, study of the verse, and skill. The audience will find the representation realistic, will be drawn into the illusion, and in the best of all worlds, will be moved to experience the emotions the actor convinces them that he is experiencing. They will forget the illusionary basis of the drama they are watching.

This dramatist's view of what constitutes excellent acting seems remarkably modern: Cervantes's advice is still valid. What should be remembered, however, is the emphasis put on the Golden Age play-text's poetry. Cervantes's Pedro refers to the expert tongue of the actor, which allows the poet's lines to impress the *oyente*. Despite the growth of the spectacular in the *comedia*, many dramatists remained convinced of the importance of the aural. Audiences could appreciate spoken poetry and follow changes in metre. The long speeches which sometimes today deter potential directors of Golden Age drama would have been enjoyed and admired for their rhetorical structuring, the beauty of their arrangement, the euphony of their rhyme or assonance.

The investigations into Golden Age acting techniques and styles remain somewhat speculative. The composition and comportment of the audience must have prevented the actors from concentrating on performance in the way they can in today's polite theatres. Nevertheless the clues from speeches such as Pedro's, from Lope's *Arte nuevo*, from other Golden Age writers who touch upon the theme, from manuals of rhetoric or preaching, from the harangues of the theologians who railed against the theatre, provide a sense of how actors and actresses may have approached their task, and also, incidentally, suggest that the study of character in the *comedia* should be taken much more seriously than it has been hitherto.

Performance

Students and admirers of Golden Age drama have shown a tendency to treat works from the period as literature to be read, rather than as drama to be performed. There are certain advantages to this approach: the poetry can be closely analysed; the underlying structure and themes of the play can be revealed; a consistency of thought or intention in the dramatist can be observed; and the ideas in the play, extracted by the literary historian, can be linked to other literary forms or the thought of the period. Cervantes and Lope de Vega both saw advantages in publishing their play-texts, although late in their careers and with ulterior motives. No longer would the memory of a play be rooted in a series of unpolished performances seen imperfectly by a diverse audience limited in number. Lope, in the guise of Teatro, takes consolation then from the printing of his *Parte XII* in 1619:

Quedo consolado, que no me pudrirá el vulgo como suele; pues en tu aposento, donde las has de leer [mis comedias], nadie consentirás que te haga ruido, ni que te diga mal de lo que tú sabrás conocer, libre de los accidentes del señor que viene tarde, del representante que se yerra, y de la mujer desagradable por fea y mal vestida, o por los años que ha frecuentado mis tablas; pues el poeta no la escribió con los que ella tiene, sino con los que tuvo en su imaginación, que fueron catorce o quince. (Vega, *Prólogos*, p. xxii)

The dramatist's frustration with audience, *autor* and actor is clear to see, and yet he imagines that his addressee will have seen the play in the *corral* before reading it and it would be a betrayal of Lope, practical man of the theatre, to assume his support for a wholly text-based study of the *comedia* (see p. 26). Indeed, whatever the benefits of slowing down the spoken poetic text through leisurely reading, an appreciation of the drama *qua* performance is surely essential to any full understanding of what the *comedia nueva* was.

The study of performance can be sub-divided into two broad areas, as it is in Shakespeare studies. These are: speculative reconstructions of primitive stagings of scenes and plays, dependent on detailed knowledge of conditions in the playhouses four centuries ago; and assessments of more recent productions which revivify these old play-texts (see Pavis, *Analyzing Performance*, pp. 198–223). Neither area has attracted the attention of *comedia* scholars until fairly recently.[15] It is still rare for an edition of a Golden Age play to deal in any depth with matters of original staging or modern productions of the work (as, indeed, it is unusual for editors to provide anything more than a cursory glance at matters of versification). The contrast with the study of Elizabethan and Jacobean theatre is again instructive.

Much more will be deduced about the original staging of Golden Age drama when plays become more regularly performed and difficulties emerge to be resolved. In the meantime Ruano, in his exemplary analysis of Golden Age staging, comes to the conclusion that:

La labor del crítico que desee reconstruir la escenificación de esta comedia [Tirso's *La mujer que manda en casa*] y otras de decorado múltiple consistirá en reproducir su 'traza', o plan de escenificación, lo cual implica establecer dónde, cómo y cuándo se descubrían estos decorados y adornos.

(Ruano de la Haza, *La puesta*, p. 324)

Many plays did make use of props and scenery for backdrops, but the setting of a particular scene was usually established on the bare *corral* boards by the actors' dialogue and costume. Thus, when the Duque de Avero and Conde de Estremoz open Tirso's *El vergonzoso en palacio* the stage direction indicates

---

[15] See my ' "Puedo yo con sola la vista oír leyendo": Reading, Seeing and Hearing the *Comedia*', for an assessment of recent approaches to performance studies of the *comedia nueva*.

that they are *de caza* and the opening speech, *in medias res*, provides the location (and simultaneously a conundrum) as Avero wonders why he has been
asked secretly to find a spot to converse with his fellow nobleman:

> De industria a esta espesura retirado
> vengo de mis monteros, que siguiendo
> un jabalí ligero, nos han dado
> el lugar que pedís . . .   (Tirso, *El vergonzoso*, lines 1–4)

There is no reason here to suppose that actual foliage would be used to represent
the thicket or that the *vestuario* would be open and decorated for the scene. The
beaters and wild boar would be taken on trust. Any substantial décor used in an
opening scene, such as the ramp that would represent the mountain from which
Rosaura descends at the start of Calderón's *La vida es sueño*, would have to stay
put until the end of the play. In a theatre without wings there is nowhere to move
it to. Ruano gives three conditions for the probable use of stage décor in a given
comedia: it is mentioned in an original stage direction; it is used, not simply
mentioned in the dialogue; and/or it has some important symbolic or thematic
function in the work (Ruano de la Haza, *La puesta*, p. 327).

Properties, when they were used, had different functions in the *corral*. It is
tempting from what we know of the use of the *vestuario*/discovery space to
assume that all revelations were made there. However, the *teatro*, or façade of
the stage (depending on the theatre), contained other curtained spaces capable of
containing adornments of one sort or another, and being used for *apariencias*
(the sudden revelation of a *tableau vivant*, a picture or other significant object,
such as a throne), especially perhaps in religious plays. The opening of one of
these spaces was often an indication that the scene had changed: for example, in
a *comedia de capa y espada*, from a street scene outside a house where a 'balcony' could be revealed, to the interior of a house or a public garden. In
Calderón's *La dama duende*, one of the few Golden Age plays to have been
subjected to detailed scrutiny in terms of its probable staging, Ruano claims
convincingly that the rooms which Doña Ángela and Don Manuel occupy (in the
same house) would be differentiated by the opening of the *vestuario* containing
furniture, including a small writing desk important for the development of the
plot. Thus by synecdoche the audience is alerted to a change of scene (Ruano de
la Haza, 'The Staging', p. 60). Close analysis of possible early stagings reveals
the flexibility of the *corral* stage, and the consequent ability of the audience to
use its imagination. Drama has always happily relied on make-believe, on the
part representing the whole, on the creation of symbolic equivalences and
conventions, and in a theatre unable to count on large casts, elaborate sound or
lighting effects, perspective scenery, and more recent technology, a realistic
theatre was not a possibility.

Nevertheless, just as the style of acting probably attempted to make the play
and its characters believable, so the other visual aspects of performance were
better developed than has sometimes been assumed. Costume, at least amongst

the official troupes, had come a long way since the days of Lope de Rueda, when the actors' wardrobe would fit comfortably in a chest and little attempt was made to avoid anachronistic dress. Large sums were lavished on spectacular costumes as the *corrales* continued to flourish, even in an age when the authorities were passing sumptuary laws, exemplified by the banning of ruffs and embroidering of clothes in 1623. At a time in Spain when appearance mattered a great deal, when a scoundrel might pass himself off as a gentleman if the picaresque novel in any way mirrors contemporary social concerns, there was an acute sensitivity to clothing: its material, its style, and its condition. An audience would instantly be able to discern rank and social standing through costume: taking an illustration from Tirso's *El vergonzoso en palacio* again, the noble-rustic Mireno suggests that he and his *pastor* side-kick Tarso swap clothes with the courtly secretary Ruy Lorenzo and his lackey Vasco, in order to save the latter pair from being instantly recognized in the countryside and handed over to the authorities. The scene doubtless originally depended on the visual comedy of the exchange to season the *gracioso*'s verbosity on the complexity of dressing in noble attire. Whilst the now 'courtly' Mireno, looking the part, begins, in his famous sonnet (see p. 66), to believe in the possibility of his own social ascension, 'que aumenta la soberbia el buen vestido' (Tirso, *El vergonzoso*, line 672), Tarso takes an age to dress, making a meal of the process 'que ha un hora que no es posible/ topar con la faltriquera' (lines 684–5). Another Tirso comedy, *Don Gil de las calzas verdes*, would have succeeded on stage only if the troupe had available four sets of green breeches to appear together in Act 3.

Costume, then, including other key markers of status – swords, capes, crowns, spurs, plumed hats, gloves, boots, ribbons, handkerchiefs – was the main visual clue to a character's status, but, along with 'stage directions' implicit in the text, it also helped the audience to pick up hints about the location of a scene, and the time of day being represented. The wearing of hats and colourful cloaks indicated street scenes (at night if the acting suggested as much); pastoral scenes, urban scenes, scenes set in *hospitales* for the mad, palaces, the church, a prison, the battlefield, a garden, would all be quickly recognizable in part through costume. In Calderón's *La vida es sueño* the vicissitudes of Segismundo's journey of self-knowledge would be rendered dramatically impotent without his changes from animal skins (in his tower) to princely attire (for the Polish court). The costume changes help the audience to separate more readily the 'dream' from the 'reality' of his experience, and thus interpret the central metaphor of the play.

Although inaccuracies and anachronisms were no doubt common enough, particularly in historical dramas, set perhaps in the Spain of the Reconquest, or *comedias de santos*, frequently set in the time of the late Roman Empire, *autores de comedias* and actors would often have attempted to suggest distinctiveness, foreignness or remoteness in time, through costume. Ruano lists dozens of professions, types, and nationalities that were conventionally distinguished by dramatists in their stage directions, including New World *indianos*, Amazons,

Asturians, *beatas*, slaves, *cautivos*, *moros*, students, and doctors (Ruano de la Haza, *La puesta*, pp. 73–100).

A favourite use of costume, attested to by Lope's *Arte nuevo* and by numerous playwrights' practice, was cross-dressing; usually female characters' dressing in male attire with the moral purpose of pursuing a recalcitrant lover and bringing him to book. The frequency of transvestism in Golden Age drama attracted the attention of the *Consejo de Castilla* on several occasions, no doubt in part because it gave men in the audience a rare chance to admire an actress's legs and feet, but it would seem their pronouncements had little effect on the frequency of dramatists' depictions of such heroines. Whilst women dressing as men can often be regarded as proto-feminist *mujeres varoniles*, the occasional men dressing as women would have been for the most part played purely for laughs, as in Lope's *La discreta enamorada*, and arguably as a deliberate attempt to subvert the norms of the *comedia de capa y espada*, as in Castaño's elaborate transvestite performance in Sor Juana's *Los empeños de una casa*.

The development of costume use throughout the Golden Age period points to an increasing concern with the visual, much lamented by Lope de Vega in the *prólogos* to the *partes* he published in the early 1620s. When, in a short dialogue, a stranger asks the figure of Teatro why the carpenters have become so important in the theatre, he replies: 'o por no haber buenos representantes, o por ser malos los poetas, o por faltar entendimiento a los oyentes; pues los autores se valen de las máquinas, los poetas de los carpinteros, y los oyentes de los ojos' (Vega, *Prólogos*, p. xxv). The importance of spectacle, of pleasing the eye rather than the ear, was reflected, to Lope's consternation, by the use of *apariencias* and especially *tramoyas* (really mechanized *apariencias*) in the *corral*. The *tramoyas*, operated from the third floor of the Madrid *corrales* using a system of pulleys and counter-weights, could move characters up and down between the stage level and the highest level of the façade, the *corredor alto*. They provoked the requisite *admiración*, for example, by showing angels descending or souls ascending vertically (horizontal movement was also possible, but more problematic). Trap-doors were regularly used, as was the *bofetón*, another sort of *tramoya*, relying on rapid mechanical gyration to make one figure disappear and another appear in its place.

Basic sound effects were possible in the *corral* theatre. Indeed in the recently re-discovered *corral* in Alcalá de Henares, there are reproduced some of the machines for generating noises, for example a stone-filled barrel which rotates with a handle to create thunder and other loud noises. However, by far the most significant sound effect in Golden Age theatre is music. Music started and ended the afternoon in the *corral*, and was essential to the *comedia nueva* itself. It had a number of functions which can be deduced from dramatic texts and their stage directions. On a practical level music helped to mark the end of one unit of action and the start of another, as well as sometimes being required to drown out the sound of the stage machinery. Additionally, certain types of instrument or music would be associated with particular kinds of scene: thus a returning monarch might enter to the sound of trumpets or drums. (In Tirso's *La venganza de Tamar* the much delayed arrival of King David is heralded by 'cajas dentro' before the princes and monarch emerge on stage 'marchando con mucha música'.) A lover might sing at his beloved's grille or balcony to the sound of a *vihuela* (an early guitar) in an attempt to move both audience and lover. A supernatural voice would often be accompanied by *chirimías* (shawms), which are very common in the *autos sacramentales* in particular. Music did not merely function, then, as a diversion or relief, but frequently shed light on the action, setting, or genre of the play. The type of song, for example a harvest or a sheep-shearing song (to return to *La venganza de Tamar*, Act 3), might help to change a mood or establish the scene of the play's action. Audiences would have instantly differentiated a popular wedding song and a courtly lyric meant, for example, to dispel a prince's melancholy. And lyrics themselves often shed light on a character and can summarize or concretize an important moment or message. The *pastores* of Absalón's estate at Balhasor, including 'Tirso', sing of 'perdón' as an alternative to vengeance for dishonour – a lesson that the rape-victim Tamar and her brother ignore, throwing the realm into further chaos and conflict.

All of the major dramatists of the Golden Age understood the importance of music as an element of drama in the *corral*. However, it was in the *auto sacramental* and court entertainments that its role took on an even greater significance, especially in the hands of Calderón, who understood well contemporary theories of music based on Pythagorean–Platonic philosophies, as Jack Sage has shown (Sage, 'The function'). Familiar with, and no doubt impressed by Italian opera, Calderón overcame his doubts over audience reaction, and introduced more sung dialogue into his dramatic works especially in the late 1650s and early 1660s. In some of his mythological plays, as we saw in chapter 4, he had the gods sing whilst the mortals spoke their verses. Then, in a small number of *zarzuelas* and operas, he left behind the compact made between music and verisimilitude, producing entirely sung dramas (see p. 111).

The lack of a performance tradition for Golden Age drama in Spain means that recent and modern productions are assessed in something of a vacuum. Audiences and critics often lack knowledge of this theatrical tradition and the collective memory of past performances common, for example, for French and English drama.[16] Studies of performances which shed light on the interpretation of Golden Age plays are rare, although growing in number, especially with the creation of the Compañía Nacional de Teatro Clásico (CNTC) in Madrid in 1986, and also the re-awakening of interest in plays by Lope and his fellow dramatists in festivals and seasons within and beyond Spain.[17] They can provide

---

[16] Even a Jacobean play such as Middleton's *Women Beware Women*, which has 'a remarkably sparse stage history', according to Ronnie Mulryne, can count on ten performances in the UK, mostly at major venues, as well as a radio and television production, all since the 1960s. See his programme notes to the RSC's production of the play, directed by Laurence Boswell in 2006.

[17] See Fischer, 'Así que pasen quince años', for an assessment of the aims and actual

a great deal of information about the *comedia* in a number of different regards. The tendency of directors and theatre professionals to approach Golden Age plays with less veneration than academics habitually do, asking questions about how to perform them convincingly and meaningfully for their audiences, provides a chance to uncover aspects and characteristics of plays that tend to remain hidden in text-based studies.

Just as dinosaur experts may be surprised by both the extent and the limitations of their knowledge of their subject when asked to help produce working models of the creatures for a television series, so *comedia* scholars can be both comforted and alarmed when they engage with actual productions of the plays whose texts they study. Modern performances may change the emphasis of a play: for example, a production of *La vida es sueño* can legitimately emphasize different, more negative responses to the perception that life is dream-like, drawing on philosophical speculation written since Calderón's play. In so doing it would exploit the ambiguities, or rather dramatic possibilities, inherent in the text. Plays will always be filtered through the vision of the director and the skills of the actor and to remain alive they must be capable of reinterpretation, and even capable of against-the-grain interpretations. However, recent productions of Golden Age works have also shed light on the creative subtleties and dramatic know-how of the playwrights who flourished in the period, justifying the scholar's faith in the quality of the theatre.

One of the problems of performance based scholarship is that its conclusions depend on an individual's inevitably imperfect viewing of a production. Another is that the play-text may have been simplified for the modern audience, as has tended to be the case with the CNTC's productions, or translated out of its original Spanish and prosified. However, repeated viewing and consultation of reviews, photographs and video recordings of particular performances, in conjunction with their texts, can offset some of the difficulties inherent to this kind of criticism. In the performances assessed below are examined some of the areas of Golden Age drama (and assumptions about them) that my own presence in the audience has forced me to consider or re-consider.

One of these areas is a play's structure. The Royal Shakespeare Company's production of *El perro del hortelano* of 2004 (to which reference has already been made), translated by David Johnston as *The Dog in the Manger*, revealed, in a practical way that the text hardly can, Lope de Vega's facility for and great concern with developing an action. The set's backdrop was a huge tapestry showing the face of a noblewoman uncannily similar to that of the actress playing the protagonist Diana. The almost permanent pictorial presence of the countess brought to the fore the number of times in the play that Lope has a

productions of the company between 1986 and 1999. The journal *Comedia Performance*, created by the Association for Hispanic Classical Theatre (AHCT) in the US in 2004, publishes articles primarily on performance of Golden Age drama. Pilar Miró's film version of *El perro del hortelano*, from 1995, also helped to raise awareness of the performative possibilities of Golden Age theatre.

character overhear others in conversation, or arrive just when least expected or desired. Walls were truly seen to have ears. Visually, the frequent attempts of characters to avoid detection or rapidly escape the stage to eschew confrontation make a strong impression. This technique, similar to that of farce, allows the love triangle of Teodoro, Marcela and Diana to develop very rapidly but coherently, especially in Act 1, and underlines the predominantly comic spirit of the play. Lope's easy command of one of the techniques of comedy-writing, evident in this performance, helps to add to the debate on the play's genre and his purposes in writing it. And the inability of characters to suppress anything they would rather keep to themselves may even hint that Teodoro's big secret is destined for revelation.

Cervantes's *Pedro de Urdemalas*, translated by Philip Osment into matching English verse as *Pedro the Great Pretender*, and directed by Mike Alfreds for the same RSC season, is equally revealing in terms of structure. Clearly, as scholars have noted, Cervantes's play is in part a parody of the *comedia nueva*, refusing to abide by the genre's conventions. What the production in 2004 made clear was that the play undermines one set of norms but provides a positive alternative, just as the novel *Don Quijote* both destroys and re-creates. This episodic, structurally loose *comedia* had been all but ignored by directors over the centuries, probably because of its apparent incoherence. A production which embraced the metatheatrical elements of the original and benefited from a strong central performance from John Ramm, as Pedro, revealed a thematic coherence that left the audience satisfied structurally and challenged intellectually.

Other productions in recent years have tended to confirm Ruano's belief that, despite frequent assertions to the contrary by scholars, Golden Age theatre does create human characters with depth (Ruano de la Haza, 'Trascendencia'). In time analyses of actual productions will prove that Golden Age theatre is concerned with character as well as theme. The production of Lope's *Peribáñez* at the Young Vic in London in 2003, directed by Rufus Norris and translated by Tanya Ronder, demonstrated how a director can build and differentiate even minor characters, such as Inés and Costanza, from a few clues in the text. And Simon Usher's production for the RSC of Tirso's *Tamar's Revenge* in 2004 (in a translation by James Fenton) demonstrated the extent to which a production can force the reconsideration of assumptions about a major character, and consequently the meaning of a well-known play. Usually Tamar is taken from the page to be an innocent daughter of King David, whose rape at the hands of her brother converts her into the avenging monster who wills and revels in his murder. By the end of the first act of Usher's production, when Amón attends and disrupts the wedding of Elisa and Josefo, there is more than a hint that this Tamar 'knows' at some level the identity of her importunate lover, or is, at least, attracted to the figure sexually. The scene tends to have been read as Tamar's flat and proper rejection of the masked man, backed up by her apparently unambiguous order to have him killed, but the production bore witness to another possibility, something to be learned from the text performed, gestures, pauses and all. Amón's continued verbal erotic assault on Tamar picks up on the mood of the previous night in the garden, the desire for union, 'puesto que la noche obscura/ también voluntades casa,/ hecho tálamo un jardín' (Tirso, *La venganza*, I, lines 773–5). The wedding, with its own inevitable sexual consummation, offers a backdrop of the imminent prize of the fruits of romantic engagement, to which Tamar has referred in the first speech of the scene. Tamar again does not recoil at the first hints of lovers' talk, although if she were committed to her lover Joab, one might expect her to. She allows Amón to convert her literal words to the language of love (especially her use of 'castigo', I, line 799), and crucially in Usher's production, she allows her body, kneeling behind a kind of low altar (made of the same benches on which she will later be raped, and Amón will be killed), to respond to her half-brother's insistent and intimate touch. The scene neatly encapsulates Usher's interpretation of Tamar as a sensuous woman, aroused by the ardour and lawlessness of a lover who shares her passionate yearning. The delayed violence of her response 'dalde muerte, o dadme nombre/ de desdichada' (I, lines 838–9) reflects only her confusion at her lover's bold-ness and her own acquiescence.

When Tamar finally brings the wedding to a chaotic conclusion with this demand that the masked man be killed, he has already escaped to safety. In the RSC's production he has exited before she reacts, as if a dream is over and she has returned to reason; in Tirso's play the stage direction reads 'Bésala, y vase' before her first exclamation (I, line 833), at least hinting at the possibility that at some level Tamar wants to let Amón escape. The character created for the stage, unexpected, though consistent with one close reading of the text, forces a funda-mental reassessment of the play. In doing so it adds to our appreciation of the depth of Tirso de Molina's theatrical skill.

Other actual productions of Golden Age plays have occasionally led scholars to re-examine assumptions and think anew about the texts they read in terms of structure and characterization, but also in terms of satirical intent, the pace of the action, the interpretation of their themes, and their genre.[18] In fact both broad areas of performance studies – the imaginative re-creation of contempor-ary staging of plays and their reinterpretation through productions on the modern stage – show welcome signs of vigour at the start of the twenty-first century.

---

[18] For perhaps the fullest scholarly analysis of a Golden Age production to date, see Fischer, 'Historicizing *Painter of Dishonour*'.

6

Types of *Comedia* and
Other Forms of Theatre

Throughout this *Companion* a number of different generic terms have been used to describe, in a kind of short-hand, some of the main kinds of play that have been discussed: *comedia de santos*, *comedia urbana*, *drama de honor*, tragedy, are a few examples. They have often been employed reluctantly or somewhat tentatively as they were either coined well after the era in which they appeared or were used somewhat imprecisely in the Golden Age itself. On balance their use has been taken to be helpful in breaking down an author's *oeuvre* into constituent parts. However, it is worth remembering that what we regard as theatre, that is (broadly defined) public or private staged performances of imaginative works written to edify and/or entertain, attracted a host of different generic names in Spain from Encina's time until the end of the seventeenth century. Most of these denominations – including *farsa*, *égloga*, *auto*, *comedia* and *representación* – are borrowed from older traditions and re-applied rather haphazardly, especially before the end of the sixteenth century, to new forms of dramatic expression. They mean different things in different contexts or to different artists and are initially confusing.

The critical urge to classify, to divide plays into precise types and then sub-genres, like that of the scientist approaching the natural world, is a fairly modern one, and is understandable, even imperative to some minds, given the mass of material to be processed and examined. Taxonomy was of limited interest to those writing drama, and, one suspects, those going to see it in the period: the classically-inspired Torres Naharro at the start of the sixteenth century and Bances Candamo at the end of the seventeenth stand out as would-be dramatic theorists. Others such as Cervantes and López Pinciano tend to discuss genre within its basic classical divisions of tragedy and comedy. The latter discusses tragicomedy too, not in anticipation of the Lopean *comedia nueva*, but using the classic case of Plautus's *Amphitruo*.

This chapter will begin by raising some of the issues taxonomy entails and discussing briefly a number of terms used by playwrights and scholars to describe Golden Age plays once the *comedia nueva* had become dominant. It then moves on to look at two other significant forms of theatre of the Golden Age, concentrating first on the minor genres, or (more happily put) short forms of theatre, such as the *entremés*, which formed part of an afternoon's entertainment at the theatre, and then on the *auto sacramental*, performed in the street at Corpus Christi in many Spanish towns and cities.

Types of *comedia*

In chapters 1 and 2 our examination of the creation of the *comedia nueva* under the inspired guidance of Lope de Vega showed how several theatrical traditions fed into his new drama. Like other dramatists of the 1580s he was familiar with classical drama (Plautus, Terence and Seneca chiefly), classical theory (especially Aristotle and Horace) as it was being re-written in the Renaissance, Humanistic comedy and Rojas's *Celestina*, Jesuit school drama, the tragic and other works of Cervantes and the Valencians, court entertainments, religious drama, the *commedia dell'arte*, and popular theatre of the type created by Lope de Rueda and his fellow professionals. In the process of synthesizing or blending these and other perhaps equally important non-dramatic ingredients, Lope can be compared to a baker: a particular element – say, Ariosto's *Orlando Furioso* – becomes the staple, the flour without which the product cannot be made, whilst other elements are added in smaller or larger quantities, depending on the type of loaf or pastry that is to be baked. Some parallels here are worth pursuing: a baker's ingredients are transformed in the making so that their original form becomes difficult to recognize; the addition and combination of different ingredients, from the savoury to the sweet, produces different end results for different occasions or palates; a good baker's initial efforts bring mixed results but his skill and confidence in his work increases over time and through experimentation. Whilst never omitting certain basic ingredients, Lope is able to create a variety of tried and tested confections that his customers savour. Others, admiring his success, first imitate him and then include their own preferred ingredients, subtly changing his recipes.

All analogies have their weak points, of course, but the reason for pursuing this one is to demonstrate some of the problems inherent in categorizing the *comedia*. Much scholarly work has been carried out in recent years on pigeon-holing works from the Golden Age, especially in France, Spain and Italy, and some of the categories that have been mooted and discussed are outlined below. The benefits of generic criticism are clear: knowing what kind of plays a particular playwright favoured helps to generalize about him or her; inspirations for and connections and influences between dramatists can be discerned more easily; older conclusions about the nature of the *comedia*, such as Menéndez y Pelayo's firm generic categorizations, or the critical tendency to see the tragic where it may be absent, can be challenged; the author's intention and the audience's horizon of expectations may be more reliably predicted; establishing genres and sub-genres ideally requires the sort of painstaking textual analyis, and comparative work, that gradually creates order from a chaotic mass.[1] On the

---

[1] See Arellano's *Convención*, chapter 2, for an exemplary study of this sort.

other hand, several factors mean that the study of genre in the *comedia* needs to be handled with care: as we have mentioned, within the Golden Age itself there is little evidence that dramatists dwelt upon distinctions between genres, let alone sub-genres, although they instinctively shared broad expectations as their collaborative experiences would indicate; dramatists were attracted by stories, not so much by the form in which they would dramatize them (and this form was anyway thought of in broad terms and was flexible and capacious); above all, the potential ingredients of any play, which, by the time of Lope's imitators, included a mass of his own works, could combine in so many ways that to insist on its firm categorization risks over-simplification; additionally one of the features of the *comedia* (as with modern film) is the constant innovation of its creators, who could set their work apart by both its variety and its novelty. To remain popular with the alert and knowledgeable *vulgo* and the expectant educated audiences of court and *corral*, a dramatist had to create *admiratio* within a model that was familiar enough. Genre was being constantly abused, parodied and re-invented as a part of the essential cycles of the *comedia* that we can only partially re-construct from this distance. The public could tell from the company's posters advertising the title of a play whether it was likely to be a comedy, a serious play, or a *comedia de santos*, but within each offering the audience would expect to be surprised by some novelty.

One further point is worth making in this preliminary discussion of dramatic genre in the Golden Age. It was made by Fernando de Rojas in the prologue to his *Tragicomedia de Calisto y Melibea* (written after he had changed the work's original title from *Comedia*), in which he discusses the mixed reception of the work, and records that readers '[dan] cada uno sentencia sobre ella a sabor de su voluntad' (Rojas, *La Celestina*, p. 80). In the end all readers and audience members, whilst sensitive to convention, have individual reactions to any work, creating meaning, and interpreting intention and formal elements for themselves and in the light of their own experiences, artistic and real.

The term *comedia* itself is the first to need explanation as it has three meanings: first it often stands for *comedia nueva* as when scholars refer to 'the *comedia*'; second, it describes any 'full-length' play, not just in the Golden Age, and is explicitly not used to denote the *auto* or examples of *teatro menor*; and third, it means 'comic play' (sometimes *comedia cómica* in Spanish to avoid confusion) as opposed to a tragic or serious play. Many printed editions in the Golden Age introduced plays with the words 'Comedia famosa de . . .', whatever the genre of the work in question. Calderón's *El pintor de su deshonra*, *El príncipe constante*, and *La vida es sueño*, for example, are unexceptional in being described thus, despite their content. It was out of the ordinary for a playwright to insist, as Lope did in the autograph manuscript of *El castigo sin venganza*, on calling a work a *tragedia*, and even then the term required a gloss from the author. When he had the play printed Lope explained that he had avoided the 'severidad' expected of classical tragedy, but he still felt he had written a modern Spanish example of the ancient genre. There was a widespread awareness amongst Golden Age playwrights that having followed Lope's lead, having mixed high and low styles, it was not possible to create proper tragedy as the ancients had understood it. This did not, however, mean that there was an inability to envisage or appreciate tragic situations, as we have seen in earlier chapters.[2] There are many plays of the period that are serious works, tragic in their action and their ending, although not all serious plays are tragedies. In addition to comedies and these serious plays, a third major group comprises religious dramas, or *comedias divinas* as Cervantes called them, of which the majority are *comedias de santos*.

Each of these three major groups of plays – which would have almost invariably announced their generic allegiance through their title, and thus suggested to a potential audience a different set of loose but identifiable expectations – will be dealt with in turn, beginning with religious plays and then moving to serious works and to comedies. The characteristics of commonly recognized sub-genres are explained but the reservations about their usefulness as interpretive tools expressed above should always be borne in mind.[3]

Religious plays

When the priest in *Don Quijote*, I, 48, rails against the abuses evident in contemporary *comedias divinas*, it would seem that he has the *comedia de santos* in mind. His reproaches concern the 'milagros falsos' (Cervantes, *Don Quijote*, I, p. 570) attributed to saints in some plays, and ignorance or confusion about which saint performed which miracle. Despite the errors of playwrights, however, the *comedia de santos* remained a fixture from the 1590s until the mid- to late eighteenth century when growing moral concerns finally saw its demise along with that of the *auto sacramental*. Works depicting the lives of saints were the most common type of religious play in the Golden Age: their aim was obviously to edify but their content was not by any means monotonously pious. Such plays might be commissioned for particular occasions or written because of a playwright's special interest in a saintly figure, real or legendary. Playwrights tended to use books extolling the lives of saints as their primary sources. In some cases, as with Cervantes's *El rufián dichoso*, which is often unproblematically called a saint's play, the holy protagonist was never in fact canonized. The dramatist's source in this case is a collection of lives of significant Dominicans. Many of these *comedias de santos*, Lope's three San Isidro plays

---

[2] Gail Bradbury makes an attempt to re-define Lopean tragedy in 'Tragedy and Tragicomedy', and finds eight plays predominantly from his mature period to call 'tragedies'. McKendrick, *Theatre*, pp. 78–83, examines the question of Golden Age tragedy with admirable common sense. The idea that Spain, as a Catholic country with a belief in the administration of divine justice after death, was incapable of producing tragedies tends now to attract few adherents. But for a forceful expression of that position with regard to Calderón's theatre, see Maestro, 'Los límites'.

[3] The norms of what is arguably another genre, the kind of musical theatre which developed particularly through Calderón's provision for the court, and included the *zarzuela*, are outlined in chapter 4.

being a case in point, are rather episodic, as one might expect with the dramatization of a biography. Here the conventions of the genre differ from the norm and less effort is made to unify action or eschew changes of place and especially leaps in time. Nevertheless, the popularity of these works is unquestionable. Apart from enjoying the chance to witness the life of a saint, perhaps known from a hagiography or a painting in church, dramatized on stage, audiences were attracted to their more elaborate staging. Many required sudden appearances, descents and ascents, and impressive tableaux because of miracles and divine interventions, and the remarkable deeds, conversions, and martyrdoms of their protagonists.

Comedias de santos demanded an additional adjustment in the normal set of expectations that the audience member would bring to the *corral*: endings were not poetically just, as they frequently were in serious and comic plays, but the positive associations of martyrdom allowed the discrepancy. No doubt the unjust, sometimes horrific, deaths of Catholic saints provoked pity, but admiration and even wishful identification would have contributed to a pious reaction to the morbid ending of the play. Despite this fundamental difference from the conventional reception of the *comedia*, many religious plays contained a large number of elements common to the other two genres: the presence of a *gracioso*, even a fairly typical love/honour plot (as in Calderón's *El mágico prodigioso*), courtly settings, and so on. In fact, as already indicated, the permeability of even the three broad generic categories outlined, means that a play such as Lope's *Lo fingido verdadero*, although it dramatizes the martyrdom of Saint Genesius, is hardly a saint's play at all. The work has attracted more attention as a kingship play and as a remarkable rumination on the *theatrum mundi* topos.

Other religious plays include those inspired by the Bible, and a looser group of those which clearly reflect church teachings in a sustained way. In the former group would be included, for example, Lope's *La hermosa Ester* and Tirso's *La venganza de Tamar*. Most Biblical *comedias* took their material from the Old Testament, primarily because dramatists could not portray Christ in the *corral*, but also because of the wealth of dramatizable material it contained. In the second group one might include Tirso's *El condenado por desconfiado*, Mira's *El ejemplo mayor de la desdicha*, Calderón's *El príncipe constante*, and arguably also his *La vida es sueño*. Again the attempt to categorize individual works creates further debate, rather than solving many problems – surely itself a sign of the richness of Golden Age theatre. When does a play on a religious theme become a *comedia de santos*? How much explicit edification does a play have to contain before it becomes 'religious' rather than 'moral' or 'philosophical'? When does a Biblical play about a monarch become a kingship play? How should early-modern understandings of 'history' (for example, the inclusion of the Bible within the reach of the term) affect categorizations?

Serious drama

Religious plays can then, on occasions, merge into the second category, that of 'serious' plays, often usefully denominated *dramas* by Spanish scholars. Within this genre, perhaps the most varied and extensive of the three, several sub-categories are regularly referred to despite the obvious overlapping between them: historical plays, honour plays (including wife-murder plays), peasant plays, kingship plays (usually but not always historical), tragedies, and mythological works. It is probably true to say that conventionally this group would develop most unpredictably for a contemporary audience. Some would follow history, often known to the Golden Age public through the ballad, so that, for example, an audience would become quickly aware of the tragic nature of Luis Vélez's *Reinar después de morir* once they had gathered who the main characters were. Yet, taking another of Vélez's plays, *El diablo está en Cantillana*, it is clear that although there are historical figures in the work, such as King Pedro himself, and although his traits are well known, the resolution of the story would not have been predictable through its generic conventions. The same can be said of the anonymous *La Estrella de Sevilla*. Golden Age playwrights were adept at building plays with a political resonance onto a historical base, sometimes flimsy, or merely suggestive.

The large number of *dramas* with their roots in history, Spanish or foreign, ancient, medieval or contemporary, requires a great deal of further study. Lope was, predictably, the most prolific exponent of this kind of drama and he often had the monarch's role and conduct in his sights.[4] Nevertheless, historical plays were also written about the Reconquest, the discovery of the New World, events in Spain's rival states, and, as propaganda, the victories of Philip IV's forces in the early years of his reign, for example, Lope's *El Brasil restituido* and Calderón's *El sitio de Breda* (both 1625). As with Shakespeare's history plays, in Spain the subject matter is not narrowly restricted and the approach taken to it is by no means uniform.

Some of the Golden Age honour plays are often (justifiably) described as tragedies. Clearly the murder of an innocent wife by an avenging husband or lover may not fit the strictest, classical definitions of the term, but the kinds of social pressures that build on the honour-conscious man and his frequently impotent, entrapped wife provide the sort of situation that an audience simultaneously sympathizes with and finds abhorrent. Calderón's *El médico de su honra* best encapsulates this world of the honour drama or tragedy, in which the place of cruel fate can be said to be taken by the irresistible force of the honour code. However, by no means all honour plays are tragedies, or rather honour is an important ingredient in many plays which end without bloodshed and horror. Even in those that do, such as Lope's *Los comendadores de Córdoba*, the drama-

---

[4] McKendrick makes clear, in her *Playing the King*, just how subtle Lope's manipulation of historical sources could be.

tist's intention may have been to make the audience laugh, so ridiculous and melodramatic does the *veinticuatro*'s revenge become. Here is another sub-category without fixed parameters.

Plays set predominantly amongst the peasantry usually involve the (attempted) dishonour of a beautiful local girl by a nobleman. They can be described as honour plays too, in the sense that they set up a fascinating conflict between two types of honour: the natural birth-right of the noble and the virtue and local prestige of the peasant. The best known of them involve deaths amongst the nobility: Lope's *Fuente Ovejuna*, well-known from chronicles of late fifteenth-century Spanish history, *Peribáñez y el comendador de Ocaña*, and *El mejor alcalde, el rey*; Calderón's *El alcalde de Zalamea*; and Luis Vélez's *La serrana de la Vera*. In each case the sustained presence of the peas-antry in these plays justifies the denomination but their themes of social discord, honour and kingship relate them to other groups within the serious genre.

Mythological plays, written from the second half of the sixteenth century, and flourishing in the court of Philip IV and beyond his death, are easier to identify and categorize but their purposes remain a matter for debate. Many of their plots come originally from Ovid's *Metamorphoses*, often via Pérez de Moya's *Philosofía secreta de la gentilidad*. Their subject matter and characters would have been well known to an educated audience. In the later period their impor-tance as court spectacle became paramount (see p. 129).

Comic plays

Comedy in the Golden Age was the dominant dramatic genre. As Ignacio Arellano has argued in recent times, this comedy has a set of generic conventions which make it quite easy to identify. Along with other influential modern schol-ars he rejects the critical stance, epitomized by Wardropper, which tended to 'tragedize' comic works from the period, perhaps through a desire to give them a greater stature within the European canon. Difficulties with comedy – worries about morality, its serious repercussions, the unsuitable character-types depicted – tend to be experienced by scholars and critics, not audiences. Indeed, although many problems arise in assigning Golden Age works to generic pigeon-holes, as we have seen, there *is* clear water between serious drama and comedy and there is rarely room for doubt as to whether a play is comic. Comedy inherits its principal subject matter of the battle for love in human society from its classical forebears; it is invariably concerned with the young, often of a middling social status; obsta-cles are conventionally overcome; and it usually ends in happiness and harmony. Thus, Tirso's *Marta la piadosa*, despite the presence of a death in the play's prehistory and other 'serious' content, is clearly comic (see p. 64). And, although a play such as Luis Vélez's *El diablo está en Cantillana* ends with the promised marriage between the lovers, Don Lope and Esperanza, it is not a comedy. Its protagonist is King Pedro and its theme his lesson in kingship, with a dramatic concentration on how he learns it and the disorder he threatens, not a prolonged focus on the lovers' story.

Golden Age comedies have been sub-divided by theme, the location of their action, their character-types or the way the characters behave, and the nature of the plot. Some of the most common types are *pastoral*, *de capa y espada*, *palatina*, *de enredo*, *de figurón*, and *burlesca*. Common enough too are references to the *comedia urbana* (usually the same as *de capa y espada*), *comedia de ingenio* (effectively an alternative to *enredo/intriga*, but see below), *amatoria* (too large a category to be helpful), *de disparates* (an alternative term for the *comedia burlesca*), and *de costumbres* (where the action might satirize a particular social class or conventional type of behaviour). Whilst prizing innovation and surprise, authors of all these types of comedy make use of the usual ingredients of the genre in language and rhetoric, staging, plot construction, thematic concerns and characterization.

Pastoral plays, typical of the early output of Lope de Vega, are love comedies set in the countryside whose noble protagonists are disguised as peasants. Like some other early manifestations of the *comedia*, they take their subject matter and some of their conventions from the prose romance – in this case Montemayor's *Diana* and its imitators. Their attraction lessened with time although the pastoral setting remained important in the *comedia*, for example in the peasant plays, and to provide an eloquent contrast to 'city life' in *La venganza de Tamar* and other works. Cloak and sword, and palace plays can usefully be dealt with together. Both have similar content and trajectories. Whilst the former are set in towns and cities of Spain (most frequently Madrid) and in a notional present day, the latter tend to be located in other lands, in a courtly setting and are peopled with characters of a higher social class: dukes, countesses and marquises. Bances Candamo set apart and defined usefully the former type in his *Theatro de los theatros*. He admired the sub-genre's elaboration in the hands of Calderón and ascribed its disappearance to the exhaustion of plot possibilities. It featured 'Caualleros particulares, como Don Juan, u Don Diego, etcétera, y los lances se reducen a duelos, a celos, a esconderse el galán, a taparse la Dama, en fin, a aquellos sucesos más caseros de un galanteo' (Bances, *Theatro*, p. 33). Typically, as in Calderón's *La dama duende* or Tirso's *La celosa de sí misma*, a young man arrives in Madrid from elsewhere in Spain and begins a courtship with a woman, the course of which is never easy because of misunderstandings, the presence of rivals, questions of family honour, changes in fortune, the stupidity (or cleverness) of the *gracioso*, and so on. Whilst the events leading to marriage are not realistic, they are played out within recognizable middle-class households and also against a well-known backdrop of churches, gardens and city streets and buildings. In *comedias palatinas*, such as Lope's *El perro del hortelano* or Calderón's *Las manos blancas no ofenden*, the events may be more distant in time and can seem more fantastic, but the kind of comic complication of plot is similar, as is the outcome.

The *enredo* is a staple of comedy, but where it is unusually complex, for example in Tirso's *Don Gil de las calzas verdes*, it can be seen as a defining element of the play's sub-classification. Similarly, if a particular character, Fenisa of Lope's *La discreta enamorada* perhaps, shows exceptional intelligence and wit in her machinations, the term *de ingenio* is frequently used to describe what is still a *comedia de capa y espada* in essence. More useful, although not to all scholars' taste, is the sub-group *comedia de figurón*: Moreto's *El lindo Don Diego* tends to be seen as ushering in dramatists' tendency to concentrate on one larger-than-life figure (see p. 119) in the way that was favoured by Molière later in seventeenth-century France. In a *comedia de figurón* the dramatist works with slightly different conventions, which is why the term is potentially illuminating: the main figure is likely to be a fool or suffer from a serious flaw (like the liar García, of Alarcón's *La verdad sospechosa*) but is also in some way attractive. In being out of the ordinary, individualistic, anti-social, larger than life, he helps to put some aspects of social life in the shade. His punishment is necessary but a part of him remains undefeated. Conventionally the ending of such plays is more ambivalent, although comedy's broad roof will still house them.

The *comedia burlesca* is a fascinating phenomenon whose study is in its infancy. Such works, usually only about two-thirds of the length of a typical play of the period, provide an antidote to some of the more serious manifestations of the *comedia nueva*. Their purpose is to cause laughter rather than moral improvement or social change as the nobler members of the comic clan can claim, and it could be argued that they are a type of *teatro menor*. Nevertheless they took on the three-act form of the *comedia* and were interrupted by *entremeses* and other entertainments as the *comedia* itself was. The fifty or so extant examples of the *comedia burlesca*, many anonymous, mostly date from the reign of Philip IV and tended to be performed on Shrove Tuesday, that is during Carnival-time when the world is turned upside-down before the privations of Lent. The desired hilarity was achieved through a parody of all the significant conventions of the *comedia*. The best known of these works is by Francisco Antonio Monteser (d. 1668) and is called *El caballero de Olmedo*. In taking aim at one of the noblest of traditional Spanish figures the play is typical: the famous 'amantes de Teruel' suffered a similar indignity. Monteser's play was performed for Philip IV in 1651. It depends on a barrage of jokes of various sorts, with quantity at least as important as quality. Some of the characters share the names of those in Lope's play but it is the conventions of the *comedia*, rather than Lope's work itself, that are systematically undermined. Don Alonso is a bullfighter who possesses none of the exquisite nobility of his namesake. He and his side-kick share the same world-view, if such it can be called. The woman he falls for, Elvira, presents herself in the 'damsel-in-distress' set-piece so common in the *comedia* with the words:

> Yo soy, como tengo dicho,
> una mujer, no lo niego.
> Nací en Medina de un parto,
> que es costumbre de aquel reino.
> Murió mi madre, y quedé
> sin ella . . .   (Monteser, *El caballero*, lines 115–20)

Parody, such as this of the self-presentation of the *dama*, must have demanded great comic timing and relies, of course, on an intimate knowledge of the norms of the dominant form. Themes such as that of honour, staging conventions such as the night scene, the *galán* in hiding and the portrait scene, characterization and language are mercilessly targeted. Even references to homosexuality and the stature of the monarch are permitted. Plot ceases to matter as the absurd and the ridiculous hold sway.

The genre has parallels in the burlesque ballads on mythological stories written by the likes of Góngora and Quevedo in the Golden Age. Indeed one notes an increase in the frequency of parody within the *comedia* itself, in the plays of Calderón and Sor Juana especially, as the genre grows old. Such deflation of the noble clearly caused great amusement in the period, and Calderón, so often presented as an austere literary and religious figure, indulged in self-parody when he wrote the *comedia burlesca, Céfalo y Pocris* (early 1660s?), in imitation of his opera *Celos aun del aire matan*. Although, unusually, if for obvious reasons, the titles of these burlesque works do not give any clue to their content, the timing of their performance at Carnival would leave no room for generic misunderstanding.

The *comedia*'s taxonomy, then, is an issue that is complicated by the existence of a plethora of generic categories, occasionally not clearly defined by those who have employed them from the sixteenth century to the present, by an unstated desire to raise the status of Spanish Golden Age theatre within the European canon, and by the theatre's vigorous development and then decline over the century of its pre-eminence. This last factor, especially, involves a lasting tension between convention and innovation, surely the cause of enjoyment to Golden Age audiences in the know, even if it leaves some modern readers in limbo. Some of Alarcón's plays as well as Calderón's, notably *No hay cosa como callar* and *El pintor de su deshonra*, even make a virtue of their engagement with genre, to the extent that the form of the play becomes one of its central concerns. Such self-consciousness should be seen as a sign not of uncertainty and weakness but of health and maturity.

Short forms of theatre

Teatro breve or *géneros menores* encompass several forms of theatre, some of ancient origin, others newly born, which became satellites of the *comedia nueva*. The best known of these is the *entremés* (or interlude), the short farce performed by members of the troupe between the acts of a full-length *comedia*. To study the *entremés* and other short theatrical forms of the Golden Age is to be reminded first that audience members did not come to the theatre solely to see the *comedia* performed, and secondly that the progress of their interpretation of the main play was interrupted and influenced by its accompaniments. Indeed at times this 'salsa/ para comer la comedia', to use the words of Luis Quiñones de Benavente (1581–1651), a specialist *entremesista*, was so appetizing that its taste dominated the main course.

A typical afternoon at the theatre might begin with music (perhaps the singing of a ballad) to welcome the audience, then continue with a *loa*, which preceded Act 1 of the *comedia*, then an *entremés*, Act 2, a *baile* or a *mojiganga*, then Act 3, and the *fin de fiesta* consisting in further music and dancing. The format was well known and well loved by the audiences, who were wont on occasions to encourage the players to move swiftly through the main event to the popular *entr'actes*. Each of these dramatic forms requires brief elucidation but it should be borne in mind that precise definitions of some of them are made difficult both by their evolution through the period and by their broad similarity in the first place. The short forms are often described understandably as 'non-literary' and yet most of the greatest writers of the period, even those generally unsuccessful in or unattracted by the theatre, tried their hand at them, perhaps because of the unusual freedom of expression they offered.

Although the *comedia* itself often started *in medias res*, perhaps with a fall or fight involving rapid action, perhaps with intriguing words or sound effects emerging from off-stage, it was the *loa* with which the company first attempted to soften and engage the audience. Rhetorically its function, certainly in the early years of the *comedia nueva*, was clearly the *captatio benevolentiae*, with the *mosqueteros* the obvious target at a *corral* performance. The *loa*'s name, employed from the late sixteenth century, suggests it has its origin in an attempt to flatter, but its precursor was the *introito* or *prólogo*, which had explained the plot of the drama to the audience in the early days of the theatre's development (for example, in the works of Torres Naharro). The link with the specific play to be performed was broken, however, by the time the *comedia*'s generic norms were established, and its content could vary greatly. Topics to be spoken on by the company's specialist deliverer of the *loa* included novelties of the day, eulogies of cities, women, art, and the theatre itself. Its form varied too, although it was written in verse, and was usually witty: a joke, a ballad, an anecdote, or a little satire. In the early days of Lope de Vega the *loa* tended to be spoken by a single actor but as the seventeenth century progressed it became a little more complex and frequently involved a dialogue. As such it took the form of a playlet, sometimes called a *loa entremesada*. The *loa* was by no means exclusive to the *corral* and one might argue that its function was different, less urgent, when it preceded an *auto* or a royal performance. Those of Antonio de Solís, who had a reputation at court as a *loa* specialist, contain mythological and allegorical figures, and involve singing and dancing. In the *Loa para la Comedia de Las Amazonas*, performed before Philip IV at Carnival-time in 1655, Solís's topic is the very usurpation of the personified figures of Comedia and Loas by Entremeses and Bailes, who outnumber them and dance all over the stage, glorifying in their new exalted status. Eventually the Loas, realizing their traditional functions are now unnecessary, join the other forms of *teatro breve*:

> ¿Nada he de pedir? Pues pido,
> que essos teques, teques,
> que cantan los Bayles,

y los Entremeses,
se buelvan en Loas.   (Solís, *Obra dramática menor*, pp. 106–7)

Two further examples of *loas*, one by Lope de Vega, a mere 40 lines long, and another by Benavente, of some 252, spoken by all the members of the troupe, should illustrate the extremes of this minor genre. In his 'Piña, de merecimiento,/ de seso y prudencia llena' Lope characteristically relates a short episode in the first person in which a hungry man destroys a beehive, having been stung extracting the honey, only to regret his actions and re-build it. More erudite members of the audience might anticipate the reason for the recounting of the short fable, but most of the *corral* audience will await the explanation of the allegory Lope has set up in suspense. He wittily equates himself, as *poeta*, with the busy bees who move from flower to flower (text to text, experience to experience) extracting the nectar to make a honeycomb (a useful and sweet poetic creation for the theatre). Then in the last two *redondillas* Lope forces the audience members to apply the lesson he has learned to themselves, asserting a moral pressure on each of them not to be the one who misses out on the honey by talking through his play:

> Pues no será, auditorio, justo,
> que un dulce panal de miel
> por un necio sepa a hiel,
> teniéndose él tan buen gusto.
> Pues el necio, con hablar,
> me quiebra el panal que crío,
> sanadle, auditorio mío,
> solamente con callar.   (Vega, *La enjambre*, loa 12, lines 33–40)

The *Loa que representó Antonio de Prado* (1635) was printed in Quiñones de Benavente's *Jocosería*, a collection of his *loas*, *jácaras* and *entremeses*, published in 1645. Its purpose is to introduce not just a single play but the freshly formed company of the *autor de comedias*, Prado, which is about to begin the new theatrical season with Lent over. Prado, whose name ('meadow') provides the author with the inspiration for his central extended metaphor, is roused from his slumber at the start of the piece and his new actors and actresses are introduced as adornments to this natural *locus amoenus*. Benavente's word-play and the ingenuity of his piece (including the parody of a series of *romances*) is a treat for the Golden Age ear but like many *loas* it depends heavily on the moment and would lose most of its meaning if performed for a modern audience.

Similar to the primitive *loa* was the *jácara*, originally a poem rather than a short drama, written in ballad form and recounting the low-life rivalries and deeds of the marginalized *hampa*, familiar from picaresque literature such as Quevedo's *El buscón* and Cervantes's *novela ejemplar*, *Rinconete y Cortadillo*. The *jácara*'s popularity encouraged innovation, and like the *loa*, it evolved into the *jácara entremesada*, in which the sung stories were danced or acted out by more than one actor. There are even records of *jácaras* developing as dialogues between actors on the stage and others hidden amongst the audience.

Other shorter forms of theatre – the *entremés*, *baile*, and *mojiganga* – are best considered together as their ludic function is similar and they are closely related. Although the latter two contain popular elements of dance and carnival respectively, these are readily embraced by the farcical theatre. Indeed elements typical of one minor genre commonly cross to another: the search for novelty stretched to the variety of terms used by Benavente and other dramatists writing from the 1620s onwards. Benavente favoured the designation 'entremés cantado' in his *Jocosería* but 'baile cantado' and 'baile entremesado' were other terms coined in the period.

The farcical *entremés* itself would have lasted some ten to fifteen minutes and would have been acted by members of the troupe with smaller parts in the main *comedia*. It portrayed peasants, *pícaros*, soldiers, mayors and local officials, old (often impotent) husbands, lascivious wives, legal professionals, students, sacristans, go-betweens, *malcasados*, old Christians, inn-keepers, kitchen-maids, fools of one sort or another, doctors, and *beatas*, and exposed them all to satire and grotesque parody. Eugenio Asensio, in his history of the form, differentiates the *entremés de enredo*, dramatizing a brief intrigue or trick, from the *entremés de costumbres* or *carácter*, where a particular class, type or individual is parodied. Whatever the subject of the farce, the characters were always (in Lope de Vega's time anyway) comic or low. Lope refers in his *Arte nuevo* to old plays as, by definition, *entremeses* because they contain a single action and are 'entre plebeya gente,/ porque entremés de rey jamás se ha visto' (Vega, *Arte nuevo*, p. 12).

The content of the *entremés* did not need to coincide at all with the content of the *comedia* which enveloped it. Nor was it necessarily by the same author: the *autor de comedias* would choose an *entremés* from the company's repertoire. Most were bought from the major playwrights of the day but there were dramatists, such as Benavente and some of the *ingenios* behind the *comedia burlesca*, who specialized in the short form. The world depicted is one of Carnival, turned upside-down, which laughs at its own social and other conventions, where women dominate their husbands, religion is mocked, moral certainties are uprooted. Asensio famously describes the genre as taking 'vacaciones morales'. The audience which applauds the endings in marriage and poetic justice in the *comedia* enjoys the riotous anarchy of the farce, applauding the adulterous wife, and the fool. There is no sewn-up ending to the *entremés*: in the early days, especially, it simply degenerated into violence and left threads untied. Many of the 'plots' of the *entremeses* came from oral tradition and consequently they have a popular feel to them; characters are rarely much more than sketched; the setting remains static and is often neutral; language and gesture dominate. The success of such works probably depended to a large extent on the virtuosity of the actors.

The history of short farcical theatre in the Golden Age is complicated by a number of factors: first, it emerged in part from folklore, oral tradition, Carnival celebrations and other performance traditions such as the *momo*, and its trajectory is thus hard to trace; secondly, its debts to the *commedia dell'arte* in the second half of the sixteenth century are naturally difficult to assess and examine; thirdly, its subsidiary status means many texts (undoubtedly the majority) were never printed and have thus been lost; fourthly, in many cases dating and attribution of texts to authors is troublesome, again because of the status and transience of the genre. The history of the term *entremés* itself is better documented (see Shergold, *A History*, pp. 113–42): in the medieval period the meaning of the term covered, or developed to include, pageants to celebrate Corpus Christi, both dishes and entertainments at banquets, then other court entertainments such as tournaments, and the floats or carts involved in these performances. For Torres Naharro, the *entremés* was a musical entertainment, and throughout most of the sixteenth century it was one of the words which could refer to any short play. Lope de Rueda used the term *pasos* to describe his short farcical scenes before the term's meaning came to be fixed later in the century. The heyday of the *entremés* was between about 1600 and 1630, during which time, without losing its essential characteristics, it evolved into a number of sub-species (mentioned above) thanks to changing tastes and Benavente's skills.

A look at a handful of farces by five important writers spanning a century and a half – Encina, Rueda, Cervantes, Quevedo and Benavente – will provide a good idea of some of the genre's characteristics and the processes of change that they underwent. In length alone several of Encina's early plays resemble *entremeses*, but it is the *Aucto del repelón*, written for Carnival, not Christmas or Easter, whose function, characters, language and action mark it out as an embryonic example of the form. The farce has just three characters, and is dominated by two *pastores*, Piernicurto and Johanparamás, who have been attacked and had their hair cut by a group of prankster-students while selling their wares in the town square. Having fled they meet up and repel another attempt at a similar *burla* by a lone student, before Johanparamás sings a *villancico* with accompaniment, to end the entertainment. The audience would have been amused not so much by the violence and rapid action that later became a staple of the *entremés* as by the comic rusticity of the dialogue between the affronted peasants, their interplay, and their individual reactions to the indignity of the attack and the loss of their goods and beasts. Crucially, however, the comedy relies on the superiority the audience feels over the characters dramatized, and, although they are subtly differentiated, they attract no empathetic identification.

A similar attitude to traditionally ignorant or foolish character-types – the defining element of the *entremés* form – is immediately discernible in Lope de Rueda's theatre, although his audience was quite different. His *pasos*, unlike the *Aucto del repelón*, were written in prose, and this became the norm for the minor form until the seventeenth century. Rueda's farces were detachable scenes, originally printed together with the whole play in which they were inserted (by Timoneda, in Valencia in 1567). Timoneda, himself an *entremesista*, clearly recognized the outstanding quality of the short scenes, denominated *pasos*, as he later published others by Rueda which stood alone. Cervantes, as we have seen, was one of the writers who remembered Rueda with affection, and he too, in the prologue to his own collection of drama, passes rapidly over the gold-beater's *comedias* to single out his farces:

> Las comedias eran unos coloquios como églogas, entre dos o tres pastores y alguna pastora; aderazábanlas y dilatábanlas con dos o tres entremeses, ya de negra, ya de rufián, ya de bobo o de vizcaíno: que de todas estas cuatro figuras y otras muchas hacía el tal Lope con la mayor excelencia y propiedad que pudiera imaginarse.   (Cervantes, *Entremeses*, pp. 91–2)

It is clear that by the late 1550s and early 1560s a number of distinct types of *entremés*, identifiable by the character-type represented, had developed, and that they were already (well before the appearance of the *corrales* and the *comedia nueva*) a much-prized part of the theatrical entertainment. Few have been preserved in written form (and those that have we owe to Timoneda), perhaps because the material was commercially sensitive, essential to Rueda's troupe's survival.

Lope de Rueda's best known *paso*, *Las aceitunas*, dramatizes another argument between peasants. The *viejo simple*, Toruvio, and his equally dim-witted wife Águeda de Toruégano, become carried away by the value of the fruit that they will harvest within several years from Toruvio's newly planted olive trees. Their discussion, already ridiculous, descends further into farce when Águeda begins to beat their daughter Mencigüela for listening to her husband's suggested market-price for the olives. The row is settled and their foolishness pointed out by their neighbour, Aloxa, who arrives on the scene to act as the voice of reason. The characters, however, are not really expected to learn from their experiences. The short play is rich in comedy but, although it gives the illusion of being an intrusion into a slice of Spanish peasant life, it is also a version of a well-known type of folk tale popular elsewhere in Europe.

In *Cornudo y contento*, and many of his other *pasos*, Rueda's characters are urban and more typical of the later *entremés* as a result: the rustic fool, or *pastor-bobo*, popular in Torres Naharro and Sánchez de Badajoz, begins to die out thanks to early-modern demographic trends and as the age of the *comedia nueva* dawns (see Brotherton, *The* Pastor Bobo). *Cornudo y contento*'s protagonist, Martín de Villalba, is still described as 'simple' but he is a husband milked by Lucio, his doctor, and deceived by his wife Bárbara, who is sleeping under his nose with her cousin, the student Gerónimo. The playlet consists of two mini-scenes: in the first Martín explains to the doctor how he has been persuaded to take his 'ill' wife's purge and suffer so that her health can improve and she can enjoy a hearty meal; in the second he meets his wife and Gerónimo out together and is again tricked because of his ignorance of the term *novena*. His wife explains that she will have to lock herself away (with her lover) for nine days and that he should feed on only bread and water during that time to help her recovery. Although the characters here are superficially town-dwellers, it is still the daftness of the universal *simple*, for example in his literal belief that he and his wife are one body as the priest told him on his wedding day, that would have caused the audience pleasure and amusement.

Cervantes may have admired Lope de Rueda greatly as a man of the theatre but it is his own sophisticated treatment of similar themes in a similar format in his *Entremeses*, published in 1615, that transforms the genre. The same character-types appear in Cervantes's eight farces, as do some of the same comic situations: the *malcasados* state their grievances before a judge in the *Juez de los divorcios*; figures from the *hampa*, local officials, a soldier and a *sacristán*, and a *vizcaíno fingido* feature in others; and the *cornudo* re-appears in both *La cueva de Salamanca* and the *Viejo celoso*. However, for Cervantes the *entremés* is not a plaything to cause hilarity for a few minutes and then be forgotten. The humour is much more sophisticated and has a purpose which goes well beyond the urgently entertaining and enters the broad area of the didactic (see Zimic, 'La ejemplaridad'). The playwright is not just putting a brave face on his inability to attract an *autor de comedias* to his plays when he writes in the *Viaje del Parnaso* that these works are better read 'para que se vea de espacio lo que passa apriessa, y se dissimula, o no se entiende, quando las representan' (Cervantes, *Viage del Parnaso*, p. 202). Cervantes, as ever, wants his reader to pause and think.

A glance at two of Cervantes's *entremeses* will demonstrate his creativity within the established form. The *Viejo celoso* takes up the well-worked topic of the deceived husband but manages to manipulate the audience's sympathies with some subtlety. The *viejo*, Cañizares, who has married Lorenza, only to find himself consumed by jealousy, has parallels with Carrizales of the *novela ejemplar*, *El celoso extremeño*. The coincidences between the two works are instructive, for Cervantes's purpose in both is to raise a moral question, to provide an example for his audience to ponder. Thus, the author builds up a portrait of Cañizares from the frustrated words of his wife, her maid Cristina and the archetypal busybody neighbour, Ortigosa, only to upset our expectations when his delayed entrance occurs. Cañizares *is* over half a century older than his wife, he *is* jealous to the point of obsession and he *is* sexually impotent, but he is also self-aware, admitting his foolishness and inadequacies, and is in fact tortured by his error in marrying and the deleterious effect it has had on his life. He discusses his situation with a *compadre*, whose voice of reason is less necessary in this play given the old man's self-knowledge, stating: 'el setentón que se casa con quince, o carece de entendimiento, o tiene gana de visitar el otro mundo lo más presto que le sea posible' (Cervantes, *Entremeses*, pp. 262–3) and explaining how he is haunted by jealous fears. Our sympathies in the farce are split, as they are between the husbands and wives in the *Juez de los divorcios*. When a young man is smuggled into the house behind a tapestry and out again as Cañizares is distracted by means of a bucket of water, we celebrate the carnivalesque triumph of youthful lust over jealous restrictions, but the old man's characterization complicates the feeling of triumph. The words of the song which all but ends the *entremés* seem inappropriate: as in the *Juez de los divorcios* their application to what the audience has witnessed is at best partial.

This is a play that engages the audience intellectually and is not for instant consumption. One hesitates to suggest that Cervantes's *entremeses* are 'realistic' but their firmer anchoring in recognizable, complex human affairs differentiates them from their precursors.

It is with his *Retablo de las maravillas* that Cervantes reveals the extent of his ambitions for the *entremés*. The central deception of the play belongs to popular tradition, but the targets of Cervantes's satire are particular as well as universal. Two confidence tricksters, Chanfalla and Chirinos, arrive in a village with the marvellous puppet-show of the title. They advertise and then begin the performance having informed the credulous villagers that only those who are legitimate and possess pure Old Christian blood are able to see the wondrous scenes created in the theatre. Even those locals, like the *gobernador*, who admit in asides that they cannot see any of what the tricksters describe to them, have to play along with the illusion or risk being mocked and ostracized. The illusion is broken, or at least a kind of conclusion is found to the play, when a quartermaster arrives in the village to billet his troops. His refusal to recognize the reality of the puppet-show leads to him being taunted as a Jew by the villagers, who make use of the theatre to disobey him in a way that would normally be impossible. As the scene becomes violent Chirinos and Chanfalla congratulate each other – 'El suceso ha sido extraordinario; la virtud del Retablo se queda en su punto' (Cervantes, *Entremeses*, p. 236) – and plan further deceptions. Cervantes satirizes the credulity of humankind, pointing to the ease with which a group can succumb to a belief and the violence which can flare as a result of its being challenged. No-one possesses the courage, or perhaps the innocence, of the child in the story of the *Emperor's New Clothes*, to denounce the illusion for what it is. More specifically the dramatist ridicules the widespread concern with purity of blood demonstrated by so many of his contemporaries. The peasants' anxiety to be thought Old Christian, that is, with no Jewish or Muslim blood in their families, leads ironically to their swearing that they can see not only the various animals but also the Jewish Biblical figures conjured up by the tricksters. Their 'negra honrilla', as the *gobernador*, the licenciado Gomecillos, puts it (p. 229), does not allow them to risk losing face and thus social status.

As an *entremés* relying on action and witty dialogue the *Retablo* works well. As a satire too, both universal and specific to honour-obsessed Spain, it is a success. However, the playlet is also, as one might expect from Cervantes the playwright, introspective, a rumination on theatre (especially audiences) in general and Golden Age theatre in particular. The succession of exciting incidents, paradoxically relying on their visual appeal, is meant to remind his reader of Cervantes's criticism of a national *comedia* too dependent upon special effects, rather than ideas. The audience's thirst for such entertainment is an indictment of the *vulgo*'s poor taste. Like the fool licensed to speak when others must hold their tongue, the carnivalesque *entremés* becomes, in the hands of Cervantes, a conscience-catcher.

A handful of *entremeses* survive by Francisco de Quevedo (of many that he no doubt wrote). The majority are in verse, which takes over from prose as the preferred medium of the genre. (Only two of Cervantes's eight *entremeses*, *La elección de los alcaldes de Daganzo* and the *Rufián viudo llamado Trampagos*, had been composed in verse.) Like Cervantes, Quevedo self-consciously mixes the low-life elements with the literary in his farcical theatre: certainly some of the jokes and other references depend on a knowledge of classical and contemporary culture. If Cervantes echoes in a burlesque fashion, at the start of *La cueva de Salamanca*, the parting of Virgil's Dido and Aeneas, Quevedo, in *La polilla de Madrid*, plays consistently with Paris's abduction of Helen of Troy. In this farce, Elena dresses up as a lady, disguises her mother, sister and *rufián* as servants, hires an actor's house, and fleeces her gentleman visitors – hence the 'robo de Elena'. A number of Quevedo's farcical figures seem to spring from the pages of picaresque fiction, or the verses of his satirical poetry, and rather than taking carnivalesque pleasure in their machinations, the playwright appears to have a moral agenda. This is not to say that the author has abandoned the central comic function of the *entremés*, it is rather that his moralizing tone, as ever, is more prominent than Cervantes's. Several of his farces do end traditionally in either song and dance or violent disorder, but the songs' lyrics often make a moral point. In *La polilla de Madrid* (probably written some ten years after Cervantes's *entremeses* were published), Mondoñedo simply steps forward to warn men about the wiles of womankind:

> Guárdese ya la gente,
> que el robo no es de Elena solamente,
> sino de Luisas y Anas,
> de Franciscas, [de] Aguedas y [de] Juanas.
> Que toda niña que se ingiere en lobo,
> ella es Elena y su galán el robo.   (Quevedo, *La polilla*, p. 122)

Luis Quiñones de Benavente, born in Toledo in 1581, moved to the court in 1617 after having taken holy orders in his home city. He became friends with Tirso de Molina, Luis Vélez de Guevara, and many other more minor poets, and flourished in the reign of Philip IV especially, until about 1640 when he gave up dramatic writing. Unusually he did not write *comedias*, but concentrated instead on the short forms of theatre which accompanied them, and for which there was such an appetite. Under Benavente the *entremés* and the *entremés cantado* (or *baile*) become more refined and courtly: they tend to be shorter and are always written in verse; the endings in violence disappear; the emphasis is on language, especially word-play; and 'realistic' elements are down-played as the genre becomes more stylized. The atmosphere of these pieces continues to be festive and satire of the usual seventeenth-century customs and character-types is common, but has arguably lost its cutting edge through familiarity. If Quevedo is a moralist first and foremost, Benavente, who often re-works the former's material, is above all an entertainer.

El murmurador is an *entremés representado* (that is, spoken, not sung) probably from the early 1630s. It is dominated by the *malcasados*, Quiteria and Pedro. The latter has been introduced by his wife as a misery: 'no hay cosa en el mundo, mala o buena,/ que no le enfade y de que no se pudra' (Quiñones de Benavente, *Entremeses completos*, p. 288), and he enters claiming that the ways of the world are indeed making him ill. Already a figure an audience is predisposed to laugh at, Pedro spends the rest of the play pontificating about slanderers. Benavente's witty novelty, however, is to have his protagonist complain about those who slander a particular group (lascivious widows, virgins, *casadas*, old women and doctors), and proceed to repeat all of the negative characteristics on which these slanderers concentrate their bile. The effect of course is to turn Pedro into a *murmurador* himself, and a hypocrite to boot. The creation of the mordant satire thus becomes secondary to the creation of the rather complex buffoon, and the result is something closer to a modern comic sketch with its single dominant amusing idea, than a full-blown, old-fashioned *entremés*.

Whilst *El murmurador* ends with a dance to distract Pedro from his cares, many other of Benavente's playlets are fully musical. These are the *bailes*, called *entremeses cantados* in the *Jocosería*, and are a further step removed from the *entremés* of earlier decades. *La paga del mundo* (1634–9?), for example, is entirely sung, and must have depended heavily on its choreography. The *gracioso*, dressed in a costume of mirrors in order to play the *mundo*, makes 'payments' of imprisonment and physical punishment to a series of low-life or vicious characters who attend him one by one. The work relies on repetition of lines, and patterns, like much musical theatre, but also on word-play and the euphony of the verse. *El doctor Juan Rana* (1635?), also almost entirely sung and danced, would have depended heavily on word-play too for its success, and also on a particular actor, the hugely popular *gracioso* Cosme Pérez, for whom Benavente tailored some of his material. The opening lines of the play, sung by the character Pérez made his own, Juan Rana, are meaningless unless the audience has seen the new doctor in other plays in which he has been *alcalde* (see Thompson, *The Triumphant*).

The *mojiganga*, the last of the minor forms to be considered, was closely related to the *baile* in the way it developed for the stage. It, too, was a short entertainment and differed from other forms in its carnivalesque, street origins. Characters, frequently singing and dancing, would play out the burlesque farce in extravagant costumes, often as animals. Like the *loa* and the *entremés*, the *mojiganga* evolved considerably over the decades: from ridiculous street procession, the sub-genre developed later in Calderón's career, into something closer to the *entremés* in nature.

Golden Age audiences' devotion to the *entremés* is attested to by the fact that so-called *follas* of playlets – shows made up only of examples of the shorter theatrical forms – became popular. Manuel Antonio de Vargas, who organized the publication of Quiñones de Benavente's *Jocosería*, claimed that 'el autor que tenía una mala comedia, con ponerle dos entremeses deste ingenio le daba muletas para que no cayese, y el que tenía una buena, le ponía alas para que se remontase' (Quiñones de Benavente, *Entremeses completos*, p. 112). Having confirmed the popularity of the genre, he goes on to borrow the authority of Horace in order to stress its moral usefulness (p. 113). (The *entremés*, like the *comedia* proper, was subject to cuts ordered by the censor.) Of course in a prologue of this period it is normal to exaggerate the didactic credentials of the work which succeeds it, and at bottom the *entremés* and its relatives, in the overwhelming majority of cases, were appreciated for the entertainment they brought. Their popularity stems from a number of ingredients whose combination has never failed to please an audience: slapstick action, human stupidity, word-play, music and dance.

The *auto sacramental*

Although the word *auto* was used by Rojas in his *Celestina* to refer to an 'act' or unit of action, it was also very commonly employed in the sixteenth century to denote a play in general. Encina and Vicente both used the term in the titles of some of their early dramas, not always ones on overtly religious subjects. By the end of the sixteenth century, however, the meaning of *auto sacramental* had settled to refer specifically to the kind of one-act play performed in the street in many Spanish towns and cities to celebrate the Feast of Corpus Christi. Pope Urban IV had instituted the Feast in 1264 and during the fourteenth century it began to be marked, especially in eastern Spain, by processions with tableaux and short plays. These were distinct from the Christmas and Easter plays associated with the liturgy and which were so important in the early development of theatre in Spain (see Shergold, *A History*, chapters 1 and 2).

The *auto* could never be confused with the *comedia* once the latter form had developed, even where the *corral* writers turned their attention to Biblical or religious themes, and the two traditions remained essentially separate in their performance spaces, in their formal norms, and within the public's mind. The primary purposes of the *auto* were to teach and to re-express dramatically (by moving the emotions and the intellect of the audience through the eye and the ear) the redemptive power of Christ, present in the Eucharist. Audiences familiar with the offerings of the court or the *corral* would naturally have adjusted their expectations during Corpus Christi performances to engage piously with the dramatic material, which communicated a predictable message. Here they were not the horde impatient for everything from Genesis to the Last Judgement, as Lope had characterized the *corral* crowds, but individuals presented with the Catholic universe in miniature and asked to consider their humble place in it. Visual and aural stimuli encouraged the faithful to re-affirm their beliefs and marvel at the perversity of humankind, the order of creation and the providential justice of God.

Before looking at the development of the content of the *auto* and in particular its apogee under Calderón, it is worth describing its performance as that evolved through the Golden Age. The form's origins as a part of the celebration of a religious feast-day are of course its most striking feature: the carts (*carros*) of the Corpus Christi procession, which were pulled through the streets to show their tableaux to the faithful, eventually became adjuncts to a temporary stage set up outside the church or in a square. They were two storeys high, elaborately decorated and designed often to produce spectacular appearances or effects.

They were pulled into position alongside the main stage before the performance could begin. In Madrid, which inevitably staged the most expensive *autos*, since the late sixteenth century two carts had been used for each of four plays, but from 1647, four were used as the number of plays performed annually was reduced to two. The splendour of the *autos* increased with the professionalization of the theatrical world: town councils ensured that they staged a fine event by commissioning the most successful dramatists (in Madrid this meant Calderón alone from 1648 until his death in 1681), paying handsome sums to those involved in the productions, including set designers and engineers, and requiring the best actors and actresses to stay in Madrid and perform. In terms of length, *autos* were usually composed of fewer than half the number of lines (of polymetric verse) of the average *comedia*, but their staging was more elaborate and their musical elements (especially later in Calderón's career when some became semi-operatic) were more extensive. Like the *comedia* the *auto* was introduced with a *loa* and interrupted by the performance of interludes, in spite of ecclesiastical condemnation of the practice.

The first performances of the *autos* in Madrid each year were to an audience of the elite: the king, members of the *Consejos*, and then the *Villa*. However, the people had ample chance to see the plays too, either in the capital or when the company took them on tour. It is just such a group of players that Cervantes's Don Quijote comes across in Part II, chapter 11 of the novel: the company's 'devil' explains to the knight how they have remained in their *auto* costumes because it is not worth changing between villages. Clearly these subsequent performances would lack some of the grandeur of the *première*.

At the time when Don Quijote and Sancho might have been wandering the highways of La Mancha, it was Lope de Vega and the priest from Toledo, José de Valdivielso (1565–1638), who were pre-eminent as *auto* writers. Their allegorical techniques, which had medieval roots and seventeenth-century parallels in the satirical and moralistic works of Quevedo and the Jesuit Gracián, would reach a new sophistication with dramatists of the second generation, most notably the Jesuit-trained Calderón de la Barca. Lope and Valdivielso unfold detailed allegories in which obstructive elements of human life, particularly abstract notions such as Deleite, Amor propio, Ignorancia, Voluntad, or Apetito, prevent Hombre or Género humano from seeing the truth of his departure from the path to salvation. Culpa (Original Sin) and Envidia, with other deadly sins, frequently join the devil or other *demonios* to tempt (as in the Garden of Eden) the innocent or foolish central character with superficially attractive worldly pleasures, but, as the audience knows he will be, the human representative is given a second chance thanks to the sacrifice and redemptive love of Christ. Sometimes humankind is supported by the allegorical figure of the Church or the intercession of the Virgin Mary, and sometimes Christ himself appears, as in Valdivielso's *El hospital de los locos*. In this typically well-worked allegory Género humano is kept locked up by Culpa and Locura in an asylum, where he is accompanied by Luzbel (the devil) and other enemies of humankind. Culpa leaves Locura in charge of the asylum (the world) and takes the attractive young

Deleite to seduce Alma and bring her into the madhouse too, thus claiming an apparently complete victory over goodness and innocence. However, San Pedro, God's *boticario*, seeks out the wounded Alma and provides redemptive medicine for her. The play ends with Christ appearing: 'Aparece Christo glorioso, con un cáliz y una hostia encima, y del costado seis cintas carmesíes que van a dar a seis Sacramentos. Caen los locos y la Culpa. San Pedro y el Alma, e Inspiración, de rodillas' (Valdivielso, *El hospital*, p. 265b), to explain the allegory:

> Vertí para tu rescate
> el tesoro de mis venas;
> sangre di, lágrimas pido,
> lágrimas tus ojos viertan.   (p. 266a)

Alma's willing repentance and Christ's love work together to produce the customary ending to the *auto*. Lope too is keen in his *autos* to produce a moment of revelation: he has a curtain drawn to reveal the sacrament in *El pastor lobo y cabaña celestial* (in which a good shepherd protects the lamb from a demonic wolf); and in *La siega* the final stage direction reveals a careful imagining of the visual climax of the play: 'Aquí, con música se abra la cabaña y se vea dentro una iglesia, y ésta también se abra, y dentro esté una fuente, en el remate de la cual esté un niño, de cuyo costado salgan siete cintas carmesíes a la primera basa, y della a la segunda, dando cada una en un Cáliz' (Vega, *La siega*, p. 195a).[5]

The *auto* writer faces a double challenge: he must construct an allegory that functions but that does not detract from the essential Eucharistic subject matter (the 'asunto' which never changes) and he must move the audience with his effects, poetic and visual. Calderón himself was well aware of the inevitable sameness of the *autos* he wrote but expressed pleasure in his achievement in writing them, employing another analogy in their justification: 'que el mayor primor de la naturaleza es que con unas mismas facciones haga tantos rostros diferentes' (Adeva, 'Estructura', p. 3). In fact, although the same limited range of characters re-appears regularly, the 'argumento' (the form the allegory or story takes) can vary considerably, and the ending does not have to reveal or refer directly to the host and the chalice, as long as the power of Christ's bodily sacrifice and its benefits to believers is clear.

Most Golden Age dramatists wrote *autos* as well as *comedias*. The financial rewards were good, especially once the festivities had become the responsibility of the town council in Madrid, and their composition was not limited to those, like Tirso de Molina, who had an advanced religious training. The greatest *auto* writer, though, combined a subtlety of mind and a theological training, to produce a corpus of plays recognized in his day as unsurpassable. Calderón's consistent brilliance at creating imaginative, varied and moving allegorical

---

[5] Orthography has been modernized in the *autos* from Arias's collection.

works meant that he monopolized the Madrid festivities for the last three decades of his life, and indeed continued to be the dramatist of choice in the eighty-four years after his death and before performance of the *auto sacramental* was at last prohibited in 1765.[6]

Perhaps because of its difference from the medieval mystery and miracle plays of other parts of Europe, perhaps because of its Catholic exoticism, perhaps because of an apparent inability to transcend its time and world-view (especially the denigration of Islam and Judaism), the *auto sacramental* has benefited from few general critical studies or histories.[7] And yet a reading of even a selection of Calderón's nearly eighty surviving *autos* reveals the great variety in their content or 'argumento', elicits admiration for the scope and ingenuity of their allegorical patterns, opens a rhetorical and poetic treasure trove, and above all disabuses one of the notion that they are dryly otherworldly, disconnected from the society in which the audience lived. Especially after he gave up writing new plays for the *corral* in the early 1650s, Calderón devoted considerable time and intellectual energy to his Corpus Christi plays, making them comprehensible to the masses yet theologically defensible, relating them to the life of his time, and ensuring that visually as well as poetically they inspired awe and renewed devotion to the faith.

One of Calderón's most remarkable achievements in the *autos* is his ability to present humans (by obvious extension, individual audience members) simultaneously within a local and an eternal context, revealing their place in society but also their importance to God. In his best known *auto, El gran teatro del mundo* (mid-1630s?), he uses the well-worn classical analogy of life as a play, to explain, first of all through the mouth of the character Mundo, how the *comedia*'s three acts represent the three stages of human history: from life in the Edenic paradise until the time of Noah; the time of the *ley escrita* of Moses to the crucifixion; and the *ley de gracia* or Christian period until the end of the world and Day of Judgement. Having explained the macrocosmic picture, Calderón has Autor (representing God) create a number of socially representative characters ranging from Rey to Pobre and leave them to interact in a separate short, unrehearsed *comedia* (which, we take it, runs for the duration of their lives). Their ability to be guided by what is Christian, to perform good works, and ultimately to have deserved God's grace to overcome Original Sin, is assessed at the end of the performance as the Autor's celestial globe opens to reveal him seated at a table with a chalice and the host displayed. Characters are sent to Heaven, Purgatory, Hell and Limbo, each with an explanation of why they have deserved their particular fate.

The attention to detail (poetic and visual) and subtle inter-relationships

---

[6] On the reasons for the suppression of the *autos*, see Parker, *The Allegorical Drama*, esp. pp. 18–27.

[7] Arellano provides a brief history of its reception in his *Estructuras dramáticas y alegóricas*, pp. 9–14. See also Parker, *The Allegorical Drama*, chapter 1, and my 'Suggestions for further reading', on the recent publication of Calderón's *autos*.

characteristic of Calderón's ingenious *comedias* are put to a more didactic use in the *auto*. Words and actions are all telling. Thus when Discreción, the female character who represents the church/religion, is about to fall, she is physically supported by the king, representing the performance of a role that is his by obligation in society. (The action later saves him from Purgatory). Characteristic too is the running commentary on the allegory, which anticipates objections and ensures the audience can follow the play easily: Autor admits, for example, that he could correct the characters' errors but 'les di/ albedrío superior/ a las pasiones humanas' (Calderón, *El gran teatro*, lines 931–3), which they must recognize and use for themselves. And Mundo too, in sonorous *octavas reales* that demonstrate that the most significant part of the play – death – has arrived, spells the lesson out in a rhetorical *tour de force* that demonstrates the parallels the *auto* has with the sermon:

> ¡Corta fue la comedia! Pero ¿cuándo
> no fue la comedia desta vida,
> y más para el que está considerando
> que toda es una entrada, una salida?
> Ya todos el teatro van dejando,
> a su primer materia reducida
> la forma que tuvieron y gozaron;
> polvo salgan de mí, pues polvo entraron.   (lines 1255–62)

The analogy of the world as a stage has neo-Stoic echoes and works quite well with the tenets of Catholic theology: the brevity of life, and its sudden ending, remarked upon by the play's characters, allows the playwright to insist that the individual keep his conscience clear before God. However, it also allows Calderón to examine specific roles available to those born in his era, and to do so critically. As well as sensing their place in the great scheme of things, audience members might recognize their seventeenth-century social roles and some advice on how to play them. Rico is irredeemable. Pobre stoically suffers a life of rejection and hardship until released by death. The king, who needs the help of Discreción to find his reward in heaven, boasts of his 'varias victorias' and the 'varios privados' (lines 1282–3) he has established. These are not innocently chosen terms, and the king's inability to comprehend the temporary nature of his earthly 'existence' is made even starker first by Mundo's criticism of his appointment of a 'limosnero mayor' (line 888) to salve his conscience, and then his mockingly disdainful undressing of him. The very grandeur of the monarch's words is thrown back at him in yet another Golden Age play which aims in part to present a mirror for a prince.

El gran teatro del mundo has appealed to scholars, and indeed to theatre directors, in modern times because it engages with the organization of society, and because it is underpinned by an allegory which has echoes in philosophy and a tradition in drama, including, of course, a presence in Shakespeare. However, for Calderón, although the *theatrum mundi* topos provided a good stream of allegorical equivalences, it was by no means his most seamless or proficient *auto sacramental*. A more obvious fount of allegorical equivalences for a man steeped in Biblical scholarship was the Old Testament and it was here that Calderón returned again and again for stories that were already read between the lines and seen to pre-figure the redemptive power of Christ. To give an example: in *La primer flor del Carmelo* (1647 or 1648) the story of Abigail placating David after Nabal's insult (I Samuel 25) represents the Virgin Mary's intercession before Christ to help to redeem ignorant humankind; *La piel de Gedeón* (1650), *Primero y segundo Isaac* (1658?), and *El cordero de Isaías* (1681) are amongst many others that bring to life the implications of Old Testament stories, foreshadowing the Christian era.

Christ's parables from the Gospels, with their allegorical bases, are also obvious sources of *auto argumentos*: *Llamados y escogidos*, written for Toledo's 1643 Corpus Christi celebrations, and starring Cosme Pérez as Verdad, is an obvious candidate given that the table of the parable of the wedding guests (Matthew 22:2–14) can double as the table of the Last Supper. Indeed the ending of the play features a *tramoya* in which the table is suddenly flipped over to reveal the usual chalice and host. Calderón is conscious that in having Daniel and Isaías invite Sinagoga and Gentilidad to the wedding of the Príncipe (Christ) to the Esposa (humankind) he is playing with Biblical chronology, and he has Rey (God) explain self-consciously that:

> uno y otro habéis de ver,
> advirtiendo que en sentido
> alegórico esto es
> una representación
> en que no importa que esté
> el tiempo alterado viendo
> lo que ha sido y ha de ser.   (Calderón, *Llamados*, lines 120–6)

Although the time of Christ's coming is anachronistically implanted into the world of the Old Testament, artistically the allegory works well, allowing for the history of the rejection and acceptance of the Christian message, with its contemporary ramifications, to be seen and understood plainly.

Such coherent and imaginative re-working of existing material was, as we have seen, typical of Calderón's *comedia* output, and his imagination worked within tighter confines to produce a similarly brilliant result where the *autos* were concerned. Thus, in *La humildad coronada*, also written for Toledo, but for the following year's celebration, and sometimes known as the *Auto sacramental de los árboles*, he takes his inspiration from Judges 9:7–21, but transforms the source almost beyond recognition. The dramatist exploits the popular 'characteristics' of trees, the mad almond, the prudent mulberry and so on, to weave an allegory in which the humble ear of corn and vine (sources of the bread and wine of the Eucharist) become monarchs amongst their more illustrious fellows for the devotion they show to the murdered cedar (representing the cross and thus Christ). In *La devoción de la misa* (1658?), an 'auto historial alegórico' in its author's words, it is indeed a historico-legendary event that inspires

Calderón: the tarrying of a soldier, called Pascual Vivas in this version of the tenth-century legend, at Mass, leads to his replacement in battle by an angel, who destroys the army of Almanzor, Muslim king of Córdoba. Even classical mythology could provide sacramental material: in *El divino Orfeo* (1663) Calderón exploits recognized echoes in the story of Orpheus's descent into the underworld to rescue Euridice, reading it as an allegorical equivalent of Christ's descent to save humankind.

Two important points regarding the *auto* remain to be discussed in more detail. The first involves the question of how contemporary these Corpus plays were in their frames of reference. Obviously the dramatist's first responsibility was to celebrate the great mystery of the transubstantiation and its implications, a universal truth for Catholics. It has been argued that propagandistically another of the *auto*'s functions may have been to counter the Protestant schism and re-affirm the tenets of post-Tridentine Catholicism. However, there remains considerable work to be carried out on the engagement of the *auto* with Golden Age society in more particular ways. By addressing individuals and asking members of the audience to examine their own consciences and observances, dramatists also commonly referred to contemporary events, or employed a double setting and time-frame. Good examples of such *autos* are Calderón's *El nuevo palacio del Retiro* (1634), written to celebrate the building of Philip IV's palace by Olivares, and *El indulto general* (1680), which refers to the pardon granted to the prisoners of the *cárcel de Atocha* by Charles II after his marriage.[8] The fascinating *auto*, *Las pruebas del linaje humano y encomienda del hombre*, ascribed to José de Valdivielso, depicts the figure of Hombre, keen to prove his nobility to the *Consejo de las Órdenes* so that he can marry Gracia, daughter of Libre Albedrío. There is undoubtedly a satirical stab aimed by the author at the arcane procedures and perverted justice of this influential seventeenth-century *Consejo*, which preferred purity of blood to Christian virtue. The procedures of the holy *Consejo* of the *auto*, by contrast, are seen to be not only just, but also merciful.

The second issue is to do with the performance of the *auto*. When he came to publish a volume of his Corpus plays in 1677, Calderón expressed concern at how they would come across when read rather than seen and heard: 'el papel no puede dar de sí, ni lo sonoro de la música, ni lo aparatoso de las tramoyas' (Parker, *The Allegorical Drama*, p. 17). Like the late mythological plays he wrote, the *autos* were always primarily dramatic events designed in detail to move an audience through its senses. Calderón was creating a set of images and aural stimuli as much as he was writing a text. In neither hearing nor seeing the *autos*, readers lose much of their essence. Primitive audiences at Corpus Christi plays would have understood oppositions expressed musically; for example, the devil's attempts to seduce man with 'sensorial', beautiful sounding music, that

---

[8] See also Greer's 'Constituting Community' for a study of two further *autos* whose performance had socio-political implications.

nevertheless fails to echo a divine harmony that *is* reflected in snatches of songs heard off-stage, as in the repeated line of *El gran teatro del mundo*: 'Obrar bien, que Dios es Dios'. Humans must ignore the superficial enjoyment to be found in music and listen instead for divine harmony: the voice of God that keeps the elements in balance and strikes a chord within the microcosm that is man. This harmony will sound different to different individuals, such as Rico and Pobre, just as a preacher's encouragement to act well may inspire or fall on deaf ears.[9] Certain instruments, such as the *chirimía*, are associated with the divine harmony, and would have had an instant effect on the *auto* audience that cannot be re-created without a performance tradition.

Visually too Calderón was a perfectionist. A number of his *memorias de apariencias* for his *autos* survive: these were instructions, in effect detailed stage directions, for what he expected from the performance in terms of costume, decoration of the carts, and special effects. Thus in *Llamados y escogidos* the *carro triunfal* which brings the Príncipe to the stage after 126 lines must be pulled by 'cuatro animales bien imitados, los delanteros un león y un toro, los otros un ángel y un águila' and the final special effect with the reversible table is anticipated thus:

> de debajo del tablado ha de salir a su tiempo una mesa grande muy bien adornada de viandas . . . y sus servicios; en medio de ella ha de haber un cordero, y todo esto ha de ser clavado de manera que pueda la mesa volverse y en lugar de todas estas viandas quedar sobre gradillas con sus luces una custodia con un cáliz y hostia.   (Calderón, *Llamados*, p. 30)

Not only could the dramatist emphasize the most significant moments of the allegory with *tramoyas*, he could also create meaningful tableaux, and make visual reference to biblical passages (as with the four animals pulling the cart, of Revelation 4:7) for an audience well able to 'read' such visual clues. Whilst all readers of plays must use their imaginations to envisage a staging, such a practice becomes essential for an appreciation of the *auto sacramental* in its allusive and spectacular complexity.

---

[9] See Sage, 'The Function', for a fine explanation of Calderón's sophisticated use of music in his *autos* and other plays.

7

A Brief History of Reception

The full history of the reception of Spanish Golden Age drama is yet to be written, and there is no space here (nor should there be in a *Companion*) to attempt to produce one. However, one of the more significant lessons that modern approaches to literature have taught us is that responses to works of art can never be fixed or eternal, and indeed they reveal at least as much about its audience (reader or spectator) as about the art itself. It is worth briefly outlining some of the characteristic and influential reactions to the works of Lope de Vega and his fellows as a curtain-call to this volume. An idea of trends in reception will help to explain the tenor of much scholarly writing on the *comedia nueva* and thus provide an essential context for further reading on the subject. We shall deal with reactions to performances and to readings of the drama from its inception to the present day.

In its early years and its heyday the *comedia nueva* attracted criticism on two main fronts: from moralists (mainly churchmen), who were scandalized in part by the inherent dangers of drama itself, and more often by the infectious depravity they saw in the world of the theatre, and from *preceptistas*, who objected on aesthetic grounds to its crowd-pleasing, unclassical form. The battle between moralists and supporters of the theatre was fought over a long period with its intensity varying in different places and at different times. In some cities, especially in the south of Castile, moralists' arguments had more success, but overall the closure of the theatres was much more likely to be occasioned by a royal death, as in 1597, 1644 and 1665, than by pressure from the anti-theatre lobby. The lobbying did intensify however, whenever the theatres were closed during a period of royal mourning (see Whicker, *The Plays*, p. 16). The silencing of Tirso de Molina in the early years of the reign of Philip IV, another time of anxiety about the role of the theatre, is further evidence of the critics' success (see p. 62). Two of the factors that worked in favour of the theatre were the court's fascination with dramatic performances throughout almost the whole of the Golden Age period, and the dependence of the hospitals on revenue from the *corrales*.

A taste of the kind of arguments marshalled against the theatre can be gleaned from an influential document in part composed by Don García de Loaisa y Girón, one-time canon of Toledo (perhaps the inspiration for Cervantes's canon of *Don Quijote*, I, 47–8?), who performed important roles in the court of Philip II. It is entitled 'Parecer . . . sobre la prohibición de las comedias', being the report of an inquiry conducted into the theatre in the realm, and outlines a series of reasons why entertainments should not recommence in 1598.[1] These include the following: actresses ensnare gentlemen, which leads to scandal and financial ruin (for the gentlemen); plays give the public a distorted view of history; other nations are ridiculed and insulted in the *comedia*; companies of actors are dissolute and full of criminals; the theatre can remind present generations of past wickedness; it encourages evil thoughts and corrupts the innocent (especially young women); it distracts people from their work (including students) and encourages them to part with their hard-earned money; and it diverts men from military pursuits, making them effeminate.

These sorts of arguments, with supporting material from theological texts recur frequently throughout the seventeenth century. By the 1640s straitened circumstances meant that the theatre was also criticized on the grounds of its excesses, for example in costume. Nevertheless, in 1648 the *Consejo de Castilla* argued for a return to dramatic performances. The theatre, the *Consejo* reminded Philip IV, was not criticized by Thomas Aquinas or by many other theologians and classical commentators. In addition, since the king approved of such entertainments they should be deemed acceptable; the people required distraction from the wars; the suspension of *corral* entertainments in 1644 had had no effect on behaviour, indeed moral turpitude was greater than ever; love comedies were not immoral but ended in Christian marriage; and anyway contemporary morals were so bad that the theatre could not teach anything new (Cotarelo y Mori, *Bibliografía*, pp. 165–9).

The *preceptistas* objected to the new kind of theatre because of its deliberate abandonment of the *arte*, by which they meant Aristotle's *Poetics* as they had been interpreted and propagated by Italians, such as Robortelli and Castelvetro, in the sixteenth century. Lope de Vega's *Arte nuevo*, with its tongue-in-cheek defence of speaking to the *vulgo* audience in its own base terms, since it actually paid to watch the drama, was published thirteen years after López Pinciano's Aristotelian *Philosophía antigua poética* (1596), just after the canon of Toledo's opinions expressed in *Don Quijote*, I (1605), and eight years before Francisco Cascales's *Tablas poéticas* and Pedro de Torres Rámila's anti-Lopean *Spongia* (both 1617), the latter of which has unfortunately not survived. The aesthetic failings of the theatre are most succinctly enumerated by the priest and the canon in *Don Quijote*: they complain about the dependence on the spectacular and the unlikely, which panders to the lowest common denominator in the audience; the canon argues for plays which follow the old 'arte' and are not 'conocidos disparates y cosas que no llevan pies ni cabeza' (Cervantes, *Don Quijote*, I, p. 568), and presents as ideal, works by the generation (including Cervantes himself) who wrote classically inspired plays in the 1580s. The *cura* goes on to criticize the theatre's standard breaches of the neo-classical unities of time and place, decorum and verisimilitude, singling out the abuses of 'comedias divinas' (p. 570) for especial opprobrium (see pp. 146–7). Plays could, in an ideal

---

[1] The document is reproduced in Cotarelo y Mori's invaluable *Bibliografía*, pp. 392–7.

world, make the audience '[salir] alegre con las burlas, enseñado con las veras, admirado de los sucesos, discreto con las razones, advertido con los embustes, sagaz con los ejemplos, airado contra el vicio y enamorado de la virtud' (p. 571). The Horatian ideal of combining profit with pleasure is thus invoked, and the priest goes on to suggest that a censor, 'una persona inteligente y discreta' (p. 572), examine all plays before they are allowed to be performed.

The views of the neo-classicists, like Cervantes's fictional Catos, and their worries for Spain's literary honour, were submerged by the tide of plays written for court and *corral* over subsequent decades, and by the sheer popularity of the theatre, which raised Lope in particular to a mythical status within his own lifetime. However, when similar voices re-emerged a century or so later, they took a long and hugely detrimental revenge on the *comedia nueva*.

Whilst Golden Age drama, particularly by writers of the second generation (especially Calderón and Moreto), continued to be performed through the eighteenth century, and was clearly commercially successful, the artistic norms of the genre were not to the taste of the intelligentsia. An air of embarrassment at, for example, the seriousness with which Lope's *Arte nuevo* might have been taken, is obvious in the neo-classicists. Ignacio de Luzán's *Poética* of 1737, for example, criticizes Lope's theoretical work: its author asserts that 'él solo basta para convencer aun a sus mismos secuaces del desorden y extravagancia de nuestro teatro'.[2] The Spain that oversaw the cessation of the performance of *autos sacramentales* in 1765 had little time for a theatre that was to the taste of the populace. Whilst there was a certain identification by the academy with the theatre of Cervantes, for its perceived classicism, that of Lope was thought to require re-writing to be acceptable. Prejudices of class also played their part in the denigration of Lope: Calderón, said Luzán, was superior as an artist to Lope because of his up-bringing and his courtly role and religious credentials.

The nineteenth century's reaction to Golden Age drama was more ambivalent. On the one hand the tendency to re-write *comedias* (creating what were termed *refundiciones*), apparent towards the end of the eighteenth century, gathered pace; on the other, there was a nascent sense of the importance of the Golden Age theatrically, its drama's status as 'clásico' in the more general, national sense, and a desire to preserve and analyse it. To elaborate on the former tendency: it became the norm for plays by Tirso, Lope, Rojas Zorrilla and their fellows to be re-worked and made to abide by neo-classical rules. Both form and content were adjusted to suit the apparently more sophisticated tastes of a bourgeois audience, and the men who undertook the re-workings became successful playwrights in their own right. The most significant was Dionisio Solís (1774–1834), who produced 25 *refundiciones* of Golden Age works and

---

2 Enrique García Santo-Tomás's fascinating *La creación del Fénix: recepción crítica y formación canónica del teatro de Lope de Vega*, in which Luzán's words are quoted (p. 198), is the fullest history of the reception of the *comedia* although it concentrates on the figure of Lope.

whose version of Lope's *El mejor alcalde, el rey*, was repeatedly a box-office success in the first half of the century (see Gies, pp. 124–6).[3]

The most significant influence on scholarly attitudes to Golden Age drama at this time was that of the German Romantics, particularly the brothers Friedrich and August Wilhelm Schlegel. The Romantics' interest, like that of Shelley in the early 1820s, was primarily in Calderón, who was praised along with Shakespeare for his creative freedom and sensitivity to the depths of human expression. Lope, by contrast, was thought of as light and superficial. In fact versions of plays by Lope (and to a lesser extent Tirso) had become more popular on the stage than adaptations of Calderón in nineteenth-century Spain. It was Adolf Friedrich, count of Schack, who was principally responsible for a more positive critical reassessment of Lope in his *Historia de la literatura y del arte dramático en España*, first published in German in 1845. Schack saw Lope as a precursor of the Romantic dramatist, keen to reject the classical rules for something more appropriate and modern. As to Lope's claim that he avoided the classical style and wrote simply what the populace demanded: that was a red herring. Whilst classicists were wont to copy another civilization's model of art (France, and ancient Rome, were guilty of this), Lope, like Shakespeare, was the example *par excellence* of the *poeta nacional popular*, that is the poetic dramatist who expressed the spirit of his age and his people without recourse to limiting models. In Schack's words: '¡cuánto aventaja el drama creado por él [Lope de Vega], en consonancia con el espíritu nacional y con la vida íntima del pueblo, a todo aquello que hubiese alcanzado sólo con el arte imitativo!' (Schack, *Historia de la literatura*, II, p. 429). Lope then, almost in spite of himself, became the voice of his people, able to remain faithful to the spirit of their history. As such he was a species of genius.[4]

This view of Lopean drama (the forbidding Calderón was always a case apart) was reflected in other German writing (for example, Bouterwek's) and in Spanish and English nineteenth-century literary histories. For Antonio Gil de Zárate the Spanish people were a block of marble containing a beauty which the poet Lope was able to perceive intuitively and then sculpt with his chisel (García Santo-Tomás, *La creación*, p. 311). The idea that Lope was an uncritical conduit for the spirit and essence of the early-modern Spaniard became a commonplace, appearing too in the American Ticknor's influential history, and it persisted well into the twentieth century. Pfandl's guide to Golden Age literature, published in German in 1928, is a case in point, as is Gerald Brenan's *The Literature of the Spanish People*, in which the author writes:

> I will sum them [Lope's plays] up by saying that they constitute a vast panegyric in praise of Spain and the Spanish way of life, and in particular of the

---

[3] For a detailed study of the phenomenon, see Ganelin, *Rewriting Theatre*. For the case of Solís's *El mejor alcalde, el rey*, see García Santo-Tomás, *La creación*, pp. 281–308.

[4] See Oleza, 'Claves románticas', for further details.

principal occupation of Spaniards at that time – love. . . . nothing is ever gone
into deeply . . . there is a lack of social criticism.

(Brenan, *The Literature*, p. 208).

Calderón, on the other hand, was seen to epitomize Spanish traditional values,
which belonged to a higher plane, and he came to be abused for political ends.
For example, the surge of enthusiasm with which the two-hundredth anniversary
of his death was celebrated in 1881 disguised a parochial attempt to re-establish
Catholic orthodoxy and absolutism in a world which was elsewhere being revo-
lutionized (Rodríguez Cuadros, *Calderón*, pp. 31–45).

Whatever the reasons in this period for scholars' interest in Golden Age
drama, and however simplistic some of these views might seem, the nineteenth
century was crucial for its preservation. Some plays of the period are still most
easily accessed in the *Biblioteca de Autores Españoles* series or in similar
collections dedicated to the works of one or more dramatists by scholars who
were committed and far-sighted.

The reception of Golden Age drama in the twentieth century cannot be
simply characterized. On the stage, within Spain, plays continued to be
performed but without what might be termed a performance tradition ever really
forming, which was perhaps due to changing political contexts, and perhaps to
the lack of a national theatre company which might have given a sense of conti-
nuity, explored the canon and educated actors in how to speak the poets' verse
and in other technical matters. The beginning of the century saw the end of the
refundición, and the 1930s the creation of companies intent on taking the theatre
to the people, to rural areas with their less educated populations. One such
enterprise was La Barraca, whose literary and artistic directors were Eduardo
Ugarte and Federico García Lorca: the student company achieved considerable
success in popularizing works by Cervantes, Lope, Calderón and others. Then in
1937, during the Civil War, Rafael Alberti staged Cervantes's *Numancia* in a
Madrid surrounded by pro-Franco forces, in a production that is probably the
best documented example of Golden Age theatre used for political purposes.
Under Franco, on stage and sometimes on screen, the canon was restricted to
works which could be made to appear to uphold the requisite models of Catholic
Spanishness – a state of affairs which requires further academic study.[5] The
Franco period has left a legacy that is beginning slowly to disappear: in some
quarters, where anti-Castilian feelings have run high in the past, there is still a
reluctance to think of Golden Age plays as *the* national drama, and to test them
on the stage. The effects of past 'pomposas y pías versiones calderonianas'
(Rodríguez Cuadros, *Calderón*, p. 42) – presented on and off the stage – are still
discernible in some monolithic readings (of Calderón, in particular) which see
the same central ideas behind all of his works whether devotional or comic.

In the democratic era, the establishment of the Compañía Nacional de Teatro

<hr />

[5] For a brief reference to this period and further bibliography, see García Lorenzo and
Muñoz Carabantes, 'El teatro de Calderón', pp. 421–2.

Clásico in Madrid in 1986 under the direction of Adolfo Marsillach, as well as the Almagro festival, running since 1978, has ensured that Golden Age plays have been allowed to breathe again. Meanwhile Pilar Miró's film version of Lope's *El perro del hortelano*, a huge box-office success in Spain, has not produced the excitement of interest in other works by Lope and his contemporaries that might have been expected from the world of the cinema. Whilst there are a large number of plays still awaiting their first modern performance, let alone adaptation to the screen, there are, however, signs in Spain and abroad that the last unopened 'treasure trove' of European theatre will gradually see its gems put on show on the world's stages. A well established festival on the Mexican–US border at El Paso, run by the Association for Hispanic Classical Theatre, attracts groups who perform several plays annually in Spanish and in English translation. In the United Kingdom, there has been a noticeable increase in productions in translation in recent years, from the award-winning season at The Gate Theatre in London in the early 1990s to the Royal Shakespeare Company's major season of four plays in 2004.[6] It would appear that major companies are beginning to appreciate the quality and thus the box-office appeal of Golden Age drama.

In chapter 5 comment was passed on the difficulty for scholars that the lack of a performance tradition causes when they come to assess and analyse the *comedia nueva*. Whilst it is taken for granted in modern times that the works of Shakespeare and his English contemporaries are open to interpretation in different fashions at the hands of directors and acting companies, 'literary' critics of the *comedia*, usually based in universities, have tended to 'considerar el fenómeno de la Comedia española como un monolito sujeto a unos mismos esquemas estructurales y obediente a unas convenciones (estéticas e ideológicas) inalterables e igualmente rígidas' (Arellano, *Convención*, p. 7). Two of the most influential of these dogmatic approaches – those of A. A. Parker and José Antonio Maravall – originated in the second half of the twentieth century. Parker developed, from his deep immersion in the literature and culture of the Golden Age, an approach (which he originally called *the* approach) to the drama which prioritized theme over character and other elements of the play:

> What the dramatist offers us, then, is not a series of complete characters, but a complete action. By a complete action I do not only mean one that hangs together, that ties up at the end all the loose strands, I mean an action that is a significant whole, one that discloses a theme that has a significant bearing on experience, a theme that can be taken out of the particular action and universalised in the form of an important judgement on some aspect of human life. (Parker, *The Approach*, p. 7)

---

6 The term 'treasure trove' was used in the publicity for the RSC's season, which played in Stratford, Newcastle, and London, and toured to Madrid, where the plays were performed with surtitles.

For Parker, poetic justice was a defining feature of the genre, which helped the audience of any period to understand the moral purpose of the theme chosen. However, for scholars who took issue with Parker, notably Pring-Mill ('Los calderonistas'), the approach was too morally and formally neat and failed to take sufficiently into account the complex relationship of plays to their historical contexts, in particular their potentially subversive function. Looking back critically at the work of British Hispanists represented by Parker and E. M. Wilson, from the vantage point of 1990, George Mariscal emphasized the need 'to see that early modern literature in Spain may have had a political function, that is, local rather than universal' (Mariscal, 'An Introduction', p. 20). This concentration on the intimacy of the work's relationship to its contexts, in some cases directly inspired by New Historicism, has become a feature of *comedia* scholarship in recent years, and is beginning to dissolve some of the old clichés about the genre.[7] Melveena McKendrick explains, for example, how Lope 'could deploy a range of manoeuvres [in his drama] to question, insinuate and probe, to explore with exactly measured diplomacy an adversarial position' (McKendrick, *Playing the King*, p. 212). And Parker's down-playing of the importance of character has also been questioned, especially by scholars who tend to emphasize the need to take performance into account in interpreting the *comedia*.[8]

The other major critical tendency in the academy has been that inspired by the work of Maravall. Put at its simplest Maravall's theory sees the *comedia* as 'una gran campaña de propaganda social, destinada a difundir y fortalecer una sociedad determinada' (Maravall, *Teatro y literatura*, p. 13). It is a political and social tool which:

> trata de imponer o de mantener la presión de un sistema de poder, y, por consiguiente, una estratificación y jerarquía de grupos, sobre un pueblo que, en virtud del amplio desarrollo de su vida durante casi dos siglos anteriores, se salía de los cuadros tradicionales del orden social, o por lo menos, parecía amenazar seriamente con ello.   (p. 18)

Whilst the nature of this connection between art and society, that is how the monarchical–seigneurial status quo is actively maintained through such a rich and varied drama written by a host of different individuals in many distinct contexts, is never adequately explained by Maravall, his ideas have continued to attract adherents within Spain and beyond its borders. Thus, for example, Anthony Cascardi nuances Maravall's views to write that 'the *comedia* may be regarded as an effort to educate the *vulgo* in the enjoyment of their condition as subjects; they are "instructed" by the genre to derive pleasure from their social

---

[7] On New Historicism, see Madrigal, ed., *New Historicism and the Comedia*. See also Evans, 'Golden Age Dramatic Criticism Now', and Thacker, 'Re-thinking Golden Age Drama', which assesses some modern critical/theoretical approaches to the *comedia*, and contains further bibliography.

[8] See, for example, Dixon, *Characterization*, and Ruano de la Haza, 'Trascendencia'.

"service" ' (Cascardi, *Ideologies*, p. 43). However, such overarching explanations of the *comedia* phenomenon are generally less enthusiastically supported
than they once were. McKendrick's words are again useful in suggesting why:
she argues that 'to claim that the theatre . . . was directly harnessed to the
purposes of government and class is seriously to underestimate the complexity
of the relationship between the Spanish theatre of the day and the society that
produced it' (McKendrick, *Playing the King*, p. 5). Research done on the history
of the period, the attempts to relate plays to particular historical moments,
recognition of differences between dramatists (some more institutionalized than
others), an acknowledgement that the play will not be uniformly received by all
the members of a socially varied *corral* audience, a growing awareness of the
generic limitations of the canon of plays habitually studied, and a slow move
away from analysing the theatre primarily as literature, have all helped to undermine a monolithic approach to the creation and role of the *comedia*.

One of the more significant developments of the last two decades has been an
increase in academics' post-structuralist approaches to Golden Age drama.
Modern 'theory' has not in fact been as pervasive, especially within Spain itself,
as it has in other disciplines or areas of Hispanic Studies. Indeed it has been
seen, for example by Arellano, as another obstacle to a fuller understanding of
the drama because of its 'anacronismo' (Arellano, *Conveción*, p. 9). It need not
be so. Some of the insights of post-structuralism, especially where they begin to
erode or undermine the authority or claim to truth of language, are as applicable
to works of the early-modern period as to those written today.[9] New Historicists
have tried, with some success, to uncover the points at which the *comedia*
exposes fault-lines in, or contests at some level, the predominant beliefs and
structures of its historical context.[10] Feminist approaches to the *comedia* have
drawn out under-researched aspects of some plays, notably Calderón's *La dama
duende* and Tirso's *El vergonzoso en palacio*, as well as ensuring that plays
written by women attract scrutiny.[11]

Late twentieth-century theoretical approaches to the *comedia* have not all
been enlightening by any means, however. Too often the application of this or
that theorist's work to a specific *comedia* has not been adequately justified, or
the results that the investigation produces have shed little or no further light on
the object under scrutiny. Much more notable in terms of the future of the study
of Golden Age drama have been the increase in productions of plays of the
period alluded to above, with the possibilities they open for performance-based
study, and the long overdue *fin-de-siècle* explosion in critical editions of works.
Lope de Vega's complete *Partes* are in the hands of the ProLope group at the
Autónoma in Barcelona; GRISO, at the Universidad de Navarra, is working on
Calderón's *Autos sacramentales completos*, and the Instituto de Estudios

---

[9] See, for example, Smith's reading of Tirso's *El burlador de Sevilla* in *Writing in the
Margin*, chapter 4, and Sullivan's 'Jacques Lacan'.

[10] See Madrigal, ed., *New Historicism*.

[11] See the two volumes edited by Stoll and Smith.

Tirsianos, at the same university, on Tirso de Molina's *Obras completas*; William Manson and George Peale are producing the works of Luis Vélez de Guevara in the US; and Mira de Amescua's drama is being edited under the direction of Agustín de la Granja at the University of Granada. All of these projects are producing the sort of scholarly editions that *comedia* readers have been short of in the past, and that will undoubtedly broaden the canon of works studied.

The two plays that have arguably most contributed to non-specialists' impressions of Golden Age drama are the canonical *Fuente Ovejuna* and *La vida es sueño*. Both are works that have transcended their contexts and have come to represent Spanish theatre of the period. Whilst both are fine plays which deserve to be edited, studied and performed, they cannot, with a handful of other old favourites, do justice to the richness of the tradition of which they form a small part. Thus if the most noteworthy development in the reception of the *comedia nueva* of recent years does turn out to be the production of scholarly editions of a host of other plays, it will be a very welcome step indeed.

APPENDIX 1

VERSE FORMS

The fact that Golden Age drama is written in verse is the first thing that a student will notice when beginning to read a play from the period. However, versification is the least discussed of the important aspects of the *comedia nueva*. Poetic drama has not been in fashion for some time and can seem daunting to a new reader, especially when it is polymetric and so obviously lacks the uniformity of appearance of French classical and Shakespearean drama. Its polymetry has probably acted as an obstacle to the performance of Golden Age theatre both in Spain, where uncertainty about how to speak the verse has been evident, and in other countries, where verse acts as an impediment to translators (see appendix 2).

In fact, once the few rules outlined below have been digested, it is not difficult, even for an inexperienced reader, to tell verse forms apart on the page.[1] What is harder to recover is the Golden Age audience's apparent ability to hear changes in metre and form and thus be sensitive to the shifts of mood and other subtleties that came with them. Verse forms often changed with the end of a *salida* or 'scene', that is after the stage had briefly emptied, or with a change in the status or objective of the speaker, or of the mood of the dialogue. They do not always have the same functions, and as fashions and personal predilections changed so different dramatists favoured different forms at different times, to the extent (as we have seen) that many of Lope de Vega's plays have been fairly reliably dated by the preponderance of certain types of verse within them.

Inevitably the starting place for the discussion of this issue is Lope's *Arte nuevo*, in which the following lines of advice occur:

> Acomode los versos con prudencia
> a los sujetos de que va tratando.
> Las décimas son buenas para quejas;
> el soneto está bien en los que aguardan;
> las relaciones piden los romances,
> aunque en octavas lucen por extremo.

---

[1] Most modern editions of Golden Age plays include an 'analysis' of their versification in the scholarly introduction. In practice this is usually presented in tabular form, and demonstrates which forms are used when, and how prevalent each form is.

> Son los tercetos para cosas graves,
> y para las de amor las redondillas.   (Vega, *Arte nuevo*, p. 17)

The prudence of the dramatic poet, alluded to in the first line here, surely refers to the need for the verse form to match the situation or speaker, so that no offence is committed against decorum. The remaining six lines provide a fascinating exemplification of this prudence rather than a complete and binding guide to *comedia* versification.[2] Thus the sonnet is not always spoken by a character awaiting some development, but it often summarizes a predicament while the scene of the action changes: similarly *redondillas* are not uniformly employed for love scenes, but were the staple form for Lope over a substantial period, whereas for Calderón the *romance* was the 'basic' form.

The verse forms used can be most readily divided into the Spanish and the Italianate. The former, which include most notably the *romance* (or ballad form), the *redondilla*, the *quintilla*, and the *décima*, are octosyllabic (lines of eight syllables) and native to Spain. Enthusiasm for the latter, represented most commonly in the *comedia* by *tercetos*, *octavas reales*, the sonnet, *versos sueltos*, the *silva*, and the *lira* forms, stemmed from the introduction of Italian verse into Spain in the sixteenth century. Garcilaso de la Vega and Juan Boscán had been encouraged by their friend Castiglione, in the 1520s and 1530s, to experiment in Spanish with forms such as the Petrarchan sonnet and their poetry was much imitated. These forms contained hendecasyllables sometimes interspersed with heptasyllables (eleven- and seven-syllable lines). Hendecasyllabic lines demanded a stress on either the sixth, or the fourth and eighth, syllables.

Before providing examples of some of the above, it is worth outlining the procedure to be adopted when counting syllables in a line as a first step to discovering the form in which it is written. A line of poetry will be either *agudo*, *llano*, or *esdrújulo*: that is, the final stress will fall (respectively) on its final, penultimate, or antepenultimate syllable. In the case of an *agudo* word, the final stressed syllable counts as two, thus the word 'amor' at the end of a verse would count as three syllables in total; in the second case, a *llano* word (the most common type), such as 'vida', would count as the expected two syllables; and in the last case, an *esdrújulo* word loses its penultimate syllable when it ends a line, so that 'mérito', despite appearances, counts only as two (and might assonate with other words, e.g. 'bueno', that end in the *e-o* vowel combination). Once these rules for line endings are accounted for, a poet has a little room for manoeuvre to ensure that a verse does not become irregular, i.e. fail to contain the correct number of syllables for the form he is employing. Where two vowels (or vowel sounds) follow each other between words, the poet can merge them into one syllable: thus the *llano* line '¡Di/cho/so al/ber/gue/ mí/o!' consists of seven syllables because the last syllable of '¡Di/cho/so' and the start of 'al/ber/gue/' naturally merge. This is called 'synaloepha' and is normal proce-

---

2   See Dixon, 'The Study of Versification', p. 385. This study also contains a useful bibliography of works dedicated to versification in the *comedia*.

dure, even bridging commas and full stops between words. Where a poet forces a separation between such mergers to attain a different syllable count, hiatus occurs. In the example quoted, the line could become '¡Di/cho/so/ al/ber/gue/ mí/o!' and have eight syllables.

This same merging or forced separation is possible within words as well. Where two vowels would usually be pronounced as two syllables in a single word, e.g. 'gran/je/**ar**', they can be made to equate to one, and where a diphthong would normally be pronounced as one syllable (because it contains the weak vowels, 'i' or 'u'), e.g. 'g**ua**r/dar', the vowels can be forced apart to make two. The former practice is called 'syneresis' and the latter 'dieresis'. The most effective way to count the syllables in a poem is to find the first line in which none of these four possibilities can intrude. Once the syllable count of the verse is made accurately, one can then look for patterns of rhyme or assonance to deduce the verse type.

The common forms

Redondilla

The following four-verse stanza is taken from Casilda's ABC of love, in Lope's *Peribáñez*. It is an intimate love-scene, well-suited to the form, especially when contrasted with the *comendador*'s later praising of her beauty in the more refined *lira* (see below):

> La/ (e)/F(e)/ de/ fá/cil/ tra/to,
> la/ G/ ga/lán/ pa/ra/ mí,
> la/ (ha/c)H(e) ho/nes/to, y /la/ I
> sin/ pen/sa/mien/to/ de in/gra/to.[3]

The *redondilla* is octosyllabic and has full consonantal rhyme in the pattern *abba* (that is, 'trato' of the first line rhymes with 'ingrato' of the last, and the middle two lines share a different rhyme). The *agudo* ending of the middle lines, in the example above, means that the final (eighth) syllable is understood. The fourth line of the *redondilla* can often pack a witty punch as we await the matching rhyme from line 1: here one can imagine the actress pausing as she struggles to think of a noble quality beginning with 'i' to describe her new husband, before cleverly reversing the implications of 'ingrato', and stretching the rules of the game. Guillén de Castro's *Los mal casados de Valencia*, which also contains a lengthy, witty word game in Act 1, is, as it happens, written entirely in *redondillas*.

---

[3] In the examples I employ I have divided some of the lines of verse up, using a '/' in order to provide further examples of syllable counting and the operation of synaloepha etc.

Romance

The ballad line, often used for narrative, was the most familiar to Spaniards as it formed a significant part of oral culture. It was also octosyllabic and depended not on consonantal rhyme but on even lines assonating in any one of a number of patterns of vowels: í-a; o-e; a-a; a-o, -í, etc. The following excerpt is the opening of Pedro's life story taken from Cervantes's *Pedro de Urdemalas*:

> Yo/ soy/ hi/jo/ de/ la/ pied/ra,
> que/ pad/re/ no/ co/no/cí:
> desdicha de las mayores
> que a un hombre pueden venir.

The assonance here is a stressed 'i' on the seventh, *agudo* (and thus final) syllable of the even lines: -cí, -ir. The effect of the *agudo* endings, especially over a long speech such as this one, is to provide a rhythmic, almost insistent beat to the lines. There is no time to dwell on the story, which, like his life, moves on regardless, and little room for a sympathy that Pedro anyway does not demand.

Quintilla

This form, also octosyllabic, was not mentioned by Lope in the *Arte nuevo*, but is heavily used by dramatists of the period. It consists of stanzas of five lines which can rhyme in any of the following patterns: *ababa, abaab, aabab, abbab*, and *aabba*. The following example of the form comes from Tirso's *El condenado por desconfiado*:

> Co/mo/ si/ fue/ra/ bo/rri/co,
> ven/go/ de/ yer/ba/ car/ga/do,
> de quien el monte está rico;
> si esto como, ¡desdichado!,
> triste fin me pronostico.

The rhyme here is clearly *ababa*, and the passage introduces us to the *gracioso*, Pedrisco, who provides light relief from the earnestness of his master, the 'hermit' Paulo, and his more *culto* styles which sandwich this soliloquy. The *quintilla* can be used in many different circumstances. Here it manages to express Pedrisco's comic frustration but, hiding behind his words, is the main theme of the play, the 'triste fin' to be predicted in fact for Paulo.

Décima

The last of the octosyllabic forms is the *décima*, which can at first look like a pair of *quintillas*. However, the rhyme scheme of the first five lines, *abbaa*, is not permissible for the *quintilla*. The ten lines have a rigid, symmetrical-looking scheme: *abbaaccddc*, and there is a break, often a full stop, after the fourth line as well as obligatory enjambement between lines 5 and 6. The opening of Act 2 of Tirso's *El vergonzoso en palacio* sees Madalena express the dilemma caused for her by the strength of her feelings for the new man at court:

> ¿Qué/ no/ve/da/des/ so/n és/tas,
> al/ta/ne/ro/ pen/sa/mien/to?
> ¿Qué torres sin fundamento
> tenéis en el aire puestas?
> ¿Cómo andáis tan descompuestas,
> imaginaciones locas?
> Siendo las causas tan pocas,
> ¿queréis exponer mis menguas
> a juicio de las lenguas
> y a la opinión de las bocas?

The heightened poetic form, the most sophisticated of the octosyllables, is well suited to the 'quejas', or at least exquisite confusion, of the aristocratic Madalena.

Soneto

This fourteen-line form has been cultivated by poets of many nations, although its precise make-up, including the rhyme scheme, varies across cultures. The Spanish form, inherited from Italy, is hendecasyllabic: the quatrains rhyme *ABBA*, *ABBA*, and the tercets usually *CDE*, *CDE*. The following example of the form shows Lope de Vega at his playful best: it is the *gracioso* Chacón's sonnet from Act 3 of *La niña de plata*:

> Un/ so/ne/to/ me/ man/da ha/cer/ Vio/lan/te,
> y en/ mi/ vi/da/ me he/ vis/to en/ tan/to a/prie/to.
> Catorce versos dicen que es soneto;
> burla burlando van los tres delante.
> Yo pensé que no hallara consonante,
> y estoy a la mitad de otro cuarteto;
> mas si me veo en el primer terceto,
> no hay cosa en los cuartetos que me espante.
> Por el primer terceto voy entrando,
> y parece que entré con pie derecho,
> pues fin con este verso le voy dando.
> Ya estoy en el segundo, y aun sospecho
> que voy los trece versos acabando;
> contad si son catorce, y está hecho.

Chacón gently parodies the *comedia* set-piece, in which lovers might compete with each other through, or set each other to write, a love sonnet. Good examples occur in *El perro del hortelano* and *La dama boba*, in the latter of which it is the *culto* form and neo-Platonic content of the sonnet that is discussed. The eleven-syllable lines of the form and its meditative content can slow down the pace of the action of the *comedia*, allowing the audience to take stock and draw breath for the next complication. Tirso's *Marta la piadosa* is extremely unusual, perhaps unique, in opening with a pair of sonnets: as a set-piece the form is usually built towards and flagged up.

Octava real

The Italianate *octava* is also exclusively constructed with hendecasyllables, rhyming *ABABABCC*. It is the form in which epic poetry (such as Ercilla's *La Araucana*) was written, and was popular with the quasi-tragic playwrights of the 1580s, such as Cueva, Virués and Cervantes, who used it heavily in *El cerco de Numancia*. A change into *octavas reales* would be understood by an audience as marking a clear shift to a loftier tone: in Calderón's *auto, El gran teatro del mundo*, as we saw in chapter 6, just as the 'play' of life ends and Mundo re-appears, the *romances* give way to the eleven-syllable form. After delivering the first two *octavas* alone to the audience as a reminder of the play's over-arching purpose, Mundo begins to oversee the departure of the individual actors, by claiming back their worldly props:

MUNDO:	Di,/ ¿qué/ pa/pel/ hi/cis/te,/ tú,/ que a/ho/ra
	el/ pri/me/ro a/ mis/ ma/nos/ has/ ve/ni/do?
REY:	Pues, ¿el Mundo quién fui tan presto ignora?
MUNDO:	El Mundo lo que fue pone en olvido.
REY:	Aquél fui que mandaba cuanto dora
	el sol, de luz y resplandor vestido,
	desde que en brazos de la aurora nace
	hasta que en brazos de la sombra yace.

The grave *octavas reales* underline the importance of the moment but also, when the poet puts them into the mouth of the king, cleverly undermine the pomposity of his conception of himself. As he grandly enumerates his achieve-ments, in appropriately flowery rhetoric and noble style, he is undressed by the indifferent Mundo. The contrast between his inflated view of his role (gleaned by the audience in part through the verse form in which he speaks) and the equality of all before God, makes clear how poorly the monarch has understood the central metaphor of the play.

Lira

The *lira* form is most commonly a six-line mixture of seven- and eleven-syllable lines, of which the sixth must be hendecasyllabic and must rhyme with the fifth. (The form that Garcilaso had introduced to Spanish was in fact a five-line one.) The rhyme scheme can vary but that of the *comendador*'s eulogy to Casilda's beauty, in Lope's *Peribáñez*, is quite usual:

> Her/mo/sa/ la/bra/do/ra,
> más/ be/lla,/ más/ lu/ci/da
> que/ ya/ del/ sol/ ves/ti/da
> la/ co/lo/ra/da au/ro/ra;

sie/rra/ de/ blan/ca/ nie/ve
que/ los/ ra/yos/ de a/mor/ ven/cer/ se a/tre/ve.

The rhyme here follows the pattern *abbacC* (the upper case '*C*' indicating the longer line). This more refined form is clearly accompanied by the diction and imagery typical of Petrarchan-style love poetry and is meant to contrast with the down-to-earth, harmonious love of Peribáñez and Casilda, as it has been expressed in the octosyllables of the former's speech at the wedding (in *quintillas*) and their alphabets of love (in *redondillas*) which immediately precede Don Fadrique's verses.

Terceto
This form consists of varying numbers of interlinked stanzas of three hendecasyllables usually rhyming *ABA BCB CDC* etc. with the last four lines concluding *EFEF*. The following example comes from Lope's *El caballero de Olmedo*:

RODRIGO: Mu/chas/ ve/ces/ ha/bí/a/ re/pa/ra/do,
              Don/ Fer/nan/do, e/n a/que/ste/ ca/ba/lle/ro,
              del corazón solícito avisado.

              El talle, el grave rostro, lo severo,
              celoso me obligaba a miralle.
FERNANDO: Efetos son de amante verdadero

              que, en viendo otra persona de buen talle,
              tienen temor que si le ve su dama
              será posible o fuerza codicialle.[4]

The exchange comes just after the scene in *romance* in which Inés has informed her father of her rejection of an arranged marriage to Rodrigo due to her religious vocation. The hope that this deception instils in Inés and Alonso will fade away, for the audience, when they hear the deliberate discussion, a 'cosa grave' in Lope's terms, between Rodrigo and Fernando which raises the possibility of a jealous revenge and a tragic outcome to a comic ploy.

Other Italianate forms are used with some frequency in the *comedia nueva*: the *silva* form usually combines seven- and eleven-syllable lines which rhyme freely; *versos sueltos* are hendecasyllables that do not have a pattern of rhyme – the *Arte nuevo* itself is written in this form (as the extract above will reveal). Occasional rhyming couplets occur in such verses and, certainly in the case of the *Arte nuevo*, they indicate a kind of closure, the end of a part of the discussion or idea; and where hendecasyllabic lines are grouped in rhyming couplets they are known as *pareados*.

[4] See Sage, *Lope de Vega*, pp. 75–80, for an analysis of the versification in this play and its implications.

APPENDIX 2

ENGLISH TRANSLATIONS OF GOLDEN AGE PLAYS

It may be useful, given the increased interest in performing Golden Age drama in English-speaking countries, to provide here a list of some of those plays that are readily available in English. A relatively small percentage of the multitude of plays from the period has been translated and translators have differing approaches to the issues surrounding their versions. Some argue strongly for translating verse as verse, others work in prose; some are happy to produce a play-text which modernizes the work, others feel there is, at some level, a betrayal of the original in such a procedure; some versions are written to be read, others with performance in mind. There are interesting discussions of these issues, written by Dixon, Round and others, in the second section of Louise and Peter Fothergill-Payne's *Prologue to Performance* and in Michael Kidd's fine introduction to his version of Calderón's *La vida es sueño* (*Life's a Dream*); for an impressive polymetric version of a Golden Age play, see Philip Osment's version of Cervantes's *Pedro de Urdemalas* (see below for both works).

The web-site of the *Association for Hispanic Classical Theatre* has a more exhaustive listing of plays from the Golden Age that have been translated into English, although some on that list are not easy to come by.

Notes:

(1) The texts published by Aris and Phillips are bilingual editions.

(2) When a text is known to have been used for a particular production, this is indicated.

(3) Entries are alphabetical by author, with collections listed first.

Pedro Calderón de la Barca

Eight Dramas of Calderón (*The Painter of his own Dishonour*; *Keep your own Secret*; *Gil Pérez the Gallician*; *Three Judgments at a Blow*; *The Mayor of Zalamea*; *Beware of Smooth Water*; *The Mighty Magician*; *Such Stuff as Dreams are Made of*), trans. Edward Fitzgerald (London: Macmillan, 1906)

Four Plays (*The Phantom Lady*; *The Mayor of Zalamea*; *Devotion to the Cross*; *Secret Vengeance for Secret Insult*), trans. Edwin Honig (New York: Hill and Wang, 1961)

Three Comedies (*A House with Two Doors is Difficult to Guard*; *Mornings of April and May*; *No Trifling with Love*), trans. Kenneth Muir and Ann L. Mackenzie (Lexington: University of Kentucky, 1985)

Calderón: Plays One (*The Surgeon of Honour; Life is a Dream; Three Judgments in One*), trans. Gwynne Edwards (London: Methuen, 1991)

Life's a Dream, trans. Michael Kidd (Boulder, CO: University Press of Colorado, 2004)

Love after Death, trans. Roy Campbell, in *The Classic Theatre*, ed. Eric Bentley (New York: Doubleday, 1959), pp. 315–405

Love is No Laughing Matter, trans. Don Cruikshank and Seán Page (Warminster: Aris and Phillips, 1986)

The Mayor of Zalamea; Life's a Dream; The Great Theatre of the World, trans. Adrian Mitchell (Bath: Absolute Press, 1984) – the first of these was performed at the National Theatre, London, 1981

The Painter of his Dishonour, ed. and trans. A. K. G. Paterson (Warminster: Aris and Phillips, 1991)

The Painter of Dishonour, trans. David Johnston and Laurence Boswell (Bath: Absolute Press, 1995) – performed by the Royal Shakespeare Company in 1995

The Physician of his Honour, trans. Dian Fox with Donald Hindley (Warminster: Aris and Phillips, 1997)

The Prodigious Magician, ed. and trans. Bruce W. Wardropper (Madrid: Porrúa, 1982)

The Schism in England, ed. Ann L. Mackenzie, trans. Kenneth Muir and Ann L. Mackenzie (Warminster: Aris and Phillips, 1990)

Miguel de Cervantes

Eight Interludes, trans. Dawn L. Smith (London: J. M. Dent, 1996)

Pedro the Great Pretender, trans. Philip Osment (London: Oberon, 2004) – performed by the Royal Shakespeare Company in 2004

The Siege of Numantia, trans. Roy Campbell, in *The Classic Theatre*, ed. Eric Bentley (New York: Doubleday, 1959), pp. 97–160

Sor Juana Inés de la Cruz

House of Desires, trans. Catherine Boyle (London: Oberon, 2004) – performed by the Royal Shakespeare Company in 2004

Mira de Amescua

The Devil's Slave, trans. Michael D. McGaha (Ottawa: Dovehouse, 1989)

Agustín Moreto

Spite for Spite, trans. Dakin Matthews (Lyne, NH: Smith and Kraus, 1995)

Juan Ruiz de Alarcón

The Truth Can't Be Trusted, trans. Dakin Matthews (New Orleans: University Press of the South, 1998) – performed at El Paso in 2000

The Walls Have Ears, trans. Dakin Matthews (New Orleans: University Press of the South, 1998)

Tirso de Molina

Damned for Despair, ed. and trans. Nicholas G. Round (Warminster: Aris and Phillips, 1986)

Damned for Despair, trans. Laurence Boswell with Jonathan Thacker; *Don Gil of the Green Breeches*, trans. Laurence Boswell with Deirdre McKenna (Bath: Absolute Press, 1992) – perfomed at the Gate Theatre, London, 1991

Don Gil of the Green Breeches, trans. Gordon Minter (Warminster: Aris and Phillips, 1991)

Tamar's Revenge, trans. J. E. Lyon (Warminster: Aris and Phillips, 1988)

Tamar's Revenge, trans. James Fenton (London: Oberon, 2004) – performed by the Royal Shakespeare Company in 2004

The Trickster of Seville and the Stone Guest, trans. Gwynne Edwards (Warminster: Aris and Phillips, 1986)

Lope de Vega

Five Plays (*Peribáñez, Justice without Revenge; The Knight from Olmedo; Fuenteovejuna; The Dog in the Manger*), trans. Jill Booty and ed. R. D. F. Pring-Mill (New York: Hill and Wang, 1961)

Three Major Plays (*Fuente Ovejuna; The Knight from Olmedo; Punishment without Revenge*), trans. Gwynne Edwards (Oxford: Oxford University Press, 1999)

The Dog in the Manger, trans. David Johnston (London: Oberon, 2004) – performed by the Royal Shakespeare Company in 2004

The Duchess of Amalfi's Steward, trans. Cynthia Rodriguez-Badendyck (Ottawa: Dovehouse, 1985)

Fuente Ovejuna, ed. and trans. Victor Dixon (Warminster: Aris and Phillips, 1989)

Fuente Ovejuna; Lost in a Mirror, trans. Adrian Mitchell (Bath: Absolute Press, 1989) – the former was performed at the National Theatre, London, in 1989

The Great Pretenders; The Gentleman from Olmedo, trans. David Johnston (Bath: Absolute Press, 1992) – the former was performed in the Gate Theatre, London, in 1991, and the latter most recently at the Watermill Theatre, Newbury, in 2004

Madness in Valencia, trans. David Johnston; *Peribáñez and the Comendador of Ocaña*, trans. Nick Drake (London: Oberon, 1998) – perfomed at the Gate Theatre, London, 1992, and the Cambridge Arts Theatre, 1997, respectively

Peribáñez and the Comendador of Ocaña, trans. James Lloyd (Warminster: Aris and Phillips, 1990)

Peribáñez, trans Tanya Ronder (London: Nick Hern Books, 2003) – performed at the Young Vic, London in 2003

María de Zayas

Friendship Betrayed, trans. Catherine Larson (Lewisburg: Bucknell University Press, 1999) – bilingual text

SUGGESTIONS FOR FURTHER READING

The following pages contain an annotated list of suggestions for further reading on the topics or authors dealt with in each chapter. Full titles and publication details of works mentioned are provided in the Bibliography, with editions of anthologies of plays mentioned listed at the start of Section A.

Introduction

This *Companion* has little space for the consideration of Golden Age history, a knowledge of which is, nevertheless, crucial to a full understanding of the drama in its context. For a one-volume general history which covers the period under consideration, see Elliott's *Imperial Spain 1468–1716*; and for a social history very useful as background to the world of the *comedia nueva*, consult Casey's *Early Modern Spain*. Other fascinating, broadly historical works which deal with aspects of the court and the culture of Golden Age Spain are Elliott's *Spain and its World*, and (for the reign of Philip III) Elizabeth Wright's *Pilgrimage to Patronage*, and (for that of Philip IV) Brown and Elliott's *A Palace for King*.

An excellent short history of the literature of the Golden Age, written by Peter Russell, is to be found in *Spain: A Companion to Spanish Studies*, pp. 265–380; and Jeremy Robbins's *The Challenges of Uncertainty*, a lively and thought-provoking introduction to seventeenth-century Spanish literature, including the theatre, is also well worth reading. On Golden Age drama specifically, the best one-volume histories are: (in Spanish) Ignacio Arellano's *Historia del teatro español del siglo XVII*; and (in English) Melveena McKendrick's *Theatre in Spain 1490–1700*. A short, very well balanced, and attractively illustrated chapter on the period's theatre, written by Victor Dixon, appears in John Russell Brown's *The Oxford Illustrated History of the Theatre*. Finally, the first volume of the multi-author *Historia del Teatro Español*, edited by Javier Huerta Calvo, provides comprehensive coverage of a host of *Siglo de Oro* dramatists and issues.

Chapter 1

Drama in the sixteenth century in Spain would arguably have been better served by scholars had the *comedia nueva* never emerged to cast its long shadow. It tends to be considered a prelude to its prodigious successor. This is a shame since there are some gifted playwrights and rewarding dramas from the period, and the dramatic output in Spain is richer than that of most other countries at this time. Alfredo Hermenegildo's *El teatro del Siglo XVI* is a good history of the theatre in the century before Lope de Vega and considers all the playwrights mentioned in this chapter. Also useful is the more recent, albeit short, *El teatro en el Renacimiento* by Miguel Ángel Pérez Priego, which provides further particularized bibliographical information on sixteenth-century dramatists. In English the best overview appears in the opening two chapters of McKendrick's *Theatre in Spain 1490–1700*. In her history McKendrick makes a point of dedicating more space than previous scholars had to the early theatre.

The most detailed and still essential study of the origins of Spanish theatre is Norman Shergold's *A History of the Spanish Stage from Medieval Times until the End of the Seventeenth Century*. This work continues to be quoted in much modern research on Spanish drama, as does Crawford's *Spanish Drama before Lope de Vega*. Miguel M. García-Bermejo Giner has recently produced a useful decade-by-decade index of sixteenth-century plays which have been preserved, lost or performed, his *Catálogo del teatro español del Siglo XVI*. Dramatic theory of the period, including of course, Lope de Vega's *Arte nuevo*, is conveniently collected in Sánchez Escribano and Porqueras Mayo's *Preceptiva dramática española del renacimiento y barroco*. Other general works on sixteenth-century drama which are worth consulting are José María Díez Borque's *Los géneros dramáticos en el siglo XVI*, which takes a fresh approach to the way playwrights described their works, and Joan Oleza's 'Hipótesis sobre la génesis de la comedia barroca' in the excellent volume *La génesis de la teatralidad barroca*. Additionally, speakers at the annual Golden Age festival in Almagro in 1994 concentrated on the birth of Spanish theatre, and the proceedings of this conference, which cover a number of areas, are collected in *Los albores del teatro español*, edited by Pedraza Jiménez and González Cañal.

Editions of texts by the early dramatists are given under their names in the bibliography, but it is worth mentioning a couple of anthologies of plays from the period. Hesse and Valencia's *El teatro anterior a Lope de Vega* contains plays by ten dramatists, including Vicente and Cervantes, and Hermenegildo's *Del palacio al corral: antología del teatro español del siglo XVI* features half a dozen works as well as a very useful bibliography and chronology of the period.

Chapter 2

There is a clear need for a new scholarly biography of Lope de Vega. The most reliable is still H. A. Rennert's with Américo Castro's additions, first published as *Vida de Lope de Vega* in 1919. Elizabeth Wright's *Pilgrimage to Patronage* neatly combines historical and literary studies to produce a convincing portrait of Lope in his middle years. S. Griswold Morley and Courtney Bruerton's work on the chronology and authenticity of Lope's dramatic works, based on analyses of the playwright's use of verse forms, remains essential to

Lope scholars. Its conclusions have been largely vindicated by more recent discoveries.

Victor Dixon provides a fine short overview of Lope's work (including the non-dramatic output) in his recent chapter of *The Cambridge History of Spanish Literature* (ed. David T. Gies); for an overview of all his plays which provides titles, locations, brief (and idiosyncratic) summaries and some other details useful to a potential director, it is worth consulting David Castillejo's *Las cuatrocientas comedias de Lope de Vega*; Enrique García Santo-Tomás has begun to trace the reception of Lope through the centuries with his fascinating and very welcome *La creación del 'Fénix': recepción crítica y formación canónica del teatro de Lope de Vega*, of 2000.

José F. Montesinos's *Estudios sobre Lope* is replete with acute observations about Lope's drama, as is R. D. F. Pring-Mill's introduction to *Lope de Vega: Five Plays*, translated by Jill Booty. Juan Oleza's 'La propuesta teatral del primer Lope de Vega', in the already cited volume *La génesis de la teatralidad barroca*, is a basic guide to some of the norms and concerns of his early drama. A number of monographs cover groups of plays and are well worth reading, but, as I suggest in chapter 2, there are huge areas that still need to be covered adequately: Donald R. Larson traces skilfully the development of the honour play in the hands of Lope in *The Honor Plays of Lope de Vega*, a very well balanced study; kingship plays are best served by Melveena McKendrick's *Playing the King*, which supersedes other studies of this grouping and argues that Lope is a much more political dramatist than previous generations have thought; Robert R. Morrison introduces the saint's plays in *Lope de Vega and the Comedia de santos*, useful principally for the summaries he gives rather than the introductory chapters.

There is a great deal of useful scholarship in individual editions of Lope's plays, notably Francisco's Rico's of *El caballero de Olmedo*, Victor Dixon's of *El perro del hortelano* and the same scholar's bilingual edition of *Fuente Ovejuna*, Ruano and Varey's of *Peribáñez y el comendador de Ocaña*, Pedraza Jiménez's of *El castigo sin venganza*, Teresa Ferrer Valls's of *La viuda valenciana*, and Stefano Arata's of *El acero de Madrid*. And there are Critical Guides to Spanish Texts (CGSTs) by Jack Sage to *El caballero de Olmedo* and J. B. Hall to *Fuente Ovejuna*.

Chapter 3

As one might expect, there are a good number of studies of Cervantes's plays, although much remains to be written. The fullest, not yet translated from the French, is Canavaggio's *Cervantès dramaturge*; but Friedman's *The Unifying Concept* and Zimic's *El teatro de Cervantes* are also full of interest. Short guides to the *comedias* (by Wardropper) and the *entremeses* (by Asensio) are published in the *Suma cervantina*, edited by Avalle-Arce and Riley, and more recently McKendrick has contributed a fine short study ('Writings for the Stage') of both genres to *The Cambridge Companion to Cervantes* (ed. Cascardi).

Luis Vázquez helps to dispel many of the myths surrounding Tirso's biography in his 'Tirso de Molina: del "enigma biográfico" ', and Ruth Lee Kennedy deals with his rivalries of the 1620s in *Studies in Tirso, I.* Three of the best book-length studies of his drama are H. W. Sullivan's wide-ranging *Tirso de Molina and the Drama of the Counter-Reformation*, Albrecht's *Irony and Theatricality*, and the excellent *Social and Literary Satire* by Halkhoree. There are very useful CGSTs to *El burlador de Sevilla* and *El condenado por desconfiado* by Rogers and Oakley, respectively.

Inevitably there exist fewer substantial studies of the works of the lesser-known dramatists of Lope's generation. Whicker's *The Plays of Juan Ruiz de Alarcón* is a fine recent guide to the Mexican-born playwright and his drama; on Castro, Wilson's *Guillén de Castro* and García Lorenzo's *El teatro de Guillén de Castro* are still useful, and the Crítica edition of *Las mocedades del Cid*, edited by Arata, is excellent; on Mira de Amescua and Luis Vélez de Guevara it is worth consulting the editions of the plays being produced under the direction of Agustín de la Granja (for the former) and Manson and Peale (for the latter) for up-to-date scholarship and further bibliographical information. On the former, see also the collection of studies edited by Arellano and de la Granja, entitled *Mira de Amescua: un teatro en la penumbra*. Plays by the female dramatists are conveniently collected in Soufas's *Women's Acts* and studied by the same scholar in her *Dramas of Distinction*.

Chapter 4

The republication of Cotarelo y Mori's 1924 *Ensayo sobre la vida y obras de D. Pedro Calderón de la Barca* at the start of the twenty-first century is indicative of the fact that, as for Lope de Vega, there is a need for a new, authoritative biography of Calderón. However, the commemorations of the 300th anniversary of the playwright's death in 1981 and the 400th of his birth in 2000 have produced a tide of conferences and publications on all aspects of his work, ensuring his place as the most studied dramatist of the Golden Age. Of these recent works, Rodríguez Cuadros's *Calderón* is a sound general guide to the man and his theatre, with chapter 2 providing some detail on his critical reception; the two-volume *Calderón 2000*, edited by Arellano, gathers together the fruits of the largest of the conferences of the anniversary year and, although the quality of papers is variable, a lot of topics are covered and most of the main Calderón scholars are represented; many important articles on Calderón have been published over the last four decades in the proceedings of the *Coloquio anglo-germano*, the most recent of which was edited in 2003 by Manfred Tietz as *Teatro calderoniano sobre el tablado*.

Three edited volumes of article-length studies on Calderón's plays stand out: Wardropper's *Critical Essays on the Theatre of Calderón* contains essays by British and North American scholars which were very influential in establishing the canon of plays studied in universities. Parker's study of the devil and Dunn's of honour against a Christian background, in particular, are often quoted; the nineteenth volume of the facsimile edition of Calderón's *comedias*, which was edited by J. E. Varey, also collected together important studies published over earlier decades, including Sage's on 'The Function of Music' and Wilson's on 'The Four Elements in the Imagery of Calderón'; and the 2000 volume in memory of John Varey, *Calderón 1600–1681*, edited by Ann L. Mackenzie, gives a good indication of some of the fields currently being ploughed by *calderonistas*. On Calderón's re-use of earlier plays, see the classic study by Sloman, *The Dramatic Craftsmanship*; for a convenient collection of many of the most influential pieces on the dramatist written by Parker, including his view of Calderonian tragedy, see *The Mind and Art of Calderón*; on mythological court plays, see Greer's *The Play of Power*; on Calderón as a Baroque artist, with a welcome emphasis on the play as theatre, see Amadei-Pulice's *Calderón y el Barroco*. Regalado's *Calderón: los orígenes de la modernidad* is an influential two-volume study of Calderón's drama. And there are three CGSTs to Calderón's plays: Halkhoree's to *El alcalde de Zalamea*, Cruikshank's to *El médico de su honra*, and Lewis-Smith's to *La vida es sueño*.

González Cañal's article 'Calderón y sus colaboradores', in the first volume of *Calderón 2000*, provides insights into the team-writing of plays. The dramatists that Calderón collaborated with and others of his generation are most succinctly examined by Arellano, in his *Calderón y su escuela dramática*. However, the most reliable source of information and further bibliography on the figures of Rojas Zorrilla, Moreto, and the several other dramatists of the later period, considered somewhat summarily in this *Companion*, is now the *Historia del Teatro Español*, volume 1, especially chapters 36, 37, 38, and 40.

Chapter 5

Much of the work on Spanish Golden Age playhouses is heavily dependent on research published in the Tamesis series *Fuentes para la historia del teatro en España*, initiated in 1971 by John Varey, who, by that year, had already been publishing the fruits of his reading in Spanish archives for over a decade. A very useful guide to the volumes in this series was published by John J. Allen in 1998, as 'Documenting the History of the Spanish Theatre'. Varey's work has been continued by a number of scholars in several countries, most notably Charles Davis. Díez Borque has conveniently edited a group of studies of several early Spanish theatres as *Teatros del Siglo de Oro*. The volume acts as a reminder that it was not only Madrid that had a vigorous dramatic scene, and that there was more than one type of playhouse.

Ruano de la Haza and Allen's *Los teatros comerciales del siglo XVII y la escenificación de la comedia* combines an excellent guide to the Golden Age playhouse with an equally fine analysis of the staging practices within it. It is the fullest one-volume guide to these aspects of Golden Age drama. However, Díez Borque's *Sociedad y teatro en la España de Lope de Vega* is also still useful in many respects, as its remit is broader. On court theatre, see McKendrick's *Theatre in Spain*, chapter 8; the *Fuentes* volume *El teatro palaciego en Madrid:*

1586–1707, edited by Greer and Varey; and, for a slightly earlier period, Teresa Ferrer Valls's *La práctica escénica cortesana*. On audiences, Catherine Connor's article 'Hacia una teoría sociocultural del espectador aurisecular' is thought-provoking, and on actors and acting, see the studies by Oehrlein, *El actor en el teatro español*, and Rodríguez Cuadros, *La técnica del actor español*, as well as Dixon's ingenious and entertaining 'Manuel Vallejo. Un actor se prepara'. Music in Golden Age theatre is dealt with very helpfully in Louise Stein's *Songs of Mortals* and in Jack Sage's far-reaching 'The Function of Music', mentioned above.

The comparative lack of studies of Golden Age drama in performance is addressed in my ' "Puedo yo con sola la vista oír leyendo" ', which also contains a list of articles by Fischer, Mujica and others who *have* produced useful research in this nascent field. And Fischer's 'Así que pasen quince años' gives an account of the history of, as well as performances by, the CNTC until the late 1990s.

Chapter 6

A good number of scholars have dealt indirectly or tangentially with questions of the genre of the *comedia nueva*, and thus *aperçus* are to be found in many articles and editions of plays. The following two works may be particularly useful as their focus remains more steadily fixed on genre in general: Margarete Newels's *Los géneros dramáticos* and James Parr's *After Its Kind: Approaches to the* comedia. Marc Vitse's 'Teoría y géneros dramáticos en el siglo XVII', chapter 24 of Huerta Calvo's *Historia del Teatro Español*, is also well worth reading. A fine study of the extent to which Golden Age dramatists left (or failed to leave) their classical models behind is to be found in Duncan Moir's 'The Classical Tradition', and Gail Bradbury discusses which of Lope's plays might be called tragic in her short article 'Tragedy and Tragicomedy'. On comedy, Bruce Wardropper's 'La comedia española del Siglo de Oro' is lively and thought-provoking, but his 'tragedizing tendency' evident in, for example, 'Calderón's Comedy and his Serious Sense of Life' needs to be read in conjunction with Arellano's corrective *Convención y recepción*. This last work, though a collection of published articles, represents a major step forward in studies of genre in the Golden Age. William Blue's *Spanish Comedy and Historical Contexts* provides a welcome focus on comedy's relationship to its social context. A brief introduction to burlesque drama can be found in the collection of plays entitled *Comedias burlescas* and edited by Arellano et al.

Short forms of theatre are conveniently defined in chapter 4 of Díez Borque's *Sociedad y teatro*. Useful studies devoted to the *entremés* and other *teatro menor* are: Asensio's *Itinerario del entremés*, which traces the genre's development and has chapters on all the major figures from Lope de Rueda to Quevedo; the 'Jornadas de Almagro' volume, edited by García Lorenzo, *Los géneros menores*; and the introduction by Antonucci and Arata to their collection of some of Lope's *loas*, *La enjambre mala soy yo*, which is a very fine guide to this fascinating form. For examples of the *entremés*, written by twelve Golden Age dramatists, conveniently gathered together, see *Antología del entremés barroco*, edited by García Valdés. And for a thought-provoking approach to Cervantes's interludes see Zimic's 1984 article 'La ejemplaridad'.

The study of the *auto sacramental*, which stalled for many decades, has begun to gather pace, principally thanks to the efforts of the GRISO team, led by Ignacio Arellano, at the Universidad de Navarra. They have been publishing, since the early 1990s, authoritative editions of Calderón's complete *autos* at a rate of three or four per year. Several of these texts are included in the bibliography. Arias's volume, *Autos sacramentales (El auto sacramental antes de Calderón)*, is still the most convenient collection of Corpus Christi theatre from before the time of Calderón's pre-eminence. A. A. Parker's *The Allegorical Drama of Calderón* remains unsurpassed as a general guide to the genre and an introduction to a selection of Calderón's Corpus Christi plays. However, chapter 9 of McKendrick's *Theatre in Spain* is also a very fine short guide to the *auto*; Adeva's 'Estructura teológica de los autos' answers several basic questions about Calderón's practice; and Arellano's *Estructuras dramáticas y alegóricas* deals very sensibly with a number of important areas.

Chapter 7

Emilio Cotarelo y Mori's *Bibliografía de las controversias sobre la licitud del teatro en España* collects together an array of documents pertaining to the history of the theatre in Spain, many from the sixteenth and seventeenth centuries. They are written by theologians, moralists, town council and *Consejo de Castilla* officials, and other interested parties, and give a fine sense of the richness of the debate over the theatre in the Golden Age.

The fullest account of the evolution in the reception of the *comedia* since the *Siglo de Oro* is Enrique García Santo-Tomás's *La creación del 'Fénix'*. Although it concentrates on the figure of Lope de Vega and does not pretend to be a history of reception, it contains a great deal of useful general information and bibliographical material. Oleza deals authoritatively with the origins and persistence of the Romantic response to Lope in his 'Claves románticas'. On Calderón, both Rodríguez Cuadros in her *Calderón* (chapter 2) and Arellano at the end of his *Calderón y su escuela dramática* assess critical responses to Lope's most important successor. On the insufficiently-studied question of *refundiciones*, see Charles Ganelin's *Rewriting Theatre*.

Two of the defining twentieth-century approaches to Golden Age theatre can be read in A. A. Parker's *The Approach to the Spanish Drama* and Maravall's *Teatro y literatura*. A selection of more recent theoretical approaches, written by scholars working in the US, is contained in Simerka's edited volume, *El arte nuevo de estudiar comedias*. And for discussions of recent directions in *comedia* studies, see Mariscal's 'An Introduction to the Ideology of Hispanism' and my 'Rethinking Golden-Age Drama'. Ruano de la Haza's 'Trascendencia y proyección' is also well worth reading for its insights into the failure of the period's drama to have achieved a higher profile.

Antonio Serrano, in chapter 42 of Huerta Calvo's *Historia del Teatro Español*, entitled 'La recepción escénica de los clásicos', provides a good brief overview of Golden Age drama on the Spanish stage, and García Gómez, in his 'Contextualización de las primeras puestas en escena', gives a fascinating account of the background and reaction to the first performance in England of *La vida es sueño*. The implications of this study go well beyond Cambridge in the 1920s.

BIBLIOGRAPHY

SECTION A: GOLDEN AGE WORKS

Anthologies

Antología del entremés barroco, ed. Celsa Carmen García Valdés (Barcelona: Plaza y Janés, 1985)

Autos sacramentales (El auto sacramental antes de Calderón), ed. Ricardo Arias (Mexico City: Porrúa, 1977)

Autos sacramentales desde su origen hasta fines del siglo XVII, ed. Eduardo González Pedroso, BAE, 58 (Madrid: Rivadeneyra, 1865)

De la comedia humanística al teatro representable, ed. José Luis Canet Vallés (Seville/Valencia: UNED, 1993)

Comedias burlescas del Siglo de Oro, eds Ignacio Arellano, Celsa García Valdés, Carlos Mata y María Carmen Pinillos (Madrid: Espasa-Calpe, 1999)

Dramáticos posteriores a Lope de Vega, ed. Ramón de Mesonero Romanos, 2 vols, BAE, 47 and 49 (Madrid: Rivadeneyra, 1858–59)

Del palacio al corral: antología del teatro español del siglo XVI, ed. Alfredo Hermenegildo (Madrid: Biblioteca Nueva, 1998)

Poetas dramáticos valencianos, ed. Eduardo Juliá Martínez, 2 vols (Madrid: RAE, 1929)

El romancero viejo, ed. Mercedes Díaz Roig (Madrid: Cátedra, 1999)

El teatro anterior a Lope de Vega, eds Everett W. Hesse and Juan O. Valencia (Madrid: Alcalá, 1971)

Women's Acts: Plays by Women Dramatists of Spain's Golden Age, ed. Teresa Scott Soufas (Lexington: University Press of Kentucky, 1997)

Individual authors

Azevedo, Ángela de, *Dicha y desdicha del juego y devoción de la virgen*, in *Women's Acts*, ed. Soufas, pp. 4–44

——, *La margarita del Tajo que dio nombre a Santarén*, in *Women's Acts*, ed. Soufas, pp. 45–90

——, *El muerto disimulado*, in *Women's Acts*, ed. Soufas, pp. 91–132

Bances Candamo, Francisco Antonio, *Cómo se curan los celos y Orlando furioso*, ed. Ignacio Arellano (Ottawa: Dovehouse, 1991)

——, *El esclavo en grillos de oro*, in *Dramáticos posteriores a Lope de Vega*, ed. Mesonero Romanos, II, pp. 305–25

——, *El esclavo en grillos de oro; La piedra filosofal*, ed. Carmen Díaz Castañón (Oviedo: Caja de Ahorros de Asturias, 1983)

——, *Por su rey y por su dama*, in *Dramáticos posteriores a Lope de Vega*, ed. Mesonero Romanos, II, pp. 369–89

——, *Theatro de los theatros de los passados y presentes siglos*, ed. Duncan W. Moir (London: Tamesis, 1970)

Calderón de la Barca, *A secreto agravio, secreta venganza*; *La dama duende* (Madrid: Espasa-Calpe, 1946)

——, *El alcalde de Zalamea*, ed. José María Díez Borque (Madrid: Castalia, 1985)

——, *Amor, honor y poder*, in *Obras completas*, ed. Valbuena Briones, II, pp. 57–86

——, *Los cabellos de Absalón*, ed. Evangelina Rodríguez Cuadros (Madrid: Espasa-Calpe, 1989)

——, *Cada uno para sí*, ed. José María Ruano de la Haza (Kassel: Reichenberger, 1982)

——, *Casa con dos puertas mala es de guardar*, eds Antonio Rey Hazas and Florencio Sevilla Arroyo (Barcelona: Planeta, 1989)

——, *Céfalo y Pocris*, in *Comedias burlescas*, eds Ignacio Arellano et al., pp. 311–421

——, *Celos aun del aire matan*, in *Obras completas*, ed. Valbuena Briones, I, pp. 1786–1814

——, *La cisma de Inglaterra*, ed. Francisco Ruiz Ramón (Madrid: Castalia, 1981)

——, *El cordero de Isaías*, ed. María Carmen Pinillos (Kassel: Reichenberger, 1996)

——, *La dama duende*, ed. Fausta Antonucci (Barcelona: Crítica, 1999)

——, *Darlo todo y no dar nada*, in *Obras completas*, ed. Valbuena Briones, I, pp. 1022–67

——, *La desdicha de la voz*, ed. T. R. A. Mason (Liverpool: Liverpool University Press, 2003)

——, *La devoción de la Cruz*, ed. Manuel Delgado (Madrid: Cátedra, 2000)

——, *La devoción de la misa*, ed. J. Enrique Duarte (Kassel: Reichenberger, 2001)

——, *El divino Orfeo*, ed. J. Enrique Duarte (Kassel: Reichenberger, 1999)

——, *Los empeños de un acaso*, in *Obras completas*, ed. Valbuena Briones, II, pp. 1039–73

——, *Entremeses, jácaras y mojigangas*, eds Evangelina Rodríguez and Antonio Tordera (Madrid: Castalia, 1982)

——, *La estatua de Prometeo*, eds Margaret R. Greer and Louise K. Stein (Kassel: Reichenberger, 1986)

——, *La fiera, el rayo y la piedra*, ed. Aurora Egido (Madrid: Cátedra, 1989)

——, *Fortunas de Andrómeda y Perseo*, in *Obras completas*, ed. Valbuena Briones, I, pp. 1641–80

——, *El galán fantasma*, in *Obras completas*, ed. Valbuena Briones, II, pp. 635–69

——, *El golfo de las sirenas*, ed. Sandra Nielsen (Kassel: Reichenberger, 1989)

——, *El gran teatro del mundo*; *El gran mercado del mundo*, ed. Eugenio Frutos Cortés (Madrid: Cátedra, 1985)

——, *Guárdate del agua mansa*; *Amar después de la muerte* (Madrid: Espasa-Calpe, 1970)

——, *La hija del aire*, ed. Francisco Ruiz Ramón (Madrid: Cátedra, 1987)

——, *El hijo del Sol, Faetón*, in *Obras completas*, ed. Valbuena Briones, I, pp. 1863–1902

——, *La humildad coronada*, ed. Ignacio Arellano (Kassel: Reichenberger, 2002)

——, *El indulto general*, eds Ignacio Arellano and J. Manuel Escudero (Kassel: Reichenberger, 1996)

——, *El laurel de Apolo*, in *Obras completas*, ed. Valbuena Briones, I, pp. 1741–63

——, *Llamados y escogidos*, eds Ignacio Arellano and Luis Galván (Kassel: Reichenberger, 2002)

——, *El mágico prodigioso*, ed. Bruce W. Wardropper (Madrid: Cátedra, 1985)

——, *El mágico prodigioso*, ed. Melveena McKendrick in association with A. A. Parker (Oxford: Clarendon Press, 1992)

——, *Las manos blancas no ofenden*, ed. Ángel Martínez Blasco (Kassel: Reichenberger, 1995)

——, *El mayor encanto, amor*, in *Obras completas*, ed. Valbuena Briones, I, pp. 1510–45

——, *El mayor monstruo del mundo*; *El príncipe constante* (Madrid: Espasa-Calpe, 1970)

——, *El médico de su honra*, ed. D. W. Cruikshank (Madrid: Castalia, 1989)

——, *El monstruo de los jardines*, in *Obras completas*, ed. Valbuena Briones, I, pp. 1985–2022

——, *El nuevo palacio del Retiro*, ed. Alan K. G. Paterson (Kassel: Reichenberger, 1998)

——, *No hay burlas con el amor*, ed. Ignacio Arellano (Pamplona: Universidad de Navarra, 1981)

——, *No hay cosa como callar*, in *Obras completas*, ed. Valbuena Briones, II, pp. 998–1035

——, *No siempre lo peor es cierto*, in *Obras completas*, ed. Valbuena Briones, II, pp. 1451–85

——, *Obras completas de Don Pedro Calderón de la Barca*, ed. A. Valbuena Briones, 3 vols (Madrid: Aguilar, 1991)

——, *La piel de Gedeón*, ed. Ana Armendáriz (Kassel: Reichenberger, 1998)

——, *El pintor de su deshonra*, ed. A. K. G. Paterson (Warminster: Aris and Phillips, 1991)

——, *La primer flor del Carmelo*, ed. Fernando Plata Parga (Kassel: Reichenberger, 1998)

——, *Primero soy yo*, in *Obras completas*, ed. Valbuena Briones, II, pp. 1167–1200

——, *Primero y segundo Isaac*, eds A. L. Cilveti and Ricardo Arias (Kassel: Reichenberger, 1997)

——, *La púrpura de la rosa*, in *Comedias de Don Pedro Calderón de la Barca*, ed. Juan Eugenio Hartzenbusch, BAE, 9 (Madrid: Rivadeneyra, 1862), pp. 673–86

——, *El sitio de Bredá*, in *Obras completas*, ed. Valbuena Briones, I, pp. 105–39

——, *Teatro cómico breve*, ed. María Luisa Lobato (Kassel: Reichenberger, 1989)

——, *La vida es sueño*, ed. Ciriaco Morón (Madrid: Cátedra, 1986)

Caro Mallén de Soto, Ana, *El conde Partinuplés*, in *Women's Acts*, ed. Soufas, pp. 137–62

——, *Valor, agravio y mujer*, ed. Lola Luna (Madrid: Castalia, 1993)

Cascales, Francisco, *Tablas poéticas*, ed. Benito Brancaforte (Madrid: Espasa-Calpe, 1975)

Castro, Guillén de, *El curioso impertinente*, in *Obras de Guillén de Castro*, ed. Juliá Martínez, II, pp. 491–533

——, *Dido y Eneas*, in *Obras de Guillén de Castro*, ed. Juliá Martínez, I, pp. 165–205

——, *Don Quijote de la Mancha*, ed. Luciano García Lorenzo (Salamanca: Anaya, 1971)

——, *La fuerza de la costumbre*, in *Obras de Guillén de Castro*, ed. Juliá Martínez, III, pp. 39–76

——, *La fuerza de la sangre*, in *Obras de Guillén de Castro*, ed. Juliá Martínez, III, pp. 236–72

——, *Las mocedades del Cid (Comedia segunda)* [*Las hazañas del Cid*], in *Obras de Guillén de Castro*, ed. Juliá Martínez, II, pp. 209–50

——, *Los mal casados de Valencia*, ed. Luciano García Lorenzo (Madrid: Castalia, 1976)

——, *Las mocedades del Cid*, ed. Stefano Arata (Barcelona: Crítica, 1996)

——, *Obras completas*, I, ed. Joan Oleza (Madrid: Biblioteca Castro, 1997)

——, *Obras de Guillén de Castro y Bellvís*, ed. Eduardo Juliá Martínez, 3 vols (Madrid: RABM, 1925–27)

Cervantes, Miguel de, *La casa de los celos*, in *Obras completas*, ed. Valbuena Prat, pp. 230–69

——, *Entremeses*, ed. Nicholas Spadaccini (Madrid: Cátedra, 1987)

——, *La entretenida*, in *Obras completas*, ed. Valbuena Prat, pp. 454–96

——, *El ingenioso hidalgo Don Quijote de la Mancha*, ed. Luis Andrés Murillo, 2 vols (Madrid: Castalia, 1982)

——, *La gran sultana*, in *Obras completas*, ed. Valbuena Prat, pp. 366–404

——, *Novelas ejemplares*, ed. Juan Bautista Avalle-Arce, 3 vols (Madrid: Castalia, 1987)

——, *Numancia*, ed. Robert Marrast (Madrid: Cátedra, 1989)

——, *Obras completas*, ed. Ángel Valbuena Prat (Madrid: Aguilar, 1949)

——, *El rufián dichoso*, ed. Florencio Sevilla Arroyo (Madrid: Castalia, 1997)

——, *El rufián dichoso*; *Pedro de Urdemalas*, eds Jenaro Talens and Nicholas Spadaccini (Madrid: Cátedra, 1986)

——, *El trato de Argel*, in *Obras completas*, ed. Valbuena Prat, pp. 112–44

——, *Viage del Parnaso*; *Poesías varias*, ed. Elias L. Rivers (Madrid: Espasa-Calpe, 1991)

Claramonte, Andrés de (attr.), *La Estrella de Sevilla*, ed. Alfredo Rodríguez López Vázquez (Madrid: Cátedra, 1991)

Coello, Antonio, *El conde de Sex*, ed. D. Schmeidel (Madrid: Playor, 1973)

Cruz, Sor Juana Inés de la, *Los empeños de una casa*, in *Dramáticos posteriores*, ed. Mesonero Romanos, II, pp. 285–303

Cubillo de Aragón, Álvaro, *Las muñecas de Marcela*; *El señor de Noches Buenas*, ed. Á. Valbuena Prat (Madrid: Clásicos olvidados, 1928)

Cueva, Juan de la, *El infamador*; *Los siete infantes de Lara*; *Ejemplar poético*, ed. Francisco A. de Icaza (Madrid: Espasa-Calpe, 1973)

Cueva y Silva, Leonor de, *La firmeza en la ausencia*, in *Women's Acts*, ed. Soufas, pp. 198–224

Encina, Juan del, *Triunfo de Amor*; *Égloga de Plácida y Vitoriano*, ed. Luisa de Aliprandini (Torrejón de Ardoz: Akal, 1995)

——, *Teatro completo*, ed. Miguel Ángel Pérez Priego (Madrid: Cátedra, 1991)

——, *Teatro*, ed. Alberto del Río (Barcelona: Crítica, 2001)

Enríquez de Guzmán, Feliciana, *Tragicomedia de los jardines y campos sabeos*, in *Women's Acts*, ed. Soufas, pp. 229–58

Fernández, Lucas, *Farsas y églogas*, ed. María Josefa Canellada (Madrid: Castalia, 1976)

Góngora, Luis de, *Las firmezas de Isabela*, ed. Robert Jammes (Madrid: Castalia, 1984)

Gracián, Baltasar, *El criticón*, ed. Santos Alonso (Madrid: Cátedra, 1993)

López Pinciano, Alonso, *Philosophía antigua poética* in *Obras completas*, ed. José Rico Verdú, 2 vols (Madrid: Biblioteca Castro, 1998), I

Matos Fragoso, Juan de, *El sabio en su retiro y villano en su rincón, Juan Labrador*, in *Dramáticos posteriores*, ed. Mesonero Romanos, I, pp. 199–218

Mira de Amescua, Antonio, *Adversa fortuna de don Álvaro de Luna*, included in Tirso de Molina, *Obras dramáticas completas*, 4 vols, ed. Blanca de los Ríos (Madrid: Aguilar, 1989), II, pp. 1056–93

——, *El arpa de David*, ed. María Concepción García Sánchez, in *Teatro completo*, ed. de la Granja, pp. 97–206

——, *El ejemplo mayor de la desdicha*, ed. Maria Grazia Profeti, in *Teatro completo*, ed. de la Granja, pp. 207–302

——, *El esclavo del demonio*, ed. James Agustín Castañeda (Madrid: Cátedra, 1980)

——, *Próspera fortuna de don Álvaro de Luna y adversa de Ruy López de Ávalos*, included in Tirso de Molina, *Obras dramáticas completas*, ed. Blanca de los Ríos, 4 vols (Madrid: Aguilar, 1989), II, pp. 1014–49

——, *Teatro completo*, ed. Agustín de la Granja (Granada: Universidad de Granada, 2001)

Monroy, Cristóbal de; Lope de Vega, *Fuente Ovejuna* (*Dos comedias*), ed. Francisco López Estrada (Madrid: Castalia, 1985)

Monteser, Francisco Antonio, *El caballero de Olmedo*, in *Comedias burlescas*, eds Ignacio Arellano et al., pp. 113–88

Morales, *Comedia de los amores y locuras del conde loco*, ed. Jean Canavaggio (Paris: Centre de Recherches Hispaniques, 1969)

Moreto, Agustín, *El desdén con el desdén*, ed. Francisco Rico (Madrid: Castalia, 1971)

——, *El lindo Don Diego*, eds Frank P. Casa and Berislav Primorac (Madrid: Cátedra, 1995)

——, *El lindo Don Diego*; *No puede ser el guardar una mujer* (Madrid: Espasa-Calpe, 1960)

——, *La ocasión hace al ladrón*, in *Comedias escogidas de Don Agustín Moreto y Cabaña*, ed. Luis Fernández-Guerra y Orbe, BAE, 39 (Madrid: Rivadeneyra, 1856), pp. 407–25

——, *El parecido en la corte*, ed. Juana de José Prados (Salamanca: Anaya, 1965)

Pérez de Montalbán, Juan, *Fama póstuma a la vida y muerte del doctor Frey Lope de Vega Carpio*, in *Obra no dramática*, ed. José Enrique Laplana Gil (Madrid: Biblioteca Castro, 1999), pp. 891–940

Pérez de Moya, Juan, *Philosofía secreta de la gentilidad*, ed. Carlos Clavería (Madrid: Cátedra, 1995)

Quevedo, Francisco de, *El buscón*, ed. Domingo Ynduráin (Madrid: Cátedra, 1985)

——, *Cómo ha de ser el privado*, in *Obra poética*, ed. Blecua, IV, pp. 149–221

——, *Obra poética*, ed. José Manuel Blecua, 4 vols (Madrid: Castalia, 1969–81)

——, *La polilla de Madrid*, in *Obra poética*, ed. Blecua, IV, pp. 111–22

Quiñones de Benavente, Luis, *Entremeses completos*, I: *Jocosería*, eds I. Arellano, J. M. Escudero, and A. Madroñal (Pamplona: Universidad de Navarra, 2001)

——, *Entremeses*, ed. Christian Andrès (Madrid: Cátedra, 1991)

Rojas, Fernando de, *La Celestina* [*Tragicomedia de Calisto y Melibea*], ed. Dorothy S. Severin (Madrid: Cátedra, 1998)

Rojas Villandrando, Agustín de, *El viaje entretenido*, ed. Jean Pierre Ressot (Madrid: Castalia, 1995)

Rojas Zorrilla, Francisco de, *Los bandos de Verona*, in *Comedias escogidas de Don Francisco de Rojas Zorrilla*, ed. Ramón de Mesonero Romanos (Madrid: Rivadeneyra, 1866), pp. 367–88

——, *Del rey abajo ninguno*; *Entre bobos anda el juego*, ed. Federico Ruiz Morcuende (Madrid: Espasa-Calpe, 1967)

——, *Entre bobos anda el juego*, ed. Maria Grazia Profeti (Barcelona: Crítica, 1998)

——, *Del rey abajo ninguno*, ed. Jean Testas (Madrid: Castalia, 1971)

——, *Persiles y Segismunda*, in *Primera parte de las comedias de Don Francisco de Rojas Zorrilla* (Madrid: María de Quiñones, 1640)

Rueda, Lope de, *Comedia Eufemia*; *Comedia Armelina*; *El deleitoso*, ed. Jesús Moreno Villa (Madrid: Espasa-Calpe, 1968)

——, *Las cuatro comedias*, ed. Alfredo Hermenegildo (Madrid: Cátedra, 2001)

——, *Pasos*, eds Fernando González Ollé and Vicente Tusón (Madrid: Cátedra, 1992)

Ruiz de Alarcón, Juan, *El examen de maridos*, ed. Maria Grazia Profeti (Kassel: Reichenberger, 1997)

——, *Obras completas de Juan Ruiz de Alarcón*, ed. Agustín Millares Carlo, 3 vols (Mexico: Fondo de Cultura Económica, 1957–68)

——, *Los pechos privilegiados*; *Ganar amigos*, ed. Agustín Millares Carlo (Madrid: Gredos, 1960)

——, *La verdad sospechosa*; *Las paredes oyen*, ed. Alfonso Reyes (Madrid: Espasa-Calpe, 1970)

——, *La verdad sospechosa*, ed. José Montero Reguera (Madrid: Castalia, 1999)

Salazar, Agustín de, *El encanto es la hermosura, y el hechizo sin hechizo*, in *Dramáticos posteriores*, ed. Mesonero Romanos, II, pp. 241–64

Sánchez de Badajoz, *Farsas*, ed. Miguel Ángel Pérez Priego (Madrid: Cátedra, 1985)

Solís, Antonio de, *Un bobo hace ciento*, in *Comedias*, ed. Sánchez Regueira, II, pp. 529–608

——, *Comedias*, ed. Manuela Sánchez Regueira, 2 vols (Madrid: CSIC, 1984)

——, *El amor al uso*, in *Comedias*, ed. Sánchez Regueira, I, pp. 223–302

——, *Obra dramática menor*, ed. Manuela Sánchez Regueira (Madrid: CSIC, 1986)

——, *Triunfos de Amor y Fortuna*, in *Comedias*, ed. Sánchez Regueira, I, pp. 49–145

Tirso de Molina, *El amor médico*, ed. Blanca Oteiza, in *Obras completas*, ed. Arellano, pp. 685–832

——, *El amor y el amistad*, in *Obras dramáticas completas*, ed. de los Ríos, I, pp. 506–47

——, *El Aquiles*, in *Obras dramáticas completas*, ed. de los Ríos, II, pp. 961–1001

——, *El árbol del mejor fruto*, in *Obras dramáticas completas*, ed. de los Ríos, IV, pp. 311–57

—— (attr.), *El burlador de Sevilla*, ed. Alfredo Rodríguez López-Vázquez (Madrid: Cátedra, 1996)

——, *La celosa de sí misma*, ed. Gregorio Torres Negrera (Madrid: Cátedra, 2005)

——, *Cigarrales de Toledo*, ed. Luis Vázquez Fernández (Madrid: Castalia, 1996)

——, *El condenado por desconfiado*, eds Ciriaco Morón and Rolena Adorno (Madrid: Cátedra, 1987)

——, *Desde Toledo a Madrid*, ed. Berta Pallares de R. Arias (Madrid: Castalia, 1999)

——, *Don Gil de las calzas verdes*, ed. Alonso Zamora Vicente (Madrid: Castalia, 1990)

——, *La huerta de Juan Fernández*, ed. Berta Pallares (Madrid: Castalia, 1982)

——, *Marta la piadosa*, ed. Eduardo Juliá Martínez (Zaragoza: Ebro, 1976)

——, *La mejor espigadera*, in *Obras dramáticas completas*, ed. de los Ríos, II, pp. 34–82

——, *La mujer que manda en casa*, ed. Dawn L. Smith (London: Tamesis, 1984)

——, *Obras completas: Cuarta parte de comedias*, ed. Ignacio Arellano (Pamplona: Instituto de Estudios Tirsianos, 1999)

——, *Obras dramáticas completas*, ed. Blanca de los Ríos, 4 vols (Madrid: Aguilar, 1989)

——, *Por el sótano y el torno*, ed. Alonso Zamora Vicente (Madrid: Castalia, 1994)

——, *La prudencia en la mujer*, in *Obras dramáticas completas*, ed. de los Ríos, IV, pp. 904–51

——, *Quien no cae no se levanta*, in *Obras dramáticas completas*, ed. de los Ríos, IV, pp. 846–92

——, *La república al revés*, in *Obras dramáticas completas*, ed. de los Ríos, I, pp. 382–428

——, *La venganza de Tamar*, ed. A. K. G. Paterson (Cambridge: Cambridge University Press, 1969)

——, *El vergonzoso en palacio*, ed. Francisco Ayala (Madrid: Castalia, 1989)

——, *La villana de la Sagra*, in *Obras dramáticas completas*, ed. de los Ríos, III, pp. 111–70

——, *La villana de Vallecas*, in *Obras dramáticas completas*, ed. de los Ríos, III, pp. 783–852

Torres Naharro, Bartolomé de, Propalladia *and Other Works of Bartolomé de Torres Naharro*, ed. Joseph E. Gillet, 4 vols (Bryn Mawr: University of Pennsylvania, 1943–61)

——, *Comedia Himenea*, in *Del palacio al corral*, ed. Hermenegildo, pp. 153–225

Valdivielso, José de, *Auto sacramental: Las pruebas del linaje humano y encomienda del hombre; Las probanzas e hidalguía del hombre*, ed. Ricardo Arias (Kassel: Reichenberger, 1995)

——, *El hospital de los locos*, in *Autos sacramentales*, ed. Arias, pp. 241–71

Vega, Lope de, *El acero de Madrid*, ed. Stefano Arata (Madrid: Castalia, 2000)

——, *Adonis y Venus*, in *Comedias escogidas*, ed. Hartzenbusch, BAE, 52, pp. 417–31

——, *Amar sin saber a quién*, ed. Carmen Bravo-Villasante (Salamanca: Anaya, 1967)

——, *Los amores de Albanio y Ismenia*, in *Obras de Lope de Vega*, ed. Cotarelo y Mori, I, pp. 1–38

——, *Arte nuevo de hacer comedias*; *La discreta enamorada* (Madrid: Espasa-Calpe, 1948)

——, *Belardo el furioso*, in *Obras de Lope de Vega*, ed. Menéndez y Pelayo, XIII, pp. 61–115

——, *El Brasil restituido*, in *Obras de Lope de Vega*, ed. Menéndez y Pelayo, XXVIII, pp. 257–96

——, *El caballero de Olmedo*, ed. Francisco Rico (Madrid: Cátedra, 1981)

——, *El casamiento en la muerte*, ed. Luigi Giuliani, in *Comedias de Lope de Vega*, eds Blecua and Serés, I, pp. 1161–1255

——, *El castigo sin venganza*, ed. A. David Kossoff (Madrid: Castalia, 1986)

——, *El castigo sin venganza*, ed. Felipe B. Pedraza Jiménez (Barcelona: Octaedro, 1999)

——, *Los celos de Rodamonte*, ed. Sabatino G. Maglione (Lanham, MD: University Press of America, 1985)

——, *Comedias de Lope de Vega*, eds Alberto Blecua and Guillermo Serés (Lerida: Milenio, 1997–)

——, *Comedias escogidas de frey Lope Félix de Vega Carpio*, ed. Juan Eugenio Hartzenbusch, BAE, 24, 34, 41, and 52 (Madrid: Rivadeneyra, 1857–72)

——, *Los comendadores de Córdoba*, in *Comedias de Lope de Vega*, eds Blecua and Serés, II, pp. 1051–1140

——, *La dama boba*, ed. Diego Marín (Madrid: Cátedra, 1985)

——, *La Dorotea*, ed. José Manuel Blecua (Madrid: Cátedra, 1996)

——, *El duque de Viseo*, in *Comedias escogidas*, ed. Hartzenbusch, BAE, 41, pp. 421–42

——, *La enjambre mala soy yo, el dulce panal mi obra: veintinueve loas inéditas de Lope de Vega y otros dramaturgos del siglo XVI*, eds Fausta Antonucci and Stefano Arata (Seville/Valencia: UNED, 1995)

——, *Lo fingido verdadero*, in *Obras de Lope de Vega*, ed. Menéndez y Pelayo, IX, pp. 51–107

——, *Fuente Ovejuna*, ed. Victor Dixon (Warminster: Aris and Phillips, 1989)

——, *Fuente Ovejuna*, ed. Francisco López Estrada (Madrid: Castalia, 1991)

——, *El grao de Valencia*, in *Obras de Lope de Vega*, ed. Cotarelo y Mori, I, pp. 513–46

——, *Los hechos de Garcilaso de la Vega y el moro Tarfe*, in *Obras de Lope de Vega*, ed. Menéndez y Pelayo, XXIII, pp. 397–423

——, *La hermosa Ester*, in *Obras de Lope de Vega*, ed. Menéndez y Pelayo, VIII, pp. 137–79

——, *La historia de Tobías*, in *Obras de Lope de Vega*, ed. Menéndez y Pelayo, VIII, pp. 87–136

——, *La juventud de San Isidro*, in *Obras de Lope de Vega*, ed. Menéndez y Pelayo, X, pp. 361–92

——, *Los locos de Valencia*, ed. Hélène Tropé (Madrid: Castalia, 2003)

——, *Los locos por el cielo*, in *Obras de Lope de Vega*, ed. Menéndez y Pelayo, IX, pp. 109–62

——, *El marqués de Mantua*, in *Obras de Lope de Vega*, ed. Menéndez y Pelayo, XXIX, pp. 135–94

——, *El mayordomo de la duquesa de Amalfi*, in *Obras de Lope de Vega*, ed. Menéndez y Pelayo, XXXII, pp. 281–340

——, *El mejor alcalde, el rey*, eds B. Morros and N. Roig (Madrid: Espasa-Calpe, 1989)

——, *La moza de cántaro*, ed. José María Díez Borque (Madrid: Espasa-Calpe, 1990)

——, *La niña de plata*, in *Comedias escogidas*, ed. Hartzenbusch, BAE, 24, pp. 273–95

——, *La niñez de San Isidro*, in *Obras de Lope de Vega*, ed. Menéndez y Pelayo, X, pp. 325–60

——, *El niño inocente de la Guardia*, ed. Anthony J. Farell (London: Tamesis, 1985)

——, *Obras de Lope de Vega*, ed. Emilio Cotarelo y Mori, 13 vols (Madrid: RAE, Nueva ed., 1916–30)

——, *Obras de Lope de Vega*, ed. Marcelino Menéndez y Pelayo, 15 vols (Madrid: Sucesores de Rivadeneyra, 1890–1913) [Plays cited in this *Companion* have been read in the BAE reprints of this ed. (Madrid: Atlas), begun with vol. VI in 1963. Vols cited are VIII (1963); IX (1964); X (1965); XIII (1965); XXIII (1968); XXVIII (1970); XXIX (1970); and XXXII (1972).]

——, *El pastor lobo y cabaña celestial*, in *Autos sacramentales*, ed. Arias, pp. 201–40

——, *Pedro de Urdemalas*, in *Obras de Lope de Vega*, ed. Cotarelo y Mori, VIII, pp. 392–428

——, *Peribáñez y el comendador de Ocaña*, ed. J. M. Ruano de la Haza and J. E. Varey (London: Tamesis, 1980)

——, *El perro del hortelano*, ed. Victor Dixon (London: Tamesis, 1981)

——, *La pobreza estimada*, in *Comedias escogidas*, ed. Hartzenbusch, BAE, 52, pp. 139–63

——, *El príncipe melancólico*, in *Obras de Lope de Vega*, ed. Cotarelo y Mori, I, pp. 336–68

——, *Prólogos de ocho tomos de comedias de Lope*, in *Comedias escogidas*, ed. Hartzenbusch, BAE, 52, pp. xxi–xxix

——, *El robo de Dina*, in *Obras de Lope de Vega*, ed. Menéndez y Pelayo, VIII, pp. 7–50

——, *San Isidro, labrador de Madrid*, in *Obras de Lope de Vega*, ed. Menéndez y Pelayo, X, pp. 393–443

——, *La selva sin amor*, ed. M. G. Profeti (Florence: Alinea, 1999)

——, *La siega*, in *Autos sacramentales*, ed. Arias, pp. 177–99

——, *La vengadora de las mujeres*, in *Obras de Lope de Vega*, ed. Cotarelo y Mori, XIII, pp. 614–46

——, *La villana de Getafe*, ed. José María Díez Borque (Madrid: Orígenes, 1990)

——, *El villano en su rincón*, ed. Juan María Marín (Madrid: Cátedra, 1987)

——, *La viuda valenciana*, ed. Teresa Ferrer Valls (Madrid: Castalia, 2001)

Vélez de Guevara, Juan, *Los celos hacen estrellas*, eds J. E. Varey, N. D. Shergold and Jack Sage (London: Tamesis, 1970)

Vélez de Guevara, Luis, *Reinar después de morir; El diablo está en Cantillana*, ed. Manuel Muñoz Cortés (Madrid: Espasa-Calpe, 1976)

——, *La serrana de la Vera*, ed. William R. Manson and C. George Peale (Fullerton: Cal. State Fullerton Press, 1997)

——, *Virtudes vencen señales*, ed. Maria Grazia Profeti (Pisa: Università di Pisa, 1965)

Vicente, Gil, *Teatro*, ed. Thomas R. Hart (Madrid: Taurus, 1983)

——, *Teatro castellano*, ed. Manuel Calderón (Barcelona: Crítica, 1996)

Virués, Cristóbal de, *La gran Semíramis*; *Elisa Dido*, ed. Alfredo Hermenegildo (Madrid: Cátedra, 2003)

——, *Tragedia de la infelice Marcela*, in *Poetas dramáticos valencianos*, ed. Juliá Martínez, I, pp. 118–45

Zabaleta, Juan de, *El día de fiesta por la mañana y por la tarde* (Madrid: Castalia, 1983)

Zayas y Sotomayor, María de, *La traición en la amistad*, in *Women's Acts*, ed. Soufas, pp. 277–308

SECTION B: SECONDARY WORKS

Adeva, Ildefonso, 'Estructura teológica de los autos sacramentales calderonianos', in Arellano, ed., *Calderón 2000*, I, pp. 3–46

Albrecht, Jane White, *Irony and Theatricality in Tirso de Molina* (Ottawa: Dovehouse, 1994)

Alcina Rovira, Juan Francisco, 'El comentario a la *Poética* de Aristóteles de Pedro Juan Núñez', *Excerpta Philologica*, 1 (1991), pp. 19–34

Allen, John J., *The Reconstruction of a Spanish Golden Age Playhouse: el corral del Príncipe, 1583–1744* (Gainesville: University Presses of Florida, 1983)

——, 'Documenting the History of Spanish Theatre: *Fuentes para la historia del teatro en España*', *MLR*, 93 (1998), pp. 997–1006

Alonso, Amado, 'Lope de Vega y sus fuentes', in *El teatro de Lope de Vega: artículos y estudios*, ed. José Francisco Gatti (Buenos Aires: EUDESA, 1962), pp. 193–218

Amadei-Pulice, María Alicia, *Calderón y el Barroco* (Amsterdam/Philadelphia: John Benjamins Publishing, 1990)

Arata, Stefano, '*La conquista de Jerusalén*, Cervantes y la generación teatral de 1580', *Crit.*, 54 (1992), pp. 9–112

Arco y Garay, Ricardo del, *La sociedad española en las obras dramáticas de Lope de Vega* (Madrid: Escelicer, 1941)

Arellano, Ignacio, *Calderón y su escuela dramática* (Madrid: Laberinto, 2001)

——, ed., *Calderón 2000: Homenaje a Kurt Reichenberger en su 80 cumpleaños*, 2 vols (Kassel: Reichenberger, 2002)

——, 'Canon dramático e interpretación de la comedia cómica del Siglo de Oro', in *El teatro del Siglo de oro ante los espacios de la crítica: encuentros y revisiones*, ed. Enrique García Santo-Tomás (Madrid: Iberoamericana, 2002), pp. 357–77

——, *Convención y recepción: estudios sobre el teatro del Siglo de Oro* (Madrid: Gredos, 1999)

——, *Estructuras dramáticas y alegóricas en los autos de Calderón* (Pamplona/Kassel: Universidad de Navarra/Reichenberger, 2001)

——, *Historia del teatro español del siglo XVII* (Madrid: Cátedra, 1995)

—— and Agustín de la Granja, eds, *Mira de Amescua: un teatro en la penumbra* (Pamplona: Universidad de Navarra, 1991)

Arroniz, Othón, *La influencia italiana en el nacimiento de la comedia española* (Madrid: Gredos, 1969)

Asensio, Eugenio, 'Entremeses', in Avalle-Arce and Riley, eds, *Suma cervantina*, pp. 171–97

——, *Itinerario del entremés desde Lope de Rueda a Quiñones de Benavente* (Madrid: Gredos, 1965)

Aubrun, Charles V., 'Las mil y ochocientas comedias de Lope', in *Lope de Vega y los orígenes del teatro español: actas del I Congreso Internacional sobre Lope de Vega*, ed. Manuel Criado de Val (Madrid: Edi-6, 1981), pp. 27–33

Avalle-Arce, J. B. and E. C. Riley, eds, *Suma cervantina* (London: Tamesis, 1973)

Bentley, Eric, *The Life of the Drama* (London: Methuen, 1965)

Bergman, Hannah E., *Luis Quiñones de Benavente y sus entremeses* (Madrid: Castalia, 1965)

Bershas, Henry N., 'Lope de Vega and the Post of Royal Chronicler', *HR*, 31 (1963), pp. 109–17

Blue, William, *Spanish Comedy and Historical Contexts in the 1620s* (University Park, PA: Pennsylvania State University Press, 1996)

Bouterwek, Frederick, *History of Spanish Literature* (London: David Bogue, 1847)

Bradbury, Gail, 'Tragedy and Tragicomedy in the Theatre of Lope de Vega', *BHS*, 58 (1981), pp. 103–11

Brenan, Gerald, *The Literature of the Spanish People* (Cambridge, Cambridge University Press, 1951)

Brotherton, John, *The* Pastor Bobo *in the Spanish Theatre before the Time of Lope de Vega* (London: Tamesis, 1975)

Brown, Jonathan and J. H. Elliott, *A Palace for a King: The Buen Retiro and the Court of Philip IV* (New Haven and London: Yale University Press, 1980)

Bruerton, Courtney, 'The Chronology of the *Comedias* of Guillén de Castro', *HR*, 12 (1944), pp. 89–151

Canavaggio, Jean, *Cervantès dramaturge: un théâtre à naître* (Paris: Presses Universitaires de France, 1977)

——, ed., *La Comedia* (Madrid: Casa de Velázquez, 1995)

Canning, Elaine M., *Lope de Vega's* Comedias de tipo religioso (London: Tamesis, 2004)

Cascardi, Anthony J., *Ideologies of History in the Spanish Golden Age* (University Park, PA: Pennsylvania State University Press, 1997)

Casey, James, *Early Modern Spain: A Social History* (London: Routledge, 1999)

Castillejo, David, *Las cuatrocientas comedias de Lope de Vega* (Madrid: Teatro Clásico Español, 1984)

Castro, Américo, *De la edad conflictiva* (Madrid: Taurus, 1972)

Chevalier, Maxime, *L'Arioste en Espagne (1530–1650): Recherches sur l'influence du* Roland furieux (Bordeaux: L'Université de Bordeaux, 1966)

Close, Anthony, 'Convergencia de comedia y novela en Tirso de Molina', in *El mundo como teatro: estudios sobre Calderón de la Barca*, ed. José Lara Garrido (Málaga: Universidad de Málaga, 2003), pp. 131–49

Connor, Catherine, 'Hacia una teoría sociocultural del espectador aurisecular', in *El texto puesto en escena: estudios sobre la comedia del Siglo de Oro en honor a Everett W. Hesse*, ed. Bárbara Mujica (London: Tamesis, 2000)

Cotarelo y Mori, Emilio, ed., *Bibliografía de las controversias sobre la licitud del teatro en España* (Madrid: RABM, 1904)

——, *Ensayo sobre la vida y obras de D. Pedro Calderón de la Barca*, facsimile edition, eds Ignacio Arellano and Juan Manuel Escudero (Madrid/Frankfurt: Iberoamericana/Vervuert, 2001)

Crawford, J. P. Wickersham, *Spanish Drama before Lope de Vega* (Philadelphia: University of Pennsylvania Press, 1922)

Cruikshank, Don, *Calderón, El médico de su honra* (London: Grant and Cutler, 2003)

Davis, Charles and J. E. Varey, *Actividad teatral en la región de Madrid según los protocolos de Juan García de Albertos, 1634–1660: estudio y documentos*, 2 vols (London: Tamesis, 2003)

——, *Los corrales de comedias y los hospitales de Madrid, 1574–1615: estudio y documentos* (Madrid: Támesis, 1997)

De Armas, Frederick A., *The Invisible Mistress: Aspects of Feminism and Fantasy in the Golden Age* (Charlottesville: Biblioteca Siglo de Oro, 1976)

Díez Borque, José María, ed., *Actor y técnica de representación del teatro clásico español* (London: Tamesis, 1989)

——, *Los géneros dramáticos en el siglo XVI: el teatro hasta Lope de Vega* (Madrid: Taurus, 1987)

——, *Sociedad y teatro en la España de Lope de Vega* (Barcelona: Bosch, 1978)

——, ed., *Teatros del Siglo de Oro: corrales y coliseos en la Península Ibérica, CTC*, 6 (1991)

Dixon, Victor, *Characterization in the* comedia *of Seventeenth-century Spain* (Manchester: Manchester Spanish and Portuguese Studies, 1994)

——, 'La intervención de Lope en la publicación de sus comedias', *ALV*, 2 (1999), pp. 45–63

——, 'Lope Félix de Vega Carpio', in *The Cambridge History of Spanish Literature*, ed. David T. Gies (Cambridge: Cambridge University Press, 2004), pp. 251–64

——, 'Manuel Vallejo. Un actor se prepara: un comediante del Siglo de Oro ante un texto (*El castigo sin venganza*)', in Díez Borque, ed., *Actor y técnica de representación del teatro clásico español* (London: Tamesis, 1989), pp. 55–74

——, 'Spanish Renaissance Theatre and Neo-Classical Theatre', in *The Oxford Illustrated History of the Theatre*, ed. John Russell Brown (Oxford: Oxford University Press, 1995), pp. 142–72

——, 'The Study of Versification as an Aid to Interpreting the *comedia*: Another Look at some Well-known Plays by Lope de Vega', in Ganelin and Mancing, eds, *The Golden Age* comedia, pp. 384–402

Elliott, J. H., *Imperial Spain 1468–1716* (Harmondsworth: Penguin, 1970)

——, *Spain and its World* (Yale: Yale University Press, 1989)

Evans, Peter W., 'Golden Age Dramatic Criticism Now', *The Seventeenth Century*, 1 (1987), pp. 49–53

Feros, Antonio, *Kingship and Favoritism in the Spain of Philip III, 1598–1621* (Cambridge: Cambridge University Press, 2000)

Ferrer Valls, Teresa, *La práctica escénica cortesana: de la época del emperador a la de Felipe III* (London: Tamesis, 1991)

Fischer, Susan L., 'Así que pasen quince años: trayectorias escénicas de la Compañía Nacional de Teatro Clásico', *ALEC*, 25 (2000), pp. 765–820

——, 'Historicizing *Painter of Dishonour* on the "Foreign" Stage: a Radical Interpretation of Tragedy', *BHS* (Glasgow), 77 (2000), pp. 183–216

Fothergill-Payne, Louise and Peter, eds, *Prologue to Performance: Spanish Classical Theatre Today* (Lewisburg: Bucknell University Press, 1991)

Friedman, Edward H., *The Unifying Concept: Approaches to the Structure of Cervantes'* comedias (York, SC: Spanish Literature Publications, 1981)

Froldi, Rinaldo, *Lope de Vega y la formación de la comedia* (Salamanca: Anaya, 1968)

Ganelin, Charles, *Rewriting Theatre: The Comedia and the Nineteenth-Century Refundición* (Lewisburg: Bucknell University Press, 1994)

—— and Howard Mancing, eds, *The Golden Age Comedia: Text, Theory and Performance* (West Lafayette: Purdue University Press, 1994)

García-Bermejo Giner, Miguel M., *Catálogo del teatro español del Siglo XVI* (Salamanca: Universidad de Salamanca, 1996)

García Gómez, Ángel María, 'Contextualización de las primeras puestas en escena de *La vida es sueño* (1925, 1929) en Inglaterra dentro del marco de la crítica anglo-irlandesa del siglo XIX', in Tietz, ed., *Teatro calderoniano sobre el tablado*, pp. 163–93

García Lorenzo, Luciano, ed., *Los géneros menores en el teatro español del Siglo de Oro* (Madrid: Ministerio de Cultura, 1988)

——, *El teatro de Guillén de Castro* (Barcelona: Planeta, 1976)

—— and Manuel Muñoz Carabantes, 'El teatro de Calderón en la escena española (1939–1999)', in Mackenzie, ed., *Calderón 1600–1681*, pp. 421–33

García Santo-Tomás, Enrique, *La creación del 'Fénix': recepción crítica y formación canónica del teatro de Lope de Vega* (Madrid: Gredos, 2000)

Gies, David Thatcher, *El teatro en la España del Siglo XIX* (Cambridge: Cambridge University Press, 1996)

González Cañal, Rafael, 'Calderón y sus colaboradores', in Arellano, ed., *Calderón 2000*, I, pp. 541–54

Greer, Margaret Rich, 'Constituting Community: a New Historical Perspective on the Autos of Calderón', in Madrigal, ed., *New Historicism*, pp. 41–67

——, *The Play of Power: Mythological Court Dramas of Calderón de la Barca* (Princeton, NJ: Princeton University Press, 1991)

—— and J. E. Varey, *El teatro palaciego en Madrid: 1586–1707. Estudio y documentos* (Madrid: Támesis, 1997)

Halkhoree, P. R. K., *Calderón de la Barca, El alcalde de Zalamea* (London: Grant and Cutler, 1972)

——, *Social and Literary Satire in the Comedies of Tirso de Molina*, eds José M. Ruano de la Haza and Henry W. Sullivan (Ottawa: Dovehouse, 1989)

Hall, J. B., *Lope de Vega, Fuenteovejuna* (London: Grant and Cutler, 1985)

Hart, Thomas R., *Gil Vicente, Casandra and Don Durados* (London: Grant and Cutler, 1981)

Hayes, Francis C., *Lope de Vega* (New York: Twayne, 1967)

Hermenegildo, Alfredo, *El teatro del siglo XVI* (Madrid: Júcar, 1994)

Herskovits, Andrew, *The Positive Image of the Jew in the* comedia (New York: Peter Lang, 2005)

Huerta Calvo, Javier, ed., *Historia del Teatro Español*, 2 vols (Madrid: Gredos, 2003), I: *De la edad media a los siglos de oro*

Kennedy, Ruth Lee, *Studies in Tirso*, I: *The Dramatist and his Competitors* (Chapel Hill: University of North Carolina Dept. of Romance Languages, 1974)

Kerr, Marie-Christine, 'The Theory and Practice of Acting in the Madrid *corrales* between 1579 and 1635', unpublished doctoral thesis, King's College, London, 1992

Kirschner, Teresa J., *Técnicas de representación en Lope de Vega* (London: Tamesis, 1998)

Larson, Donald R., *The Honor Plays of Lope de Vega* (Cambridge, MA: Harvard University Press, 1977)

Lewis-Smith, P., *Calderón de la Barca, La vida es sueño* (London: Grant and Cutler, 1998)

Lihani, John, *Bartolomé de Torres Naharro* (Boston: Twayne, 1979)

McKendrick, Melveena, 'Calderón and the Politics of Honour', *BHS*, 70 (1993), pp. 135–46

——, 'Honour/Vengeance in the Spanish *comedia*: a Case of Mimetic Transference?', *MLR*, 79 (1984), pp. 313–35

——, *Playing the King: Lope de Vega and the Limits of Conformity* (London: Tamesis, 2000)

——, *Theatre in Spain 1490–1700* (Cambridge: Cambridge University Press, 1989)

——, *Woman and Society in the Spanish Drama of the Golden Age: A Study of the mujer varonil* (London: Cambridge University Press, 1974)

——, 'Writings for the Stage', in *The Cambridge Companion to Cervantes*, ed. Anthony J. Cascardi (Cambridge: Cambridge University Press, 2002), pp. 131–59

Mackenzie, Ann L., ed., *Calderón 1600–1681: Quatercentenary Studies in Memory of John E. Varey* (Abingdon: Carfax, 2000)

Madrigal, José A., ed., *New Historicism and the Comedia: Poetics, Politics and Praxis* (Boulder, CO: Society of Spanish and Spanish-American Studies, 1997)

Maestro, Jesús G., *La escena imaginaria: poética del teatro de Miguel de Cervantes* (Madrid/Frankfurt: Iberoamericana/Vervuert, 2000)

——, 'Los límites de una interpretación trágica y contemporánea del teatro calderoniano: *El príncipe constante*', in Tietz, ed., *Teatro calderoniano sobre el tablado*, pp. 285–327

Maravall, José Antonio, *Teatro y literatura en la sociedad barroca* (Barcelona: Editorial Crítica, 1990)

Mariscal, George, 'An Introduction to the Ideology of Hispanism in the US and Britain', in Peter W. Evans, ed., *Conflicts of Discourse: Spanish Literature in the Golden Age* (Manchester: Manchester University Press, 1990), pp. 1–25

Marsillach, Adolfo, 'Distancia de diez años', *Diez años de la Compañía Nacional de Teatro Clásico: 1986–1996* (Madrid: Ministerio de Cultura, 1996), pp. 11–13

——, 'Teatro clásico hoy: la experiencia de un director', in Díez Borque, ed., *Actor y técnica de representación*, pp. 167–9

Metford, J. C. J., 'Tirso de Molina's Old Testament plays', *BHS*, 27 (1950), pp. 149–63

Miñana, Rogelio, ' "Veréis el monstruo": la nueva comedia de Cervantes', *BCom*, 56 (2004), pp. 387–411

Moir, Duncan, 'The Classical Tradition in Spanish Dramatic Theory and Practice in the Seventeenth Century', in *Classical Drama and its Influence: Essays presented to H. D. F. Kitto*, ed. M. J. Anderson (London: Methuen, 1965), pp. 191–228

Montesinos, José F., 'Algunas observaciones sobre la figura del donaire en el teatro de Lope de Vega', in *Estudios sobre Lope*, pp. 21–64

——, *Estudios sobre Lope* (Salamanca: Anaya, 1967)

Morley, S. Griswold, 'Lope de Vega's *Peregrino* lists', *University of California Publications in Modern Philology*, 14 (1930), pp. 345–66

——, 'The Pseudonyms and Literary Disguises of Lope de Vega', *University of California Publications in Modern Philology*, 33 (1951), pp. 421–84

—— and Courtney Bruerton, *The Chronology of Lope de Vega's* Comedias (New York: Modern Language Association of America, 1940)

Morrison, Robert R., *Lope de Vega and the* Comedia de santos (New York: Peter Lang, 2000)

Newels, Margarete, *Los géneros dramáticos en las poéticas del Siglo de Oro* (London: Tamesis, 1974)

Oakley, R. J., *Tirso de Molina*, El condenado por desconfiado (London: Grant and Cutler, 1994)

Oehrlein, Josef, *El actor en el teatro español del Siglo de Oro* (Madrid: Castalia, 1993)

Oleza, Juan, 'Claves románticas para la primera interpretación moderna del teatro de Lope de Vega', *ALV,* I (1995), pp. 119–35

——, 'Hipótesis sobre la génesis de la comedia barroca', in *La génesis de la teatralidad barroca*, Cuadernos de Filología, III, 1–2 (1981), pp. 9–44

——, 'La propuesta teatral del primer Lope de Vega, in *La génesis de la teatralidad barroca*, Cuadernos de Filología, III, 1–2 (1981), pp. 153–223

Orozco Díaz, Emilio, *El teatro y la teatralidad del Barroco* (Barcelona: Planeta, 1969)

Parker, A. A., *The Allegorical Drama of Calderón: An Introduction to the* autos sacramentales (Oxford: Dolphin, 1943)

——, *The Approach to the Spanish Drama of the Golden Age* (London: Hispanic and Luso-Brazilian Councils, 1957)

——, *The Mind and Art of Calderón* (Cambridge: Cambridge University Press, 1988)

——, 'Towards a Definition of Calderonian Tragedy', *BHS*, 39 (1962), pp. 222–37

Parker, J. H., *Gil Vicente* (New York: Twayne, 1967)

Parr, James A., *After Its Kind: Approaches to the* comedia (Kassel: Reichenberger, 1991)

Pavis, Patrice, *Analyzing Performance: Theatre, Dance and Film* (Ann Arbor: University of Michigan Press, 2003)

Pedraza Jiménez, Felipe B., *Lope de Vega* (Barcelona: Teide, 1990)

—— and Rafael González Cañal, *Los albores del teatro español: actas de las XVII Jornadas de Teatro Clásico* (Almagro: Universidad de Castilla-La Mancha, 1995)

Pérez Priego, Miguel Ángel, *El teatro en el Renacimiento* (Madrid: Laberinto, 2003)

Pfandl, Ludwig, *Historia de la literatura nacional española en la Edad de Oro* (Barcelona: Gustavo Gili, 1952)

Pring-Mill, Robert, *Calderón: Estructura y ejemplaridad*, ed. Nigel Griffin (London: Tamesis, 2001)

——, 'Los calderonistas de habla inglesa y *La vida es sueño*: métodos del análisis temático-estructural', in *Calderón: Estructura y ejemplaridad*, pp. 13–47

——, 'Introduction' to *Lope de Vega: Five Plays*, trans. Jill Booty (New York: Hill and Wang, 1961)

Regalado García, Antonio, *Calderón: los orígenes de la modernidad en la España del Siglo de Oro*, 2 vols (Barcelona: Destino, 1995)

Rennert, Hugo Albert, *The Spanish Stage in the Time of Lope de Vega* (New York: Dover Publications, 1963)

—— with Américo Castro, *Vida de Lope de Vega (1562–1635)* (Salamanca: Anaya, 1967)

Robbins, Jeremy, *The Challenges of Uncertainty: An Introduction to Seventeenth-Century Spanish Literature* (London: Duckworth, 1998)

——, 'Performing Doubt: the Epistemology of Honour in Calderón's *El médico de su honra*', *JIRS*, 7 (1999), pp. 63–74

——, 'Review Article: Baltasar Gracián (1601–2001)', *BHS*, 80 (2003), pp. 41–55

Rodríguez Cuadros, Evangelina, *La técnica del actor español en el Barroco: hipótesis y documentos* (Madrid: Castalia, 1998)

——, *Calderón* (Madrid: Síntesis, 2002)

Rogers, Daniel, *Tirso de Molina*, El burlador de Sevilla (London: Grant and Cutler, 1977)

Rozas, Juan Manuel, *Estudios sobre Lope de Vega*, ed. Jesús Cañas Murillo (Madrid: Cátedra, 1990)

Ruano de la Haza, José María, *La puesta en escena en los teatros comerciales del Siglo de Oro* (Madrid: Castalia, 2000)

——, 'The Staging of Calderón's *La vida es sueño* and *La dama duende*', *BHS*, 64 (1987), pp. 51–63

——, 'Trascendencia y proyección del teatro clásico español en el mundo anglosajón', in *Significados y proyección internacional del Teatro Clásico Español*, ed. José María Díez Borque (Madrid: Seacex, 2004), pp. 171–82

——, and John J. Allen, *Los teatros comerciales del siglo XVII y la escenificación de la comedia* (Madrid: Castalia, 1994)

Russell, P. E., 'Spanish Literature (1474–1681)', in *Spain: A Companion to Spanish Studies*, ed. P. E. Russell (London: Methuen, 1980), pp. 265–380

Sage, J. W., 'The Context of Comedy: Lope de Vega's *El perro del hortelano* and Related Plays', in *Studies in Spanish Literature of the Golden Age presented to Edward M. Wilson*, ed. R. O. Jones (London: Tamesis, 1973), pp. 247–66

——, 'The Function of Music in the Theatre of Calderón', in Varey, ed., *Critical Studies*, pp. 209–30

——, *Lope de Vega*, El caballero de Olmedo (London: Grant and Cutler, 1974)

Sánchez, Alberto, 'Aproximación al teatro de Cervantes', *Cervantes y el teatro*, *CTC*, 7 (1992), pp. 11–30

Sánchez Escribano, Federico and Alberto Porqueras Mayo, *Preceptiva dramática española del Renacimiento y Barroco* (Madrid: Gredos, 1972)

Schack, Conde de, *Historia de la literatura y del arte dramático en España*, 5 vols (Madrid: Tello, 1885–7)

Shergold, N. D., 'Ganassa and the *Commedia dell'Arte* in sixteenth-century Spain', *MLR*, 51 (1956), pp. 359–68

——, *A History of the Spanish Stage from Medieval Times until the End of the Seventeenth Century* (Oxford: Clarendon, 1967)

—— and J. E. Varey, eds, *Genealogía, origen y noticias de los comediantes de España*, (London: Tamesis, 1985)

Simerka, Barbara, ed., *El arte nuevo de estudiar comedias: Literary Theory and Spanish Golden Age Drama* (Lewisburg: Bucknell University Press, 1996)

Sloman, Albert E., *The Dramatic Craftsmanship of Calderón* (Oxford: Dolphin, 1969)

Smith, Paul Julian, *Writing in the Margin: Spanish Literature of the Golden Age* (Oxford: Clarendon, 1988)

Soufas, Teresa Scott, *Dramas of Distinction: A Study of Plays by Golden Age Women* (Lexington: University Press of Kentucky, 1997)

Stein, Louise K., *Songs of Mortals, Dialogues of the Gods: Music and Theatre in Seventeenth-Century Spain* (Oxford: Clarendon, 1993)

Stoll, Anita K. and Dawn L. Smith, eds, *Gender, Identity, and Representation in Spain's Golden Age* (Lewisburg: Bucknell University Press, 2000)

——, *The Perception of Women in Spanish Theater of the Golden Age* (Lewisburg: Bucknell University Press, 1991)

Sullivan, H. W., 'Jacques Lacan and the Golden Age Drama', in Simerka, ed., *El arte nuevo de estudiar comedias*, pp. 105–24

——, 'Love, Matrimony and Desire in the Theatre of Tirso de Molina', *BCom*, 37 (1985), pp. 83–99

——, *Tirso de Molina and the Drama of the Counter-Reformation* (Amsterdam: Rodopi, 1976)

Thacker, Jonathan, 'Comedy's Social Compromise: Tirso's *Marta la piadosa* and the Refashioning of Role', *BCom*, 47 (1995), pp. 267–89

——, 'La locura en las obras dramáticas tempranas de Lope de Vega', in *Memoria de la palabra: Actas del VI Congreso de la Asociación Internacional Siglo de Oro*, eds María Luisa Lobato and Francisco Domínguez Matito, 2 vols (Frankfurt and Madrid: Iberoamericana, 2004), II, pp. 1717–30

——, ' "Puedo yo con sola la vista oír leyendo": Reading, Seeing and Hearing the *Comedia*', *Comedia Performance*, 1 (2004), pp. 143–73

——, 'Rethinking Golden-Age Drama: The *Comedia* and its Contexts', *Paragraph*, 22 (1999), pp. 14–34

——, *Role-play and the World as Stage in the* comedia (Liverpool: Liverpool University Press, 2002)

Thompson, I. A. A., 'Castile', in *Absolutism in Seventeenth-Century Europe*, ed. John Miller (London: Macmillan, 1990), pp. 69–98

Thompson, Peter E., *The Triumphant Juan Rana: A Gay Actor of the Spanish Golden Age* (Toronto: University of Toronto Press, 2006)

Ticknor, G., *History of Spanish Literature*, 3 vols (London: Murray, 1863)

Tietz, Manfred, ed., *Teatro calderoniano sobre el tablado: Calderón y su puesta en escena a través de los siglos*, Archivum calderonianum, 10 (Stuttgart: Franz Steiner Verlag, 2003)

Tomillo, D. A. and D. C. Pérez Pastor, eds, *Proceso de Lope de Vega por libelos contra unos cómicos* (Madrid: Establecimiento tipográfico de Fontanet, 1901)

Trambaioli, Marcella, 'Una protocomedia burlesca de Cervantes: *La casa de los celos*, parodia de algunas piezas del primer Lope de Vega', in *Cervantes y su mundo*, eds Eva and Kurt Reichenberger, I (Kassel: Reichenberger, 2004), pp. 407–38

Urzáiz Tortajada, Héctor, *Catálogo de autores teatrales del siglo XVII*, 2 vols (Madrid: Fundación Universitaria Española, 2002)

Varey, J. E., 'The Audience and the Play at Court Spectacles: the Role of the King', *BHS*, 61 (1984), pp. 398–406

——, '*Casa con dos puertas*: Towards a Definition of Calderón's View of Comedy', *MLR*, 67 (1972), pp. 83–94

——, *Critical Studies of Calderón's Comedias*, vol. 19 of *The Comedias of Calderón*, ed. D. W. Cruickshank and J. E. Varey, 19 vols (Farnborough: Gregg International, 1973)

—— and Charles Davis, *Los corrales de comedias y los hospitales de Madrid, 1615–1849: estudio y documentos* (Madrid: Támesis, 1997)

Vázquez, Luis, 'Tirso de Molina: del "enigma biográfico" a la biografía documentada', in *Tirso de Molina: del Siglo de Oro al siglo XX*, eds Ignacio Arellano, Blanca Oteiza, María Carmen Pinillos, and Miguel Zugasti (Madrid: Revista Estudios, 1995)

Vitse, Marc, *Éléments pour une théorie du théâtre espagnol du XVIIe siècle* (Toulouse: Université de Toulouse le Mirail, 1990)

Wardropper, Bruce W., 'Calderón's Comedy and his Serious Sense of Life', in *Hispanic Studies in Honor of Nicholas B. Adams* (Chapel Hill: University of North Carolina, 1966), pp. 179–93

——, 'Cervantes' Theory of the Drama', *MP*, 52 (1955), pp. 217–21

——, 'La comedia española del Siglo de Oro', addendum to Elder Olsen, *Teoría de la comedia* (Barcelona: Ariel, 1978)

——, 'Comedias', in Avalle-Arce and Riley, eds, *Suma cervantina*, pp. 147–69

——, ed., *Critical Essays on the Theatre of Calderón* (New York: New York University Press, 1965)

——, 'El problema de la responsabilidad en la comedia de capa y espada de Calderón', in *Actas del Segundo Congreso Internacional de Hispanistas*, eds Jaime Sánchez Romeralo and Norbert Poulussen (Njimegen: Instituto Español de la Universidad de Nimega, 1967), pp. 689–94

Weber de Kurlat, Frida, 'Lope-Lope y Lope-PreLope: formación del sub-código de la comedia de Lope y su época', *Segismundo*, 12 (1976), pp. 111–31

Weiger, John G., 'Lope de Vega según Lope: ¿creador de la comedia?', in *La génesis de la teatralidad barroca*, Cuadernos de Filología, III, 1–2 (1981), pp. 225–45

Whicker, Jules, *The Plays of Juan Ruiz de Alarcón* (Woodbridge: Tamesis, 2003)

Wilson, Edward M., 'The Four Elements in the Imagery of Calderón', in Varey, ed., *Critical Studies*, pp. 191–207

—— and Duncan Moir, *A Literary History of Spain*, ed. R. O. Jones, *The Golden Age: Drama, 1492–1700* (London: Ernest Benn, 1971), a vol. of *A Literary History of Spain*, ed. R. O. Jones

Wilson, Margaret, *Spanish Drama of the Golden Age* (Oxford: Pergamon, 1969)

Wilson, William E., *Guillén de Castro* (New York: Twayne, 1973)

Wright, Elizabeth, *Pilgrimage to Patronage: Lope de Vega and the Court of Philip III* (Lewisburg: Bucknell University Press, 2001)

Zamora Vicente, Alonso, *Lope de Vega: su vida y su obra* (Madrid: Gredos, 1961)

Zimic, Stanislav, 'Cervantes frente a Lope y la comedia nueva (observaciones sobre *La entretenida*)', *AC*, 15 (1976), pp. 19–119

——, 'La ejemplaridad de los entremeses de Cervantes', *BHS*, 61 (1984), pp. 444–53

——, *El teatro de Cervantes* (Madrid: Castalia, 1992)

INDEX

Printed and bound by CPI Group (UK) Ltd, Croydon, CR0 4YY

25/03/2025

14647332-0002